SELECTED PRAISE FOR THE FIRST EDITION OF
LORDS OF CHAOS

"The authors of *Lords of Chaos* clearly know the international Metal/Satanism picture and, largely through interviews, have brought information to light of which religion scholars as well as the general public ought to be aware ... highly recommended."

—ROBERT ELLWOOD, HISTORIAN OF RELIGION, WRITING IN *NOVA RELIGIO*

"With *Lords of Chaos* Michael Moynihan and Didrik Søderlind paint a portrait of a fantastic realm where Satanism, neo-paganism and National Socialism energized a musical scene in which fantasy was actualized in the burning of medieval churches in Norway ... a uniquely valuable history of Black Metal music in general and of the Norwegian scene in particular as it is viewed by the participants themselves. *Lords of Chaos* is a compelling work deserving of a wide readership on both sides of the Atlantic."

—DR. JEFFREY KAPLAN, AUTHOR OF *RADICAL RELIGION IN AMERICA*

"This definitive study of Black Metal bridges the gap between fans and students of music subcultures, avoiding the twin evils of fanzine hype and academic detachment. Wise, witty and informative, Moynihan and Søderlind have written a model genre study in an engagingly accessible style through which their deep understandings shine."

—DEENA WEINSTEIN, AUTHOR OF *HEAVY METAL: A CULTURAL SOCIOLOGY*

"An unusual combination of true crime journalism, rock and roll reporting and underground obsessiveness, *Lords of Chaos* turns into one of the more fascinating reads in a long time. This unpredictable collection of interviews, histories, quotes and anecdotes stares long and hard into the dark heart of the Satanic Black Metal movement and returns with a sober analysis on the subject.

"To their credit, Moynihan and Søderlind manage to avoid both the frequent flippancy of the mainstream media as well as the backward bending apologizing of the counter culture press. For them, the world of Black Metal offers legitimate insights into art, ethics and politics, but they never forget just how strange these people are..."

—DAVID THOMAS, *THE DENVER POST*

"A fascinating study in extremism… *Lords of Chaos* is the rare exception, proving of interest not just to fans of the genre, but also to any students of true crime, sociology, and cultism. This both intelligent and accessible book will definitely serve as the textbook on the black metal scene for years to come."
—*Bay Area Music News*

"Gripping stuff, a book about scary rock that is really scary."
—*Booklist*

"Long the source of rumors, wildly exaggerated stories, and misinformation, the saga of black metal has finally been been chronicled intelligently and accurately … [shows] the blood-red dividing line between the drama of antichrist superstars and the limits of human reality."
—*Bikini*

"A meticulously researched exposé … a fascinating read. If you thought the feuds associated with Death Row Records were a bit over-the-top, then take a glimpse into the dark corners of the metal underground."
—*The Face*

"This exhaustive, near-academic look at metal's satanic underground simultaneously traces the Devil's ascent through rock history and provides cultural antecedents for music-related violence and paganism."
—*Alternative Press*

"*Lords of Chaos* is a brilliantly interwoven, if unlikely, bundle of journalistic branches—music, true-crime, occult, and subcultural anthropology. [It] benefits immeasurably from the authors' commitment to long-term study, and the care they've taken to convey the contradictions and differences within the scene, demolishing the oversimplified coverage in the sensationalistic press."
—*Brutarian*

"Well-written and highly academic… A non-fiction take on the cultural, political, and social implications of a music realm gone mad… I was somewhat hesitant in picking up a book which might fall into a trap of adding to the notoriety of the sporadically violent media pariahs it portrays, but Moynihan and Søderlind don't do them any favors."
—*Wet Ink*

"*Lords of Chaos* is the definitive study of the Black Metal subculture, the events which issued from it, and the divergent and convergent trends which it impacted. Its value goes much further."
—*Rúna*

"Paints a grim picture of the infamous Norwegian death metal scene in the early '90s… Testimonies reveal a lethal brand of childish, psychopathic obsession vastly more scary than the ponderous and deliberately offensive music scene that spawned them."

—*Bizarre*

"[*Lords of Chaos*] includes not only the sensationalistic, fiery, blood-and-guts side of the black metal story, but the elegant and passionate side as well; the life-and-death struggle by a few dedicated young people to rise above the mediocrity and complacence that surrounded them."

—*Flipside*

"A fascinating and deeply tragic story supported by hilarious photographs."

—*Loaded*

"A riveting read, equal parts history, sociopolitical analysis, and true crime."

—*Spin*

"The most exciting book since the Old Testament … a masterwork of music history."

—*Spex* (Germany)

"Finally someone has compiled an exhaustive resource regarding the seamy and Satanic side of pop music and culture. Whatever your musical or religious outlook, this book has the facts you need to understand what's going on in Death Metal music."

—Bob Larson, radio & TV personality, author of numerous Christian-oriented books on Satanism, the occult, and contemporary culture.

"Speaking of dark and twisted reads, Michael Moynihan and Didrik Søderlind's *Lords of Chaos: The Bloody Rise of the Satanic Metal Underground* has everything: wacky Norwegians burning down churches to get back at Christians for stamping out Odin worship, murder, suicide, more than you ever wanted to know about the Norway vs. Sweden black-metal rivalries, and the (d)evolution from theatrical Satanic to slightly-more-serious Wotanic Nazi metal. Plenty of interviews—from the late Anton LaVey to Norwegian metal villain Varg Vikernes—make this a mighty entertaining bedtime reader."

—*Pulse*

"With its numerous original documents and informative interviews with all the important representatives of the scene, *Lords of Chaos* is the first serious history of the rise of a music scene that was first marginalized as exotic and extreme, and in the end was hushed up by the press on account of its criminal element."

—*Financial Times* (Germany)

"*Lords of Chaos* brings much light into a realm of darkness where previously rumors and mystical transfigurations had reigned."

—*Visions* (Germany)

"Rev up a chainsaw. Flick on the blender and a couple of power drills. Stand directly behind an F-16, right before it blasts off into space. A jackhammer should do to set the tempo. Now get down on all fours, contort your face into the wickedest grimace you can muster, and scream until your vocal cords collapse. If all of this makes you feel just the least bit ridiculous, hit yourself in the face with a roofing hammer until you can't laugh anymore. There now. Listen carefully. This is what Black Metal sounds like.

"Black Metal's 'medieval Satanism' is the logical fulfillment of Christianity's worst apocalyptic fantasies, or at least the ones the media have irresponsibly legitimized. It is rebellion taken to its natural conclusion ... destruction for its own sake, an adrenalized nihilism that revels in every toppled steeple. *Lords of Chaos* ... lets the genre's more luminous personalities speak for themselves, stringing countless first-hand interviews into a seamless chronological narrative. It's a task few other writers could have pulled off, whether geeked-up music journalists or academic outsiders. Surprisingly balanced, exhaustingly thorough, and—lest we forget that a lot of these folks come across more like professional wrestlers than terrorists—darkly humorous, it is a comprehensive look at a phenomenon that's rarely been scrutinized."

—*Vor Tru*

LORDS OF CHAOS:
THE BLOODY RISE OF THE
SATANIC METAL UNDERGROUND

MICHAEL MOYNIHAN
DIDRIK SØDERLIND

FERAL HOUSE

Lords of Chaos:

The Bloody Rise of the
Satanic Metal Underground
Revised and Expanded Edition

Published by Feral House
All Rights Reserved.

Cover and interior design by Sean Tejaratchi.
Cover photograph by Heimer Andersson.

ISBN: 0-922915-94-6
ISBN: 978-0-922915-94-1

Library of Congress Cataloging-in-Publication Data available.

For catalogue of publications, write Feral House's new address:

Feral House
1240 W. Sims Way Suite 124
Port Townsend, WA 98368

www.FeralHouse.com

10   9

TABLE OF CONTENTS

★ ★ ★ ★ ★

APPENDICES

★ ★ ★ ★ ★

ACKNOWLEDGMENTS

THIS BOOK HAS BEEN A NUMBER OF YEARS IN THE MAKING, AND IS THE RESULT of collaborations both close-at-hand and long distance. Most of the interviews with the Norwegians in the book were done in person in the fall of 1995 by myself, assisted and abetted by my co-author, Didrik Søderlind. Most were conducted in English, which should explain the occasionally awkward turn-of-phrase from some of our subjects. However, like the Scandinavians in general, their usage of English is often frighteningly superior to the average American youth of today. A few of the interviews, with Lene Bore and Snorre Ruch most notably, were done in Norwegian and translated by Didrik Søderlind. More recently in 1997 he also conducted the interviews with Asbjørn Dyrendal, Katrine Fangen, Henrik Lunde, Martin Alvsvåg, Ketil Sveen, Per Anders Nordengen, Kjetil Wiedswang, and Willy Kobbhaug.

The remaining interviews were all conducted by myself, either by phone or mail, during the period of 1995–97. The bulk of the book was written and organized by myself, with important editorial contributions from Didrik. A few key sections of the book were written by him, specifically the material on the religious/social situation in Norway, and the current trends in political extremism there. The descriptions of the Helvete shop were also written by Didrik, much of it based on his own recollections from the period, having met and spoken with Øystein Aarseth a number of times.

We have provided endnotes which attempt to document as many of the statements in this book as was humanly possible. The citations are as detailed as we were able to make them. We were unable to track down the exact date of a few newspaper or fanzine articles, especially the latter which were often provided to us in the form of photocopies. There is also a lengthy bibliography comprised of both general works and specifically cited works which were crucial to our effort.

There are a multitude of friends and acquaintances who have contributed to this book in some manner, and hopefully I will have remembered them all below. My apologies to anyone who has been overlooked.

An initial and sincere word of thanks is due to my good friend Peter Sotos, at whose suggestive encouragement many years ago I first began to investigate much of the material which later wound up documented in these pages. Likewise to editor and publisher Adam Parfrey, who supported its development into a full-length book. Beyond his aforementioned contributions, my co-author Didrik Søderlind provided assistance in too many other ways to count, as well as hospitality and generosity during my weeks in Norway. My parents also deserve thanks for their help and support of this endeavor in numerous ways. Gratitude is due to this book's designer Sean Tejaratchi for his putting his invaluable and indelible visual stamp on the appearance of its cover and contents.

Those who consented to be interviewed during my visit to Norway deserve special thanks: Varg Vikernes, Lene Bore, Simen Midgaard (also for permission to reprint his fine article on "Satanism in Norway"), Pål Mathiesen, Ihsahn and Samoth of Emperor, Snorre Ruch, Bård Eithun, and Metalion. Thanks are due as well to the helpful liaisons at the Ila, Ullersmo, and Tønsberg prisons.

Sincere thanks to Elden M. for allowing me to use his interview with Abaddon of Venom; to Finn Bjørn Tønder for permission to reproduce his revealing *Bergens Tidende* interview with Varg Vikernes; to Kadmon for the kind permission to reprint his excellent "Oskorei" essay; to David Walsten for permission to reprint his Fantoft Stave Church photos; to Nihil for generous access to some of his vast photographic archives; likewise to Samoth, Bård Eithun, Hendrik and Wolf Möbus, Rikke Lundgreen, Metalion, Lene Bore, and Rayshele Teige for providing photographs.

Pictures in the book have been credited to the photographer whenever possible, although some wished to remain anonymous. Uncredited illustrations are from my own archives.

Others who were interviewed and/or provided crucial insight or information without which this book would be vastly inferior include: Anton LaVey and Blanche Barton, Hendrik Möbus, Jan Axel Blomberg, Erik and Garm of Ulver, King Diamond, M.W. Daoloth, Quorthon, Kerry Bolton, "Gungnir," Johnny Hedlund, Dani from Cradle of Filth, Asbjørn Dyrendal (and for permission to quote at length from his incisive report "Media Constructions of 'Satanism' in Norway"), Willy Kobbhaug, Larry King of the Ft. Myers Sheriff's Dept., Henrik Lunde, and Katrine Fangen.

Invaluable suggestions, material, or other assistance was provided by: R.N. Taylor and Karen Taylor, Tiziana Stupia, Jan Rune Bruun, David Thomas, Linn and Hugo Lundhaug, Andrea Meyer, Anne Bergestrand, Mårten Björkman, Torsten Cornils, Matt Ward, Eric Stenflo, George Petros and Steve Blush at *Seconds*, Robert Ward, Jim Goad, Peter Gilmore and Peggy Nadramia, Carl Abrahamsson, Josh Buckley, Donovan Ives, Pascal Schubert, Werner Linke, Paula Hogan at Fierce Records, Sophie Diamantis at Roadrunner Records, Rayshele Teige at Osmose USA, Marco Barbieri, Stephen O'Malley, Chad Hensley, Ed Balog, Neil Sceeny, Ben Solis, Carrie Petersen, "Wolf" of Burznazg Productions, Paul Thind and Necropolis Records, Moribund Records, and Thomas Thorn.

Important assistance with the translation of foreign newspaper articles and texts was generously given by Henry Möller, Markus Wolff, and Eric Owens.

Deepest gratitude is due to Cornelia Moynihan and especially Annabel Lee for taking considerable time to read and offer suggestions to the manuscript. Their thoughtful criticisms laid the basis for essential improvements in the final book.

For suggestions and contributions that have helped to improve the new edition, we would like to thank Stephen Flowers, Max Fredriksson, Tyler Davis, Kola Krauze, Jürgen Bäuerle, Stephan Pockrandt, Timo Kölling, Timo Kötter, Thor Wanzek, Martin Kreischer, Melanie Aschenbrenner, Martin Köller, and Christoph Dzur. Didrik extends gratitude to Ike Vil and Antti Litmanen from the Babylon Whores for help with lodging in Helsinki and translation of articles, and also to Tania Stene for lodging in Trondheim.

Last but not least, for the new edition we thank Jacob Jervell, Mattias Gardell, Michael Rothstein, Asbjørn Slettemark, Merja Hermonen, Per Bangsund, Eivind Eckbo, and Yorck Eysel for their interviews.

— MICHAEL MOYNIHAN

PREFACE TO THE NEW EDITION

L ORDS OF CHAOS WAS RESEARCHED AND WRITTEN IN THE YEARS 1994–97 and published in 1998. It became a subcultural sensation almost immediately. Somewhat to our surprise, it caught the interest of an astonishingly wide range of readers. The book has been hailed as a revelation by both underground fan and ivory tower academic alike. Many people who would otherwise have zero interest in a topic like Black Metal have been fascinated to gaze into this otherwise hidden underworld. Well-dressed businessmen were spotted reading it on the London Underground.

The attention did not stop there. At the American national publishing convention, it won the coveted independent press Firecracker Award for "Best Music Book" of the year. We were widely interviewed by the mainstream media both in Europe and across America, appearing in magazine articles, television documentaries, and radio programs which ran the gamut from Howard Stern to Christian talk shows. It was not long before we became de facto experts on the modern phenomenon of "unexplained youth violence." The day of the infamous Columbine school shootings, a major radio news program had us on to provide live, real-time commentary as part of their effort to help listeners understand the real motivations behind such a seemingly senseless, brutal event.

Earlier this year, a long-awaited German edition of *Lords of Chaos* appeared, accompanied by a double-CD compilation of music which provided the soundtrack to the book's contents. In a major press blitz, both releases were widely reviewed across Europe; full-page pieces on the history of Black Metal appeared in the strangest of places, from daily papers to the *Financial Times*, the German equivalent of the *Wall Street Journal*. When the anniversary of Germany's own bloody school shooting at Erfurt came around, our comments wound up in newspaper editorials on the subject.

In essence, this is a radical book. Radical in the true sense of the word (deriving from the Latin *radix*, "root"), it explores the roots of the matter at hand in an unflinching fashion. It is not our job to pass judgment on our subjects; we expect the readers to have the intelligence to do that for themselves. This reluctance to overtly criticize those whom we interview and document has occasionally been a source of consternation for reviewers who harbor their own moralistic agendas, who claim that by neglecting to "properly"—read: politically correctly—interpret this material for the reader, we are allowing potentially dangerous ideas a free voice. In a sense, they may be right. Our world, increasingly homogenized and with the entire spectrum of its cultural creations adulterated for palatable mass-consumption, needs dangerous ideas more than ever. It may not need the often ill-formed and destructive ideas expressed by some of the protagonists in *Lords of Chaos*, but we felt all along that this is an issue for the individual reader to decide.

However, at times we simply couldn't resist commenting on our subjects' views. Case in point: the claim (made by Varg Vikernes and some of his fellow travelers) that Norway is run by a Jewish conspiracy. The notion of a "Protocols of the Elders of Zion"-style Jewish cabal running the world is absurd to begin with, but all the more so in a country with practically no Jewish population, and we felt the need to point this out. In many instances, the reader will also find that the outrageous points being made by one person are soon commented upon and put into a different light by other interview subjects.

We do not claim to offer any cut-and-dried rationale for why these events all happened, or continue to happen. There is no simple or single answer. While a certain amount of what is found in these pages can be ascribed to age-old impulses of teenage rebellion, undoubtedly there was and is something deeper going on, a certain energy twisting and erupting from below the ground—something from the roots.

A few critics have accused us of overemphasizing the extreme political rhetoric that marks some quarters of the Black Metal scene. The implication is that we did so for sinister reasons. An example is Hendrik Möbus of the German band Absurd (whose exploits are detailed in chapter 11). Möbus was an obvious focal point for us since, in many respects, this volume became a true crime book. But the effects of *Lords of Chaos* can also clearly be seen here. In the interview he granted to us for the first edition, Möbus made numerous extreme statements and the accusation was leveled at us on more than one occasion that we had unwisely given a obscure and insignificant figure a platform to express extremist political views. As things turned out, many of Möbus's remarks were ultimately used against him as evidence during subsequent legal proceedings that resulted in an additional sentence he received for

GERMAN HEADLINE AFTER MÖBUS VIOLATES PAROLE, PRIOR TO BECOMING AN INTERNATIONAL FUGITIVE: "SATAN MURDERER TO GET THREE YEARS BEHIND BARS"

NORWEGIAN HEADLINE: "IT'S THE ULTIMATE ACT, BECAUSE IT CAN'T GET MUCH WORSE"

publicly deriding the victim of his crime. This was not the end of the matter. In order to avoid being sent back to prison, Möbus fled the country. He flew to the U.S., eventually finding safehousing with Dr. William Pierce, author of the notorious *Turner Diaries* and the director of the National Alliance, which is widely considered the most serious and "potentially dangerous" racialist organization in the country. It was not long before Möbus was apprehended by U.S. authorities and ultimately extradited to Germany. The obscure, insignificant figure had now reached the status of a notorious international fugitive, commanding headlines in major papers. These events demonstrate that our attention was warranted.

There is no question that things have quieted down a bit in the Black Metal scene—at least insofar as its extra-musical activities go. The popularity of the music seems undiminished; indeed it has become a serious cash cow for the Norwegian music industry, and underground music in general. The major groups sell impressive quantities of records and draw multitudes of fans on their extensive worldwide tours. The Satyricon single "Fuel for Hatred" received heavy airplay on one of Norway's three biggest radio stations, and just before this revised edition went to press we heard that Dimmu Borgir's new album will be hawked to the public through TV advertising spots. Today most of the genre's protagonists hold no interest in committing crimes. Fully aware they have a viable commercial and artistic product to sell, they take their musical careers seriously. For all the morbid cachet it might provide one's reputation among the demi-monde, being locked up in a jail cell does not facilitate recording and playing music—in other words, making a living.

Nevertheless, recent events in Finland and Norway bear witness to the fact that Black Metal can still inspire fear and apprehension. Among the new sections in this revised edition is a chronicle of the particularly lurid crimes committed near Helsinki by Black Metal youths, news of which was heavily suppressed by the authorities for fear of copycat incidents.

And more recently in June 2003, Black Metal was back on the front pages in Norway. A 26-year-old man with a past as a member of a relatively unknown Black Metal band had been arrested in a case that was guaranteed to capture the nation's imagination. Along with some younger compatriots, the former bass player had broken into a chapel where bodies were awaiting cremation. The group opened coffins and abused the deceased by cutting, beating, and stomping on the bodies; this was supplemented with a thorough vandalism of the chapel itself. The corpse of an older man was decapitated, and the severed head brought to a party for show-and-tell. The grotesque conversation piece was later retrieved from the basement of a young man who was totally unaware it had been deposited there.

The results were predictable: the case dominated the media for days, and even seemed to overshadow murders of living people and important world events. In a fit of hysteria the tabloids went into full gear, speculating upon whether the desecrations were part of Satanic rituals. Some urged that Black Metal music should be outlawed.

As might be expected, several key points were overlooked in the coverage of the case. In fact, the culprit wasn't even really part of the Black Metal scene. He had long since been fired from his band for musical reasons, and was furthermore such a misfit that he had been more or less ostracized from the scene in general. His extensive abuse of drugs like ecstasy and GHB probably hadn't helped his sorry situation. It is more likely that the prime contributing factors behind his extreme behavior were psychological and pharmacological rather than anything to do with music or Satanism.

But one thing had changed in the decade since Black Metal first shocked Norway. Since those early outrages it has become a both critically acclaimed and commercially appealing genre of music—the upshot of this being that the sub-culture now has mainstream media people ready to defend it. "Nobody in this scene would gain in status from chopping the head off a corpse," claimed a prominent radio DJ who plays a lot of Black Metal. While this might make a good interview soundbite, it is no more true than tabloid rantings that paint all metal fans as potential corpse violators.

A significant degree of Black Metal's allure and stature does not derive from the accomplished musical achievements and originality of the artists playing the music. The grisly crimes have contributed as much, and maybe even more, to its appeal. And while most Black Metal people are law-abiding citizens, they can hardly claim that the criminal element merely represents a clique of confused hangers-on. Those responsible for the murders, church burnings, and so forth have often been the prime movers and shakers of the scene. Underscoring this is the fact that key Black Metal magazines publish articles that treat real killers as cozy celebrities, or proclaim them to be outright heroes.

This new edition of *Lords of Chaos* has been revised in various places throughout, with corrections made, sections updated, and new material, interviews, and illustrations added. The format and the majority of the text from the original edition have been retained, for we feel they capture well the wild world of Black Metal—not to mention what is undoubtedly the strangest saga ever told in the history of popular music. Here blood, fire, and music were the volatile ingredients that fueled an alchemical explosion which still continues to loudly reverberate through the apocalypse culture of the modern world.

— MICHAEL MOYNIHAN AND DIDRIK SØDERLIND

LOS ANGELES AND OSLO, JULY 2003

FROM DEVASTATED EARTH

NEW FORMS WILL RISE

BUT WHAT AT FIRST OFFENDS OUR EYES

WILL AT LAST BE SEEN AS WELCOME BIRTH

HOW LONG DID WE CRY VAINLY

IN THE LONG AND ENDLESS NIGHTS?

NOT EVEN SECONDS.

IN THE DARK, NO ONE CRIES IN VAIN—

WE ONLY FAIL TO SEE.

WE BEWAIL THE RUINS IN OUR VIEW

AND STREW OURSELVES WITH ASHES

AND DO NOT SEE THE PHOENIX

IN THE FLAMES.

DO YOU STILL CRY?

DO YOU STILL CRY OUT?

— TARJEI VESAAS, "THE BIRD IN THE FLAME," *LAND OF HIDDEN FIRES*[1]

PREAMBLE:
INTO THAT DARKNESS

APRIL, 1997 (OSLO)—THE HEADLINES OF THE NATION'S NEWSPAPERS SCREAM with the revelation of a sinister plot to slaughter progressive politicians and religious leaders in Norway. The perpetrators, possessed of not only weapons but significant sums of money, allegedly planned further actions beyond the list of assassinations. On their agenda is the liberation of an imprisoned comrade, whom they hope to safely smuggle out of the country. Is this prisoner-of-war another extreme nationalist with a long history of underground political activism like themselves? No. He is 24-year-old Varg Vikernes, the most infamous Black Metal musician in the world.

It is a winding path which leads from the world of Pop music to political terrorism. This is not the first time Rock and Roll has assumed a revolutionary mode, but it is the most fanatical and uncompromising such outbreak yet. It is also just the tip of the iceberg. Upon closer scrutiny, the plot to free Varg Vikernes becomes only the latest development in one of the most bizarre and outrageous sagas in musical history. Until now, it has remained largely unwritten.

The annals of Black Metal are fraught with violence—exploding in both self-administered suicidal shotgun blasts and cold-blooded, knife-blade murders. The number of deaths incurred worldwide is hard to calculate, but the frenzied nature of the killings bestows them with an unmistakable essence. As merciless as the murders have been, the ongoing campaign of church arsons adds psychological terror and religious intimidation to the list of Black Metal's arsenal. It is a legacy comprised of innumerable strands of virulent rhetoric, from Satanism to fascism—some of it mere pomp, some stated in deadly earnest. Pulling back the genre's dark veil reveals a few certifiable loose cannons amidst numerous poseurs; the share of cartoon characters is counterbalanced by some genuine "demons" in human form. They all share a common desire to boldly step beyond the perimeters of acceptable society, be it in image or in deed, and plant their flags of defiance. All this is accomplished to the militant sound of Black Metal itself—a roaring cacophony of mind-bending dimensions. Black Metal adopts the basic framework of the hardest strain of Heavy Metal, ripping it down to a poisoned, jagged splinter of aural hate. As if to add further confusion for an unwary listener, some Black Metal bands have also taken to recording sounds which could rightly be described as "beautiful," and have branched into the territories of Ambient Electronic, Traditional Folk, and even neo-Classical music.

Rock music has always held seeds of the forbidden. As decades passed and the business swelled, the multinational corporations who came to control it could not allow such seeds to develop into uncontrollable stalks and vines. Simultaneous with Rock's descent into a commodity, sold through endless magazine advertisements and glitzy videos, a façade of pseudo-rebellion has been carefully cultivated, but Rock's "garden of earthly delights" is very well manicured indeed. Yet there are those who attempt to kick down the boundaries and allow it to rejuvenate its limbs in the fertile, blood-soaked fields of real danger.

Heavy Metal exists on the periphery of Pop music, isolated in its exaggerated imagery and venting of masculine lusts. Often ignored, scorned, or castigated by critics and parents, Heavy Metal has been forced to create its own underworld. It plays by its own rules, follows its own aesthetic prerogatives. Born from the nihilism of the 1970s, the music has followed a singular course. Now in the latter half of the 1990s it is often considered passé and irrelevant, a costume parade of the worst traits in Rock. Metal is no longer a staple of FM radio, nor are record labels pushing it like they used to. Watching MTV and reading popular music magazines, one might not even realize Heavy Metal still existed at all.

Rumors of its demise are greatly exaggerated, however, as the Metal underground boils and seethes worldwide. Essentially left to its own devices and relegated to independent labels run by the hardcore fans themselves, this has allowed Metal's most antisocial and aggressive tendencies to develop unburdened by any system of moral checks and balances, which society provides—at least tenuously—for other significant forms of music.

In Europe, Heavy Metal has always kept up a certain level of popularity, despite its pariah-like status in the eyes of the public. In the Far North of that continent, the molten nature of extreme Metal met with the icy climes of Norway and Sweden, and the result was a creation of explosively volatile proportions: Black Metal. The North, rigidly controlled by the natural elements, its seasons dominated by darkness and cold, ironically provided the desolate environment which would spark Black Metal to marshal its forces and gather up weapons in a coming unholy war.

Rock and Roll has long been an adversary to many of the basic tenets of Christianity, but underground Heavy Metal took this to the ultimate extreme. Christianity was not to be slowly eroded through steady incursions of increasing immorality, rather it should be abruptly uprooted and incinerated to its very last breath. Black Metal would provide foot soldiers ready to plunge headlong into battle, firebrands in hand, to brazenly set alight the cathedrals and churches of Europe.

The justifications for this onslaught are many. Some declare allegiance to Satan, that ancient enemy of Christ, and honor his name in song and deed. Others draw fortitude from the pagan ways of old and claim to continue a battle left unfinished 1,000 years ago when Christianity invaded Europe. "A furore normannorum, libera nos, domine. 'From the fury of the Northmen, O Lord, deliver us' was a litany without need of vellum. It was graven on the hearts of men wherever and for as long as that fury fell," wrote Gwyn Jones in his A History of the Vikings.[2] Such sentiments on the lips of the early church fathers are just as relevant now as then.

Saint Columcille, the founder of the Iona monastery in the British Isles in 563, foretold a dire prophecy concerning the establishment of the new religion of peace. According to Manus O'Donnell's hagiography, certain morbid images had entered the Saint's consciousness. "'My mind and heart have been sore troubled' saith Columcille, 'by a vision that hath been given me... for at the end of time men will besiege my churches, and they will kill my monks and violate my sanctuary, and ravage and desecrate my burial grounds.'"[3]

His words would be fulfilled only a few centuries later, when Viking raiders from the Norwegian coasts descended upon the monasteries of Britain, "like stinging hornets, and overran the country in all directions, like fierce wolves, plundering, tearing, and killing not only sheep and oxen, but priests and Levits, and choirs of monks and nuns..."[4] In the end, the newly established forces of God and Christ quelled and subdued their heathen resisters. Europe became a Christian continent to its furthest borders. But the wolves and hornets were only sleeping in their caves and nests, and they would be inflamed again.

Slightly over a millennium later, Columcille's prophecy was due for a second coming, this time on a worldwide scale. The antagonists were no longer the warrior class of an untamed heathen society, but rather the well-bred youth of the most civilized Christian nations on earth.

The connection between such recurring events is blurred, its details obscured in the mists of pre-Christian myth and allegory. Black Metal has taken the fire of Loki and used it as fuel, the accelerant for a one-way ride to hell. Have the terrifying gods of old reawakened, thirsty for blood after years of dormancy? Or is this simply their last stand, a *Götterdämmerung* of Wagnerian proportions as they gasp before the final curtain?

A historian of the Germanic people wrote, "There is not only a Twilight for the Gods, there is a deep, dark impenetrable night."[5] In the flaming glint of real or imagined sword blades, Black Metal's legions have made their own desperate attempt to illumine the darkness. Their weapons are blasphemy and fire, coupled with heavy sonic artillery and spurred on by powerful internal and infernal impulses. Their methods and approach may be inopportune, the tactics crude and thoughtless, but the resulting unprecedented and unexpected crimes warrant an inquest. The implications of their behavior ripple far beyond the borders of music, youth culture, even esoteric religion. Their experiments in "evil" provide the opportunity to understand the dynamic impetus which lies behind hate-driven destruction itself.

In order to fully understand the present and future, one must gaze back into the past. Thus, we will begin our explication of a modern eruption of musical terrorism a few generations ago, before Rock and Roll had even entered the picture. Once a quick overview of Black Metal's instinctual and visceral pedigree has been gained, the rest of the insanity quickly falls into place.

THE SABBATS OF THE OLD DAYS HAVE COME TO LIFE IN A NEW FORM—
THE OUTDOOR ROCK FESTIVAL. BOTH SERVE AS A CATHARTIC RELEASE FROM THE
DRUDGERIES OF DAILY SECULAR EXISTENCE. THOSE YOUNG PEOPLE IN ATTENDANCE AT
THE CONCERTS ARE, FOR THE MOST PART, THOSE WHO LABEL THEMSELVES PROUDLY THE
"NEW GENERATION," THOSE WHO, LIKE THE EUROPEAN SERF, FEEL A PROFOUND SCHISM
BETWEEN THEMSELVES AND THE ESTABLISHMENT. AT THE CONCERTS, AS AT THE
SABBATS, THERE IS THROBBING, HYPNOTIC MUSIC, WIDESPREAD USE OF HALLUCINO-
GENIC DRUGS BY THE CELEBRANTS, AN ESCAPE INTO ANIMALITY...
—ARTHUR LYONS, *THE SECOND COMING*[1]

SYMPATHIES
FOR THE DEVIL

THE DEVIL HAS ALWAYS TREASURED MUSIC. WHAT BETTER ARENA to inspire, cultivate, and propagate his will into the affairs of man? Music serves as both balm and excitant, soothing the savage or awakening dormant passions. In spiritual terms music is a magical operation, a vehicle for man to communicate with the gods. Depending on whom the celebrants invoke, this can mean soaring to heaven on the voices of angels or raising beasts from the pits of hell.

With the ascendency of Christianity in the Western world over the past two millennia, music has always been a problematic area for both religious and secular authority. While song has often served to bind the Lord's supplicants, its seductive words and cadences may just as easily sow seeds of doubt in the mind. Mephistopheles and the Muse go hand in hand, and the folk songs of old often extol wine, women, and song—all three the Devil's playthings. Many of the oldest known songs in European tradition derive from heathen, pre-Christian roots, and spin tales of magic, necromancy, and superstition. It is no wonder the Christian Church did its best to try to supplant such songs of the people with hymns extolling its own icons and ideals; nevertheless, tradition dies hard and has a way of resurfacing despite all attempts to discourage or silence it.

Self-proclaimed moral authorities continue to frown upon the ecstasies of revelry and lusty song, attempting to root them out. In the first half of the twentieth century, Jazz was considered particularly dangerous, with its imagined potential to unleash animal passions, especially among unsuspecting white folk. Theosophical writers on the occult significance of music even go so far as to state that the force ushering Jazz into the nightclubs could be none other than that which allows evil to operate on earth. In his book on the Rolling Stones, *Dance With the Devil*, Stanley Booth quotes the *New Orleans Times-Picayune* in 1918: "On certain natures sound loud and meaningless has an exciting, almost an intoxicating effect, like crude colors and strong perfumes, the sight of flesh or the sadic pleasure in blood. To such as these the jass music is a delight [sic]."[2] Early lurid scare tactics had little effect, and Jazz attracted a more genteel audience as time went on.

More directly tied to deviltry than Jazz, and likewise imbued with the potency of its racial origins, was Blues. Black slaves often adopted Christianity after their enforced arrival in America, but melded it with native or Voudoun strains. Blues songs abound with references to devils, demons, and spirits. One of the most influential Blues singers of all time, Robert Johnson, is said to have sold his soul to the Devil at a crossroads in the Mississippi Delta, and the surviving recordings of his haunting songs give credence to the legend that Satan rewarded his pact with the ability to play. Johnson recorded only twenty-nine tunes, some of the more famous being "Crossroads Blues," "Me and the Devil Blues," and "Hellhound on My Trail." The leaden resignation of his music is a genuine reflection of his existence. Life for Johnson began on the plantations, wound through years of carousing and playing juke joints, ending abruptly in 1938 when at the age of 27 he was poisoned in a bar, probably as a result of an affair with the club owner's wife. Johnson's musical legacy would fade into obscurity until reissued on LPs in the '60s, when it found a new excited audience among the Blues Rock musicians of that era. From the demonic songs of Delta Blues one can trace a line to the present world of Satanic Rock and Roll.

LUCIFER TURNS UP THE VOLUME

Most early Rock—despite the power commanded over youth by Elvis "the pelvis" Presley and the Beatles—was, in reality, only mildly threatening to the status quo. Its most anti-social element came from the thugs and delinquents who latched onto Rockabilly, but chances are these youths would have been stealing cars and rolling bums no matter what kind of music they listened to. As the '60s spiraled onward, musical experimentation coupled with drug use, and a decidedly darker element came to the fore.

The Beatles appeared downright tidy next to Rolling Stones, who reveled in the role of international bad boys—boozers, fighters, and satyr-like icons of sensual excess. By no accident the Stones traced their musical lineage back to

Robert Johnson and his infernal Delta swamp Blues. The Stones took their diabolical inspiration seriously, deliberately cultivating a Satanic image, from wearing Devil masks in promotional photos to conjuring up sinister album titles such as *Their Satanic Majesties Request* and *Let it Bleed*. The band's lyrics ambivalently explored drug addiction, rape, murder, and predation. The infamous culmination of these flirtations revealed itself at the Altamont Speedway outdoor festival on December 6, 1969. Inadvertently captured on film in the live documentary *Gimme Shelter,* it was only moments into the song "Sympathy for the Devil" before all hell broke loose between the legion of Hell's Angels "security guards" and members of the audience, ending with the fatal stabbing of Meredith Hunter, a gun-wielding black man in the crowd. The infernal, violent chaos of the event at Altamont made it abundantly clear the peace and love of the '60s wouldn't survive the transition to a new decade.

Simultaneously with the ascension of the Rolling Stones to world fame, other English Rock groups entered the scene, bringing with them even more developed elements of the occult and black magic. Flower Power was a period of spiritual desperation for a vast section of youth in Britain and America, throwing off the Christianity of previous generations while seeking something truer to their nature with dabbling in Eastern mysticism and innumerable cults and sects. Occult faddism, largely dormant since the first decades of the century, began to manifest widely.

English black magician Aleister Crowley, dubbed the "wickedest man in the world" by the press in the 1930s, now rose to higher influence and prominence than he had ever experienced in his own lifetime. Through the underground films of Kenneth Anger, Crowley's specter began to loom large over the end of the '60s and early '70s. Both Mick Jagger of the Stones and Jimmy Page, guitarist of Led Zeppelin, scored soundtracks for Anger's Crowley-inspired films *Invocation of My Demon Brother* and *Lucifer Rising,* the titles of which betray their mystical concerns. Page's interest in Crowley developed to a far more serious level than the Satanic dabbling of the Stones; his collection of original Crowley books and manuscripts is among the best in the world. Page held a financial share in the Equinox occult bookshop (named after the hefty journal of "magick" Crowley edited and published between 1909–14) in London and at one point even purchased Crowley's former Scottish Loch Ness estate, Boleskine. The property continued to perpetuate its sinister reputation under new ownership, as caretakers were confined to mental asylums, or worse, committed suicide during their tenures there.

The bad vibes came with the territory. Speaking of his attraction to the strong-arm philosophy of Machiavelli in an interview, Page declared, "He was a master of evil, but you can't ignore evil if you study the supernatural as I do ... I want to go on studying it."[8] He was also straightforward in admiration for his spiritual mentor: "I think Aleister Crowley's completely relevant to today. We're all still seeking for truth—the search goes on ... Magic is very important if people can go through with it."[4]

ALEISTER CROWLEY

Imagery of Crowley's Thelemic religion can be found woven throughout the albums of Led Zeppelin, along with influences drawn from Anglo-Saxon and Norse heathen folklore and traditional music, and the mythology of J.R.R. Tolkien's literary works. If there is any early Rock band bearing exemplifying the basic themes that would later preoccupy many of the Black Metal bands in the '90s, it is Led Zeppelin. Stephen Davis, author of the Zeppelin rockography *Hammer of the Gods,* remarks that the music for the song "No Quarter," which Page composed, "inspired Robert [Plant] to write lyrics with provocative images of Led Zeppelin as a Viking death squad riding the winds of Thor to some awful Satanic destiny."[5]

The group encouraged such impressions with some of their antics, staging a record release party in the guise of a mock Black Mass. The event was held in the underground caves which formerly housed similar rites perpetrated by Sir Francis Dashwood and his debauched Hellfire Club two centuries earlier. In their heyday, the band—and Page especially—knew the value of a nasty reputation, much as Crowley had in his own generation. The resulting rumors ranged from the old standby of an alleged pact with the Devil signed by the group in return for success, to stories of Page's experiments with black magic effecting the death of drummer John Bonham. In recent years the former members of Led Zeppelin have tried to downplay such interests, with Plant and Page dismissing the Boleskine property as nothing more than an old "pig farm."[6]

Whether Zeppelin was in fact a "Heavy Metal" band is a point of debate, although they pioneered a sound which must be acknowledged as such in its more thunderous moments. Whether Black Sabbath is a Heavy Metal group there is no room for doubt. Sabbath slowed the contemporary framework of Blues-based Rock down to a lurching, sinister pace which perfectly suited their lyrical themes of insanity, war, and alienation. Singer Ozzy Ozbourne pioneered a haunting wail and the rest of the band made little effort to concede to any of the cheery sentiments still floating on hippy lips. Sabbath's cover art brought Satanic imagery to its apex in mainstream pop culture of the early '70s, with eerie demons attacking sleeping humans on albums like *Sabbath, Bloody Sabbath.*

Although members of the band talk of the occult, and Ozzy Ozbourne later in his solo career wrote his own paean to the "Great Beast" with the song "Mr. Crowley," a closer look at the lyrics of Black Sabbath does not uncover any serious Satanic philosophy. To the contrary, it reveals an almost Christian fear of demons and sorcery. In a 1996 interview with journalist Steve Blush in *Seconds* magazine, Sabbath bassist Geezer Butler explains the truth of the band's connection to the occult:

I was really interested because I was brought up Catholic. When I was a kid, I was a religious maniac. I loved anything to do with religion and God. Being a Catholic, every week you hear what the Devil does and "Satan's this" and "Satan's that," so you really believe in it. What sparked my interest was when I was in London around 1966–67. There was a whole new culture happening and this one guy used to sell these black magic magazines. I read a magazine and thought, "Oh yeah, I never thought of it like that"—Satan's point of view. I just started reading more and more; I read a lot of Dennis Wheatley's books, stuff about astral planes. I'd been having loads of these experiences since I was a child and finally I was reading stuff that was explaining them. It lead me into reading about the whole thing—black magic, white magic, every sort of magic. I found out Satanism was around before any Christian or Jewish religion. It's an incredibly interesting subject. I sort of got more into the black side of it and was putting upside-down crosses on my wall and pictures of Satan all over. I painted my apartment black. I was getting really involved in it and all these horrible things started happening to me. You come to a point where you cross over and totally follow it and totally forget about Jesus and God. "Are you going to do it? Yes or no?" No, I don't think so.[7]

Black Sabbath's flirtation with evil, filtered to their fans through a haze of barbiturates and Quaaludes, cemented them as a band tapped into the dark current. Like Led Zeppelin, the sinister image took hold and would be with them forever. Without respect or support from the press, Black Sabbath were filling arenas around the world, leaving their mark on impressionable kids who swarmed to have their eardrums pummeled in these rituals of crushing sound and volume.

Groups further from the spotlight than Black Sabbath—such as Black Widow and Coven—could afford to be even more obsessive in their imagery. The English sextet Black Widow released three diaphanous Hard Rock albums between 1970–72, and later appear as a footnote in books that cover the history of

occultism in pop culture. The chanting refrain of their song "Come to the Sabbat" evokes images of their concerts which featured a mock ritual sacrifice as part of the show. Beyond sketchy tales of such events, and the few recordings and photos they've left behind, Black Widow remains shrouded in mystery.

Coven are just as obscure, but deserve greater attention for their overtly diabolic album *Witchcraft: Destroys Minds and Reaps Souls.* Presented in a stunning gatefold sleeve with the possessed visages of the three band members on the front, the cover hints at a true Black Mass, showing a photo with a nude girl as the living altar. The packaging undoubtedly caused consternation for the promotional department of Mercury Records, the major label who released it, and the album quickly faded into obscurity. Today it fetches large sums from collectors, clearly due more to its bizarre impression than for any other reason. The songs themselves are standard end-of-the-'60s Rock, not far removed from Jefferson Airplane; the infusion of unabashed Satanism throughout the album's lyrics and artwork makes up for its lack of strong musical impact. In addition to the normal tracks, the album closes with a thirteen minute "Satanic Mass." The inside cover warns:

> To the best of our knowledge, this is the first Black Mass to be recorded, either in written words or in audio. It is as authentic as hundreds of hours of research in every known source can make it. We do not recommend its use by anyone who has not thoroughly studied Black Magic and is aware of the risks and dangers involved.[8]

Coven included the attractive female lead singer Jinx as well as a man by the name of Oz Osbourne, who bore no relation to the British vocalist "Ozzy." In an additional coincidental twist, the first track on the Coven album is titled "Black Sabbath." The *Witchcraft* album was released a year or two before Sabbath's eponymous debut in 1970, but the hidden links that exist between the two are up for speculation. Like their English counterparts in Black Widow, Coven devised a live show that puts many of the modern Satanic bands to shame. In a 1996 interview, former member Osbourne recounted the grandiose proceedings to *Descent* magazine as follows:

> We did a lot of our album and other things as our stage show, intermixing the Black Mass, or Satanic Mass, as kind of a segue between the songs. Behind the stage we had an altar and on top of the altar we had what we called a Christian cross and we had one of our road people hanging on the Christian cross as Jesus, and he just kind of stayed there during the whole show. Our stage was lit with obviously a lot of reds, and we had candles and that kind of thing. Then we would do our whole album and other materials that all dealt with interesting stories of witchcraft. Of course we were costumed. ... right at the end of our set we did a Procol Harum song that was just appropriate, called "Walpurgis." And right in the middle of it we break into the "Ave Maria." At that point Jinx would do the benediction of the Black Mass and she'd recite the Latin bits and she would go, "Do what thou wilt shall be the whole of the law," which is Crowley ... She'd say the Crowley bit then would hail Satan and

would turn around and scream "Hail Satan!" at the cross and altar, at which point the guy (Jesus) would pull his arms off the cross, get down, invert the cross into the Satanic symbol, and would go dancing off the stage while the music was still playing.[9]

After their outrageous debut, Coven recorded a few more major label albums, the diabolism drastically toning down with each succeeding release. Stories persisted for a time of a planned "Satanic Woodstock" in the early '70s where Coven was to play as a prelude to an address by Anton LaVey, High Priest of the Church of Satan. This rumor is verified in Arthur Lyons's book *The Second Coming: Satanism in America* (later revised and reissued as *Satan Wants You)*. Lyons traveled with LaVey to Detroit, where the festival was due to take place on Halloween, only to find the show cancelled due to controversy. Coven did manage to perform their full Black Mass spectacle at a Detroit nightclub the next evening, which frightened the living hell of out an acid-tripping Timothy Leary in attendance. The band's only widespread recognition came years later with the unexpected national hit single "One Tin Soldier," which some (predictably) spec-

ulated was the result of their pact with the Prince of Darkness whom they had once so boldly acknowledged. Despite Coven's obscurity, the *Witchcraft* album was striking enough to be discovered by some of the more important Satanic musicians in recent years, illustrating another link in the continuum of demonic Rock over the decades. King Diamond, the singer and driving force behind Mercyful Fate, one of the most important openly Satanic Metal bands of the '80s, acknowledges he received dramatic influences from a Black Sabbath concert he attended as a kid in his native Denmark in 1971. He also tells of finding inspiration from Coven's lead vocalist Jinx:

> An amazing singer, her voice, her range... not that I stand up for the viewpoints on their *Witchcraft* record, which was like good old Christian Satanism. But they had something about them that I liked...[10]

ENTER THE BLACK POPE

As integral to Satanic popular culture as any of the aforementioned music groups was Anton Szandor LaVey himself. Following years of observing the seamier folds of life as a carny, police photographer, burlesque organ accompanist, and occultist, LaVey made headlines when he founded the first official Church of Satan

PHOTO: NICK BOUGAS

ANTON LAVEY

on the dark evening of Walpurgisnacht, April 30, 1966. The fundamentals of the Church were based not on shallow blasphemy, but opposition to herd mentality and dedication to a Nietzschean ethic of the anti-egalitarian development of man as a veritable god on earth, freed from the chains of Christian morality. LaVey's Church was tailor-made for unending media attention, which soon made it a household word around the globe. In 1968 he released a *Satanic Mass* LP, which also broadcast a "Black Mass" from its grooves. Not centered on the medieval imagery found on the Coven album, it functioned instead as an exercise in the rejection of Christian doctrine. LaVey explains:

I don't think it was originally released as propaganda, but rather to set the record straight as to what a Satanic Mass is, opposed to a Black Mass, the latter of course just an inversion of a Christian rite. It was also an opportunity to reach a certain element at that time. There was no such forum for performance art at that time. The recording was done live with different tracks—it was recorded as performed. But I guess you could say it turned out to be propaganda ... it was subsequently distributed by Lyle Stuart [the publisher] and Howard Hughes funded some of that. He was quite sympathetic to what we were doing.[11]

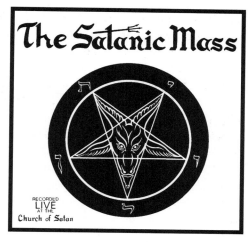

Looking back today on the relevance and influence of the *Satanic Mass,* LaVey notes, "I can see and appreciate it more than I could for years. For awhile I thought of it just as a documentary, similar to the LPs that came out in the early '70s like *The Occult Experience.* But now I realize it was a first for the kind of visuals which you're seeing all over today. It really was twenty years ahead of its time in many respects."[12] Following the "mass" ceremony, the B-side of the album also contained a number of Satanic declarations by LaVey, recited over the strains of Wagner and other bombastic scores. These texts were gleanings from LaVey's essays that would later form the framework of his infamous book the *Satanic Bible* which appeared in 1969. The only openly Satanic manual of thought to be widely distributed to the masses, it is impossible to accurately gauge the impact LaVey's book has had on society since its appearance almost thirty years ago. Readily obtainable, the book inevitably influenced the more prominent Rock musicians exploring themes of demonism and the occult in their personas, songs, and stage shows. In the heyday of such experimentation, a bizarre LP of entirely electronic synthesizer pieces devoted to the Devil even surfaced in 1971 on MCA Records, entitled *Black Mass Lucifer.* By the end of the '70s only a few of the major Metal acts were paying homage to sinister forces, and this was usually done superficially or with tongue in cheek, as on Sabbath albums like *We Sold Our Souls for Rock and Roll,* and AC-DC's *Highway to Hell.* But it was LaVey's *Satanic Bible* that ensured the Devil a permanent place on hundreds of thousands of bookshelves the world over. With a decade of

BLACK MASS LUCIFER LOGO

mainstream coverage for Satanism as a religion, and many of Hollywood's rich and famous converting to the new creed, others would be quick to follow.

THE NEW WAVE OF BLASPHEMY

The most discernible roots of the modern wave of Black Metal arising in Norway and elsewhere in the beginning of the 1990s can be clearly seen in the pioneers ten years earlier—Venom, Mercyful Fate, and Bathory. In tracing this lineage we have already stepped onto subjective territory, and others would argue for the inclusion of Slayer, Hellhammer, and Sodom alongside the above triumvirate. These bands made their undeniable mark as well, and will be noted in the next chapter. But by dint of chronology and primary impact both in terms of music, appearance, and philosophy, our focus concentrates on the former three.

THE UNHOLY TRINITY: VENOM

Venom began in 1979–80 in Newcastle, England, the result of three Metal fans and musicians deciding to take things one step further than their contemporaries. Even their mortal names were not intimidating enough to reveal, thus Conrad Lant, Jeff Dunn, and Tony Bray respectively adopted the more evil-sounding *noms de guerre* of Cronos, Mantas, and Abaddon. Their music was to be as over-the-top as their stage names, with equally abnormal lyrical content. Their beginnings and influences go straight back to the earliest Heavy Metal bands such as Black Sabbath and Deep Purple, as Abaddon explains:

> I was about nineteen. We were all into the older stuff—Judas Priest, Deep Purple, Motorhead, Black Sabbath. Mantas has always been a huge Kiss fan. We were drawing inspiration from these bands. We'd take some of the diabolical content of Black Sabbath and we'd mix it with some of the stage presence of Kiss, and with the originality of Deep Purple. That's where we got Venom from. Venom was never meant to be a blacker Iron Maiden or anything, it was really based on older bands and what little pieces of those bands we wanted to emulate.[13]

Venom took the heaviness and dark mysticism of these progenitors and gave it their own youthful punch-in-the-face to bring it up-to-date, as by this time the original Metal bands had settled into lavish lifestyles resulting from their success, losing most of the rawness that had once made them exciting. On close analysis, Venom was still playing fast Blues-based Rock, but with the primitive aggression which at that time was generally considered the property of the Punk bands. "Our music was born on the back of the Punk explosion in England," states Abaddon, "if you drew back Venom's influences I guess you'd find bands like Deep Purple and the Sex Pistols, Led Zeppelin, and Black Sabbath."[14] Thus it was not surprising that an array of their early fans were drawn from areas beyond the standard Metal crowd (many of whom considered Venom pointlessly offensive and untalented noise-makers). Abaddon remembers:

We played to skinheads and punks and hairies—everybody. Where some guy with long hair couldn't come into a Punk gig, all of the sudden it was really cool to go to a Venom gig for anybody. That's why the audience grew really quick and became very strong; they were always religiously behind Venom and they've always stayed the same.[15]

VENOM

PHOTO: FRATER NIHIL

CRONOS OF VENOM

In America indeed a large percentage of Venom's early fans came out of the nascent Hardcore Punk scene which was gathering momentum contemporaneously with the release of the band's first singles. Old Venom standards like "Die Hard" echo the caustic, violent sound of early '80s Black Flag more than any of the band's fellow English Metal acts, although if you discount the low-fi recording, overly distorted guitars, and barked vocals of Cronos, one realizes Venom is arguably not much more than classic Sabbath warp-speeded to 78 rpm.

Besides pioneering a dirtier sound than any other extant Punk or Metal band in Europe, Venom's notoriety was doubly assured with their elaborate endorsement of Satanism to a degree which would have caused wet dreams for medieval inquisitors. Given the level of blasphemy they made their trademark, it is not surprising the band could be embraced as panacea for the soul by kids brought up in stifling Christian environments, and looking for any possible way out. Whether or not Venom's members really practiced such rites in private was altogether irrelevant for listeners who could revel in the statements found on their album sleeves:

> We drink the vomit of the priest
> Make love with the dying whore
> We suck the blood of the beast
> And hold the key to death's door[16]

Such polemics struck a chord with their fans, and the vintage Venom albums *Welcome to Hell* (1981), *Black Metal* (1982), and *At War with Satan* (1983) have gone on to sell hundreds of thousands of copies over the years. With the title of their second album, *Black Metal*, a future style of Satanic music had found a name. The record also carved in stone some of the genre's essential features. Primary among these would be an open policy of violent opposition to Judeo-Christianity, endless blasphemy, and the abandonment of all subtlety in favor of grandiose theater which teetered over an abyss of kitsch and self-caricature. The magnitude of Venom's overwrought image was tempered considerably by some of the songs which wound up on their early LPs. Despite the Satanic trappings, they were still a Rock band after all, and numbers like "Teacher's Pet," "Angel Dust," and "Red Light Fever" are little more than shockingly low-brow paeans to sex, drugs, and cheap thrills.

PHOTO: FRATER NIHIL

MANTAS OF VENOM

Early interviews with the members of Venom make it clear they themselves were beer-swilling Rock and Rollers out to have a good time. The Satanism projected in their presentation and lyrics was primarily an image they stumbled upon, guaranteed to assure them attention and notoriety. There is no real philosophy behind it, beyond the juvenile rebellion of presenting anti-Christian blasphemy in the most lurid manner one's imagination can muster. Abaddon's reply to the question of whether he considers himself a Satanist is honest, but at the same time demonstrates it was probably never a real concern for him:

I certainly have in the past. I haven't spent a lot time on any one religion for quite a few years. It's something that I'm getting back towards, and I get a lot from people like LaVey. I'm a firm believer in all religions. Religion has become money now, and it's a very dangerous area because people can become very persuasive. We've always tried to make Venom as powerful and as loud and unmissable as we possibly can, but without preaching to people. We're very conscious about that. All the fans are called Legions and we are at their behest, but we don't want to preach. It's quite a difficult thing. We don't want to be seen as some kind of organized religion whereby you have to buy the T-shirt or the album to keep funding the thing that is Venom. If you don't want to listen to Venom anymore, so be it.[17]

In a 1985 *Kerrang!* interview, Cronos was even more blunt: "Look, I don't preach Satanism, occultism, witchcraft, or anything. Rock and Roll is basically entertainment and that's as far as it goes."[18] If one were to reduce Satanism simply down to the credo of "doing your own thing," then Venom may be "Satanists"—but by that criterion the Beach Boys probably are as well. After *At War with Satan* Venom diluted much of its image, and personnel changes wrought havoc on the integrity of their later recordings. Still, the band's vintage albums had caught the ears of thousands of feisty kids, and their (fabricated) image as vehement desecrators of the holy set the stage for the next generation to carry the newly lit Black Metal torch forward.

A MERCYFUL KING

The bands from the early 1980s who would have the most profound influence on the development of Black Metal as a genre have all on occasion acknowledged their familiarity with LaVey's *Satanic Bible,* and in the case of King Diamond and his band Mercyful Fate, it served as powerful inspiration. After stumbling across it in an occult bookstore, Diamond recalls:

> I read the book and thought, hey, this is the way I live my life—this is the way I feel inside! It's not like it was a major religion or anything like that, it was a lifestyle that I could relate to 500%. And it's just nice to see your own views and thoughts in words, in a book. It comforts you in some way. And that is how I felt. ... and you'll see it reflected in our early lyrics with King Diamond and Mercyful Fate. I used the word Satan at that time, and it had a very specific meaning for me—not the one that other people had.[19]

Drawing musical influences from the godfathers of Heavy Metal such as Sabbath and Deep Purple, combined with King Diamond's trademark operatic vocals, Mercyful Fate debuted with an eponymous mini-LP in 1982 which featured the anthem "Nuns Have No Fun."

This was followed by two more advanced albums, *Melissa* (1983) and *Don't Break the Oath* (1984), brimming with stories of magical rites, nightmarish fantasies of the consequences of broken pacts, and declarations of Satanic allegiance: *"If you say Heaven, I say a Castle of Lies / You say forgive him, I say revenge / My sweet Satan, You are the One."*[20]

Adding a cleverly conceived stage presence, King Diamond sang out such blasphemous provocations under a mask of theatrically sinister black-and-white face paint, his microphone lashed

MERCYFUL FATE'S KING DIAMOND

onto a cross fashioned of two human legbones. In many respects the records of Mercyful Fate would exert the same influence on their fans that groups such as Black Sabbath had commanded on Diamond's own musical beginnings. Diamond received occasional tabloid attention and much criticism for his promotion of evil subjects through his music, but he was always willing to declare his personal dedication to the LaVeyan brand of Satanism. He points out

that the outlandish and gruesome imagery in some of his lyrics was nothing to be taken seriously:

I make pretty sure that nobody can come and say, hey, you are trying to influence people into doing this or doing that, or you want to convert people and so on. No way. I raise a lot of questions, definitely. But I try not to give—in straight words—an answer of what I feel about it... You'll never see me doing things like that. People have got to make up their own minds. And if people are not interested in getting anything deeper out of words on an album, that's fine too. We are entertainers— we're not priests. I have my way of life and of course that will influence my music and my lyrics. I put all my feelings into both.[21]

MERCYFUL FATE

Diamond represents one of the only performers of the '80s Satanic Metal who was more than just a poseur using a devilish image for shock value. Between his openness about his personal commitments and the masked theater of his stage persona, his influence would be apparent when Black Metal was resuscitated with new blood in 1990–91. It's difficult to imagine King Diamond causing anyone to commit atrocities in emulation of his down-to-earth philosophy. The required stimulus would come in the more overt blasphemies of bands who pushed the themes to further extremes, and provided a vastly more volatile cocktail for teenage fans to imbibe.

THUNDER GODS: BATHORY

The Swedish group Bathory, along with Venom, are torch bearers in the evolution of modern Black Metal. Bathory takes its name from the "Blood Countess" Erzebet Bathory, a Hungarian noblewoman in the 1700s put on trial for the murder of hundreds of young girls, in whose blood she alleged bathed to maintain her youthful beauty. It is highly probable that an early Venom number, "Countess Bathory" on the *Black Metal* album, may have provided the direct inspiration for the name, as Bathory owes much of its initial sound and look to the English founders of Black Metal. The driving force behind the group is a man who uses the stage name of Quorthon (although, in point of fact, Bathory have never in their career played a live concert before the public). He describes the band's first efforts:

At that time I must have been 15, and I was helping a record company out with listening to new bands because there was some kind of Metal wave going on, I believe due to the "New Wave of British Heavy Metal." At that time I found out they were going to put together a Metal compilation album with

five or six Swedish bands, and I asked, "Please can you listen to my band, because we play a really exciting type of new Heavy Metal." That was January, 1984.

I never thought we'd be able to enter a studio again after that because we were really dirty sounding. But it turned out that 85-90% of all the fan mail that came to the record company from that record [the compilation was titled *Scandinavian Metal Attack*] was about our songs. So the guy from the record company called me up and said, "Hey, you really need to put your band together again and write some songs, because you have a full-length album to record this summer."

BATHORY'S FIRST ALBUM

VVORNTH
Drums & Cymbals

QUORTHON
Lead & Backing Vocals
Electric & Acoustic Guitars
Percussion · FX

KOTHAAR
Electric Bass Guitar

BATHORY GO VIKING

I thought we'd be selling two or three thousand copies; that album is still selling like crazy nine years later. I'm still really amazed about it, especially since when it was recorded it cost me about two hundred dollars and was recorded in fifty-six hours in a twelve-track demo studio south of Stockholm. From then on we just recorded every album on more or less "borrowed time" because we didn't really have any ambitions whatsoever, up until Important Records asked us to come over and do some kind of tour together with Celtic Frost and Destruction in the summer of '86. While all this was happening I of course didn't have a line-up together because, if you know anything about Swedish music at that time, the musicians were bound to look like the band Europe [an effeminate Hard Rock band popular in the mid-80s]! So when I'd drag a drummer down to my rehearsal place and play him the first record of Bathory, he'd go, "Oh no, oh no!" There just wasn't any atmosphere or tradition for Death Metal at that time, as there is today. ... Everybody seems to think that I'm a megalomaniac with a big head or something, but it wasn't really my fault— I should have been born in some place like San Francisco or London where I would have had a real easy time putting this band together.[22]

AN EARLY BATHORY PROMO PHOTO

Bathory's first three albums follow a similar mode of expression as Venom, though the music is made even more vicious by a potent arsenal of noisy effects and distortion. The hyperkinetic rhythm section blurs into a whirling maelstrom of frequencies—a perfect backdrop for the barked vocals of an undecipherable nature. Much of the explanation for this sound was simply the circumstances of recording an entire album in two-and-a-half days on only a few hundred dollars. The end result was more extreme than anything else being done in 1984 (save maybe for some of the more violent English Industrial "power electronics" bands like Whitehouse, Ramleh, and Sutcliffe Jugend) and made a huge impact on the underground Metal scene. In retrospect Quorthon says of Bathory's first self-titled album, "If you listen to it today, it doesn't make you tickled or frightened, but in those days it must have made a hell of an impression. Thinking back on how it was recorded, it's amazing how big things can be made with small measures sometimes."[23] The lyrics were centered on black magic and Satanism à la Venom, although funneled through a bit of Scandinavian innocence and teenage melodrama which made them come off as even more extreme in the end. Quorthon is very honest in his assessment of the Satanism on the early records:

Well, at the time it was very serious, because today, ten years later, I don't think I know anything more about it than I did then. I'm not one inch deeper into it than I was at that time, but your mind was younger and more innocent and you tend to put more reality toward horror stories than there is really. Of course there was a huge interest and fascination, just because you are at the same time trying to rebel against the adult world, you want to show everybody that I'd rather turn to Satan than to Christ, by wearing all these crosses upside down and so forth. Initially the lyrics were not trying to put some message across or anything, they were just like horror stories and very innocent. But nevertheless at the time you thought that you were very serious, and of course you were not.[24]

As Bathory matured over the course of their subsequent records, *The Return...* (1985) and *Under the Sign of the Black Mark* (1987), the music slowed down noticeably, songs became more elaborate, and the subject matter began to convey a degree of subtlety and ambiguity a far cry from the earliest singles. At this point came a remarkable shift of focus which, like their early primitivity, would also greatly influence the Black Metal scene of the future. *Blood Fire Death,* Bathory's fourth LP, hit record shops in 1988 and was eagerly grabbed by extreme Metal fans around the world. Instead of the B-grade horror cover art of the previous album, an entirely different image greeted them: a swarming, airborne army of enraged valkyries on black horses, spurred on by the Nordic god Thor, hammer held aloft in righteous defiance as a wolfskin-cloaked warrior drags a naked girl up from the scorched earth below. This remarkable romantic painting by Norwegian artist Peter Nicolai Arbo, depicting the infamous "Wild Hunt" or *Oskorei* of Scandinavian and Teutonic folklore, was the ideal entryway into Bathory's new sound which lay on the vinyl inside it. More accessible than the band's previous noisefests, the new album was, nevertheless, just as brutal. *Blood*

Fire Death employed the same amount of raw aggression, but channeled it through orchestrated songs and understandable vocals, which were helped along by more realistic and thoughtful lyrics. The first track was an evocative instrumental, "Odens Ride Over Nordland," which recreates the soundtrack of sorts to the cover art, with the father of the Norse heathen gods, Odin (also called Oden, Wotan, and other names, depending on the Germanic language) riding his eight-legged horse Sleipnir across the heavens. The Norse gods are again invoked on the final track of the record, the title song:

Children of all slaves / United, be proud / Rise out of darkness and pain
A chariot of thunder and gold will come loud / And a warrior with thunder and rain
With hair as white as snow / Hammer of steel / To set you free of your chains
And to lead you all / Where horses run free / And the souls of your ancient ones reign.[25]

With *Blood Fire Death* Bathory had forsaken the childish and foreign Satanism of their original inspiration but uncovered something just as compelling and fertile—the heathen mythological legacy of their own forefathers. The tapping of ancestral archetypes would become a matter of primary importance for the generation of Black Metal to follow, and an essential component of the genre.

The same inspiration resurfaced intensely on the next release, 1990's *Hammerheart,* with the songs written from a more personal point of view. The record is, to a deeper and more romantic degree than its predecessor, an attempt to seriously explore the mindset of a Viking Age practitioner of Ásatrú religion. Ásatrú, which translates to "loyalty to the Æsir [the pantheon of pre-Christian Nordic gods]," is the modern word for the revival and reconstruction of the religious beliefs of the Norse and Teutonic Northern Europeans. It is often accompanied by a strong hatred of Christianity, considered to be an alien religion forced on one's ancestors under threat of death. Bathory was not the only Swedish band of the period to advocate a return to Ásatrú (the singer of the heavy biker-oriented Punk group the Leather Nun in fact led an Ásatrú organization for a time), but they would have the most impact with their actions.

On *Hammerheart,* Bathory's music undergoes an epic restructuring. Most of the songs clock in at ten minutes apiece, the vocals are clearly sung and even surrounded by chanted choral backdrops. Richard Wagner is thanked in the credits. The cover art, a romantic oil painting titled "A Viking's Last Journey," depicts a Viking ship burial of a nobleman, where the corpse is pushed to sea in a longship, set alight by torches. Ironically it was not long after this that many a Norwegian Bathory fan would pick up real-life firebrands, and employ them in their own neo-Viking fantasy.

The final release in Bathory's "Ásatrú trilogy" came with 1991's *Twilight of the Gods,* which further emphasized the musical elements of European Classical composition. Lyrical themes were drawn from Nietzsche's dire warnings about the

spiritual malady afflicting contemporary mankind. Beside this came veiled references to the SS divisions of World War II Germany in the song "Under the Runes," which Quorthon admits was a deliberate provocation:

> I wrote it in a way so that it would create a little havoc. "Under the Runes" is, to begin with, just my way of saying that regardless if it's in the sky, the land, or deep down in the oceans, we will fight for my father's gods'

right to have a place in any form of discussion when we discuss Sweden...

We tend to think of ourselves as modern, down-to-earth Protestant Christians—healthy Christians. And we never talk about how Sweden was prior to that, more than 900 years ago, because we have a history of 2,000 years of being Ása-faithful, and just 970 years of Christianity. And if they don't want to talk about it, I'm prepared to fight any kind of war by the great hail, under the runes, for my father's gods. Because there are certain values, from those times, worth fighting for.

And in creating havoc, being able to talk about what the song is all about, I wrote it so that it would be able to be taken as a Second World War song. Because then I knew people would keep on picking out that lyric, and then I would keep having to answer questions about it, and would get the idea out there.[26]

This was not the first time Bathory trod onto questionable ground with symbolism. *Hammerheart* featured a sunwheel cross emblazoned on its back cover, an oft-used icon of radical right-wing organizations. Quorthon professes some naiveté in the matter, but it's hard to believe he wasn't aware of the full potency of such visual elements. As he explains:

In Sweden that's also the symbol for archeology, but in Germany it means something completely different. And the original colors for the logo and titles were black, white, and red—the original
German colors. I didn't even think about it, but people went berserk, so we had to print them in gold.[27]

Though not conscious of its influence, Bathory managed to create the blueprint for Scandinavian Black Metal in all its myriad facets: from frenzied cacophony to orchestrated, melodic bombast; reveling in excesses of medieval Devil
worship to thoughtful explorations of ancient Viking heathenism; drawing inspiration from European traditions to deliberately flirting with the iconography of
fascism and National Socialism. Bathory's first six albums encapsulated the
themes which would stir unprecedented eruptions from the youth of Scandinavia
and beyond.

Bathory's bizarre bloodline of demonic inheritance—and that of Black
Metal itself—can be traced straight back through Venom, Mercyful Fate, and
other darker-themed Metal bands of the early '80s, to the Heavy doom-ridden
sounds of Black Sabbath and the mystical Hard Rock of Led Zeppelin, to their
bluesy antecedents the Rolling Stones, and all the way to a poor black guitarist
from the American South who may have sold his soul to Satan in a lone act of

desperation. An unlikely Black Metal pedigree, but there it stands, helped along the way by countless others who poured their own creative juices into an evolving witches' brew.

Only a few years and a few more selective ingredients were needed to push the cauldron of Black Metal from the edge of the hearth and into the fire...

DEATH METAL DIES, BLACK METAL ARRIVES

BLACK METAL IS A BASTARD CHILD, CONCEIVED FROM THE PROMISCUOUS intermingling of a number of evil seeds, with only the general formula of Heavy Metal as its fecund womb. Abaddon notes the reality of the situation when discussing how many of the Metal sub-genres of the '80s and '90s came in the wake of Venom's outbursts:

I don't think any band sets out to become an institution. A band sets out simply to fulfill different goals at different times in their career. ... We were interviewed once and somebody said, "Venom's obviously not a Heavy Metal band. You don't sound like Heavy Metal and you don't look particularly Heavy Metal; you look like punks with long hair." We said Venom *is* Heavy Metal—it's Black Metal, it's Power Metal, it's Speed Metal, it's Death Metal. And all of these sub-genres had never been heard of before. All of the sudden one band is considered a Speed Metal band, one is considered a Death Metal band, and another is considered a Black Metal or a Power Metal band. What we meant is that Venom is *all* of these things, and all of these genres could emanate from Venom. We didn't mean for it to happen, but that's how it turned out. A band like Pantera have nothing in common with a Scandinavian band, or a band from England like Cradle of Filth—they don't sound like them. But when you draw back to where their all influences come from, you find Venom.[2]

By the closing years of the '80s, cutting-edge Metal groups had absorbed influences from both the bombastic "New Wave of British Metal," with ultra-masculine bands like Saxon and Judas Priest (the latter so much so they often crossed over the line of homoeroticism, with singer Rob Halford's leatherman get-ups), and the burgeoning Hardcore scene, with its lack of pretentiousness and gritty depictions of reality. The gnarlier second generation of Punk, Hardcore mirrored the same angst of the lost generation of American youth as did Metal; both thrived and cross-pollinated in the sprawling no man's lands of suburbia. Punk's do-it-yourself ethos carried over into everything and increasing numbers of kids formed their own bands, pressed their own albums, and organized concerts. Hardcore began to merge with elements of Heavy Metal and vice versa. Boundaries blurred and—as in the early days of Venom—kids from both scenes liked the same bands, attended the same shows, and voiced the same simple slogans of teenage turmoil and rebellion.

UNITED SATANIC AMERICA

Overt expressions of Satanism remained buried deep in the Metal underground, and Venom never reached the same visibility in the U.S. they had achieved in England. The closest American parallel to Venom was L.A.'s Slayer,

PHOTO: FRATER NIHIL

SLAYER ONSTAGE

with their odes to bloody sacrifices and moonlit rituals on the early records *Show No Mercy* (1983), *Haunting the Chapel* (1984), and *Hell Awaits* (1985). Bands from the States never seemed to achieve quite the unadulterated level of blasphemy wielded by the British founders of Black Metal, but they did their best. Slayer penned endless songs about Satan and black magic, but interspersed these with vague attempts to comment on the horrors of warfare and other social ills. After some initial promo photos dressed up in spikes, leather, and makeup, feigning the bloody sacrifice of a blond female, the band opted for a more realistic image of beer-drinking everyday Metalheads.

While most of the harder American Metal bands of the period stuck to less ornery lyrical themes, Slayer were not the only ones dabbling in diabolism. Another California band, Possessed, released its *Seven Churches* album in 1985, destined to be a influential slab of proto-Black Metal, and others waited in the wings to emerge. Even Mötley Crüe, later to devolve into Glam Rock sissies, began with a punkified debut and followed it up with *Shout at the Devil*, bringing a watered-down taste of the demonic to hundreds of thousands of impressionable suburban kids.

Equally important are the Misfits, Glenn Danzig's Punk band from the early '80s. They never sang of political problems (like the rest of their Punk and Hardcore peers) but rather a realm of B-grade horror films and space aliens. Beginning with a campy image of ghoulish makeup and "Devil locks" (a pointed clump of hair hanging down in front of their faces), the Misfits mutated into Samhain, injected more Metal into their sound, and sang pagan hymns to dark forces in nature. By 1988 the group had changed names again, to simply Danzig. They continue to this day, pumping out impious Blues-based Metal and walking much the same tightrope of spiritual and moral ambivalence as Black Sabbath did two decades ago.

SOUNDLY THRASHED

The late '80s saw the brief ascendency of Thrash Metal, exemplified by bands like Anthrax, M.O.D., Metallica, and even the more extreme Slayer. In Europe, the German groups Kreator and Sodom left a strong mark, along with Swiss ensemble Celtic Frost, who started out as the seminal outfit Hellhammer. Sodom toyed with Satanic themes on their first few albums, and band members adopted pseudo-

Possessed *Seven Churches*

nyms of "Angelripper," "Witchhunter," and "Grave Violator"—the last of these
bearing an ominous ring in light of the real-life activities Black Metalers would
partake in a few years later. Hellhammer/Celtic Frost flirted with darker occult
subjects for lyrical fodder, but eventually turned into something resembling a
metalized Art Rock band. Like any style hyped incessantly by the music industry,
Thrash Metal's days were ultimately numbered. The genre became too big for its
own good and major labels scrambled to sign Thrash bands, who promptly
cleaned up their sound or lost their original focus in self-indulgent demonstra-
tions of technical ability.

　　Peter Steele of gothic Metal band Type O Negative (and former frontman of
the late '80s "neo-barbarian" Speed Metal act Carnivore) accurately characterizes
Thrash Metal as a form of "urban blight music," a palefaced cousin of Rap.[3] His
remark is astute, and it wasn't long before Thrash bands like Anthrax actually
began collaborating with Rappers and incorporating elements of Hip Hop into
their songs. The less compromising underground watched such developments
with dismay, and eagerly awaited for its phoenix to arise from the ashes of the
now dead Thrash genre.

　　Innovations in the louder forms of music have almost always come at the
hands of the fans—fans who pick up instruments of their own, determined to do
one better over their mentors, or disgusted with seeing their favorite music
swamped in the wake of commercial sell-outs and corporate record labels meddling
in the affairs of the underground. Speaking about the longevity of extreme Metal,
Abaddon of Venom observes, "This kind of music always fractures, but the most

CELTIC FROST

important thing is that it always has a lot of passion in it, from the fans, which keeps it together. It's the power of the fan base that will always keep it there."[4]

DEATH THROES

Concurrently emerging in both the U.S. and Europe, Death Metal was the antidote the underground had awaited, reintroducing a sense of immediacy and danger otherwise lost after the early demise of Thrash. Death Metal took the speed of both Hardcore and Thrash to build its skeleton, and fleshed this out with churning, down-tuned guitars and a growling style of singing which provided a dramatic antithesis to the falsettos and high-pitched lead vocals dominating mainstream Metal at the time. Death Metal's subject matter was not far off from that of the Misfits, but instead of B-grade '50s horror, one now found the Z-grade slasher movie violence of the '70s and '80s served up in endless rotation. Songs detailing infinite varieties of murder, torture, rape, and dismemberment were spewed out from the growing army of Death Metal acts around the globe. The related genre of Grindcore, more heavily indebted to the politics of English anarchist and "peace Punk" pioneers like Crass and Rudimentary Peni, produced its own massively popular groups Extreme Noise Terror, Napalm Death, and Carcass. The latter are noteworthy for their graphically nauseating cover art on records like *Symphonies of Sickness*—collaged photographs of butchered meat and human autopsy photos, accompanied by lyrics drawn from textbooks on medical pathology.

EARLY SLAYER PROMO PHOTO

MORBID ANGEL

The two world capitals of Death Metal were the unlikely locations of Tampa, Florida and Stockholm, Sweden. From these extremes of fire and ice, the genre produced its most influential acts: Entombed, Hypocrisy, Dismember, and Unleashed from Sweden; Morbid Angel, Death, Obituary, and Deicide from the swampy netherworld of Florida. Other areas of the States also spat out bands of notoriety—misogynist gore fans Cannibal Corpse from upstate New York, equally rude and savage Autopsy from California—but the two afore-mentioned cities had specific record-ing studios and record producers which indelibly shaped the sonic boundaries of the genre. Death Metal eschewed the theatrics of its musical predecessors, instead opting for a "dude-next-door" look which remained unchanged on stage or off. Ripped jeans or sweatpants, high-top sneakers and plain leather jackets became the Death

Metal uniform, and band members were assured of never being recognized by fans on the street since they looked no different than a thousand other sallow-faced urban hoods.

A few exceptions came from the overtly Satanic bands who made up a small segment of Death Metal overall. The flamboyant singer of Deicide, Glen Benton, ceremoniously branded an upside-down cross into his fore-head, threw bloody entrails into con-cert crowds, and sported homemade armor on stage; fellow Floridians Morbid Angel began donning paramil-itary clothes for their live appearances, courting a neo-fascist demeanor, and reinforcing it with inopportune and illiberal comments in magazine inter-views. For the most part however, the

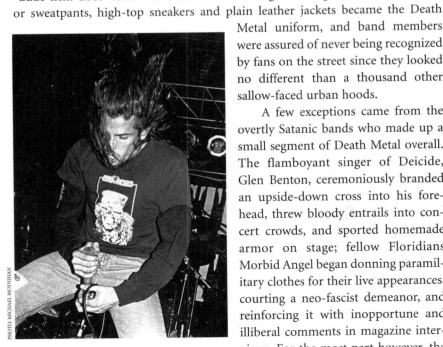

CANNIBAL CORPSE

DISMEMBER

genre rested on its laurels of unbridled sonic brutality and lyrical glorification of all things morbid and decaying.

As Death Metal gained momentum, only a few bands from the Thrash days remained who commanded any respect from the younger generation. Slayer continued to be revered as godfathers of the scene, and in turn the band kept fans interested as they shifted subject matter from juvenile Satanism to an open-ended fascination with violence in general. Serial killers, genocide, religious persecution, and other apocalyptic topics all became grist for Slayer's lyrical mill. Additionally they often employed the long-standing Metal tradition of invoking specters of Nazism and fascism in their lyrics and packaging. Slayer's fans were dubbed the "Slaytanic Wehrmacht," Nazi eagles were incorporated into the

PHOTO: MICHAEL MOYNIHAN

OBITUARY

DEICIDE

band's logo, songs were penned about Josef "Angel of Death" Mengele, and Jeff Hanneman adorned his guitar with photos of concentration camp corpses. They gained an added following from neo-Nazi skinheads as as a result, but it would be difficult to take much of this seriously upon closer examination of the group—despite his last name, there is nothing remotely "Aryan" about lead singer Tom Araya, who in fact comes from a Hispanic South American background.

VIKING DEATH SQUADS

One Scandinavian Death Metal group in particular set a precedent for certain of the Black Metal bands to appear some years later. This was Stockholm's Unleashed, who emerged after the breakup of early Swedish Death Metal group Nihilist. Unleashed never concerned themselves with the gory interests of their fellow bands, but instead made a similar discovery to Bathory and drew creative stimulus from the pre-Christian heathenism of their native Sweden.

From their first CD, *Where No Evil Dwells*, to the present, Unleashed have dedicated a significant number of their songs to themes drawn from the Viking Age and the old Norse religion. Their live concerts appear no different at first from a typical Death Metal show, until lead singer and bassist Johnny Hedlund starts making fervent declarations on the necessity of destroying the Christian religion of weakness and exhortations that "self preservation is the highest law!" This is certainly not the usual banter of a Metal band between songs, but they are sentiments that would be taken up by prominent Black Metalers soon enough. The band members proudly wear amulets of *Mjöllnir*, the Hammer of Thor, and at a certain point in every show

Hedlund leaves the stage, to return seconds later clutching a huge Viking drinking horn filled with ale (or on special occasions, mead, the traditional sacred honey wine of ancient Europe). He will then dedicate a song, such as "Into Glory Ride," to his Viking ancestors, drink from the horn and pour some of the libation onto fans in front of the stage. By incorporating such elements of tradition into their performances, Unleashed tap into the same atavistic well of energy which serves as a focal point for many of the most significant Black Metal bands.

PHOTO: MICHAEL MOYNIHAN

Unleashed are also noteworthy as one of a small handful of Death Metal acts who have managed to survive the demise of the genre they themselves forged. Between 1989–93 Death Metal had become immensely popular

UNLEASHED

worldwide, with bands drawing crowds in the thousands on an average night. The underground had been again pushed above the surface into commercial daylight, and it would—in typical fashion—react with a vengeance. As greedy record labels tried to cash in on the Death Metal trend by signing up untalented bands and releasing an endless stream of mediocre and remarkably unoriginal albums, the market was quickly swamped in a morass of interchangeable sludge. The irritated denizens of the underground began fomenting a new progeny they hoped would prove resistant to all attempts at co-option and dilution.

In Norway, bleak clouds on the horizon brought with them cheerless portents of a storm to come. Sweden's Death Metal underground had for years been in the world spotlight; it was considered the forefront of one of the most extreme varieties of music

THOR'S HAMMER, *MJÖLLNIR*

yet conceived. Norway also had its share of Death Metal bands, with names like Mayhem, Old Funeral, and Darkthrone. The leaders of the Norwegian scene realized—wisely—that in order to grab the attention of minds and souls they would need to willfully take things one step further. The fanciful violence and bloodlust of Death Metal wasn't anything in itself—it must be made real, and become a means to an end, if it was to hold greater purpose. Otherwise it was nothing more than the audio equivalent of a comic book for kids to aimlessly gloat over. Venom had set an example with their exaggerated blasphemy, and had pointed out organized religion as a worthy target for assault. Raised amidst a complacent acceptance of Christianity as something inherently good, surrounded by an oppressive and numbing social democracy which dominated Norwegian political life, these youths would proudly adopt Black Metal as their own. Picking up where Bathory and Venom had left off, they injected their efforts with a grim seriousness the likes of which even the extreme Metal underground had never dreamt possible. The mistakes of Death and Thrash Metal would not be repeated. No, this would be something else entirely—something so pure and unsparingly severe it would sear a mark in the history books forever.

A BLAZE IN THE
NORTHERN SKY

THE PRINCIPAL ELEMENTS OF BLACK METAL IN NORWAY RESIDE AS MUCH
in belief and outlook as they do in the music itself. There is a considerable
berth given toward sonic experimentation as long as certain
attitudes are prominently displayed by the musicians. At the same time, there is
no set "rule book" to be followed, and the boundaries of the ideology shift as time
passes. Such changes are usually effected at the hands of the more important
members of the scene, for the genre is in many ways entirely defined by the
dramatic personalities who have comprised it—and continue to forge its destiny.

In much the same manner as Venom are considered the fathers of Black
Metal worldwide, Mayhem holds a similar position in Norway itself. Their infamy
has long since spread into an international cult status. Mayhem were there before
anyone else and—albeit in a rather different form—they still exist today. Mayhem
will always remain associated with their late founder Øystein Aarseth, aka
"Euronymous," brutally stabbed to death in 1993. Long before this startling
setback, the band was already legendary due to all the rumors it had engendered
since its inception.

Synonymous with the rise of Norwegian Black Metal is *Slayer* magazine,
published for the last seventeen years by Jon "Metalion" Kristiansen out of his
home in Sarpsborg, a quiet area not far from Oslo. He has been both observer and
participant in the underground world of extreme Metal for as long as anyone in
Norway, and his recollections are quite valuable in piecing together the birth
pangs and key events of Black Metal there.

Metalion is quick to proudly point out how important and essential Black and
Death Metal are to him, "This is the blood which runs through my veins ... this is
me, this my destiny ... no options—total dedication," he says.² His excitement for
the music came in 1982, only a year after Venom had released their first singles:

PHOTO: NIHIL ARCHIVES

MAYHEM

There was nothing going on in Norway at that time. I was getting into the music all alone, and I was influenced by no one, because no one I knew was interested in this music. It took a few years before I found people who had similar interests in the same music. The first issue of *Slayer* magazine came out in 1985.[3]

METALION

Although Venom had a large cult following in Europe, Black Metal was yet to develop as its own style. During this period Metalion discovered the existence of Mayhem, then a severely raw and primitive Death Metal band, when he met them outside a Motorhead concert that year in the city:

I met them at the concert and they told me about their band. I was selling my magazine, so I got to know about them. After a few months we came in closer contact. At that time they didn't even have any demo tapes. They recorded the first one in the summer of '86—the *Pure Fucking Armageddon* demo. It was much more extreme than everything else; the sound was very, very primitive and much more brutal. You couldn't hear anything as extreme as Mayhem at that time.[4]

BATHORY ON THE COVER OF AN EARLY ISSUE OF *SLAYER*

Mayhem had played only one live show, shortly before Metalion's chance encounter with them. "But that was nothing...They did only covers of Celtic Frost, Bathory, and Venom I think—no real songs of their own. That was with their original singer, who was called 'Messiah.'"[5] Metalion remembers no other band in Norway with the intensity of Mayhem at the time, although another group called Vomit existed briefly, and had also provided Mayhem with a vocalist and session musicians for some rehearsals.

Mayhem released a second demo and then their *Deathcrush* mini-album in 1987, now a much sought-after rarity. It was only at this point the band had managed to build a name for itself and attract a circle of serious fans, for Aarseth was excruciatingly slow in releasing material, either due to financial problems or his insistence on maintaining total control over all aspects of the band's productions. Likewise there were few live shows, but the ones that did occur are still infamous milestones. Metalion

MAYHEM LOGO

PHOTO: METALION ARCHIVES

CELTIC FROST IN PROTO-CORPSEPAINT

recalls the early image of Mayhem "wasn't so serious at that time. They just dressed as they were—black hair, leather jackets, black clothes. That was just normal."[6] Soon enough Aarseth would adopt the concept of wearing "corpsepaint" during concerts and in band photos—stylized black-and-white makeup which created a gruesome, macabre appearance and became one of the trademarks of Norwegian Black Metal.

The origins of this practice are puzzling. More theatrical Metal and Punk performers like King Diamond and Glen Danzig's Misfits had all worn ghoulish makeup for their live shows in years prior to 1985; Celtic Frost from Switzerland adopted the style as well. One could even trace the seeds of the corpsepaint idea back to how KISS or Alice Cooper appeared during their giant stage spectacles of the '70s. Metalion has another theory about the specific source:

> I think it was really from a band called Sarcofago from Brazil. A very extreme Metal band, they released an album and Euronymous was totally obsessed with them because they wore lots of spikes and corpsepaint. He said he wanted every band to be like this, because he was so against the Death Metal trend from the USA and Sweden. Death Metal bands would play shows wearing jogging suits and he was totally against that.[7]

In 1988, a Swede named Per Yngve Ohlin, alias "Dead," joined as a new vocalist for Mayhem, having previously been a member of a horror-themed Death Metal group called Morbid. Dead would become the first keynote in the saga of Norse Black Metal when he blew out his brains in 1991, living up to his nickname at the same moment as he died with it. By the time of Dead's involvement in Mayhem, the

MORBID, WITH DEAD ON FAR LEFT

Norwegian Black Metal scene in Oslo was beginning to coalesce into a tiny but tangible network of dedicated people. They formed new bands, attended each other's shows, traded influences, and now had standards of extremity close at hand to measure themselves against.

New fans of the music began to make contact with those in Oslo, and especially with Aarseth. They were often teenagers still living at home in smaller towns and more isolated areas of Norway. An obsession with the same ideals, hatreds, and attitudes was enough to unite disparate young musicians to keep in contact primarily through correspondence and telephone, only meeting in person at an occasional concert when a more popular or mainstream Metal band would play a major city.

On the west coast of Norway stands the old city of Bergen, notable for its aristocratic attitude of independence from other areas of the country—especially Oslo. Bergen was the home of Kristian Vikernes (later to legally change his first name to Varg), a charismatic teenager

ADVERTISEMENT IN *SLAYER*
FOR FIRST MAYHEM MINI-LP

DARK THRONE LOGO

exploding with enthusiasm for whatever his current fixation happened to be. Having played guitar for years, he joined the Death Metal band Old Funeral, but tired quickly of their superficiality and juvenile concerns. Through playing with the group Vikernes came into contact with many who would become important in the realm of Black Metal. He met the musicians who later formed the band Immortal, as well as the legendary Euronymous. After leaving Old Funeral, Vikernes formed a one-man band in order to have complete control over his own work. Originally called Uruk-Hai after a J.R.R. Tolkien reference, he then changed the name of the project to Burzum, another coinage from Tolkien meaning "darkness." Metalion recalls Vikernes's entry into the Black Metal scene at this point:

> Nobody knew who he was. He was starting to talk about his band Burzum at the same time, and all the sudden he had recorded an album, the first Burzum album, and Euronymous was totally excited about it, because it was something extreme and new. They became very close friends.[8]

Burzum was not the only new Black Metal band to appear. An Oslo group, Darkthrone, was beginning to attract attention and played a few shows around this time. Some members of the band still dressed in jogging suits, betraying their Death Metal origins; others began wearing clothes more in line with the developing aesthetics of Black Metal. One of these concerts took place in the left-wing anarchist venue Café Strofal (A play on the Norwegian for "Catastrophic")—ironic, in retrospect, since their drummer Gylve Nagell, aka "Fenriz," would later exert significant influence of his own for a series of outspoken fascistic statements. Other groups who soon claimed the Black Metal title for themselves included Immortal (who also emerged from the remains of Old Funeral) and a young group from the Telemark countryside, Emperor. The latter outfit, along with Vikernes, was destined to play an important role in bringing the music genre to the attention of police departments as well as record collectors.

After the untimely demise of Dead, Euronymous continued plowing ahead with his projects, primary of which was to open a record shop. This was soon realized with the ominous title of Helvete ("Hell"). The shop was housed in too large and costly a space, didn't ever make much money to speak of, but functioned as an expression of Euronymous himself—it became the focal point of the scene. Metalion is quite clear in his assessment of the importance of the shop to the rest of the bands, and how it served as an extension of Euronymous's ability to influence those around him:

The opening of the record store Helvete happened a few months after [Dead's suicide]. That's the creation of the whole Norwegian Black Metal scene—it's connected with that shop, the influence Euronymous had on the young customers in the shop, and how he convinced them what was real and not real in this world. A lot of the guys in Immortal and Dark Throne were all into normal Death Metal and Euronymous showed them what Black Metal was really like, how things should be, and they followed him. Looking at the first Dark Throne album compared with the second, you can see Euronymous's influence on the second one, *A Blaze in the Northern Sky*. That's the first Norwegian Black Metal album after *Deathcrush* which was really big and an influence on the rest of the scene.

EMPEROR

Then followed Immortal, which was a Death Metal band who changed toward Black Metal, also under the influence of Euronymous. Even if they don't admit it, it's the truth. Also with Emperor—they had a band called Thou Shalt Suffer, which was Death Metal, and it changed to Emperor, which was Black Metal. The whole Norwegian scene is based on Euronymous and his testimony from this shop. He convinced them what was right and what was wrong. He was always telling what he thought, following his own instincts to the true Black Metal stuff like corpsepaint and spikes, worshipping death, and being extreme. That's what he was telling everyone about.[9]

WHY NORWAY?

It is difficult to offer an explanation of how Norway, a country on the outskirts of Europe with less than 4.5 million people, should become the epicenter of blasphemous Black Metal. The theories might range from the most prosaic to the spectacularly speculative. For example, one of the reasons suggested for why so many churches burned in Norway is that, compared to other Scandinavian countries, a much higher percentage of Norwegian churches are constructed of wood. It is much easier to set fire to a wooden church than one of stone—but even then it is not an entirely simple affair, as many failed arson attempts have proven.

There is an early example of church arson with diabolical overtones which was recorded in 1739. An eighteen-year-old youth from the Norwegian coastal city of Kristiansand named Anders Suhm allegedly renounced his baptism, blasphemed against God, and offered himself to the Devil. He also attempted unsuccessfully to set fire to a church. He was charged under Norway's strict blasphemy laws, which allowed for capital punishment. And even though beheading was rarely used for such offenses, Suhm ran away rather than face trial and was never heard of again. However, the case of Anders Suhm seems to be an isolated occurrence, and there is no evidence that would suggest a deep-seated Satanic tradition in Norway.

Since anti-Christian actions have played an important part in Black Metal, it might be useful to look at how Christianity functions in Norwegian society. Norway's official religion is Protestantism, organized through a Norwegian Church under the State. This has deep historical roots and a membership encompassing approximately 88% of Norway's population. However, only about 2-3% of the population are involved enough to attend regular church services. A saying goes that most Norwegians will visit church on three occasions in their lives—and on two of them, they will be carried in. Many Norwegians retain their membership in the Church "just in case," but will not actually sit and listen to sermons. There are also

laws on the books that require half of the government at any given time to be members of this Church. However, apart from these formalities, the Church's role has been steadily diminishing in Norwegian society.

The lack of religious fervor in the formal, State-run institutions has left a vacuum that is being filled by all kinds of religious and secular orientations. Evangelism is strong in Norway; few other countries have sent out more missionaries per capita. The Evangelical culture is particularly active on the southern and western coasts, where the Christian denominations tend to be extremely conservative. Here, drinking alcohol and sometimes even dancing is frowned upon. In the North, especially in Lappish areas, Christian communities exist which enact strict taboos against owning curtains and TV sets. An

BLACK METAL MAKES HEADLINES:
"THE CHURCH FIRE WAS SET. SATANIST
ALARM FOR PENTECOST"

example of the conservative Christian influence in Norway was the banning of Monty Python's classic comedy *The Life of Brian* as blasphemous. The amicable rivalry and fun-making between Norwegians and Swedes led to the movie being advertised in Sweden as "a film so funny it's banned in Norway."

The cultural legacy of Norwegian folktales presents a grotesque world of trolls, witches, and foreboding forests. These have had a profound influence on many younger Black Metal groups. Some bands, like Ulver, have altogether dropped traditional Black Metal imagery and symbolism for "trollish" atmospheres. Today there even exists a band called Troll. Modern folklore has had a more difficult time in Norway and horror culture has never been allowed a place here. While America has figures like Edgar Allan Poe as a part of the literary heritage, and slasher movies are screened on National TV, Norway's otherwise highly prolific movie industry has produced but one horror film in its seventy-year history. Horror films from abroad are routinely heavily censored, if not banned outright. This taboo against violence and horror permeates every part of Norwegian media. In one case, Norwegian National Broadcasting stopped a transmission of the popular children's TV series *Colargol the Singing Bear* on the grounds that the particular episode featured a gun.

The resulting void from cultural censorship of violence and the macabre may have made a significant contribution to Black Metal's overweening appetite for such imagery. When denied something, one tends to gorge on it when access is finally gained. Black Metal adherents tend to be those in their late teens to early twenties who have recently gained a relative degree of freedom and independence from their parents and other moral authorities. They are finally in a position to indulge their own interests without the interference of those who might frown upon such behavior.

The cultural distance from Europe might be part of the explanation why Black Metal was carried to its logical, or illogical, conclusion in Norway. Early Black Metal bands like Venom might not have been very serious about their image, but many young Norwegians may been unable to realize this. So when Venom were tongue-in-cheek, Norwegian kids took them dead seriously. Similar things have happened before. The Sex Pistols, for example, being the product of

PLATE FROM A NORWEGIAN FAIRYTALE BOOK

Count Grishnackh at the Winter Olympics in Lillehammer.

CARTOON SATIRIZING BLACK METAL'S HUMORLESSNESS

GEORGE MORAGEMOS

a smart manager who knew how to make a buck off Rock music, spawned a generation of bands who took Punk Rock, and the anarcho-politics that had been convenient slogans for the Pistols, very earnestly indeed. One strange aspect of the Black Metal mentality of the earlier days was the insistence on suffering. Unlike other belief systems, where damnation is usually reserved for one's enemies, the Black Metalers thought that they, too, deserved eternal torment. They were also eager to begin this suffering long before meeting their master in hell.

This gave rise to popular jokes like: "Why don't Satanists drive cars? Because walking is really hellish." Funny enough, to be sure, but reality was more bizarre. In an interview the February, 1993, edition of the now defunct Norwegian magazine *Rock Furore*, Varg Vikernes talked about his arrest for suspected church burning. When asked if this world wasn't already hellish enough, and therefore no grounds existed for romanticizing a metaphysical Hell, Vikernes lashed out against the prison system:

> It's much too nice here. It's not hell at all. In this country prisoners get a bed, toilet, and shower. It's completely ridiculous. I asked the police to throw me in a real dungeon, and also encouraged them to use violence.[10]

There is no one satisfactory explanation why the music reached such an epidemic proportion in Norway and was taken to such extremes. The only reasonable solution to the puzzle of Black Metal lies in all of these pieces forming a whole. Those who have attempted to understand Black Metal generally agree upon this.

Martin Alvsvåg is a graduate from the Theological Seminary in Oslo. His thesis about Black Metal was reworked into the book *Rock and Satanism*. Alvsvåg is one of the few in Christian circles in Norway—indeed one of the few from any background—who has taken the time to look at the subject closely. In addition to his research he has also encountered Black Metal through his work with young people in other Church contexts.

MARTIN ALVSVÅG

IS THERE A SIMPLE EXPLANATION FOR THE RISE OF NORWEGIAN BLACK METAL?

I don't think its right to point to one specific factor. It might just have been that Norway came up with one or two good Black Metal bands that gave Norwegian Metal a good name abroad and made it easier to sell. This would have been very conducive for a scene to be established.

IS THERE SOMETHING TO THE NORWEGIAN HISTORY OR PSYCHE THAT WOULD HELP PEOPLE MAKE GOOD DARK MUSIC HERE?

Some of the Black Metal people themselves seem to feel it's the fact that we have dark woods and long winters with virtually no light. This might make people attracted to darkness. On the other hand, Norway is the land of the midnight sun so I think it's a bit more complicated.

THIS COUNTRY IS A VERY SAFE PLACE TO GROW UP. COULD THIS HAVE UNDESIRED CONSEQUENCES?

I think Norway, being a very wealthy country with a high standard of living, makes young kids very blasé. It's not enough to just play pinball anymore. They need something strong, and Black Metal provides really strong impulses if you get into it. They're looking for something more in life than what they have already, and might feel that it's better to identify with evil than not to identify with anything at all. Black Metal is something strong that gives you respect and a sense of belonging in certain circles.

Ketil Sveen is one of the founders of the record label Voices of Wonder. His company has been involved with selling Black Metal music since 1991, when it started distributing the releases on Øystein Aarseth's label Deathlike Silence Productions. While Black Metal has often done its best to avoid commercial recognition, without record sales most of the bands would quickly cease to exist. Sveen was able to explain its development from the angle of the independent music business.

KETIL SVEEN

IS BLACK METAL AS POPULAR IN NORWAY AS IT WOULD APPEAR?

Black Metal has never really been that big in Norway, compared to how it sells abroad. One of the reasons that it appeals so much to foreign audiences might be that, for them, Norway and the Far North are really exotic. In Norway, it's basically been a circle of musicians and lots of bands.

WHERE IS IT MOST SUCCESSFUL?

Black Metal sells a little everywhere. If you are in a Pop or Rock band, it has traditionally been very important to be from the US or England to get really big. That's not so important in Metal. You can even be from a country like Brazil— look at Sepultura.

HAS THE DEMAND FOR THE MUSIC CHANGED OVER RECENT YEARS?

A few years ago, you could record anything and label it Norwegian Black Metal, and it would sell. Today, people are far more critical. Shoddily recorded and bad records won't sell. All musical waves will develop after a while; Punk matured, too.

Due to its excesses, Black Metal has become synonymous with Scandinavia, and Norway in particular. Somehow, through a combination of subtle and not-so-subtle factors, it coagulated and took shape. The drive toward violence could have just as easily been dissipated in less cathartic ways if the same people had become involved in an already established genre like Hardcore Punk instead. But this was not to be. With a frozen yet fertile garden in place, all it took was the effort of a few visionaries to sow the seeds of barbarity.

The scene owes itself to Euronymous more than anyone, that is beyond doubt. As he is no longer here to speak, we shall never know how deeply or seriously aware Øystein Aarseth was of the monster he was bringing to life. But animate it he did, and therefore his activities and associations deserve a closer scrutiny in order to reveal the path of the sparks which ignited the blaze in the northern sky.

A MAN'S DEAD BODY MUST ALWAYS HAVE BEEN A SOURCE OF

INTEREST TO THOSE WHOSE COMPANION HE WAS WHILE HE LIVED...

—GEORGES BATAILLE, *DEATH AND SENSUALITY*[1]

MAYHEM IN THE DEAD ZONE

MANY WILL ATTEST THE VERACITY OF THE OLD ADAGE, "BE CAREFUL WHAT you wish—it may come true," and for those who descend into the netherworlds of the occult it assumes even more portentous weight. A sensible magician who has opened up the currents of the supernatural knows that the smallest signs may be omens of a future miracle or catastrophe, and indeed every name, symbol, and event may have hidden meaning beyond the ken of the common man. In the realm of Black Metal, so thoroughly impregnated with the iconography of the occult by its perpetrators, names and pseudonyms appear to achieve a magical significance, and become indelibly welded to the personalities of their bearers—*nomen est omen*. This can be a blessing or curse, depending on the elements involved.

Do the names eerily reflect the karma of the personalities they denote? Or are the people destined to fulfill the fate foretold in titles they (ir)reverently adopt? These are questions that will never be answered. Regardless, in the case of Øystein Aarseth and his band Mayhem, the connection between such elements and outcomes is startling.

Mayhem began in 1984, inspired by the likes of Black Metal pioneers Venom, and later Bathory and Hellhammer. Judging from an early issue of Metalion's *Slayer* magazine, Aarseth initially adopted "Destructor" for his stage name as guitarist. The other members of the earliest incarnation of the band were bassist "Necro Butcher," "Manheim" on drums, and lead vocalist "Messiah." Not long after this Aarseth took on "Euronymous" as his own personal mantle—presumably it sounded less comical and more exotic than his previous pseudonym. His new name was a Greek title mentioned in occult reference books as corresponding to a "prince of death."

PHOTO: NIHIL ARCHIVES

MAYHEM CIRCA 1986

In early interviews Mayhem always refer to themselves as "Total" Death Metal, although in the fashion of many other Norwegian groups, Aarseth

HELLHAMMER

would later claim the band exclusively played Black Metal from the beginning. There was also no religious angle to Mayhem, beyond band members sprinkling their signatures with upside-down crosses. Their image mainly emphasized an obsession with death, violence, and having "a fuckin' good time."[2]

Mayhem played their first show in 1985. Their debut demo tape, *Pure Fucking Armageddon,* appeared a year later in a limited edition of 100 numbered copies. By 1987 someone called "Maniac" replaced the previous singer, whom Aarseth henceforth referred to as a "former session vocalist," despite his appearance on the demo as well as the first proper release, that year's *Deathcrush* mini-LP. Released in an edition of 1,000 on their own label Posercorpse Music, the vinyl sold out fairly soon, demonstrating Mayhem's small but increasing position of importance in the underground. Aarseth commanded a powerful role among disenchanted younger music fans, as Mayhem was considered the most extreme band existing in an otherwise quiet, conservative land. After the release of *Deathcrush*, vocal duties were exchanged once again and Dead, the distinctive singer for the Stockholm cult act Morbid, joined

NECRO BUTCHER

Mayhem and moved to Oslo. A new drummer was found in Jan Axel "Hellhammer" Blomberg, one of the most talented musicians in the underground. Even with the mini-LP selling briskly, and Mayhem's bestial reputation increasing, the band and its members remained dirt poor.

HELLHAMMER

HOW DID YOU BECOME INVOLVED WITH MAYHEM?

I started out in Mayhem in 1988 —early, together with Dead.

YOU KNEW HIM?

I didn't know him before—he was a Swedish guy—but we joined Mayhem at about the same time. I'd heard from some friends of mine that Mayhem was seeking a new drummer. I hadn't heard about Mayhem back then, but people had said it was the real stuff.

PHOTO: METALION ARCHIVES

DEAD ONSTAGE

MAYHEM LIVE ONSTAGE

I got in contact with Euronymous, and he wanted to hear a demo tape, so I brought one to the meeting and he said, "Yes, of course!" and was very pleased with it. Then I just moved to Ski, outside Oslo, where they were living and rehearsing. Dead had started out in the band a few months earlier than me.

EURONYMOUS

HOW LONG WAS IT BEFORE HE WAS LITERALLY DEAD?

It was in April, 1991, three years later.

HOW WOULD YOU DESCRIBE HIM?

He was a very strange personality. He was from Sweden, the old vocalist in a band called Morbid—some of the guys play in the shit band Entombed now. But he was an okay guy, a very nice fellow, but a bit melancholic and depressive.

WHAT WERE THE CIRCUMSTANCES OF HIS DEATH?

Me and Euro and Dead were living in an old house outside of Oslo where we rehearsed, but I was at my parent's house in Oslo when it happened. I was planning to go back, but Euronymous called me and said, "You can't go back because the police have closed the house."

"Why?" I said.

"Because Dead has gone home."

"He went back to Sweden?" I asked.

"No, he blew his brains out."

Euronymous found him. We only had one key to the door and it was locked, and he had to go in the window. The only window that was open was in Dead's room, so he climbed in there and found him with half of his head blown away. So he went out and drove to the nearest store to buy a camera to take some pictures of him, and then he called the police.

WHAT HAPPENED TO THE PHOTOS?

We had them the whole time, but when Euronymous was killed his father found them in his apartment and threw them away.

DEAD AND EURONYMOUS CIRCA 1990

EURONYMOUS

BUT YOU SAW THEM?

Yes, I was the one who took them to be developed. They were in color, real sharp photos. Dead was sitting half up, with the shotgun on his knee. His brain had fallen out and was lying on the bed. Euronymous was taking pictures from above, with details of the skull.

DEAD HAD BEEN SITTING ON THE EDGE OF HIS BED?

Yes, that's right. He had a shotgun, which was Euronymous's. We had a lot of weapons in our house.

WAS THERE ANY ADVANCE WARNING HE WAS GOING TO KILL HIMSELF?

I'd thought about it, because I saw him earlier that day and he told me he'd bought a knife. I said, "Okay." Then he told me it was very sharp, and I said, "Yeah, so what?" But I didn't know then. The same night he committed suicide he was talking to a friend near our house, and they were talking very much about it, about suicide in general, and when he left that night he'd seemed very happy.

HE WAS LOOKING FORWARD TO IT?

Yeah.

IT FIT IN WITH HIS PERSONALITY?

Yes, depressed, melancholic, and dark—very special.

WAS HE UPSET ABOUT HIS SITUATION WITH THE BAND?

Yes, because Euronymous was always telling him—lying to him—that, "Yeah, we're going to be very rich, just wait..." But in fact they were very poor and had no food to eat. Euronymous was a dreamer. The goals he set were far too high.

WERE YOU ALSO ANGRY AT THE TIME?

No, I didn't care about them fighting because I would just go to Oslo. I didn't care about it. I was concerned about the band, but not in the same

DEAD IN ISSUE 10 OF *SLAYER*

MAYHEM

way Dead was. He was far away from Sweden and didn't know anyone because he wasn't the kind of fellow who could get in touch with people very easily. He just sat in his room and became more and more depressed, and there was a lot of fighting. One time Euronymous was playing some synth music that Dead hated, so he just took his pillow outside, to go sleep in the woods, and after awhile Euronymous went out with a shotgun to shoot some birds or something and Dead was upset because he couldn't sleep out in the woods either because Euronymous was there too, making noises.

WHAT WAS DEAD DOING WHEN HE WASN'T WORKING ON THE BAND?

He was writing letters, mainly, and drawing pictures all the time.

Bård Eithun, alias "Faust," was the former drummer for the Black Metal band Emperor, now one of the most respected and popular groups in the genre worldwide. Eithun has long been involved in the inner core of the scene in Norway, and published a seminal fanzine, *Orcustus,* at the beginning of the '90s. He would later become even more infamous for his extra-musical activities.

BÅRD EITHUN

WHAT WERE YOUR FIRST IMPRESSIONS ABOUT MAYHEM?

I was very excited about it because Mayhem was already a big legend in Norway. It might sound a bit weird, but Mayhem was the band that everyone had heard of, but not many people had actually heard because they had released the demos which were quite limited and the mini-LP itself was very limited. But I was lucky because I knew Maniac, the vocalist, so he had some extra copies of the mini-album and he gave me one. I was very impressed because it was the most violent stuff I had ever heard, very brutal. I remember I thought that these people like Euronymous, Maniac, and Necro Butcher were very mysterious, because they didn't do many interviews but they were always in

BÅRD "FAUST" EITHUN

magazines and I saw pictures of them. They had long black hair and you couldn't see their faces, it was mysterious and atmospheric. That made a big impression on me back then.

WHEN DID YOU FIRST MEET EURONYMOUS?

I met Euronymous and Dead at a gig in Oslo in 1989; it was an Anthrax concert and I met them outside, where Øystein had some records to sell.

WHAT WERE THEY LIKE COMPARED TO THE IMAGE YOU HAD OF THEM?

They looked exactly as I expected them to. Dead was about as tall as me and very, very thin. He had long hair draped down and lots of symbols on his jacket, and band logos on the back. They acted how I had expected them to as well, they didn't talk too much and it was mostly about business, about the records, but they were nice guys.

YOU ATTENDED THE MAYHEM GIG IN 1990, WHICH WAS ONE OF THEIR RARE PUBLIC SHOWS.

Yes, it was their first official gig. Dead cut himself very badly—intentionally of course—because he crushed a bottle and took it and cut himself, leaving a big scar. He was supposed to go to the hospital afterward but he arrived too late so it was no use to give him stitches. I remember after the gig he was very sick and in pain because he lost a lot of blood.

Was this the infamous gig with the pigs' heads?

Yes, pigs' heads on stakes. When this gig occurred I was living with Mayhem and they had to make these pig heads, putting stakes into them. Dead was having big difficulty in getting the stake through the skull of the pig. I remember at the gig one person ate some piece of the pig head, which was very old so he got very sick.

Where did they get the heads from?

The local butcher, very cheap. It was some leftovers that would be put in the rubbish. But this gig made a big impression on people.

When did Dead mutilate himself?

It was in the middle, during the set. He had been talking about it before the set, so expectations were high and he had to do it. It was during a track with almost no vocals, so he had time to do it. He took a bottle and crushed it, took a sharp edge and did it.

How well did you know Dead?

He wasn't a guy that you could know very well. I think even the other members of Mayhem didn't know him very well. He was hard to get close to. I met him two weeks before he died. I'd met him maybe six to eight times, all in all. That's something I appreciate. He had a lot of weird ideas. I remember Aarseth was talking about him and said he did not have any humor. He did, but it was very obscure. Honestly I don't think he was enjoying living in this world, which of course resulted in the suicide.

What were his weird ideas?

He hated cats. I remember one night he was trying to sleep. A cat was outside his apartment, so he ran outside with a big knife to get the cat. The cat ran into a shed and he went after it. Then you heard lots of noise, and screaming, and there was a hole in the shed where the cat came out again, and Dead ran after it with his big knife, screaming, hunting the cat, only dressed in his underwear. That was his idea of how to deal with a cat.

Some believe Øystein killed him. Did Dead really kill himself?

He did. I know that afterwards Aarseth heard these rumors that he might have killed him. I remember Aarseth told me, "Dead did it himself, but it is

MAYHEM

okay to let people believe that I might have done it because that will create more rumors about Mayhem." That's also why he didn't tell people about how he took the brain pieces and made necklaces and ate part of the brain, because he wanted people to make up their own image of what he might have done. He didn't want to say yes or no about this, he was a quite obscure person. But he did use some stuff from the brain to make necklaces.

DID YOU EVER SEE THESE?

Yes. His skull was blown into many pieces, and Aarseth gave them to different people who could make necklaces.

CAN YOU SEE ANY CONNECTION BETWEEN HIS SUICIDE AND THE LYRICS HE WROTE?

It was his own choice really. People back then were expecting him to do it. I remember people were talking about how one day he would take his own life. It wasn't any big surprise.

WERE PEOPLE UPSET?

People who knew him didn't like it, because he was a good guy. The Mayhem guys were upset because they lost a good vocalist. He was supposed to record the album, so he delayed the whole recording. It was an unfortunate thing, because he was one of the best vocalists, at least in my opinion.

METALION

WHAT MAYHEM CONCERTS WERE YOU AWARE OF?

There was a Jessheim gig in '89. They played in February in '90 in Sarpsborg, where I live. I organized the gig. Euronymous always wanted to have an extreme stage show, and Dead was also into this, having as extreme a live show as possible. Corpsepaint, blood, and everything else. Dead ripped

PHOTO: NIHIL ARCHIVES

DEAD

up his shirt with a bottle. Mayhem also did a surprise gig at a place called Bootleg in Oslo; they only played a few songs.

HOW MANY PEOPLE WOULD GO TO THESE SHOWS?

The gig in Sarpsborg was with other bands, and was quite a big show. I reckon there were 300 people. There is a bootleg of the Sarpsborg show called *Dawn of the Black Hearts,* released by someone in South America.

THE CONCERTS MUST HAVE INFLUENCED MANY PEOPLE.

Yes, I think the guys from Darkthrone and Immortal were there.

WHAT WAS DEAD LIKE?

He was a very special person, a good friend. Very shy, very quiet. He didn't talk to many people. He stuck to himself and a few people he knew. I got to know him in 1987 when he was recording a demo with his former band Morbid, and I got him in touch with Euronymous and he joined Mayhem in early '88, because his band Morbid was folding. He and Euronymous had the same ideas about music and the stage show, so they fit well with each other. Dead had extreme views about everything: he talked about being non-human, not belonging on earth. He told me stories that he was almost dying when he was a kid, because he was sleeping so deeply and his face turned blue, and he wanted to die when he was only two or three years old. They couldn't wake him when he was sleeping; I think it was something between deep sleep and unconsciousness.

HOW DID EURONYMOUS DESCRIBE WHAT HAPPENED AFTER THE SUICIDE?

Euronymous wasn't worried about it. It was just like a car accident: "Yeah, Dead killed himself." That's one thing about worshipping death—why worry when people die? Maybe he was upset, but he didn't show it.

VARG VIKERNES

DID YOU KNOW ØYSTEIN VERY WELL BEFORE BURZUM SIGNED TO HIS LABEL?

No, not at all. I didn't talk to him at all, just a few sentences. I talked with Hellhammer a bit, and I was talking with Dead. Dead actually stabbed Øystein with a knife once; he hated Øystein.

SLAYER #9 WITH DEAD ON COVER

YOU WERE IN CONTACT WITH DEAD?

I didn't know him at all, I wasn't interested. I sent him some ammunition and stuff like that. And he actually shot himself with my ammunition, Dead did!

WHERE WAS HE LIVING THEN?

He was living in a house with Øystein and Hellhammer, southeast of Oslo. I met them in March 1991, and drove back home and we didn't have any contact, except I sent them the ammo in a Christmas present, with detonators and shotgun shells.

DEAD END

Dead's name was an ever-looming portent of his destiny. In letters written shortly prior to his suicide, he talked in detail about his obsession with snuff films:

What I prefer in movies is when they're underground-produced or of the classical HORROR sort—not "gore" but ESPECIALLY snuff, although I haven't seen many snuff movies... I like to research how one reacts when watching real deaths, or preferably real corpses (not on video...). A friend of mine who works in a morgue has told me that those who used to work with preparing autopsies, after a long day's or night's work have to "return to reality" before they just can walk out from there to go home...[3]

Describing what appears to have been a Near Death Experience, Dead once stated about himself:

I had a weird experience once. I had inner bleeding and it couldn't be found at X-rays so when it continued to bleed and bleed I finally fainted and dropped down to the floor cos I run out of blood. The heart had no blood left to beat and my veins/arteries almost emptied of blood. "Technically" I was dead. At that moment when I fell down (into a door, I heard later), I saw a strange blue color everywhere—it was transparent so I could for a short moment see everything in blue, till something shining white and "hot" surrounded me.

...it's someone I know who's had many out-of-body experiences and knows much more than I do about "supernatural" experience, that I asked [about] this cos it was so strange about those colors. She told me that the first "plane" in the astral world has the color of blue. The earthly plane has the color of black. Then comes a gray that is very near the earthly one and is easy to come to. The next one further is blue, then it gets brighter and brighter till it "stops" at a white shining one that can't be entered by mortals. If any mortal succeeds in entering it, that one is no longer mortal and can not come back to the earthly planes nor back to this earth. After the white plane ... it goes further with other colors that I don't know of—there only spirits and great sorcerers can travel. I was told that the white plane I then entered, without knowing it, was the deadworld and I had died.[4]

Dead would return to his own reality soon enough. Stian "Occultus," the vocalist who briefly replaced Dead in Mayhem after the suicide, recalls, "Dead didn't see himself as human; he saw himself as a creature from another world. He was very much into death and the other world. He said he had many visions that his blood has frozen in his veins, that he was dead. That is the reason he took that name. He knew he would die..."[5]

Dead was a truly unusual personality, judging from the words of all those who did know him. No one speaks ill of him, which is rare in such an insular and competitive realm as the extreme music underground. As many will testify, however, Aarseth appeared to feel little sorrow over the loss of Dead, instead glorifying his violent departure in order to cultivate a further mystique of catastrophe surrounding the band.

Besides photographing the body before the police arrived and collecting pieces of the skull which later became talismanic jewelry for Aarseth's close associates, Hellhammer remembers: "We also found some of the brain, and Euronymous took it, cooked it in a stew, and ate it so he could claim himself to be a cannibal."[6] There was even a fleeting idea to retain other parts of Dead before the police arrived. "[Aarseth] thought of sawing his arm off and putting it under a glass display case, but he figured it wouldn't be very smart because the police would probably ask where his arm was."[7]

Aarseth also chalked up his bandmate's demise as part of an ongoing war against the other music scenes from which Mayhem had now fully distanced itself. Interviewed in 1992 by Bård Eithun for his *Orcustus* fanzine, Euronymous declared:

We have declared WAR. Dead died because the trend people have destroyed everything from the old black metal/death metal scene. Today "death" metal is something normal, accepted and FUNNY (argh) and we HATE it. It used to be spikes, chains, leather and black clothes, and this was the only thing Dead lived for as he hated this world and everything which lives on it.[8]

Writing shortly after the suicide, Euronymous told a correspondent:

We have no vocalist anymore! Dead killed himself two weeks ago! It was really brutal, first he cut open all his arteries in the wrists and then he had blown off his brains with a shotgun [sic]. I found him and it looked fucking grim, the upper half of his head was all over the room, and the lower part of the brain had fallen out of the rest of the head and down on the bed. I of course grabbed my camera immediately and made some photos; we'll use them in the next Mayhem LP. I and Hellhammer were so lucky that we found two big pieces of his skull and we have hung them on necklaces as a memory.

Dead killed himself because he lived only for the true old black metal scene and lifestyle. It means black clothes, spikes, crosses and so on... But today there are only children in jogging suits and skateboards and hardcore moral ideals, they try to look as normal as possible. This has nothing to do with black, these stupid people must fear black metal! But instead they love shitty bands like Deicide, Benediction, Napalm Death, Sepultura and all that shit!! We must take this scene to what it was in the past! Dead died for this cause and now I have declared war! I'm angry, but at the same time I have to admit that it was interesting to examine a human brain in rigor mortis. Death to false black metal or death metal!! Also to the trendy hardcore people... Aarrgghh![9]

As usual, Euronymous proves himself a historical revisionist of unparalleled ability when it comes to anything connected to Mayhem. According to others who knew him, Dead wasn't excited enough about black clothes to ever wear them much of the time. He died wearing a white T-shirt with "I ❤ Transylvania" stenciled across it. Hellhammer adds, "Euronymous spread the rumor that [Dead] committed suicide because of the scene. That was not the reason for it, but he wanted it to look that way because then he could make more money and make him look more evil than he really was."[10]

Øystein was quickly realizing the power of creating a militantly sinister image for the band, as part of his stated plan to "spread evil" to the masses. As far as their musical endeavors were concerned, the only circumstances where Mayhem really lived up to their image was during the rare live performance they could arrange. The 1990 Sarpsborg concert became legendary, later spawning a bootleg CD—the cover of which bears a very clear reproduction of Dead's shotgun-detonated head and slumped torso, brains emptied onto his lap. No one should have been shocked that Dead chose to blast himself to oblivion, given his disposition. Speaking shortly after the Sarpsborg show in an interview done by Werner Linke of *C.O.T.I.M.* magazine, the singer revealed his own peculiar obsession with mutilated heads:

Pigheads, as well as other heads, is what we try to have at all gigs. It needs sick ideas and also money as well as it's gotta suit the place we're playing at. For example, if we use impaled pigheads in an Islamic country we'll surely get killed then. Another thing is that what's the most disgusting thing to do right here to fuck with the wimps might not be the same effect somewhere else... if we ever come to, for example, India, the most evil thing that we can do there that I have in mind will be to sacrifice a "holy cow" on stage.

I wanna have stage equipment at our shows of Transylvania landscapes, instruments of torture that are from the 12th Century, real trees from a dead forest, spotlights that are used to "paint" dark colors of dusk and later moonshine... different animal heads and human craniums hanging in meat hooks by chains from the dead trees and heads that have huge screws in their eyes... that's what I think would make the perfect mood...

[Another aspect of the live show] is when I cut myself up. Something I study is how people react when my blood is streaming everywhere, but that's not why I do it. I like to cut, in others preferably, but it's mostly in myself. That I can't do it too often ... makes me a bit mournful. The nearest thing is three gigs in Sweden which will probably be in the end of May and I think if I can take a highly tuned kitchen saw machine that's cutting and saw-

"DEAD"

ing faster than it's possible to control—that would be a nice thing to have there. Another band there ... will try to get a goat that they shall sacrifice on stage with a fireman's axe.[11]

Such interviews of the period demonstrate that by early 1990 the modern face of Black Metal had now reared its grimly corpsepainted face. It was a far cry from the vintage days of Venom concerts and their banks of flashing strobe lights, pyrotechnics, and cheesy outfits fashioned of studs and spandex. Norwegian Black Metal had found its soul, and was happy to just settle for a few decapitated heads, self mutilation, and an opposition to everything considered "good" or life-affirming.

The concerts Dead fantasized about for his homeland of Sweden would never reach fruition, nor would the promises of live animal sacrifice and demented rites involving table saws. For on that 8th day of April, in the house on Sørumveien Road in Kråkstad, the 21-year-old Per Ohlin picked up one of the many weapons in the house, loaded with ammunition provided by Varg "Grishnackh" Vikernes as a friendly gift the previous Christmas, and discharged himself abruptly from this mortal coil. Often accused of being humorless, he rectified this with a last scrawl of *Schadenfreude* on his succinct suicide note: "Excuse all the blood."[12]

WELCOME
TO HELL

Ø YSTEIN AARSETH WAS UNDAUNTED AND ODDLY INSPIRED BY DEAD'S dramatic departure from Mayhem. He continued with his program to slowly take control of the extreme underground in Norway. He had already re-established his record label under the name Deathlike Silence Productions (DSP) and released an LP by the band Merciless. He hoped to soon re-release the now legendary *Deathcrush* mini-LP, but realized in order to raise the capital to continue with his projects, he would have to make additional money with less uncompromising releases than his own. In the 1992 *Orcustus* interview he explained:

If we had the economic possibility to do it, we should meet up at concerts and beat up ALL trend people ALL the time until they would be too scared to go to concerts at all; now we need their money instead. It's impossible to stop the trend no matter how much we want. We have to do the best out of it and sell lots of trend shit to them.[2]

With such thoughts in his mind, he rented a space in Oslo for a record shop. Even if he would have to sell less extreme music to pay the bills, the orientation of the business would be around Black Metal—thus it was christened "Helvete," the Norse word for Hell. Aarseth would create something unique of his new venture, even if he had to make some concessions to popular taste:

The original idea was to make a specialist shop for metal in general, but that's a long time ago. Normal metal isn't very popular anymore, all the children are listening to "death" metal now. I'd rather be selling Judas Priest than Napalm Death, but at least now we can be specialized within "death" metal

EURONYMOUS

and make a shop where all the trend people will know that they will find all the trend music. This will help us earning money so that we can order more EVIL records for the evil people. But no matter how much shitty music we have to sell, we'll make a BLACK METAL look for the shop. We've had a couple of "actions" in churches lately, and the shop is going to look like a black church in the future. We've also thought about having total darkness inside, so that people would have to carry torches to be able to see the records.[3]

The space was much too large for his limited stock of wares, so Aarseth closed off a smaller section of the building to house the store. The walls were painted black with the Helvete logo on the door in blood red paint. A former associate of Aarseth's, Stian "Occultus," remembers, "It was far too big, and the rent was too high. That's the reason why it never did well."[4] Metalion concurs, "It was like renting a big house and only using one room. That was all they used."[5] He also clarifies that Aarseth's plan for the customers to have to illuminate the shelves by carrying

PHOTO: TOMAS HAUGEN

INSIDE HELVETE

torches remained wishful thinking. "That was just a rumor again. It *was* very dark. Euronymous wanted people to go around with torches to look, but that was never a reality."[6]

BURZUM'S FIRST ALBUM

Nevertheless, with Aarseth's prominent position in the new Black Metal scene, the store began to gather energy as a focal point, even if it wasn't generating much wealth. More and more Norwegian bands were shifting over to Black Metal, following the example of Mayhem. Now they would dedicate themselves fully to the "evil" and anti-social inclinations which made the Death Metal bands look like humanists in comparison.

By mid-1991 the groups Darkthrone, Burzum, Immortal, Thorns, Enslaved, Arcturus, and later Emperor were all in contact with Øystein Aarseth, who had plans to release most of them via Deathlike Silence. The inner core of friends and casual acquaintances who made up these bands would later be termed the "Norwegian Black Circle" by Aarseth when he spoke to the press about the church burnings destined to start before the year's end. Ihsahn, the singer of Emperor, recalls the dynamics that were operating at that time:

There's no discipline in the scene anymore, like earlier on around the shop—you had to be kind of accepted. You came there and if you were trusted, if they knew that you were serious in your views, you were accepted. There was a lot of respect for the shop, and people came there with corpsepaint on, which in some cases was quite stupid as it was daytime, and people were out shopping. But it was a very complex and very hard atmosphere, you felt this once you came in there—it was very powerful. The shop was an environment ... People wanted to be accepted, and they were kind of humble before Euronymous and the older guys from the scene.[7]

obscuritatem advoco amplectère me

ABRUPTUM'S DEBUT CD

One of the more recent arrivals to the scene was Varg Vikernes, also known as "Count Grishnackh," with his one-man band Burzum, who lived in Bergen on the West Coast. It was a long six- to seven-hour trip over mountains by car or train from there to Oslo. Vikernes would come for extended visits, during which he and Aarseth became fast friends. Details were sorted out for DSP to sign Varg's band, for which a debut album was already recorded. Aarseth was immensely excited about the sound and presentation of Burzum; the band fit perfectly into his scheme to release only "truly evil" music. With its depressed atmosphere and wailing, painfully hoarse, high-pitched vocals, Burzum sounded quite distinct from any other band in the scene.

Aarseth also kept in touch with a growing number of extreme bands from out-side Norway whom he likewise encouraged and made plans to release records by: Japan's Sigh, Monumentum from Italy, and the bizarre Swedish entity Abruptum.

Only a few of these schemes would ever be realized before Aarseth's death, mostly because he was never cut out to be a businessman. He ran his label ineptly, and the capital to invest in new releases was simply not there.

BÅRD EITHUN

WHAT WAS YOUR RELATION TO THE RECORD STORE?

He opened the shop in May or June of '91 and I started working there from July, '92, until July, '93. In the beginning he was doing the shop with two other guys, but it didn't work out very well. Then he asked if I would work there, because we could get some

PHOTO: FRATER NIHIL

JAPANESE BLACK METAL BAND SIGH

money from the Labor Exchange system; it was quite easy for me to get money and he could have someone working in the shop. It was also interesting for me to work there.

WHEN DID YOU MEET VIKERNES?

That was before I moved to Oslo, it was before a Morbid Angel gig. The shop was kind of a meeting place for people. I think it was in '91. It was at that gig that Vikernes was introduced to the scene, because people hadn't met him before.

IMMORTAL

WHAT WAS YOUR IMPRESSION?

I liked him because he was able to do things. He also often wanted to overdo stuff. If he did something that went well, then he wanted to do it ten times more that evening if it was possible. He didn't know how to stop and take a break. He was okay then, but when he was arrested the first time, in January, '93, and he became more of a known person in Norway, then he got more difficult to be with because he was a prominent person and such.

WHAT SORT OF IDEAS DID HE HAVE WHEN YOU FIRST MET HIM?

He was a Devil worshipper and he was against Nazis, for reasons I don't know, but that's what he said. After the arrest in early '93 then he got into this Nazi stuff.

PHOTO: FRATER NIHIL

IMMORTAL ONSTAGE

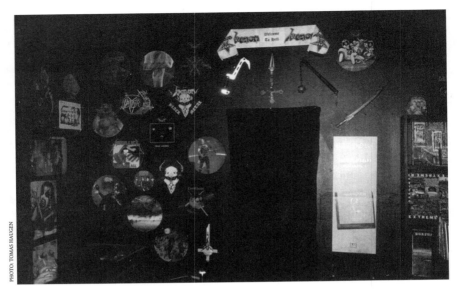

HELVETE

WHAT WAS THE "BLACK CIRCLE"?

It's just a name that was invented for the people who hung around the shop—the people in these bands and some others too. People kept asking who were the members of this Black Circle, but it didn't really have members. We just had some people we knew who were able to do things but there wasn't anything like members and membership cards and official meetings. We just knew who was able to do what and just asked them if they might be interested to come around the shop. It was very easy stuff, there wasn't anything more behind it.

WAS THE IDEA THAT IT WAS ORGANIZED CREATED BY THE NEWSPAPER ARTICLES?

If it was "organized," it must have been because we had this shop that made it possible to have an economic background for the actions. But yes, the media made it look lots more organized than it was in reality. The media loves these big scandals and always try to make the most out of it.

THE SHOP WAS JUST A CENTRAL PLACE...

Yes, a meeting place. That's the most organized the Black Circle was.

HOW DID SO MUCH HAPPEN WITHOUT ANY ORGANIZATION?

I don't know. I guess after the first church burned down in Bergen, people got very enthusiastic about it.

EXPERIMENTS IN EVIL

There are fanciful stories that have circulated about Euronymous setting up a laboratory of sorts in the basement of the house he shared with Hellhammer and Dead. Allegedly he would descend into the cellar for hours, concocting recipes with volatile chemicals, attired all the while in his white lab coat. Some of Euronymous's experiments were rumored to have caused dangerous combustions, creating fiery results with almost supernatural qualities. The same could be said of the Helvete shop, although the consequences would reach far beyond the black walls that enclosed it. The chemistry of impetuous personalities and impatient enthusiasms would play off each other in an escalating drama that quickly made national headlines.

Smaller "actions" had occurred before someone in the scene decided to torch the ancient Fantoft Stave Church in Bergen. Aarseth proudly alluded to church break-ins done to provide interior decorating props for the record shop, and a few such minor crimes were probably committed from mid-1991 onward.

In late '91 an Oslo concert by the popular Satanic Death Metal band Morbid Angel was a meeting point for fans who would become integral to the inner core of the Black Metal scene. It was also linked to a rash of cemetery grave desecrations. The media would later paint a picture of the profanations occurring as a result of the excitement generated by the concert, but Vikernes clarified, "It wasn't *after* the concert, really it was the day before. I was accused of it, but they didn't have any witnesses. The witness withdrew his testimony, so I was actually freed of the charge."[8]

Other small, fledgling crimes included a threatening attack against Stian "Occultus," the temporary member of Mayhem who Euronymous later disowned entirely. In an old German fanzine interview from 1991, Vikernes boasted, "Under a fullmoon of June a cross was burnt in Occultus's garden. His window shattered under the raging stormclouds by the hands of evil beings tossing an iron crucifix. The false will be given a sign before they DIE! One night!"[9] When recently asked about the nature of the incident, Vikernes explains there was "some idiot who said, 'I'll kill you.' We just took a cross which said 'My girl' on it, put it in his garden with gasoline all over it and lit it, and threw rocks through his bedroom window. Nothing came of it."[10]

METALION

HOW DID YOU HEAR ABOUT THE CHURCH BURNINGS—FROM THE MEDIA?

No, first hand information you could say. From Euronymous—he told me that Grishnackh had burned a church, yes, great. It was the first one in Bergen.

DID VIKERNES SAY ANYTHING ABOUT IT TO YOU?

There was a certain understanding between us. We were not talking directly, but I got the impression of what he was saying. It was no problem to understand what he meant and vice-versa, but he didn't say directly.

DID YOU KNOW ABOUT WHO WAS DOING THE DIFFERENT ACTIONS?

Yes, but how interesting is that?

I'M CURIOUS ABOUT HOW MANY PEOPLE KNEW WHAT WAS GOING ON.

Too many people, anyway!

INSIDE HELVETE

BÅRD EITHUN

WAS THERE ANY SERIOUS PHILOSOPHY BEHIND WHAT BEGAN TO HAPPEN?

Many people were happy about all the attention we got. A lot of people wanted attention, and as they got it they wanted to go further into it and do more things. I also believe that many people were really into it because of the music, Black Metal philosophy, working against Christianity and organized religion. They believed in it.

WHERE DID YOU PICK UP THE IDEOLOGY?

The feeling around the shop was that we worked against all these organized religions that were in Norway—Christianity and also the new ones like Islam. That was at least my intention...

The idea was that we would make an organization which was mostly basing its action on illegal activities and not legal ones. We wanted to get in touch with people on the illegal market who could get us weapons. We had a guy who lived near the shop who could get us all sorts of weapons. He could also get amphetamines and heroin, but that wasn't interesting to us.

HELL ON EARTH

Helvete was by no means a normal record shop. Situated in the Old Town in Oslo's East End, a lower-income area with a high percentage of immigrants and young people, it was rather inconspicuous from the outside. With its blackened windows it could easily be mistaken for one of the many porn shops or brothels posing as massage parlors that thrive in Oslo's low-rent neighborhoods.

Once the visitor was inside, any confusion as to where he was would be quickly dispelled. The purpose of the interior decoration was to live up to the shop's name in every respect. One of the first things to catch your eyes was a

PHOTO: RIKKE LUNDGREEN

STREET ENTRANCE LEADING TO HELVETE SHOP

female mannequin dressed in a hooded cloak, the kind one would expect to see members of a witch coven wearing in a Hammer horror film. Other paraphernalia that helped set the mood included a skull proudly displayed on the counter. Aarseth's more grandiose interior decorating schemes, like making tombstones from polystyrene, were never carried through.

Add to this a gloomy ambience enhanced by lit candles, and the resulting atmosphere was tailor-made for scaring the occasional Christian who would drop in to check out the machinations of the Devil on earth. To other people, it was downright silly. Aarseth was not unaware of this, and somehow cultivated it too. He had always been cognizant of the theatrical side to Heavy Metal, as the Kiss picture discs on the wall attested.

Additionally, Helvete had a spacious basement that would be used for photo sessions, parties, and other social gatherings. It functioned as spare lodging space for guests and those that lived too far away to get home after an excessive night about town. The basement was where Varg Vikernes lived when he was visiting Oslo. The reins were, however, gradually tightened on what the room could be employed for, since some would use it as a place to take girls they picked up while out drinking. Eventually, the cellar became too damp and clammy to serve any function at all.

Helvete quickly gained a substantial cult following. Specialist record shops are often able to make more money than the number of their customers would suggest, as members of subcultures defined by music tend to buy everything within "their" genre. Thus, the shop became a meeting point for the nascent Black

Metal scene as well as for all kinds of people interested in the harder ends of the music spectrum. As Helvete coincided with the boom of Death Metal music, the shop attracted music fans that would in no way share the Black Metal scene's outlook. Aarseth was not above making money by selling music to them, and the shelves contained bands like Metallica and Godflesh.

Aarseth tried to be like his shop. He realized the responsibility that comes with being in a band that has decided to maintain a certain image. Like Helvete, Aarseth would be a manifestation of the Black Metal aesthetic. He was always dressed in black from head to foot, his hair dyed black for added effect. He sported long, aristocratic mustaches and wore knee-high boots. His black leather biker jacket was decorated with badges. His rather slim frame bore the mark of many hours in the gym, but could not hide the fact that his height was hardly imposing. When talking, he seemed stern and serious, sometimes with pomposity verging on the theatrical. He would do his best to maintain this façade towards outsiders and the younger members of the developing scene.

Anyone conversing with him for more than a few minutes would get an impression of a man very different from his carefully constructed image. If he took a liking to you, that side would be revealed in full. Aarseth was an enthusiast by nature, hardly appearing "evil" as he would run around his shop like an

CELLAR OF HELVETE, 1992

overgrown kid. You could be treated to listening to goodies from his private record collection, fetched from the back room where Aarseth lived for a time before he could raise the money to buy his own apartment. There he kept his sizable hoard of records, books, videos, and other personal possessions.

Having been a music fan for so long, his record collection also included lots of material that was hardly standard Metal fare; he had a specific taste for German electronic music like Kraftwerk. This was not popular within the scene in its more orthodox days. His stern appearance was also probably influenced by Kraftwerk's image as faceless and machine-like. Such obsessions on Aarseth's behalf had the rather strange effect that many people in the scene would later claim to be huge fans of electronic music.

Politically, Aarseth was a long way from the nationalist and often pseudo-right-wing sentiments that are so prominent in Black Metal today. He proclaimed himself a communist, and for a while had been a member of the Rød Ungdom (Red Youth), the youth wing of the Arbeidernes Kommunist Parti (Marxist-Leninistene)—The Marxist/Leninist Communist Workers Party. Though rather few in number, the party had an appeal for intellectuals, including many prominent writers and politicians, and thus maintained a strong grip on Norwegian cultural life for many years. Rød Ungdom was aggressively anti-Soviet, and looked to China and Albania for inspiration. Despots like Pol Pot were also viewed as models of resistance against Western imperialism.

While the Party no longer glorifies these dictatorships, no formal excuse or apology has never been made for these ideological excesses in the '70s and '80s. This was what attracted Aarseth; the idea of strong leaders shaping the world appealed to him greatly. He eventually broke with Rød Ungdom, allegedly because he realized at a certain point they were "just a bunch of humanists." However, he would keep his convictions, if that was the right word, for it is hard to say how much of this was truly heartfelt and how much of it was part of his "evil" act.

He was an ardent collector of Eastern Bloc memorabilia and political trinkets like badges and flags, some of them picked up on Mayhem's travels (before Dead's suicide the band had played a few shows in East Germany and Turkey on one ill-fated tour). His correspondence with people from those areas would also help him tremendously. Some of the treasured objects in his collection were heroic photographs of Nicolae Ceaucescu, the former dictator of Rumania and one of Aarseth's idols. "Albania is the future," he would muse to anyone willing to listen.

It is hard to say why Aarseth's particular brand of communism never caught on in the scene. An explanation might be that with leftism's strong tradition in Norway, and prominent public figures having defended Pol Pot and Stalin in the past, the trappings of communist dictatorships are not shocking to the Norwegian mind in the way that a runic symbol would be for its association with the Quisling regime of World War II.

The aura surrounding Helvete attracted many young people later to gain fame in the scene. They would start their Black career by lingering in the shop, literally hanging around there for hours. It would be extremely annoying for Aarseth to have teenagers hovering in the shadows of his store all day perfecting their "evil" act, but he was too polite to tell them to beat it. After Aarseth's death, many of these same peripheral young fans would claim to have been his close confidants.

An intriguing question is who or what produced the sudden and severely intensified "pro-evil," Devil worship ideas that both Øystein

VIKERNES IN CORPSEPAINT

Aarseth and Varg Vikernes began projecting in underground interviews and toward their companions. Many in the scene today blame it on Varg, but judging by interviews with Aarseth from this period he was on a similar track. In reality, it was probably a case of two charismatic personalities egging each other on. Vikernes takes credit for this, although he disassociates himself from the sexual proclivities he claims Aarseth engaged in as a result:

We were joking about the Satanism. Øystein and all these guys in Oslo were saying how they were Satanists. I reasoned that if you're a Satanist then you invert everything that Christianity was. Øystein wasn't serious about Satanism at all, though. But I tried to provoke him, in a way to say, "You're not a Satanist, you don't follow anything." So I was provoking him about what Satanism was, and he was following me. He was having anal sex... because in the Bible it says that you shall not let the sperm fall to the ground, and we reasoned that if you shoved it up someone's ass, into the sewer, then that's the worst thing you can do—that's Satanism. And he said "Yes!" We didn't realize he was bisexual and actually homosexual. Some weeks before I killed Øystein, another guy joined me on a trip to Oslo, and he told me that he had once searched Øystein's drawers and had actually found a dildo with shit on it. He was a homo, always saying how pussy was disgusting. We didn't want anything to do with him.[11]

Vikernes also later wrote down his recollections about Aarseth's video collection and the type of material he was fascinated by, stating that Øystein

spent large parts of his time watching child pornography—disgusting films with hermaphrodites having anal intercourse with "men," so-called "snuff" films where ordinary people are kidnapped and tortured to death in front of the camera. For example—I have been eagerly told descriptions of what these films are like from [Aarseth]—dildos with nails are pushed into women's crotches, or they are nailed to tables through their labias.[12]

PHOTO: NIHIL ARCHIVES

One of the Famous Euronymous
Promotional Pictures for Mayhem, 1991

In its basic form, the type of Satanism preached in the early stages of Black Metal was just an inversion of doctrinal Christianity. Whereas international Satanic groups like the Church of Satan view Satan in an archetypal or symbolic sense, to the Norwegian teenagers he was most certainly real. In a similar manner to fundamentalist Christians, they viewed the world as eternally locked in a struggle between good and evil— the only real difference being which side they chose to fight on. However, in many ways the Black Metalers were more sternly "Christian" than the average follower of the Norwegian State Church.

In the late 1950s, conservative theologian Ole

Hallesby asked a Norwegian radio audience: "If you die in your sleep tonight, do you know where you will go?" His provocative question had the effect of pouring gasoline on a debate that had already been ignited regarding the existence of Hell. Even then, subjects such as this were becoming something of an embarrassment within the Church. In later years, overt acknowledgment of Hell and Satan have been nearly taboo in Church circles. Like exorcism, they are topics that are simply not discussed.

Ironically, this is the State Church of a country where "Hell" was placed in the center of the capital city, in the form of a record shop which became the focal point of the gestating Black Metal scene. So while Satan might be nearly dead in the Norwegian Church, he was alive and kicking elsewhere. Jacob Jervell, a retired professor of theology at the university and a minister in the State Church, feels it unfortunate that many people involved in organized Christianity in Norway are reluctant to address uncomfortable issues. He is now primarily a writer of books on theological subjects.

JACOB JERVELL

HOW DO YOU EXPLAIN WHY SOME YOUNG PEOPLE WOULD BECOME INVOLVED IN AN EXTREME MOVEMENT LIKE BLACK METAL, AND WHY THE CHURCH WOULD HOLD NO INTEREST FOR THEM?

When young people encounter the flat moralism of the Church, they get the feeling that it doesn't make sense. It is a very idyllic world that is preached about in the sermons. Black Metal music awakens powerful destructive forces in its listeners, forces that are not dealt with in church preaching, where they never received an answer to the question about what evil is. Instead they get rather idyllic, utopian sermons about sin. Young people don't feel that this is relevant, so they become alienated. It is counterproductive; we end up with a lost generation. Young people might see the Satanic version of Christianity as more realistic than the one they have been taught by the Church. They feel it is something they can connect to—powerful forces that have a resonance within themselves.

WHAT IS THE POSITION OF THE CHURCH WITH REGARD TO SATAN?

The Church dutifully trots Satan out once in a while, but only because it has to confirm that the Church believes in him too, since he's mentioned in the Bible. But when he's trotted out, he's just a harmless ghost, a ridiculous character. This leaves the church without any ability to formulate what evil is. And that is perhaps the biggest problem we have. The figure of Satan has enormous symbolic power. The word that is used as a substitute for it, "destructive," has nowhere near the same content. And when the real sources are lost, evil can start to look attractive. On the occasions when I am asked to lecture about evil, it is never in a Church context—it is always for university students. So the word "evil" is coming back, but not in the Church. It is a pity that historians look at the Christian texts in a wholly different way than the Church itself does.

COULD VIOLENTLY ANTI-CHRISTIAN ACTS LIKE THE BURNING OF CHURCHES BE SEEN AS A REACTION TO A CHURCH THAT HAS BECOME MORE LIBERAL— WHICH MIGHT BE INTERPRETED AS A CASE OF THE CHURCH ABANDONING ITS OWN THEOLOGY AND BASIC PRINCIPLES?

Yes, as well as a reaction to it becoming more secular. As a result, if you want to "find yourself," you don't go to church. Incitement to thinking doesn't come from the Church anymore; not even the incitement to behave morally. We are not able to expose modern society for what it is.

HOW HAS THE CHURCH REACTED TO THESE EVENTS?

The Church has not reacted at all, at least not in any sense that I can see, theologically. They are unable to make clear what evil is—even in a century as evil as ours, in which evil has been industrialized. The moralism is too strong, and the Church is unable to see that some things are beyond good and evil. The campaigns where refugees at risk of deportation were provided safehouses by local churches, on the other hand, elevated the Church's consciousness.

BUT WOULDN'T THE CHURCH FEEL THAT THE CHURCH FIRES ARE THE TIP OF AN ICEBERG, THE MOST EXTREME MANIFESTATIONS OF A TREND WHICH JUST SHOWS HOW FAR YOUNG PEOPLE HAVE FALLEN OUTSIDE THE CHURCH'S SPHERE OF INFLUENCE?

No, then the Church officials start talking about how well they are doing with Christian youth choirs and getting young people to go to summer camps and so on. The Church is more preoccupied with arguing about whether they should bless homosexual partnerships.

SPREADING THE FEAR

During the period when Aarseth was releasing the first Burzum records on DSP and running Helvete, Vikernes had not arrived at any of the above judgements about his then close friend. Varg came to Oslo for a time and moved into the basement of the record shop, living in the barren space there along with "Samoth," the guitarist of Emperor. The line-ups of many of the Norwegian Black Metal bands were extremely incestuous at this point, and Vikernes was even a stand-in bassist for Mayhem, and played on the debut full-length album they were endlessly trying to complete, *De Mysteriis Dom Sathanas,* "Lord Satan's Secret Rites."

In a Mayhem interview from this period, actually answered by Vikernes, he lauds his bandmates, saying, "the 'new' Mayhem is, as I see it, better than ever! Hellhammer is the best drummer ever and Euronymous is a musical genius. Could it be better?"[13] A few sentences later he promises that Hellhammer will also play drums for Burzum, although this never came to pass. On the second Burzum release, *Aske* ("Ashes"), bass playing would be done by Samoth, but with this sole exception Vikernes maintained his project entirely alone.

Promotional photos of Aarseth were taken shortly after the opening of Helvete. They show him cloaked in a black cape, candle or sword in hand, his face austerely decorated in corpsepaint, obscuring his small dark goatee under white make-up. There are also many earlier photos of Dead and Euronymous similarly decorated. Very few such corpsepainted portraits of Vikernes exist— the fashion seems to be something more particular to Aarseth. If it is true that Vikernes introduced the ideology of medieval-style Devil worship to Norwegian Black Metal, it must be also acknowledged that not a moment was lost before Aarseth began trumpeting it as his own. He summed up his attitude at the time:

I don't think people should respect each other. I don't want to see trend people respecting me, I want them to HATE and to FEAR. If people don't accept our ideas as their own, they can fuck off because then they belong to a musical scene which has NOTHING to do with ours. They could just as well be Madonna fans. There is an ABYSS between us and the rest. Remember—one of the Hardcore [Punk] rules is that you must be open-minded (except for themselves), so we must be careful and avoid being open-minded ourselves. The Hardcore pigs have correctly made themselves guardians of morality, but we must kick them in the face and become guardians of anti-morality.[14]

In the months following the opening of Helvete, the tone of such proclamations by Aarseth and Vikernes steadily intensified. They were not confining their viewpoints to themselves, but publicly stating them in fanzine interviews as well. People in the Metal underground began to take notice of these vociferous Satanic extremists from the remote North, and wondered if they could possibly be sincere. Aarseth and Vikernes were smart enough to realize that unless more serious actions were undertaken in the real world, their words would be seen as nothing more than empty rhetoric—or worse, a bad joke. They would simply have to prove Black Metal was no laughing matter...

ASHES

ONE OF NORWAY'S GREATEST HISTORICAL TREASURES IS THE STAVE CHURCH. These unique wooden congregation houses were built soon after the arrival of Christianity in Scandinavia around 1000 C.E. They continued to be erected up until the end of the Black Death, the bubonic plague which swept through medieval Europe in the 1300s. The name stave church is derived from the manner of their construction, which utilizes a strong post (*stav* in Norwegian) in the four corners of the main room.

The exterior of a stave church is commanding, often distinguished by gabled roofs and windows, with these smaller configurations leading to a sharp steeple. Entirely fashioned of wood, sometimes darkened or tinted blue-black from pitch, the more elaborate stave churches also bear intricate carved portals in *ringarike*-style Nordic interlace and interior motifs displaying remnants of heathen iconography. A dramatic example is a one-eyed carved head at Hegge and its vivid echoes of Odin in a state of ecstasy.

Sheathed in scaled, reptilian wood shingles, stylized dragon heads often rear up from the upper gable-points of the churches, adding to the foreboding effect. The external aura of the more elaborate stave churches conveys an impression of part wooden cathedral, part haunted house. Although not entirely exclusive to Norway (two less distinctive examples exist in Sweden and England), the stave church has become synonymous with that country. As many as 1,200 stave churches may have existed in the early Middle Ages; only thirty-two original examples survived in the second half of this century. That total has since been revised to thirty-one.

Before its day of judgement by fire in June, 1992, Fantoft arguably possessed the most ominous visage of any extant stave church. Dating from the twelfth century, it originally stood at Fortun, near the Luster Fjord in Central Norway. Like a number of stave churches, it also contained old runic inscriptions. At the close of the 1800s it was scheduled to be demolished to make room for a new burial ground. Unlike like many other stave churches that were destroyed during this period (before the realization of their great historical and cultural value), the church was saved when it was dismantled and moved to Fantoft, five miles south of Bergen on the west coast of Norway.

The groundplan of the building was slightly altered at the time of its recon-

struction in 1883, and the entire exterior renewed. The church sat on a thickly wooded hilltop, where according to David Walsten, author of *Stave Churches of the World*, "The trees were so dense that from some vantage points the church could not be seen until one was nearly upon it."[2] The wooden construction of the traditional stave churches has always made them vulnerable to destruction by causes natural and unnatural, and the obscured location of Fantoft made the work of an arsonist even easier. Thus, early in the morning on the 6th of June, 1992, it was fatally torched, and while Vikernes is strongly suspected as the culprit, no conviction has ever been made in the crime.

PHOTO: DAVID WALSTEN

FANTOFT IN 1990

News of the destruction of one of Norway's cultural landmarks made national headlines. It would not be long before other churches began to ignite in nighttime blazes. On August 1st of the same year the Revheim Church in southern Norway was torched; twenty days later the Holmenkollen Chapel in Oslo also erupted in flames. On September 1st the Ormøya Church caught fire, and on the 13th of that month Skjold Church likewise. In October the Hauketo Church burned with the others. After a short pause of a few months' time, Åsane Church in Bergen was consumed in flames, and the Sarpsborg Church was destroyed only two days later. In battling the blaze at Sarpsborg a member of the fire department was killed in the line of duty. Some would later consider this death the responsibility of the Black Circle.

Beginning with a small, ineffectual fire at Storetveit Church in the month preceding the Fantoft blaze, there have since been a total of at least forty-five to sixty church fires, near-fires, and attempted arson attacks in Norway. Roughly a third have a documented connection to the Black Metal scene, according to Sjur Helseth, head of the Technical Department of the Directorate for Cultural Heritage. The authori-

PHOTO: DAVID WALSTEN

Fantoft

PHOTO OF FANTOFT ALLEGEDLY TAKEN BY VIKERNES
HIMSELF SHORTLY AFTER THE ARSON

ties are reluctant to discuss the details of many of these incidents, fearing that undue attention may literally spark other firebugs or copycats to join the assault which Vikernes and his associates began in 1992.

Church fires themselves are not a wholly new phenomenon. On average, one or two churches have burned down per year in Norway in the past, most due to natural occurrences such as lightning strikes. Fire security at churches has been notoriously bad, and faulty electrical wiring can therefore also account for many of these fires.

However, there have also been cases of arson in the past. Churches are prime targets for pyromaniacs, and prior to 1992 there have been nine instances in Norway since World War II where churches have been deliberately set alight, for various reasons. Since pyromaniacs generally prefer uninhabited buildings, not really wanting to harm anyone, churches are ideal since they are usually situated away from residences—an added advantage to this being that it is easy to carry out the deed unnoticed. Finally, churches make very attractive fires, as the spire will cause flames to leap dramatically into the sky, creating a rather spectacular sight.

According to the law enforcement manual *Fire and Arson Investigation*, "Arson as a crime predates the written history of common law," and they note it "has always been regarded by the law as a heinous and most aggravated offense. It endangers human life and the security of habitations. It evidences a moral recklessness and depravity in the perpetrator."[3] This attitude is certainly present in Northern Europe, and arson is specifically mentioned in the oldest extant Norse codes of law. In eleventh-century England, arson was a crime punishable by death. Later, during the reign of King Henry II, a person convicted of arson would be exiled from the community after they had suffered the amputation of one hand and one foot.

FIRE IN THE MIND'S EYE

Arson often afflicts a community due to the presence of a pyromaniac or pathological firesetter. These individuals have a psychological—rather than monetary—impulse behind the acts of arson they commit, and this often drives them to repeat the crime until caught. It is difficult to generalize about pyromania, and casebooks on the subject categorize different types of pyromaniacs according to their apparent motives: jealousy, paranoia, revenge, suicidal urges, and so forth.

On top of this, fire—especially in its destructive aspect—is a source of instinctual fascination for human beings in general. The 1951 study *Pathological Firesetting* by Lewis and Yarnell remarks:

> Religion is only one outlet in which man indulges his hereditary fascination for fire carried in the racial unconscious, according to Jung. There are more practical methods of utilization. Everyone vicariously enjoys witnessing a devastating fire, and its appeal is sufficiently elemental to surmount intellectual and cultural differences. Adolescent boys out looking for excitement like a good fire. Angry mobs derive pleasure from burning the victims' property; revolutionaries burn their oppressors' estates; and warring men find in fire their greatest outlet for these destructive tendencies. In fact, some

PHOTO: MARTEN BJORKMAN

FROGN CHURCH BURNED

aviators describe with ecstatic fervor the joy and satisfaction they derive from watching the countryside burst into flames from their bombings; of course here is a reaction of justified revenge, but it still
satisfies an instinctive urge.[4]

In reviewing the case literature, basic parallels can be found between the
recent Scandinavian church-burners and certain classes of pyromaniacs,
although the actions of the former are to a large degree unprecedented. In general they appear to fit into the classification of pyromaniacs motivated by "revenge."
The common viewpoint shared by Vikernes and others convicted of burning
Norwegian churches is that their crimes were a form of justified retaliation
against Christianity.

Lewis and Yarnell's study of American arsonists found that among 457 cases
of "revenge-spite firesetters," churches were only the objects of attack in ten
instances. In their overview of this classification of cases they write:

> The conflagration is the most spectacular feature of revenge-motivated incendiarism. The fire-
> setters are usually colorless figures who remain in the background. A woman is rarely directly involved
> ... Theirs is a deep-seated grievance, and literal revenge is desired. Hence their firesetting is not con-
> fined to gestures or playful attempts, but is intended to become destructive. Inflammable agents may
> be used.
>
> Revenge is the strongest and most durable of all possible motives for firesetting, and revenge fires
> are set by offenders of any age, though the greatest incidence occurs in the 16–20 year old group.
> Adolescents will work as a group in setting this type of fire ... but the usual fire is made by a solitary
> individual.[5]

In the discussion of "Boys Over 16 Who Make Fires in Groups," similarities
are evident with the dynamics of the Black Circle and its loosely-knit coterie with
common interests, inspired and incited by a few of the more charismatic individuals within it. In forty cases of group arson activity studied:

> The majority of these were 17–18 year old boys, most of whom worked in pairs, and where more
> were included, we find that the extra members were chiefly "hangers-on" and were usually not indict-
> ed or given a suspended sentence. In some cases, a large group of inadequate boys were completely
> under the influence of a leader.[6]

One should bear in mind, however, that the same scenario is probably true
of any juvenile group engaging in anti-social behavior or crime.

None but a few of the offenders in Lewis and Yarnell's book mention burning down a church for ideological reasons. One of them states, "I can't tell you
why I [set fires], I just do. I didn't pick on Catholic churches because I hated the
Catholics. They were just easy places to get into."[7] However, in a later state hospital examination it was determined this 17-year-old had possibly chosen the
specific churches as a symbolic gesture against his estranged, Catholic father.

"Pyromaniac" is a classification which technically denotes someone who set fires for no other ostensible reason than some kind of sensual satisfaction. One intriguing case in *Pathological Firesetting* describes the actions and sentiments of a 20-year-old pyromaniac who set fire to a church where he had served as an usher during his youth:

After the morning service he unlocked a basement window, through which he entered the church that evening. The first match he struck went out—"It gave me a sensation when it went out. Something told me to continue and light the second match and I did. I couldn't think of anything that would happen. As I entered the dark room it gave me a great thrill. It was so magnificently beautiful there and I thought it would be great to be more beautiful and magnificent still and I thought if the fire was set, no harm would be done and the building would probably be more magnificent than ever. As I continued on, it seems as though in every move I made there was more pleasure out of it. I felt a different person after I set the fire."[8]

The man later added: "I felt a double personality when I went into the choir room. I was filled with great enjoyment. I thought such a beautiful edifice should be destroyed. It should be destroyed to be created into a thing even more beautiful."[9]

While there are slight similarities between some of these comments and the sentiments of Norwegian Black Metal church burners who viewed church fires as aesthetically beautiful, it would be inaccurate to lump them in the same category. True pyromaniacs tend to have a sexual impulse behind their action, according to psychologist Wilhelm Stekel, whose *Peculiarities of Behavior* covers the affliction in detail. He believes "awakening and ungratified sexuality impels the individual to seek a symbolic solution of his conflict between instinct and reality," resulting in pyromania in extreme cases.[10] Stekel further writes:

But in the case of the pyromaniac a second determinant [beyond sexual impulse] is also involved—revenge. Arson is an act of hatred. It is the expression of a destructive tendency. Love is creative, hatred destroys. But the question remains: against who is the hatred directed? Is it directed against the employers, or against the owners of the property set on fire? This should be accurately ascertained in every instance. Certain arsons have the immediate persons for objective, they are expressions of revenge for unrequited love, other deeds of this character aim at the pyromaniac's own family, the parents, etc. They shall see to what their lack of heart has led. They are responsible for everything![11]

In the case of Varg Vikernes, he has often stated that he holds the Christian church responsible for destroying everything that was once beautiful in what he considers Norway's true culture—that of the heathen age. He refers to the wave of arsons as an organic, instinctual uprising or revolution against the alien shackles of Christianity, and feels his music project Burzum to be a weapon in encouraging such outbursts. Curiously, he has also declared that Burzum is "a dream without holds in reality. It's to stimulate the fantasy of mortals—to make them dream."[12] In light of such beliefs proclaimed by Vikernes, one of Stekel's remarks becomes intriguing:

> We must also bear in mind that the pyromaniacs, as a rule ... attach considerable significance to their dreams and such individuals easily transpose into the impulse to set fire any impulsion to an asocial deed which may oppress them. What they hear is the voice of their own blood, transposed into a voice calling from within.[13]

Stekel allocates some of his study to pyromania with overtones of sadism or cruelty. While Vikernes and the others apprehended for setting church fires have given reasons other than mere cruelty as a motive, none of them have expressed any degree of remorse for the suffering they caused in the lives of priests and churchgoers, or the painful impact on the surrounding communities. At the time of his first arrest in relation to any of the fires, Vikernes did make a number of extremely sadistic comments to newspapers and magazines which reflected the initial Norwegian Black Metal preoccupations with spreading "evil" and pain. When discussing the findings of fellow psychologist Iwan Bloch, Stekel summarizes:

> Bloch in his endeavor to explain the pyromaniac tendency, has recourse to the assumption of a sadistic impulse and of a sexually toned destructive tendency. He points out that red is a color which plays a tremendous role in our *vita sexualis*. The thought or sight of dark red flames exerts a sexually exhilarating influence, similar to the sight of the reddened body parts during flagellation, or of the flowing blood in sadistic indulgences.[14]

Even while acknowledging that violent or criminal sexual drives may be an important factor in pyromania, as a psychologist Stekel approaches the issue of the crime quite differently than would a police officer or fireman. His attitude toward the arsonist is a far cry from the days of the courts severing hands or feet, and ordering excommunication. Speaking of a pyromaniac, Stekel asks:

Pro-Grishnackh Flyer

> Is he a criminal? Is his arson a crime deserving punishment? My reply to both questions is a decided negative. Anyone who has read through the whole account must understand that

the act was symbolic, there was no criminal motive behind it. It is desirable that similar cases be sub-jected to careful analytic investigation. Then it will be seen that many of these crimes are but the off-shoots of faulty training and morbid environment.[15]

The youths involved in the Norwegian Black Metal scene had certainly immersed themselves in a morbid environment. There is no evidence that Vikernes or the others felt any "sexually exhilarating" influences when burning churches, or desecrating graves for that matter, but one could assume that a certain degree of sadism was inherent to these provocative acts. Their primary motivation was indeed symbolic, and they voice no regret for what they see as righteous revenge against Christianity, which they believe glorifies and caters to the "weak."

The value of the burned churches in Norway is difficult to estimate. The loss of cultural and historical significance in a specific community (whose members were baptized, married, and buried there) can never be replaced. Even when the church burnings occurred in their own cities, where the repercussions would be impossible to ignore, the perpetrators have expressed no pity for the results of their handiwork.

Some of the most famous recent examples of church burning in Norway were at Fantoft and Holmenkollen, although neither had any congregation as such. They were more like museum pieces. In contrast, Hauketo Church outside Oslo had an active congregation. The night before October 3, 1992, the parish church was burnt to the ground. Per Anders Nordengen was parishioner of the Hauketo and Prinsdal congrega-tions.

Per Anders Nordengen

What happened at Hauketo?

I was awakened by my daughter who said there was a phone call for me, at 4:30 in the morning. I was told that the church was burning. I don't think I've ever gotten into my clothes so fast. I drove down to the church, just a kilo-meter away, hoping that it was just a small fire. But seeing the flames rise into the air was quite a shock.

The day after was an incredible experience. It was a state of mourning

Pro-Grishnackh Flyer

in Hauketo and Prinsdal, and it wasn't just us, the active churchgoers. I suddenly realized what a church means to a community. The church is a symbol of security. Everyone had been baptized or confirmed or married there. Lots of people who didn't really go to church were crying and speaking of "our church." Later, lots of people helped out and contributed money. So we kept going in makeshift localities; we didn't cancel one service, one choir practice, or one activity. But it was hard work, and wore me out. That is one of the reasons why I have quit being a minister now.

WHEN WAS ARSON SUSPECTED?

At the beginning of the investigation, the police didn't believe in theories about Satanism. They wouldn't have any talk about Satanism, and talk about arson was hushed up. This was shocking, since it was right after Holmenkollen was burnt. The policeman who led the investigation worked from a theory that young members of the congregation had left a waffle iron or coffee machine on the night before. He even repeated this on the TV news the day after. This was a hard blow for many.

During the investigation, it turned out that there were footprints leading to one of the windows, and the window had then been shattered. Later on, I was looking for a silver crucifix that had been at the altar. I had hoped it wouldn't be completely destroyed or melted, but couldn't find it. Then we found it by the exit. So the police accepted that someone had been in the church, and that there was foul play involved. The crucifix, still blackened with soot, now occupies the place of honor in our new church.

It turned out that there was a 19-year-old from the suburb next to Hauketo that was responsible. He had bought two cans of gasoline at a nearby gas station, broken into the church and set fire to it. He also took psalm books with him, which the police found in his home later.

HOW DO YOU FEEL ABOUT THE ARSONIST?

I was asked by radio and TV to meet him, and wanted to do it. But when I heard that he didn't regret what he had done, I felt that it was pointless to make a confrontation out of it.

I don't think this was very ideologically motivated. I think he ended up in this scene because it was the only one in which he could gain recognition. I've also heard that he had a difficult upbringing. I feel more sorry for him and feel that he has been punished too harshly. The prison sentence wasn't that hard, a year or so, but he got a damage claim of 5 million Kronor. That will destroy the boy's future, and I think a sentence should be such that you can keep on living after atoning for your actions.

THE BURNING TIMES

For the churches that were completely destroyed, the only thing which can be done is to raise a new structure that will somehow correspond to the function of the old church. The Norwegian Directorate for Cultural Heritage estimates the value of each full reconstruction at between 15 and 30 million Kroner (between 2 and 4 million dollars). Thus, the expenses of repairing the totally damaged churches alone could run up into 300 million Kroner (40 million dollars). In addition, there come the expenses incurred by the damages on churches that were only partially harmed. The figures also do not cover the costs of the artistic decorations.

The city of Oslo took Vikernes to court to reclaim damages for the burning

SATANISME: Kirkebrannene satte for alvor black metal-miljøene i medias fokus. Her er restene av Fantoft stavkirke.

SVART ALVOR

Vi får møte ungdommer fra de såkalte black metal-miljøene i programmet «Samtid: Det svarte alvor», som sendes i kveld. Dokumentarprogrammet gir et innblikk i de unge svartkleddes tankeverden, en tankeverden preget av fascinasjon for det dystre og mørke.

Av OLE MORTEN ERIKSEN

Det norske black metal-miljøet

kom for alvor i søkelyset til både de norsk og utenlandsk media etter en rekke kirkebranner i

20.30

NRK TV

fjor og forfjor. Det hele toppet seg da innehaveren av platebutikken «Helvete»,

sataniske ritualer. De tilber ikke satan, men de ønsker å spre mørke og ondskap gjennom livsstil og musikk. Mange gir

NORWEGIAN HEADLINE: "BLACKLY SERIOUS"

of Holmenkollen Chapel. The insurance company Gjensidige did the same for Skjold church and Åsane Church. The original charge was that Vikernes should compensate the entire cost of rebuilding the churches, which amounted to nearly 40 million Kroner (5 million dollars). Later, however, the sum was reduced so that Vikernes would not have to pay for the actual consecrations of the rebuilt churches, nor the cake parties later. Still, around 37 million Kroner remained to be paid, and Vikernes, unsurprisingly, did not accept the charges. He would have to go through the court system again.

In the courtroom, Vikernes once more played the role of Public Enemy No. 1, wearing green fatigues and leering. A certain tone was also set by the fact that all who were admitted to the courtroom were searched with metal detectors (which is not the common practice in Norway). During the trial, Vikernes's defense attorney claimed that he had been wrongly convicted of the church burnings, the charges were outdated, and furthermore, his client had no money to pay the damages. He pressed for acquittal on all counts.

Vikernes's protestations of innocence were not accepted by the court, and in December, 1997 he was ordered to pay 8 million Kroner (1 million dollars) in damages. Vikernes would also have to endure a 12% interest rate on the money owed, calculated from the summer of 1996. By the time of the trial the interest alone had already amounted to nearly one million Kroner.

Fantoft Stave Church became, in many ways, the primary symbol of church burnings in Norway. It was a church museum and a prominent attraction for tourists visiting Bergen. It was also used for special weddings and services on important occasions. Fantoft is under private ownership, and this would probably be the most expensive reconstruction of them all. Stave church historian David Walsten noted in 1994, "Like the legendary phoenix bird, a new Fantoft Stave Church began rising from the ashes of the old soon after the tragic fire. The owner's intention was to construct a faithful copy of the original."[16] The family which owns Fantoft wishes to keep the exact cost of this massive undertaking confidential.

VARG VIKERNES

HOW ORGANIZED WERE MOST OF THESE ACTIVITIES IN REALITY? WERE YOU REALLY SOME KIND OF RINGLEADER?

It was nothing like that, nothing at all. There was no such organization. I was a person who—I'm not going to say I burnt any churches, but let's put it this way: there was one person who started it. I was not found guilty of burning the Fantoft Stave Church in Bergen, but anyways that was what triggered the whole thing. That was the 6th of June, and everyone linked it to Satanism, because of the 6-6 and it was on the 6th day of the week.

What everyone overlooked was that on the 6th of June, year 793, in

Lindisfarne in Britain was the site of the first known Viking raid in history, with Vikings from Hordaland, which is my county. Nobody linked it to that—*nobody.*

That church is built on holy ground, a natural circle and a stone *horg* [a heathen altar]. They planted a big cross on the top of the *horg* and built the church in the midst of the holy place.

That was where it started, that was the first church. From then on it just continued. After that a church in Stavanger, south of Bergen, burned. We had no contact with them in any way. They were just another group who saw this in the newspaper and thought, wow, it was cool and we'll do the same. They burnt the church and set fire to a small chapel. The next church that burned was Holmenkollen in Oslo, it burnt to the ground. Earlier actually, before August, another church was set on fire in Bergen, but the fire didn't develop so it just burnt a little, and there was nothing in the newspaper, to keep it silent. Anyway, I'm actually found guilty in doing that. I was found guilty in three successful— and one unsuccessful—church burnings.

WHAT ARE THE THREE YOU ARE FOUND GUILTY OF?

Holmenkollen, Skjold Church in southern Hordaland, and Åsane Church. When I was in prison in Bergen, that church was just one kilometer away, and the under-warden came and stared at me—though he wouldn't look in my eyes— and said: "Every day I drive to work I go past the ruins of the Åsane church and every time I think of you." That was the first thing he told me. I was put in isolation for one year. That was a bad trip—it wasn't the right place to come to prison. He'd been married and baptized in that church.

YOU CLAIM THE CHURCH BURNINGS ARE LINKED TO ODINISM OR ÁSATRÚ?

The point is that all these churches are linked to one person. Everything was linked to that one person, who was not Øystein obviously. All the church burnings, with the exception of Stavanger because that was another group (who, by the way, have also turned into nationalistic pagans).

CAN YOU EXPLAIN IN AN ABSTRACT WAY HOW THINGS MIGHT HAVE FUNCTIONED?

Just like I said to the journalists, I might know what happened. If it turns out to be correct, well it was just a lucky guess! The first church burned on the 6th of June, with the intention probably to light a flame, to put dried grass and branches on the coal and the fire to make it big. It's a psychological picture—an almost dead fire, a symbol of our heathen consciousness. The point was to throw dry wood and branches on that, to light it up and reach toward the sky again, as a growing force. That was the point, and it worked.

I'M INTERESTED IN THE IDEA THAT THERE WAS A GOAL BEHIND THE BURNINGS.

It would be extremely childish in any other case. The Greek guy [Vikernes is referring to the person found guilty in the arson of Hauketo Church] was influenced by us; he was trying to be one of our friends. I was just in Oslo a couple of times, coincidentally every time we burned a church. The group in Stavanger, they were doing it of their free will, of their own interest and hatred towards the church. I think the Greek guy was the only one who was doing it to impress. The people in Stavanger did it without our influence. That was in '92. They were caught right afterwards. They were 16–17 years old, heavily into drugs and Anton LaVey.

YOU CLAIM THERE IS A GENUINE CONNECTION TO NATIONALISM.

I've always had that, more or less. It's not a Satanic thing, it's a national heathen thing. It's not a rebellion against my parents or something, it's serious. My mother totally agrees with it. She doesn't mind if someone burns a church down. She hates the Church quite a lot. Also about the murder [of Øystein Aarseth], she thinks that he deserved it, he asked for it. So she thinks it's wrong to punish me for it. There's no conflict between us at all about these things. The only thing she disliked was that I liked weapons and wanted to buy weapons, and suddenly she got a box of helmets at her place because I ordered them! Bulletproof vests, all this stuff...

THE COUNT'S EMISSARY

Churches were not the only things being disturbed by the middle of 1992. On July 26th, an 18-year-old girl, Suuvi Mariotta Puurunen, nicknamed "Maria," crept up to a quiet house belonging to Christopher Jonsson in Upplands Väsby, near Stockholm, Sweden. She attempted to set the domicile on fire and left a note tacked to the door with a knife which read, "The Count was here and he will come back."[17] Someone inside the house awakened at the smell of smoke and the fire was quickly put out before any serious harm was done. Jonsson is the frontman of the Death Metal band Therion. He had been involved in an argument with Vikernes. Shortly after the attempted arson on his house, Jonsson received a letter from Norway:

Hello victim! This is Count Grish-nackh of Burzum. I have just come home from a journey to Sweden (northwest of Stockholm) and I think I lost a match and a signed Burzum LP, ha ha! Perhaps I will make a return trip soon and maybe this time you won't wake up in the middle of the night. I will give you a lesson in fear. We are really mentally deranged, our methods are death and torture, our victims will die slowly, they must die slowly.[18]

The actual perpetrator of the attack, Maria, would later be arrested and her diary discovered by the Swedish authorities. In speaking of her actions, she wrote, "I did it on a mission for our leader, The Count. I love The Count. His fantasies are the best. I want a knife, a fine knife, sharp and cruel... he-he."[19] She would later be sentenced to one year's observation in a mental hospital for her activities in connection with the Black Circle.

SWEDISH HEADLINE: "'I AM GUILTY OF ARSON.'
MARIA'S DIARY REVEALS HER TO BE
A DEVIL WORSHIPPER"

BLACK METAL MEETS THE PRESS

In January, 1993, after seven major churches had burned in Norway, Vikernes spoke to a reporter at the *Bergens Tidende* daily newspaper. According to Vikernes, his interview was absurd and revealed nothing that could prove his involvement in any crime.

However, this article in all its demented glory would in fact bring intense scrutiny upon the Black Metal scene—at that point an otherwise unknown byway of underground youth culture—and link it to the burgeoning wave of inexplicable church burnings. Vikernes also provided connections to an unsolved murder of a homosexual the previous August in the Winter Olympic park in Lillehammer, a crime which the police had exhausted all their leads on and given up investigating.

VARG VIKERNES

WHAT LED TO YOU ACTUALLY BEING ARRESTED?

That was January of 1993. It was an interview and I simply said, "I know who burned the churches." It was very simple psychology: *show Odin to the people and Odin will be lit in their souls.* And this is exactly what happened in Norway today, there's a big trend in interest in Norse mythology, in all these things. And I dare say that one of the main reasons is just because of that case. I truly believe that. Why else should it be?

WHAT DID YOU SAY IN THIS INTERVIEW?

I said, "I know who burned the churches," to the journalist, and I was making a lot of fun with him because we told him on the phone, we have a gun and if you try to bring anybody we'll shoot you. Come meet me at midnight and all this, it was very theatrical. He was a Christian, and I fed him a lot of amusing info. Very amusing! Of course he twisted the words like usual. After he left we lay on the floor laughing.

We thought it would be some tiny interview in the paper and it was a big front page. The same day, an hour or so after I talked to him on the phone, the police came and arrested me. That was why I was arrested. I didn't tell them anything. I talked to the police that time and I told them, "I know who burned the churches—so what?" They tried to say, "We've seen you at the site," and all this, and I said, "No you haven't!"

They bugged my friends a lot, like the Immortal guys, one of them was taken into custody. They were messing a lot with them, but they were dealing okay with it. And actually this murder that Bård Faust did, I was interviewed about that as well—they believed *I did it.* Then they suddenly suspected him, but I talked him so well out of it, that when he turned up to the police and said, "I want to give you an interview," they didn't even bother to listen to him. They said, "Who are you? We don't want to talk to you," and *he'd done it!* And of course, after some while, they had to release him, because they didn't have anything on him. But later when he was in a cell, after twenty minutes he was crying into his lawyer's tie and told everything. That's the loyalty you get.

The Black Metal scene first came to the attention of mainstream, middle Norway through a cover story in the *Bergens Tidende* daily newspaper on January 20, 1993. Vikernes's brooding gaze covered the front page of the newspaper under the headline "WE LIT THE FIRES." [The text of this story is reproduced in its entirety as Appendix I.]

In the article, Varg Vikernes set the tone for the Black Metal scene's subsequent interaction with, and portrayal by the media. In flamboyant phrases he unveiled the story of a grand conspiracy aiming to overthrow the forces of good in Norway and slaughter innocent rabbits. With quotes like "Our purpose is to spread fear and evil," he left no doubt about his feelings toward society.[20] The article gives unique insight into how the Black Metal scene was developing at the time, and particularly how Vikernes tried to construct his image in the media.

Journalist Finn Bjørn Tønder was approached by two youths who had grown up with Vikernes. As his band Burzum was set to release a new album, they had conducted an interview with Vikernes which they hoped Bergens Tidende would print. The article closed with the remark that Vikernes had burned eight churches and killed a homosexual at Lillehammer—the latter act being the crime that Bård Eithun would later be jailed for.

Unsurprisingly, Bergens Tidende did not buy the article. However, Tønder sensed a story and set up a meeting with Vikernes with help from the two youths. In the agreement, there was the understanding that Vikernes was to read through and okay the final article. With everything thus arranged, the midnight madness at Vikernes's pad ensued.

Tønder called Vikernes early in the evening the day afterward to read an unfinished version of the article to him on the phone. Vikernes said that it was completely in keeping with his spirit, but that he also feared that it would lead the police to him. He explained that if he didn't pick up the phone when Tønder called him back later with the full version, he might have already escaped to Poland—supposedly to comrades there. When Tønder called back, Vikernes didn't answer, but he had not gone into exile. He was already downtown being questioned by the police, who had managed to find him on their own.

In an unrelated event, the police had come across some flyers for Burzum's Aske mini-album. The flyers, like the record sleeve, proudly displayed a picture of the smoldering ruins of Fantoft Stave Church. This caught the eye and interest of the police, who simply went to the address on the flyer, where they found Vikernes.

By time the article was printed, the Bergen police had Vikernes in custody and realized that this was the youth interviewed by Tønder. In the subsequent interrogations by the police, Vikernes both claimed that he never spoke to Bergens Tidende, and that the article was incorrect. But the newspaper had four representatives present during the interview, and therefore plenty of witnesses to attest to the accuracy of the piece.

In addition to boldly presenting himself as a probable suspect in the rash of church arsons, Vikernes's statements in the newspaper would have other residual effects. In the article, Vikernes calls the accomplice in the arson of Åsane church a "less intelligent individual" who was "utilized" by the Black Circle.[21] The person he was referring to, Jørn Inge Tunsberg from the Bergen Black Metal band Hades, ironically later talked to the police partially due to irritation at Vikernes's unflattering description of him.

Vikernes later claimed that during questioning at his initial arrest he was also suspected for an unsolved murder in late 1992. An older black exchange student in Bergen had been reported missing some months earlier. Varg referred to his disappearance as a "murder" in a number of fanzine interviews, implying that he might have been involved with the crime. In reality, the whole incident was just a red herring. The police found out that the man had withdrawn money from his bank account after he was presumed dead. The man had a family, and in the end police concluded he'd simply run away to escape his responsibilities.

Vikernes maintained his innocence on all counts during police interrogations, and was eventually released in March for lack of evidence. Although he often intimates his involvement in the arson of the Fantoft Stave Church, it has never been proven that he committed this crime, which is considered one of the most serious and callous of the fires.

In the wake of Varg's interrogation at the hands of the Bergen cops, a number of others in the Black Metal scene were also rounded up by different police departments and questioned regarding church arson and the murder of the homosexual in Lillehammer, including Samoth and Bård Eithun of Emperor, the latter of whom was in fact guilty of the killing. Still, evidence was scarce and all were released after being interviewed.

Bård Eithun

Was the murder you committed in Lillehammer on the news?

He was discovered two days later by a schoolgirl who was jogging in the area. It wasn't on the news until then. So I talked to Øystein and I talked to Vikernes too, and when he heard about this he made some other plans about burning down a church. When I came back to Oslo the evening after I was supposed to go with him and Øystein to burn down a church. So that's what we did.

You participated in burning of the Holmenkollen Chapel?

At least that one, yes. It was not anything big really. They were in the shop in Oslo talking about it. They asked me if I wanted to come with them, and yes, of course—I'd already killed a man so it's okay to be involved in this too, to burn down a church. We went up to a church and we had bombs, but they didn't work so we had to come back. The bomb was something that he [presumably Eithun is referring here to Vikernes] made at home. Some kind of simple bomb, it was supposed to work so that when it exploded it would light some gasoline. We broke into the church and placed the bomb on the altar of the church, surrounded by papers and gasoline. The bomb exploded but flew from where it was laying all the way into the other room inside the church. It didn't work and did not light the gas. So we had to go up again to the church and light it by hand with a lighter. We put a lot of books, notebooks, and stuff up against the wall and we lit it. That was successful.

DID THE CHURCH BURN DOWN?

Yes, it burned down completely. Later we were watching the news. The first story in the news was about the murder which I did and the second story was about the burning, so that evening I was in the two main reports on the news. I was quite nervous, but the cops didn't have any traces or evidence.

UGLY TRUTHS,
SCREAMING HEADLINES

Once the anti-Christian crime wave was seen as emanating in some fashion from the Black Metal movement, media attention began to escalate at an exponential rate, much to the glee of the prime movers in the scene, Vikernes and Aarseth. The most infamous article published at that time is a cover feature of issue 436 of glossy U.K. Metal magazine *Kerrang!*, which hit the newsstands on March 27, 1993.

Dominated by a striking shot of Vikernes glaring through long locks of his darkly dyed hair, with two huge knives crossed in his fists, the cover also featured a blazing church and smaller inset photo of the band Emperor, decked out with corpsepaint, a cowled robe, and medieval weaponry. The tabloid-style headline promises: "ARSON... DEATH... SATANIC RITUAL... The Ugly Truth About Black Metal."[22] Inside, the five-page article luridly presented the Norwegian version of Black Metal to the rest of the world. The author, Jason Arnopp, described his subjects with sensational gusto, but the bulk of the article is entirely based on alleged comments from Vikernes and Aarseth.

Under a giant quote spreading across two pages, "We are but slaves to the one with horns..." the article begins.[23] It relates the rise of church burnings, commenting that in Norway, "Black Metal has become a national menace."[24] Along with details on Mayhem and Burzum, the America bands Deicide and VON are also mentioned as representative of the dangerous new trend. VON were merely an obscure group who managed to release one raw-sounding demo tape, *Satanic Blood*, which became legendary within the Norwegian scene. In *Kerrang!*, Vikernes is quoted as claiming VON was an acronym for "Victory-Orgasm-Nazis," although this appears to be a fanciful notion on his part.

THE INFAMOUS *KERRANG!* COVER

The entire article is reminiscent of the earlier *Bergens Tidende* piece about Vikernes. In it both Aarseth and Vikernes refer to an organization behind the crime wave in Norway, the "Satanic Terrorists," which they are part of. Arnopp makes an interesting aside that Aarseth claims he and Vikernes "are of equal standing" within the group.[25] Aarseth also brags of ten "inner circle" members who in turn direct and manipulate a larger body of Black Metal "slaves," and that the Helvete shop provides an economic basis for the terrorism.[26] He says he does not involve himself in the actual crimes because if he was arrested the movement would fall apart. This could support Vikernes's later contention that Aarseth was actually afraid to take part in any of the riskier activities.

Regarding his own deeds, Vikernes is quoted by Arnopp as saying, "I'm accused of child abuse, church burnings, some murders, possession of illegal weapons... a lot of things," but refuses to comment about any guilt on his part.[27] He describes Burzum's *Aske* mini-album as "a hymn to church burning ... It's saying, 'Do this. You can do this too.' And we convert the souls of kids with our music..."[28] He declares his biggest fear above all is being committed to a mental institution.

Regarding the arson motives, Vikernes states: "We support Christianity because it oppresses people, and we burn churches to make it stronger. We can then eventually make war with it."[29] This curious quote is revealing, and similar sentiments became part of Black Metal ideology. The Church should not be opposed for its cosmology *per se,* but rather its contemporary state of weakness and its *rejection* of its former draconian conduct (such as the Inquisition). Both Vikernes and Aarseth told the *Kerrang!* journalist they had been raised as either agnostics or atheists.

An intriguing passage in the article discusses the genesis of the interests held by the Satanic Terrorists. Arnopp asserts that both Vikernes and Aarseth cited Venom and Bathory as early influences, and when he pointed out that Venom's use of Satanism was purely a gimmick, Aarseth insisted the Norwegians "choose

KERRANG! SPREAD

to believe otherwise."[30] Aarseth then claims knowledge of ten assorted deaths tied to the influence of Venom's music. "I hope Venom know about this, and they think it's terrible. It is their legacy," he gloats.[31]

The *Kerrang!* exposé is also notable as it appears to be the first media story which labels the Black Metal scene as "neo-fascist." Arnopp quotes members of Venom and mainstream U.K. Metal band Paradise Lost (who the article claims were haphazardly attacked by teenage Black Metalers while on tour in Norway), referring to the Satanic Terrorists as Hitlerian Nazis. Vikernes makes only one comment in the article which might imply any truth to this allegation: "I support all dictatorships—Stalin, Hitler, Ceaucescu... and I will become the dictator of Scandinavia myself."[32] The last statement of this exclamation would be recycled in many of the later mass-media articles on Vikernes and Black Metal.

The *Kerrang!* cover story must have electrified everyone in the Norwegian underground. In addition to their newfound extracurricular activities, Vikernes, Aarseth, and the other key personalities in prominent bands like Emperor were still very much involved in their music projects—and now the biggest Heavy Metal magazine in the world had just given them an unprecedented amount of sensational coverage.

Years later in retrospect, all involved realize the absurdity of much that was said. Vikernes now insists vehemently (with what is undoubtedly significant validity) that many of his remarks were fabricated, misunderstood, misquoted, or taken out of context; others reflect back on the mentality of the scene at that time and see it as naive and deluded. Like it or not, however, the *Kerrang!* article was what brought Norwegian Black Metal to the rest of the world's attention. It probably meant the crimes would eternally overshadow the music, but it was undoubtedly the best piece of international P.R. the scene would ever receive.

IHSAHN OF EMPEROR

WHY WERE THE CHURCHES BURNED?

To be honest, I think that many of the things that were done and said were just for the shock value of it. Some burned churches as a symbol against Christianity, and some burned churches just to prove themselves worthy, to say to the respected persons, "Look, I burned a church, I'm really true." Some did it just for the sake of burning a church, just to be bad.

HOW DID YOU FIRST HEAR WHAT WAS HAPPENING?

I first heard about the church burnings on the news. Then I ran into Vikernes and he said, "Look, I burned a church!" and showed me photos. I don't know if he showed them to everybody, but I don't think he was very discreet about it. It was impressive—it was very evil to have burned a church, if you look at it that way. I guess I was excited about it, since anti-Christian thoughts had been discussed and I got very into it. I still have anti-Christian views, but for other reasons than I had before. I guess that's just part of the progression.

WHAT WERE THE REACTIONS IN THE SCENE?

I remember that everybody was very inspired, thinking, "Yeah, I want to do a thing like that." Everyone was very drawn into it, because it was our thing. It became very personal; it was almost like us against everybody. You felt that brotherhood you get when you have people who are your friends, they agree with you, and you create something together. You felt part of something very strong. Like in a band, you create something together that you're all very fond of and you personally get very attached to the creation, or in this case, the destruction. In a sense you create war.

DID YOU FEEL THINGS WERE GETTING OUT OF HAND?

I didn't care much about the value of human life. Nothing was too extreme. That there were burned churches, and people were killed, I didn't react at all. I just thought, "Excellent!" I never thought, "Oh, this is getting out of hand," and I still don't. Burning churches is okay; I don't care that much anymore because I think that point was proven. Burning churches isn't the way to get Christianity out of Norway. More sophisticated ways should be used if you really want to get rid of it.

IN RETROSPECT, IS THERE VALUE IN WHAT WAS DONE?

Burning churches was a symbolic act, and it proved that some people in Norway were very much against Christianity. I also have very much respect for extreme things. Things that are extreme are fascinating, as long as they don't go against me or those I care about. I like extreme things. It underlined and strengthened my individual feelings. It was one step further away from normal daily life for me, as for many other people.

SAMOTH OF EMPEROR

HOW ORGANIZED WERE THESE ACTIVITIES THAT WERE CONNECTED TO THE NORWEGIAN BLACK METAL SCENE?

Most of the actions were more or less "let's do it tonight" kinds of things. But that didn't make them any less serious. It was not like "Knights around the Round Table"... there was not a formal meeting before any act would take place, where people were told what to do and things like that. For a little while there was unity and some some strong ideas, but it soon became too unserious. Way too many people knew what was going on.

WHEN DID YOU FIRST BECOME AWARE OF THE IDEA TO BURN CHURCHES, AND FROM WHERE DID THIS ORIGINATE?

I think it was from something Vikernes hinted in a letter that made me aware of the idea. This was in '92. Later I was shown some photos at the Helvete shop of some church ruins. I participated in the church burnings because it felt right to do so. It all happened quite spontaneously, even though the thought of doing it had been lurking in my mind for awhile. I did not really think much about it afterwards, and still don't.

I view my arson as a sociopathic outburst, an extreme act towards the church and society. That was the intention. I still find the concept of reducing a church into a pile of ashes appealing. However, I'm not concerned about it anymore, nor do I think it's the way to get rid of Christianity. These church fires didn't awaken much more than a huge media hysteria and even stronger prejudice among the common people, which in the end was quite negative for us. It also led to a Black Metal hype, based upon the media, who are well-known for sensationalizing everything. Of course, we did prove a point and people are aware that there are anti-Christian forces around. Still, I think serious, intelligent propaganda is maybe a more effective way to get through to people.

DID YOU EVER HAVE THE FEELING THINGS WERE GETTING OUT OF CONTROL OR GOING TOO FAR?

I realized of course that everything had taken a very extreme turn. Anyway, I had chosen my way, so it did not disturb me really.

WHAT ARE YOUR FEELINGS ABOUT CHRISTIANITY IN NORWAY?

We cannot control nature! In the big picture we are but small cosmic dust. We have no control whatsoever on the universe. The earth can strike us down and crush us all. When, or if this will happen we know not—only time will tell. I think humanity has gone "off the edge." I don't see any major changes amongst people of today's world. People choose not to think. It's a difficult thing to try to change things in the world. Christianity, for example—I think it would be close to impossible to actually wipe out Christian belief and dogma; it's very deeply rooted in society. In retrospect to all the talk about what to do to destroy Christianity, I think there's a lot of naiveté going around. To actually gather people and weapons for a total war against Christianity and the common society is a nice dream indeed, but hardly the reality. I even see church burning as a finished chapter. It was a good symbolic anti-Christian act, but now it's nothing of any value at all—even the shock effect is gone. But the fact is that Christianity and all the other monotheistic religions are such destructive and false belief systems. Some people might actually open their eyes to serious and intelligent anti-Christian propaganda. The problem is that the common people don't really care; they don't think. It doesn't matter for them if they are a member of the State Church or not. They are so caught up with being normal and being like

SAMOTH OF EMPEROR

everyone else, so they baptize their children in the church for that reason only. The same goes for confirmation and marriage. Most of these people have no strong religious belief, they just do it. If that "trend" would change then the Church would lose a lot of its power, because in Norway much of that power is based upon a bunch of stupid statistics. Let's hope the next generation, our generation that is, will bring in more open- and strong-minded people who believe in individual and religious freedom, rather than narrow-minded conservatives, who believe in a type of society that we truly despise.

FLAMMENES ROV: Seegård kirke i flammer. Det tragiske synet gjorde et dypt inntrykk på folk i bygda, som forgjeves forsøkte å slukke den voldsomme brannen. Kirken brant ned til grunnen. *(Foto: Kari Østegård)*

KIRKEN BRANT BRYLLUPSNATTA

FOR BRANNEN: Hilde Anny Østegård ga torsdag ettermiddag sitt ja til Øistein Nettum i Seegård kirke for Brylupsbildene er de siste som er tatt før brannen. *(Foto: Trzli Østegård)*

SNERTINGDAL (Dagbladet): Bryllupsnatta ble svært dramatisk for Hilde Anny (25) og Øistein Nettum (28). Få timer etter at de hadde gitt hverandre sitt ja i Seegård kirke i Snertingdal nord for Gjøvik, så de kirken bli flammenes rov. Bare ruinene er tilbake.

NORWEGIAN HEADLINE:
"THE CHURCH BURNED ON THE WEDDING NIGHT"

★ ★ ★ ★ ★

HELLHAMMER

HOW STRONG IS CHRISTIANITY IN NORWAY NOW?

It's the biggest belief here.

IS A LOT OF THE "SATANISM" JUST A REACTION AGAINST THAT?

I don't know, because from the first time I was against the burning of the Norwegian churches. Totally. I told them, why not burn up a mosque, the foreign churches from the Hindu and Islamic jerks—why not take those out instead of setting fires to some very old Norwegian artworks? They could have taken mosques instead, with plenty of people in them!

FANNING THE FLAMES

The church burnings which began in the spring of 1992 would continue until the present, although they have not received as much publicity after the court trials were concluded in 1994. When we interviewed him in 1995, Vikernes claimed he knew of approximately thirty church arsons which had occurred the previous year, and stated that they continue to take place. Asked why there was little media coverage of the ongoing trend, he explained:

> Most of [the churches] are just damaged. If something burns to the ground you usually hear about it. But there are a lot of smaller chapels which have been burned, and Christian schools, and we read almost daily in the papers about grave desecrations. A week doesn't go by without a report of grave desecrations.[33]

A November 7, 1995 article in Norway's *Aftenposten* newspaper focused on the history of the church burnings, listing the following "official statistics": 1992—thirteen fires, ten cases solved; 1993—ten fires, five cases solved; 1994—fourteen fires, seven cases solved; 1995—seven fires, three cases solved at the time of the article. These figures vary considerably from some of Vikernes's claims, although they add up to a startling forty-four church attacks over four years. If Varg is to be believed, the number could be even higher, and more arsons have occurred since the end of 1995. A spokesman for the Kripos (roughly the Norwegian equivalent of the FBI) stated to *Aftenposten* that in *every case* which was solved, the culprits were Black Metal "Satanists."

Whether the church burnings and other acts of vandalism

The Bureau of Alcohol, Tobacco and Firearms
National Church Arson Task Force

NATIONAL CHURCH ARSON TASK FORCE

Church Threat
Assessment Guide

Department of the Treasury

Department of Justice

Federal Emergency Management Agency

Bureau of Alcohol, Tobacco and Firearms

BATF ARSON PREVENTION BOOKLET

Hjemmebrenning med GA:

BRENN DIN EGEN KIRKE

Er du en av de frustrerte? En av de som hater de kristne? En satanist, kanskje? Føler du store oppsamlinger av aggresjon hver gang du hører morgenandakten og føler at du vil gjøre noe skikkelig ondt? Da kan du herved få muligheten for å få ut dine innestengte følelser uten å la det gå ut over hverken mennesker eller nasjonale kulturskatter. Vi tilbyr deg nemlig denne lille miniatyrkirken i papir, som du kan leke deg med hjemme i dine mørkeste stunder. Det eneste du trenger er en saks, litt lim og en eske fyrstikker. Det kan være litt lurt å sette kirka på et brannsikkert underlag så du ikke tenner på leiligheten din samtidig. Det ville jo være ille om du skulle skade deg selv eller kanskje brenne inne bare fordi du har lyst å være litt ond iblant.

Klipp ut - Lim sammen - Tenn på

"Burn Your Own Church" Kit From Oslo Magazine, *Gate Avisa*

in Norway will eventually stop is difficult to say. As chapter 12 will reveal, the trend has spread to nearby Sweden and into some countries in Central Europe. A purely coincidental development would appear to be the rash of churches recently hit by arson in the United States. While this trend appears to have begun in the early 1990s, it has been escalating. In 1995–96 there were investigations into 429 incidences of church arsons, bombings, or attempted bombings. The epidemic mostly afflicted poor black churches in the South, and public outrage against a presumed conspiracy of racist terrorism resulted in the President's formation of a National Church Arson Task Force in June, 1996. The Task Force has since concluded that no nationwide conspiracy exists, and suspects arrested in relation to the the fires have been blacks and Hispanics as well as whites. The motives in specific incidents have ranged widely, from revenge to vandalism to racial hatred.

Church arson has also been used as an element of intimidation in the centuries-old conflict between Protestants and Catholics in Northern Ireland. The April, 1997 issue of *An Phoblacht,* a pro-Republican newspaper, features photos of the burnt-out remains of two Catholic churches hit with firebombs, and the accompanying article refers to at least eight different arson attacks on Catholic churches or religious buildings. A quote from Sinn Fein representative Gerry Adams indicates that the terrorist strategy of church burnings is utilized by both sides in the ongoing civil war: "Attacks on Catholic churches are just as wrong and sectarian as those carried out on Protestant churches."[34]

Most observers might find it an inapt comparison to speak of church burnings by Norwegian teenagers in the same breath with those committed by the

BURNED CATHOLIC CHURCH FROM AN IRA NEWSPAPER

Ulster Defense Association or Irish Republican Army in Ireland. No matter the country or context, however, the tangible effect of a destroyed church on its congregation and surrounding community is the same. And if Varg Vikernes is to be believed, the church burnings in his country serve a similar *function* to those in Northern Ireland—that of terrorism aimed toward the spiritual sanctuaries of one's enemy. According to Vikernes, the Norwegian arsons are symptoms of a religious struggle even more deep-seated and long-standing than the Catholic/Protestant sectarian conflict in Ireland. They are symbolic acts of terror against Christianity itself, and Vikernes sees no reason to apologize for that. To him, the torching of a House of God is simply one more weapon to be utilized in the arsenal of an unholy war.

...THE WOUNDS
WERE RUSHING RED WITH BLOOD
WHILST THE MEN FELL LIFELESS...

—SNORRE STURLASON, *HEIMSKRINGLA*[1]

DEATHLIKE
SILENCES

DESPITE AN INCREASING GLARE OF MEDIA ATTENTION—AND PARTIALLY DUE to it—Norwegian Black Metal had distinguished itself as its own genre. Defined at the time by an extreme form of Devil worship that demanded escalating levels of "evil" from its adherents, the scene had engineered a grim destiny for itself which would be fulfilled with installments of fire and blood.

Along with Aarseth and Vikernes, others would also violently make their imprint on the scene. One of the most important among these is Bård Eithun, know among comrades as "Faust." His initiation into Black Metal was similar to many others who sought increasingly intense rewards from the music they listened to. An experienced and talented drummer, Bård was enthusiastic when he discovered the extremity of Mayhem, and was in turn quickly welcomed into the core of the scene.

BÅRD EITHUN

HOW DID YOU ORIGINALLY GET INVOLVED IN BLACK METAL?

I grew up in Kvikne, a little village in the middle of Norway in the Østerdalen valley, and I lived there until I was 15 or 16 years old. Then I moved to Lillehammer and lived there two years, and then my last year outside I lived in Oslo. I worked in the shop with Aarseth, and the last half of this year I even had an apartment in the building where the shop was and lived there. I remember that the first bands I was writing to were Mayhem, Aggressor from France, and a

BÅRD EITHUN

Norwegian band, Imposter. When I wrote to Mayhem I came in touch with Aarseth and started to correspond with him. That was in '87, and was when my contact with the Black Metal underground scene started. Up until that time I had been listening to bands like Voivod, Venom, Metallica, and such, but it was when I wrote to Aarseth that I first got involved in the underground scene. From that point I became very much a part of the scene, because I started to know different people—I wrote lots of letters, got magazines, and all that shit.

WERE THERE A LOT OF PEOPLE INVOLVED DIRECTLY IN THE SCENE?

There were always people who wanted to hang out and be inside the shop around Mayhem and the bands. It was these people that Øystein didn't like and after he was killed they started to talk about how they were the great people who knew Euronymous back then, saying things like, "Me and Aarseth were doing things together back then, he liked me and he liked my band," and all this. That's what I expected when he was killed—all the people who weren't liked by Aarseth would start talking like this. Now you have a hundred people in Oslo saying how great it was being friends with Aarseth when maybe eight of them were people he liked.

HOMOSEXUAL MURDER

Besides playing in the bands Stigma Diabolicum, Thorns, and Emperor, Eithun was involved in the scene in other ways. He published his fanzine *Orcustus*, corresponding with and interviewing anyone of importance in

Norwegian Black Metal. The combination of his well-established obsession with murder and violence, and the increasing atmosphere of pushing behavior to the limits in the Black Metal scene, accelerated by the first church burnings in May and June, all seem to have contributed to Eithun's state of mind which led him to commit cold-blooded murder. Ihsahn, vocalist and guitarist in Emperor, comments about his former bandmate, "[Bård] had been very fascinated by serial killers for a long time, and I guess he wanted to know what it's like to kill a person, another human being. I think that was basically the reason for him doing it."[2]

ORCUSTUS

Visiting his family in Lillehammer in August, '92, Bård went out walking late at night to a pub and had a pint of beer. The atmosphere at the bar didn't suit him, and decided to head home. He wandered through the nearby park that had been set up for the Winter Olympics. He carried a knife with him because, as he once explained in an interview, "I lived in Oslo at the time, so it was natural for me to carry a knife. I don't consider that a weapon, more like an insurance in case something unexpected happens. It's better to have a knife you don't need than to not have one when you need it. The strange thing about [the night of the murder] is that I *didn't* need it, but someone got killed anyway. Quite incredible."[3] Eithun was neither inebriated nor under the influence of any drugs. At a certain point during his late night stroll he encountered another man who approached him. After a few moments of interaction, it became clear both of them were seeking quite different stimulation, and each would soon find radically divergent destinies as a result.

BÅRD EITHUN

WHEN DID YOUR CRIME HAPPEN?

This man I killed, that was on the 21st of August, 1992. I moved to Oslo in July, '92, and one month later I killed this man when I went back to visit my mother for a weekend.

What happened?

I was outside, I went to go out to drink but I didn't want to because there were too many people, so I was walking back home again. This man approached me—he was obviously drunk and obviously a faggot. He wanted to talk to me. "Okay, I'm talking to you," I responded. I understood that he was a homosexual very quickly. He was asking if I had a light, but he was already smoking. It was obvious that he wanted to have some contact. Then he asked me if we could leave this place and go up to the woods. So I agreed, because already then I had decided that I wanted to kill him, which was very weird because I'm not like this—I don't go around and kill people. So he was walking; it was quite a long way. This long walk was used against me in court, since the prosecutor wanted me to be charged with first degree murder—because it was a long way and I didn't take him up to the woods to beat him up, but rather to take his life. That's what the prosecutor said, and that's what I wanted of course, but I didn't mention that in court. I was saying that I wanted to beat him up and take his money, but of course it's not reasonable to go such a long way into the woods just to beat up a guy. So we walked into the woods, in a big park where the opening of the Olympic Winter Games was.

You had a knife?

I always used to have a knife in my back pocket. It was a black knife with a handgrip, a folding kind that locked.

Did you feel this was enough of a weapon to kill someone with?

I don't remember really what I was thinking, but at least I knew that if I didn't do it now, I would not get another opportunity. Then I took out the knife and turned around and stabbed him. He was walking behind me and I turned and stabbed him in the stomach. After that I don't remember much, only that it was like looking at this whole incident through eyes outside of my body. It was as if I was looking at two people who were having a fight—and one had a knife, so it was easy to kill the other person. If something happens that is obscure, it's easier for the mind to react if it acts like it is watching it from outside of yourself.

Murder Victim Magne Andreassen

YOUR SENSE OF TIME CHANGES TOO, AND EVERYTHING SLOWS DOWN...

Yes. If it happened in a minute or a much longer time, I can't recall. I was stabbing him in the stomach and he went down on his knees. I started stabbing him in the neck and face. Then he lay down and I was standing over him, stabbing. My intention was to take his life completely. I didn't want him to manage to live through this and go to the hospital and report me. It was easier to take his life and then go and hope that everything would be okay.

DID HE FIGHT BACK?

Not much. He tried to take me down to the ground but it's not easy when the other person has a knife. He was laying down and I wanted to take his life. I stabbed him very hard in the back so it went through the shoulder blades. I had to brace my foot against him to get it out again, because the knife was stuck between the bones. That's most likely when he died. After this I wanted to walk, and I did a little bit, but then he made some sounds. I thought, "He's not really dead," and walked back and kicked him in the back of the head with my boots, many times. I wanted to know that he was dead. After that I walked away.

BÅRD EITHUN (RIGHT) AND UNIDENTIFIED BRITISH FAN

WERE YOU NERVOUS?

I don't remember. I had to walk back through the woods very fast, in case some people might have heard him. I suppose I was quite nervous, but it's not that easy to remember. I went down to a river and washed my hands—they were of course red with blood—and then walked on again. It didn't help to only wash my hands, because I had blood all on my face and my hair was sticky with blood.

NO ONE SAW YOU?

Luckily! I was walking through an area where there were lots of people outside, coming back from town, but I didn't meet anyone. When I got home my mother was not awake, so I got in and washed off all the blood and washed my clothes. The day after I was talking to Aarseth on the phone and let him know what had happened.

DID YOU HAVE ANY REMORSE ABOUT THE MURDER?

No, I didn't have any remorse. I have to stand up for what I've done and do my time. There's no remorse. I took his life and I paid for it. It's not a big deal, at least not in my opinion.

PHOTO: MICHAEL MOYNIHAN

BÅRD EITHUN IN PRISON, 1995

WHY DID YOU HAVE THE IDEA YOU DESIRED TO KILL SOMEONE?

It's not easy to answer that. Lots of people have asked me. I was outside, just waiting to get out some aggression. It's not easy to describe why it happened. It was meant to happen, and if it was this man or another man, that's not really important.

DID THE FACT THAT HE WAS A HOMOSEXUAL HAVE MUCH TO DO WITH IT?

I don't like it when they're trying to get people who aren't homosexual. It's okay if they want to be homosexuals, but at least they must stay with their own people. They should not expect that every man they see around is homosexual.

THERE WEREN'T SPECIFIC THINGS THAT YOU WERE READING THAT HAD AN INFLUENCE ON YOU?

No, there wasn't. I remember Øystein asked me if I had been listening to some music before. I had been listening to Hellhammer, but it's really not important what I'd been doing before. If I'd been reading books or watching videos or listening to music it's not important because it had to happen anyway.

BÅRD WITH MACHETE

YOU DON'T THINK THE BLACK METAL CULTURE CREATED A CERTAIN CLIMATE?

Of course it might have influenced me a bit and made it easier. But all this really could happen to anyone if you get approached by a homosexual. Whether you are like me into this underground scene, or if you were working in a bank— you might react the same way.

THERE WAS A LONG PERIOD BEFORE YOU WERE CAUGHT.

Yes, I was free for a year and a week.

NOBODY HAD A CLUE?

Not really. The cops were checking homosexual scenes. They

BÅRD EITHUN IN PRISON, 1995

didn't have any traces toward us. It wasn't until Vikernes was arrested the first time, and he was giving an interview to the newspaper in Bergen, talking about how he knew who had killed someone. Then they made a connection between us and this murder; though they weren't investigating it anymore, they at least had it in their minds.

VARG WAS JUST BRAGGING?

He was bragging. The night after it happened he had already been bragging to a girl, who he didn't know, about this murder. I was still up in Lillehammer but I had talked to Øystein first and Vikernes afterward. That evening Vikernes was outside in Oslo bragging to a girl about this murder. It was not a very wise thing to do, but he liked to talk to people about what he and his friends had done.

DID YOU TELL OTHER PEOPLE?

Yes, a few.

SO IT WAS KIND OF A LEGENDARY ACTION?

Yes, I guess so, because I suppose it made other actions occur too. People were very enthusiastic about it. They thought we would not get caught, because I had done this murder and I was still outside.

DID YOU THINK YOU WOULDN'T BE CAUGHT?

Yes, because in the beginning I was expecting to get arrested, but after the months passed I was convinced that the cops didn't have any interest and I was maybe going to get away with it.

EXIT THE PRINCE OF DEATH

It is rare for a serious crime to go unsolved in Norway, but the murder of homosexual Magne Andreassen was truly a dead end for the police. There was no rhyme or reason to why it happened and no significant evidence—just a lone body found lying in the woods, dead from loss of blood through thirty-seven puncture wounds.

With the police investigation pursuing futile leads in the homosexual milieu, the "action" taken by Bård appeared to be one of impunity. His participation in the burning of the Holmenkollen Chapel the next day after the slaying, together with Vikernes and Aarseth, was again accomplished without any ill consequences. He is quoted in an interview talking about what occurred as soon as they had accomplished the arson. After the church was alight, "We rode up the mountain to watch it burn. It was very beautiful and exciting—when we got back to the record store we could hardly sleep."[4]

As the gravity of the Black Circle's forays into crime and transgression was increasing unhindered over the course of late 1992 and early 1993, similar events began to take place in Sweden. On February 7, 1993, the Lundby New Church in Gothenburg was burnt down. Built in stone

"IT" OF ABRUPTUM—
TOO EVIL TO HAVE A HUMAN NAME

in 1886, it was renowned for its good acoustics. The same night another Christian building nearby was also desecrated.

Øystein Aarseth had long been in contact with the personalities of the Swedish Black Metal scene, some of whom rivalled the Norwegians in their dedication to perversity. The bizarre duo Abruptum, who allegedly recorded their music during bouts of self-inflicted torture, was praised by Aarseth as "the audial essence of Pure Black Evil."[5] He released their debut album *Obscuritatem Advoco Amplectère Me* on Deathlike Silence in 1992. Øystein had also managed, with financial assistance from Varg Vikernes, to release the first Burzum CD on DSP. The second Burzum effort, *Aske*, was released in early 1993, some months after the burning of the Fantoft Stave Church. It was around this time, in the first months of the year, that bad blood arose between Vikernes and Aarseth. Their disagreement appears to come at the same period when Øystein was also arguing with members of the Swedish scene, causing a general animosity to surface between Black Metalers in the two neighboring countries.

The nature of an underground music genre invariably fosters rivalry among specific scenes from different localities, countries, or the individual bands themselves. Such was the case with the Swedish and Norwegian Black Metal crowds, with leading members of both groups competing for primacy in the ambiguous, amorphous "Black Circle." Samoth of Emperor recalls, "Several people from Sweden were in Norway on occasion. There's no doubt that what happened in Norway made an impact on several other countries."[6] There was a certain degree of cooperation between the two groups, but the recent frictions had been strong enough that when Øystein Aarseth was found slaughtered in the stairwell of his apartment building on August 10, 1993, the initial suspicion of many was directed at the Swedes.

The death of "Euronymous" shook the Black Metal scene to its core. Until that point, many felt they could continue to escape the repercussions of their deeds unscathed—deeds which by now had become a veritable shopping list of church arson, murder, burglary, death threats, grave desecration, and vandalism.

METALION

DID YOU HEAR ANYTHING BEFORE THE MURDER?

I didn't expect it at all. I hadn't spoken to Euronymous for a while before, and things were very quiet. All of the sudden this happened, and it was very surprising to me. I didn't even think it was Grishnackh who did it. I was confused and it took a very long time before I realized anything.

It was very strange. A cop came to my place and I was brought in for questioning. They raided my place and were looking through all my stuff. I wrote a letter to Grishnackh and told him about the stupid police coming to my place, and he gave me total support. He said, "Fuck them, just tell them nothing," and stuff like this. So I didn't know. I was surprised, I must say so.

WHO DID YOU THINK KILLED HIM?

I thought it was just some lunatic who was living in Oslo, or some drug people had killed him for some stupid reason. I didn't have any reason to suspect anyone, because the people in Sweden I didn't think were capable of doing anything like this.

THE NEWSPAPERS SUGGESTED HE MIGHT HAVE BEEN KILLED BY SWEDES?

I never believed that. I knew those people and they weren't capable of it.

DID YOU THINK IT COULD BE SOMEONE FROM THE BLACK METAL SCENE?

I didn't really know what to think. At first I thought it was some druggies, people who killed him for some money or something. Some crazy accident or incident. Because I couldn't think of anyone who wanted to kill him.

WHAT EFFECT DID IT HAVE ON THE BLACK METAL SCENE?

The effect was that a lot more people were attracted to Black Metal because it was in the newspapers. People who never knew what Black Metal was, or Death Metal, or Metal at all, were attracted to this because they thought it was cool. People who never knew Grishnackh and never knew Euronymous. "Oh yeah, Black Metal—that's the new thing." There were so many new bands starting at this time in '93 who were influenced by the writing in the newspapers. People braindead who are not capable of thinking for themselves, who just follow trends. Maybe now the worst trend people who have followed it have switched to something else. I hope these people get another hobby.

In the days following the fateful, late-night murder in Oslo, police launched an investigation into Øystein Aarseth's death, interviewing numerous personalities in the Black Metal scene which he had almost single-handedly founded. Vikernes allegedly told police the murder was surely the handiwork of Swedish pseudo-Satanists, who were envious of the more hardcore Norwegian Black Metal ideology. At one point a police spokesman even stated about the rivalry, "These groups really hate each other and they are capable of using almost any method to punish one another."[7]

Investigators also questioned many who hung on the coattails of Black Metal, and on August 13th they spent eight hours talking with Ilsa Raluce Anghel, a 16-year-old Swedish girl who had lived for a brief time with Aarseth. She cryptically told police:

I am quite sure that I know who killed Øystein. The murderer was jealous and wished to take over Øystein's leading position in the scene. ... I do not believe that Øystein was killed by Swedish Satanists. Most of the Swedes are too cowardly to ever commit a murder. I will not reveal the name of the real killer. The Black Metal scene will exact its own revenge against him.[8]

She also explained that in recent conversations Aarseth had told her the feud between the Swedish and Norwegian Satanists had ended; thus there was no motive for them to have murdered him. She elaborated on the background of the murderer:

The one who I think is the killer is part of the Norwegian scene. Many of the others I have been talking to in the Norwegian scene have already reached the same conclusion. I cannot give the name of the person I believe to be the killer because I would be risking my life.

The nature of the killing itself confirmed her suspicions, she said. "I don't think [Øystein] would have let a stranger into his apartment; that wasn't his style. That makes me even more sure about who the killer was."[9]

Of course she was alluding to Varg Vikernes, and it didn't take long for the police to piece together what had actually transpired. Many in the scene knew of a feud between Vikernes and Aarseth, but they didn't suspect it could have reached such intense proportions. Some were more cynical, and assumed the killer must have come from "within" the scene, and there were few possibilities about who it could be. Ihsahn of Emperor first heard about the murder on the evening news:

> I turned on the TV at home, and heard the words "Øystein Aarseth," and I wondered—what could he be doing on TV? Oh shit, *Grishnackh killed him*, I thought. Then I called Samoth and said, "I think Grishnackh killed Euronymous." We knew that they weren't friends anymore and that they hated each other, but Samoth didn't think it could be so. I was kind of shocked, because I knew him quite well at the time. But it didn't change anything else for me, Euronymous being dead.[10]

Aarseth had been forced to close the Helvete store a few months earlier, due to overwhelming attention from the media and police after the initial Black Metal church fire revelations. His parents were upset about all the negative publicity and, since they had helped him finance the shop, they successfully leaned on him to shut it down. Vikernes sarcastically points out how Aarseth's inconsistent nature often resulted in deference to his parents' wishes instead of adhering to the black and "evil" image he supposedly embodied: "Øystein once came to one of the newspapers wearing a white sweater, and later apologized to the scene, in case he had insulted anybody! It was all because of his parents. He was 26 years old!"[11]

After only four days of investigative work following the interview with Ilsa, the police had enough evidence and testimony to confidently make their move against the slayer of Øystein Aarseth. On August 19, 1993, they arrested Varg Vikernes in Bergen. As the case unfolded, they would eventually be able to bring charges against him for far more than just the killing.

There are endless speculations on the motives for the killing of Aarseth. Certainly the relations between him and Vikernes had soured. Øystein owed Varg a significant sum of royalty payments from the Burzum releases on Deathlike Silence, although given the poorly-run nature of the record label, this was hardly unusual or unexpected. Vikernes denies there was any monetary motive behind his actions. Others claim the attack came about as a result of a power struggle for dominance of the Black Metal scene, although astute insiders like Metalion are skeptical: "That's stupid reasoning, because you can't expect to kill someone and have everyone think of you as the king and forget about him. That's very, very primitive. It's something more than that, I think."[12]

IHSAHN: I knew they had a conflict. Euronymous had said he thought Grishnackh was an asshole. Grishnackh thought Euronymous was an asshole. To some degree I think it was a fight for leadership. In some way they both wanted power, and to be the leading man. They had both done a lot; Grishnackh started the church burning, but Euronymous had the shop and kind of started the scene up. They were both important people for the progression of the scene. Maybe I'm speculating too much.

SAMOTH: It did not come as a shock really. I was hoping that it wasn't Vikernes who did it, because I knew that this would lead to a lot of shit. But Vikernes was arrested shortly after, and then the ball started to roll. The police began a huge investigation of the whole scene, both in Norway and Sweden. The fact that Euronymous died did not affect me much personally. But because of his murder, the whole thing collapsed and we all got bloody arrested and ended up in prison. I was okay with Euronymous, but I was also okay with Vikernes. I'd heard Vikernes talk shit about Euronymous and vice-versa, but I didn't want to take any sides. After the confessions and trials there was a lot of tribulation between some of us. Vikernes was obviously pissed off, as he went down for a lot of stuff. These days I'm hardly concerned about the death of Euronymous at all. I think some people made a little bit too much fuss about him being "the king" and all that. He was once important for the scene, but I am my own master.

METALION: The final recordings of the Mayhem album and the financial situation between Grishnackh and Euronymous—I think that was the thing that started it all, and ended it all. Øystein never mentioned Grishnackh, he would just say he was having problems with certain elements in the Norwegian Black Metal scene, but of course it was him he was talking about. It was only financial matters— he owed him royalties from the first two Burzum albums, which I think Grishnackh never received. That's because Euronymous wasn't a good businessman and I don't think he had the cash to pay him. Also Grishnackh's

"I PISS ON HIS GRAVE!"
Count Grishnacht slams murdered Black Metal 'godfather' Euronymous!

VIKERNES IN *KERRANG!*

ØYSTEIN "EURONYMOUS" AARSETH

mother paid for the studio recording of the first album, and Euronymous owed her money which she was supposed to get back. I don't think it ever happened. All this added up with the aggression between them. And Grishnackh wanted to sign with another record label, Candlelight or Earache.

BÅRD EITHUN

HOW DID YOU FIND OUT ABOUT ØYSTEIN'S MURDER?

I was supposed to visit Øystein, the night he was killed, but instead I waited and went to visit him the day after. I was walking up to his apartment and then I was in the middle of the investigation by the cops. There were people there from the TV and newspapers and that's how I heard that Øystein was killed.

WERE YOU SURPRISED?

Of course, because I didn't expect it at all. It was like something that doesn't happen to people you know, only to those you don't know. I tried to pick out who might have been there to do it, but I couldn't recall.

YOU DIDN'T THINK IT WAS VIKERNES?

I didn't, not at all. I didn't know he was so stupid that he could do it.

DID YOU KNOW ABOUT A FEUD BETWEEN HIM AND ØYSTEIN?

I knew there were disagreements between them, but I don't think Øystein took it very seriously. Vikernes was very much into making war with Øystein. He didn't like him anymore, because obviously Øystein got more attention in the underground scene than Vikernes, and he couldn't handle it. For Øystein it wasn't any big deal really, because he was an easy going, very controlled person. There

EMPEROR LIVE IN ENGLAND, 1993

was also a disagreement about some money that Vikernes had lent to Øystein. Øystein had needed money to release the first Burzum record, which of course he didn't have the ability to pay back. Vikernes was angry about all that. But he knew that Øystein needed time to pay back the money because he had to get the business into a good condition. Anyway, it wasn't any reason in that to kill him, just for some money... at least he can't get it back now!

WHAT ABOUT THE STORY THAT ØYSTEIN WAS PLANNING TO KILL VIKERNES?

I don't know because I was in England at that time with my band, Emperor. I heard that Øystein called Mortiis [Emperor's bassist at the time] and was talking about how he wanted to kill Vikernes, but I heard this after the murder. But honestly, I can't see any reason for him to want to kill Vikernes. Maybe something happened when I was in England, I don't know.

WHAT ABOUT THE SELF-DEFENSE STORY?

That's bullshit. There's no reason why Øystein would attack Vikernes after he'd just woken up, still in his underwear. He wouldn't do it.

I can understand it though, because Vikernes wanted to get away from a twenty-one-year, first-degree murder sentence. It's a natural move—it was the same with me in court, I tried to get away from it by claiming self-defense. But it's not easy in Norway to get away with such stuff.

VIKERNES PROMO PHOTO, 1993

DID YOU HAVE ANY CONTACT WITH VIKERNES AFTER THAT?

None at all. He was arrested after the murder and I was arrested two weeks later. We were in different prisons and I had no interest in writing to him because he killed Øystein, who I had known for six years and who I liked more than Vikernes at that time. Vikernes had started to get a very big ego, after he had been in the news at that time, and he believed he was important. Øystein was more down-to-earth. Vikernes always had all these plans about all kinds of shit. One night it was plans about killing different people, one night it was about burning stuff, and then it would change again. He was always talking about burning down churches. It wasn't very realistic.

VARG VIKERNES

WHERE DOES THE INCIDENT WITH ØYSTEIN COME INTO EVERYTHING?

Øystein has nothing to do with anything! He knew us, and every time someone burned a church he was going around talking to everybody, boasting that *we* have burned another church. He was always saying "we" because he wanted to be part of it. The only criminal thing that I know he's done was a burglary, a break-in of a church, and then the terrorizing of another Black Metal guy [this was the threat made against Stian "Occultus"], which actually I convinced him to join in on.

He was just following me. Øystein was just a big mouth—of course we used that consciously. If I wanted to implant a meaning into the whole scene, I could just tell him and he'd say, "Okay, yeah, that's right!" and he'd tell everybody "I've got a new idea." Suddenly everybody knew the same. It was the simple way. He was a big mouth, and we joked about him being the "mouth of Grishnackh." I told this to Øystein before he died, and that was one of the reasons he was so against me—because I revealed his true nature.

ØYSTEIN WASN'T INVOLVED IN ANY OF THE CHURCH BURNINGS?

Not the crimes. He did not plan or do anything else either. He did nothing.

DID OTHERS DISLIKE HIM IN THE SCENE?

Darkthrone realized what a jerk he was. They didn't want anything to do with him. Fenriz liked Øystein, but the other guys hated him. That's damn sure. They cursed him in rituals—they were Satanists.

WHY DID PEOPLE HATE HIM?

Because he was nothing of what he presented himself as. More and more people realized that he was just lying. When he was sitting in his shop drinking Coca-Cola and eating Kebab from the Paki shop next door, it was all our money he bought everything with. It was dishonest pay. He was a parasite. Also he was half Lappish, a Sami, so that was a bonus. Bastard!

He was ripping everyone off, all of us. When he gave records away and people thought, "Oh, Øystein is so cool, I got a free record from him," it was *us* who paid for it. More and more people got pissed as he ripped people off. I got orders in advance for the *Aske* mini-album, and since I was in prison I just gave the orders to him so he could have them. He just took all the money and didn't send one single album out.

YOU WERE GETTING MORE AND MORE FED UP WITH ØYSTEIN?

Yeah. We didn't want anything to do with him, and he was always phoning up and asking, "Can I stay at your place when I'm in Bergen?" We'd say, "No." But the reason I tried to kill him is actually quite simple: *he tried to kill me.*

He also told Samoth and some people—and one of them phoned me and said Øystein was planning to kill me. And he [Øystein] did not tell everyone about it, which he usually did. So this time it was serious, obviously. Also because he didn't boast about it or say anything (except to those people he trusted, who of course reported to me) I thought, okay, maybe that's serious.

So I just drove straight to his home and asked, "What the fuck are you thinking?" and he panicked. If you plan to kill someone and the guy turns up at your apartment at three o'clock at night, you panic, quite simple. He planned to kill me, but when I turned up at his place he probably thought I was going to kill him, so he panicked. And in his panic he attacked me.

He kicked me in the chest, and I was quite stunned. Then I threw him to the floor. Suddenly he tried to run for a knife in the kitchen. I said, okay, if he's going to have his knife then I'm going to have a knife, and I pulled my knife. I managed to stop him before he got his knife and I stabbed him. Then he tried to go to the bedroom where he had his shotgun—the gun Dead shot himself with.

HE HAD THAT GUN?

I don't know now if it was. Perhaps he didn't have it, but the point is that at that time I believed he did. Also he had his stun-gun. I thought, okay, he's gonna have that, and I chased him and then suddenly he was running out and he started to scream, "Heeelllp!" and rang the doorbells of his neighbors. That pissed me off—such cowardice. And I knew that he was going to kill me; I can kill him now or I can kill him later—because someday he would try, and perhaps succeed. So why wait? So I killed him.

Also I'd been told about this plan he had, to shoot me with his stun-gun, tie me up, and torture me to death.

YOU HAD HEARD THIS?

In detail, in detail! That pissed me off, obviously! A normal person, they would run away, right? They would be afraid. But I did not react that way. I went straight to his place. I had also gotten a letter and in the letter he was *so* kind and *so* positive, and I thought, "What is this?" Also he talked with another guy about "getting rid" of me, at the same time I got this sweet, pink, cozy letter from him. All the other reasons [people theorize for the murder] are just bullshit.

WHAT ARE SOME OF THE OTHER EXPLANATIONS PEOPLE HAVE SPECULATED?

The newspapers wanted it to be some kind of struggle between rivals, but that's just bullshit. That's how they *want* it to be, so they can make it seem like a big danger. Like Christianity depends on Satan. Without Satan, what the hell do you need Christianity for? So they had to portray us as Satanists, to get more followers for themselves. That's the problem.

YOU HAD NO PLAN THAT THIS WOULD HAPPEN WHEN YOU WENT TO ØYSTEIN'S?

No. They claimed I made the car very clean. I *never* washed the car. It was so dirty when my mother got it back, there were layers of shit and mud in the car. I never cleaned, there was no point to do so. But they claimed I cleaned my car very, very carefully. That's absolute bullshit.

THE "OFFICIAL" STORY IS THAT YOU PLANNED THE KILLING—CREATING AN ALIBI BY RENTING A VIDEO YOU SUPPOSEDLY WATCHED THAT NIGHT IN BERGEN, PLANNING FOR A FRIEND TO MAKE AN ATM WITHDRAWAL WITH YOUR CARD WHILE YOU WERE IN OSLO, AND SO FORTH, SO THAT IT LOOKED LIKE YOU NEVER LEFT BERGEN AT ALL.

Well, I have *never* had a card. The card belonged to the other guy and I had nothing to do with any of this. The point is that it doesn't matter if we planned it at all or not, because what happened is that he attacked me out of fear, and that makes it not first degree, because he attacked me. The conviction is wrong. I had military shooting gloves in my pocket—if this was a first-degree murder wouldn't I have worn the gloves? Of course! I came into the building with gloves halfway out of my pocket and he attacked. If I was going to kill him I would have put on the gloves and then attacked. That would have been first degree.

WHAT DID YOU DO WHEN YOU GOT TO HIS BUILDING?

I rang his doorbell. He was on the fourth floor. I was talking into the intercom. "Hello, who is it?"
"It's Varg, let me in."
"Why?"
"I want to talk to you."
And he let me in! I walked up to the fourth floor; the other guy was standing outside smoking. I knocked on the door upstairs. He was still in his underwear. I walked up four flights of stairs and he was still in his underwear!
I was out of breath when I got up there and he was standing there. The neighbors said they heard everything. They told the police they heard a woman screaming! I was laughing when I read about it. He ran away, pressing the doorbells and calling "Help!" They said there were twenty-three or twenty-four stab wounds, but that's not true. I was running after him, stabbing, and it was four or five stabs. The first stab was in the chest. The whole time he was trying to run away, so I had to stab him in the back.
He was running down the stairwell, barefoot. I'd just been sleeping during an eight-hour drive and was wearing heavy army boots. I had to run like hell to catch up with him, and at the same time I was stabbing and he was running as fast as he could. There were a couple of stabs in the back.

He broke a lamp in the stairwell in the chase and fell down on his back into the glass fragments, which of course makes a lot of wounds, which they said were knife cuts. He also had the glass fragments under his feet because he fell and got up afterwards. The autopsy was bullshit. They said he died of blood loss. The real point is that he died from one stab to the head. He died momentarily. *Bam!* he was dead. Through his skull. I actually had to knock the knife out. It was stuck in his skull and I had to pry it out, he was hanging on it—and then he fell down the stairs. I hit him directly into his skull and his eyes went *boing!* and he was dead.

Also I read an autopsy report and there was a wound through his chest which came out in the back! Which means of course I was angry and hit him hard. It was a very sharp knife. If you cut someone with a sharp knife you get a nice cut, if you use a blunt knife you rip his fucking flesh up. The autopsy report was wrong, because he died momentarily. They even managed to get that wrong.

WHERE DID HE DIE?

That was on the first floor. I chased him and he fell down in the glass fragments, and I ran past him. I turned around to face him again. He was standing and the other guy came running up. I didn't know whether he was going to attack me too; he was Øystein's best friend. He was with me accidentally. I thought he might attack me because he was Øystein's best friend, I was waiting for it. Øystein got up and the other guy just ran past. Then everything was clear to me. Øystein came against me and I attacked him, quite simply. I got his chest and then I pounded his skull. He just sat down, dying momentarily.

NONE OF THE NEIGHBORS OPENED THEIR DOORS?

They didn't dare. They thought it was some drunken fight. It's the worst neighborhood in Oslo—60% colored people.

ONCE IT STARTED THERE WAS NO TURNING BACK?

No, no mercy. You don't give mercy to someone who would never give it to you. That's the moral. I will treat a person honorably who I expect will treat me honorably, but I knew he was going to tie me up, and shoot me with an electro stun-pistol. Where's the honor in that? He was just some scum who deserved no honor, no mercy, no nothing. That's why I didn't treat him right.

ANATOMY OF A SLAYING

According to testimony that would later be given at Vikernes's trial, the killing of Aarseth was a premeditated act. Varg had the help of two accomplices, 21-year-old Snorre Westvold Ruch aka "Blackthorn" (who was also a member of Bård Eithun's band Thorns), and another friend in Bergen. Ruch accompanied Vikernes on the long seven-hour drive to Oslo that night; the third accomplice remained in Varg's apartment in Bergen.

It would be alleged in court that a video had been rented that day which was played in the apartment while Vikernes and Ruch were gone. It was a film both had already seen; this was allegedly so they could describe the details of the movie if ever questioned on what they did that night. An ATM card was also left with the friend in Bergen, who was to withdraw money from Varg's account late at night; this would be further evidence that Vikernes never left town. However, in the haste of their departure, the wrong card was left and the ATM withdrawal couldn't be carried out.

Vikernes also brought along a contract for the release of Burzum material on Aarseth's DSP label with him to Oslo that night. The contracts had already been

PHOTO: RIKKE LUNDGREEN

AARSETH'S APARTMENT BUILDING DOOR

signed and sent to him by Øystein who, despite their disputes, still hoped to keep Burzum on his label. Vikernes dated the contracts on the 9th, which he would later say was in error. Snorre Ruch claims the documents were brought along as another part of the subterfuge; they would make it seem as if Varg and Øystein had met on friendly terms shortly before the latter's death. Vikernes has written his own explanation:

> Before I left for Oslo I burned a picture of [Øystein] on which a friend—who didn't like him either—had written "death to the red rat" with a special magic script. I burned it because I wanted nothing to do with him, I wouldn't even have this picture of him, and I went to Oslo to deliver a contract to him to avoid having any contact with him at all. I had arranged it so that I got money from the record label right above him, and in that way I wouldn't even have to receive checks from him. To give him the contract would mean that he would never write or call me anymore.[13]

SNORRE RUCH

WHAT WAS YOUR PERSONAL SITUATION BEFORE THE MURDER?

I lived in Trondheim from Christmas '92 to summer '93. In the summer of '93 I had a few psychiatric problems and was almost committed to an institution. But instead of being committed, I ran off to Bergen. And then what happened, happened.

WHO FIRST PUT FORTH THE IDEA?

It was the Count. It was he who wanted it; I was neither for nor against it. I didn't give a shit about Øystein, I had nothing to do with him.

BUT YOU JOINED IN ON IT?

Not at the beginning. I didn't really want to go. The original idea was that I should drive the car for the Count. It was then that we got a third man. I wanted the Count to take him along instead of me. I put forth the suggestion, but the Count put pressure on me to get me to come.

WHAT KIND OF PRESSURE?

He is very authoritarian. He gets people to go along with him.

WHAT HAPPENED?

We settled on the idea that he would go alone. But a few hours before he left, he decided that he was so well-known, so famous, that people would recognize him when he drove through Oslo or Bergen. Therefore, he wanted me to drive. So he talked me into coming with him. He lay in the back of his Volkswagen Golf under a lot of T-shirts.

It wasn't intended that I should come with Vikernes into the apartment either. I asked him, before we left the car, if he wanted me to come with him as "moral support" and so it meant me coming with him. I never went with him into the apartment, because I loitered in the stairway. I walked to the top of the stairs, and as I stood in front of Øystein's door I shuddered. When I stood outside Øystein's door I heard noise inside and Øystein came out, with the Count on his heels, covered in blood, rushing down the stairway.

I realized that this was going to hell. We had intended this to happen in the apartment, and fast—no big, dramatic thing with a hundred knife-stabs or something. So I ran down the stairs, past them, and into the square outside the building. I started walking towards the car and the Count came right after me.

How did you get into the building?

Øystein didn't know I was there. The Count rang the bell [and spoke through the intercom] that only he was coming. Øystein didn't want to let the Count in. He had gone to bed, and seemed nervous. I was standing right next to the Count so I could hear this. Øystein said it was late, that he had gone to bed and that the Count should come back another day. The Count then said he had brought the contract with him, and that Øystein should let him in.

I took the last draws from my cigarette, crushed it and put it back in its packet, and turned the door handle. Then I had to polish it to remove the fingerprints. I had to walk up the stairs without touching the railing. The Count had gloves, but he forgot to wear them. That's why he left fingerprints in the blood after the fighting. He also forgot the contracts, and left them in the apartment. They are dated August 9th, '93, and signed by Varg Vikernes.

Øystein had written the contract and signed it, then sent it off to the Count for him to sign and send back. It was to be used as an excuse for the visit. On the way to the car I asked him if he'd remembered the contract, because I could see that it wasn't in his hand. He said he had it with him.

Did you do anything on the drive home?

On our way to Oslo we had seen that there was a big traffic control of cars going out. At one point on our way back we stopped at a small place near Nittedal [about 25 km from Oslo] to call the person in [Varg's] apartment.

At that time we were not sure whether Øystein was dead or not. The Count said he stabbed him many times, and that he was sure that Øystein was dead. I asked, what if he was alive and someone had heard what happened? What if Øystein told them that the Count has been there? Then the police would go to his apartment in Bergen and wait for him. So we were going to call the guy in the apartment to ask him to go home.

We stopped by a phone booth, but that didn't work. Right then a uniformed police car drove by. It turned around, probably thinking that we looked rather suspicious. We drove off with the police on our heels. It became a car chase, and we outran the police.

BUT THIS WAS NEVER REPORTED?

It was never connected to the case.

THE POLICE DIDN'T TAKE YOUR LICENSE NUMBER?

No, probably not. But the story was later checked and it was correct. We were afraid they were looking for us so we were quite nervous. When we came to Bergen we imagined we saw plainclothes policemen everywhere, looking for us.

SO YOU STOPPED SOMEWHERE AND GOT RID OF THE MURDER WEAPON?

SNORRE RUCH IN PRISON, 1995

Yes, a small pond in Nittedal. I slept on the way back and he slept on the way to Oslo. I was sick with fever, by the way. So we drove with the heat on maximum and Dead Can Dance on the stereo real loud. It was quite atmospheric. We drove back to Bergen, and drove right out to run an errand at the printers the morning after. And we returned the video too, to get as tight an alibi as possible.

WHAT OCCURRED WHEN YOU WERE TAKEN IN FOR QUESTIONING?

After a while, the story we made up began to spring leaks. When three people are going to tell the same story to the police, in interrogations lasting seven hours, it will go to hell. In addition, I was sure that they knew, and I was just waiting for them to get to us. In the end I didn't bother to keep up any more.

BUT THE COUNT CLAIMS THAT IF YOU HADN'T CONFESSED YOU WOULDN'T HAVE BEEN CAUGHT?

That is not correct. He left behind fingerprints in the blood, and the contract. His excuse about the contract was going to be that he wrote the wrong date. He claimed in the media to have difficulty knowing what day it was.

VARG VIKERNES: The first thing that happened is that I was arrested after a guy snitched on me, Snorre. He's a nobody, a loser. A sick, feeble guy. I was arrested and in prison with no contact with anything and they said in the newspapers that I had killed him.

Of course the moment a guy dies, then everybody says they were friends with him. Nobody knew Dead, nobody has even heard of him, but once he's dead he's cool. That's typical.

So they started to arrest others, because one stupid bitch from Rumania, a so-called Swede named Ilsa, she confessed that Bård had killed a guy, exactly what he'd told her. He was arrested. Of course they didn't have any proof at all, but he admitted everything. They didn't have any clues, except for this stupid 16-year-old Gypsy girl—what court would believe her? But he admitted everything. Then it went on to the next guy, and to the next guy, until everything was revealed. It's typical, these unimportant people could be important this way, by ratting each other off. So they did. Of course I was the big bad guy.

SNORRE RUCH

HOW DO YOU REACT TO VARG'S VERSION OF THE EVENTS?

I don't understand what he wants with his story. He got me into this mess. But I don't blame him as long as he doesn't put the blame on me.

WHAT DO YOU THINK WAS VIKERNES'S REASON TO KILL ØYSTEIN?

One thing was that he was envious of Bård, because Bård had killed a man. Varg hadn't done that. Varg was saying that what Bård had done was uncool, but inside the scene Bård's actions commanded respect. "Bård has just killed a stupid homo, it's nothing to brag about at all," Vikernes thought. Bragging about killing someone is a pretty extreme thing to do. The Count said it was no big deal to kill someone.

THAT WAS THE WHOLE REASON?

And it was that he didn't care much for Øystein. But the rumors about it being because he was a communist or homosexual have nothing to do with it.

DO YOU REGRET WHAT HAPPENED?

I don't have a bad conscience. Maybe I would feel that if I met his parents. But I haven't met them, so I don't think about it. I don't have any sleepless nights or anything. I regret coming here [to jail] a bit, though.

ØYSTEIN SEEMED TO DIE IN ACCORDANCE WITH HIS IDEALS...

Yes, it's not as if a little girl was run over in the road or something.

HE LIVED AND DIED BY THE SWORD...

But the thing is, he was not a swordsman. He wasn't as tough as he claimed. He didn't receive a just death—that would be too stupid to say—but he got a just death according to who he posed as.

I liked Øystein for what he was, but he refused to admit that he was like that. He took away what I found to be sympathetic about him. After a while, when we were in the same room, he refused to be the cool guy that I knew. He refused to let go of his mask.

★ ★ ★ ★ ★

Snorre today maintains the same story which he told in court, presenting himself as the ambivalent accessory to Varg's crime. However, his comments in the above interview are made questionable with his remark about the murder when he states, "I was neither for nor against it. I didn't give a shit about Øystein, I had nothing to do with him."

The truth of the matter is that Snorre had shortly before joined Mayhem as a second guitar player. It is difficult to believe that he could have cared less about killing the founder of the band he was in—doubly difficult given Mayhem's position as such a legendary group in the underground. In hearing his and Vikernes's versions of the story, both are flawed. With his history of mental problems, one far-fetched explanation may be that Snorre was too daft to comprehend what he was actually participating in.

VARG VIKERNES

IT SEEMS ODD YOU WOULD GO TO MURDER SOMEONE WITH AN ACCOMPLICE WHO WAS THEIR FRIEND.

The guy who went with me joined me because he was going to show Øystein some new riffs on the guitar! They were playing in the same band. He was in Mayhem at the time, he was the second guitarist besides Øystein. He was his best friend.

DID THAT COME UP IN COURT?

I tried to bring it up; they just suppressed it. ... [Snorre] testified against me. He did his best to nail me. But he did it so well that he nailed himself—he got eight years for doing nothing. Just because he was with me. They said that he supported me *psychologically*. They sent him to prison for eight years, for doing nothing. He regrets it very deeply now, but it's too late. He didn't think about that then—too bad.

HE LIVED IN BERGEN?

He was living in my apartment for a limited time. He was a common friend of ours; Øystein's best friend—my worst friend! But I'm not blaming others, because I'm the fool who socialized with such idiots. I must have been quite a fool to not realize these guys were just losers. The only foolish thing I did and the only thing I regret, is not killing [Snorre] as well. If I'd killed him as well I would not have gotten any more punishment if I was caught, and secondly, *I wouldn't have been caught*. That's what I regret.

PRO-VIKERNES FLYER

HELLHAMMER

WAS THE GUITARIST IN MAYHEM DIRECTLY INVOLVED IN THE KILLING OF EURONYMOUS?

Varg and Blackthorn were living in Bergen, about seven hours' drive from Oslo. It was planned that they were going to kill him. So he was part of the murder but he didn't stab him, he just stood and watched.

YOU DON'T SOUND SO UPSET ABOUT THIS YOURSELF.

I'm not.

WEREN'T YOU CLOSE TO EURONYMOUS?

Well, I liked him a lot, but the fact that he was a communist offended me. Euronymous wanted to be the most extreme person, and he thought that communism was very extreme, with the things in Soviet Russia you know? But after awhile, a couple of years, he found out that communism was total shit. He realized this and then claimed to be a fascist, but I don't know about that. He was a communist, sadly.

BARBARIAN ETHICS

Although he steadfastly maintains that Øystein's death came about as partial self-defense (based on a pre-emptive strike), Vikernes is quick to point out other justifications for ridding the world of Aarseth. Communism and homosexuality are mentioned, along with Øystein's dishonesty (which friends of Aarseth dismiss as merely the result of ineptitude in business affairs), false nature and weakness, summing him up as "the god of laziness in earthly communist manifestation."[14]

Once asked why he did not realize these extreme flaws in Aarseth's character earlier, Vikernes replied:

Because Euronymous lived five hundred kilo-meters from Bergen; so seldomly did I meet him. It took me half a year of weekly contact by phone, mail, and some visits, to find out what a loser he truly was. But he was a good actor, and a good liar for sure.[15]

Many who knew Aarseth concur that the extreme Satanic image he projected was, in fact, just that—a projection which bore little resemblance to his real person-ality. Vikernes also asserts that many in the Black Metal scene applauded when they heard about Aarseth's death, and this is no doubt true. Vikernes also appears genuinely perplexed that anyone cares about Øystein's premature departure from the scene, and in this Varg fails to real-ize that even if they did not always like him personally, Euronymous fulfilled the role of figurehead for the music genre which had held so many in sway during their younger, impressionable years.

What is striking about members of the Scandinavian Black Metal circles in general is how little they cared about the lives or deaths of one another. When Dead killed himself, it became merely an opportunity for Aarseth to hype Mayhem to a new level. When he himself died violently two years later, his own bandmates speak of the killing with a tone of indifference more suited to a court stenographer.

After enough time extolling "death and evil," some began to take it seri-ously indeed. Vikernes stated frankly from jail while on trial: "Basically I am a worshipper of Odin, the god of war and death. Burzum exists exclusively for Odin, the one-eyed enemy of the Christian God."[16] Varg's obsession with war and death is shared by others, or so

COUNT

Grishnackh

ANTI-VIKERNES FLYER

they proclaim in the pages of fanzines and CD booklets.

A number of prominent Black Metalers have sworn to avenge Aarseth's death on the day Vikernes is finally released from his twenty-one year sentence. Aware of such sentiments, Varg's reply is a mocking one:

We shall all die and I fear it not. In a way we are all dying, for indeed life is a slow death. We grow old, fade away, grow weak. I say let the weak die. My time shall come when I am weak, as with all the others. If I am shot in the back, I'm a fool not to foresee that a sniper may lurk in the shadows behind me. If I am stabbed to death with a knife or dagger, I am a weaker warrior than my foe. If I am poisoned, I am a fool to let my enemy near my food. If a car hits me, I am too unobservant to deserve survival. If I die of disease it is my destiny. Alas, if anybody wants me dead let them try; I enjoy a good fight and if they win (which they won't! HAH!), they win—so what? I'll die fighting. Reincarnation in Valhalla awaits. Eternal strife![17]

With the killings committed by Bård Eithun and Varg Vikernes, members of the Black Metal scene had proven their willingness to match the violent rhetoric with bloody deeds. In the eerie phenomenon which haunts the movement, Øystein Aarseth had now followed tradition and managed to live up to his name—he was indeed Euronymous, "the prince of death." He had achieved his ideal of "deathlike silence."

With the exception of Darkthrone, the major Norwegian Black Metal bands were now in hiatus, their key members facing prison sentences for arson, grave desecration, and murder. The legal proceedings that would follow disrupted the entire scene and pitted different factions against one another. People felt forced to choose sides: pro-Vikernes or pro-Euronymous. At this point a cult developed around the memory of Euronymous, hailed as "the King" or "Godfather of Black Metal." As many have commented in the preceding interviews, much of this was hyperbole, emanating from a second generation of musicians trying to gain credibility by riding on the back of the legend of Aarseth's Black Metal legacy.

At this point Vikernes began to vehemently disassociate himself from his former friends. He stated he had nothing to do with the Black Metal scene—his interests lay elsewhere in the realms of nationalism and the worship of Odin. It was true Vikernes had upheld a far more uncompromised attitude in his interactions with the police than many of his former colleagues (although his *Bergens Tidende* interview had triggered the police interest in Black Metal to begin with). He simply refused to cooperate with the authorities, and maintained he was innocent until proven guilty. He followed the advice of his lawyer and never testified in court.

Kerrang! Headline

The same cannot be said of the other offenders, most of whom confessed in detail once they were pressured by the police. On the one hand, this is understandable given their young age, relative naivety, and fear of worse punishments if they refused to admit their wrongdoing. Samoth explains his own experiences with the police, and reasons for confessing, which are probably similar to some of the others:

I was arrested in September '93 and put into custody. I had on several occasions been in for questioning. The first time was right after Vikernes for some reason openly stated in a major Bergen newspaper that it was the "Black Circle" who were behind all the church burnings, and also that he knew something about the "Olympic Park Murder." I didn't tell the police shit then. Next time was during August '93, right after the murder of Euronymous, in connection with Bård Eithun's murder, as well as the many church burnings. I said nothing relevant to the police at this point. By the time I was arrested, everyone else had been arrested and Eithun had already confessed to his actions. I was arrested on the basis of some statements made by three other guys in the scene. I realize now that these statements weren't that strong. However, at that time I was not very familiar with the law and how it all worked. I listened way too much to my lawyer, which was my first mistake. During my time in custody, another stronger statement against me came up. My main mistake was of course trying to explain myself out of it. The best thing is obviously to keep your mouth shut. Anyway, in the end, the statements that I had given to the police were so full of shit, so I decided to confess. I guess in a way

I gave up. Also my instincts told me it was the best possible way, because as I had understood it, I would go down for this no matter what. I also figured Vikernes was so deep in it already, so it would make no bigger difference. Egoistic maybe, but I had to put myself on top of the ladder.[18]

Bård Eithun

What was the chain of events that led to you finally getting caught?

It was when Øystein was killed, because he was killed almost like this homosexual, with many stabbings. Then the cops started to question people in the scene about this homosexual murder. They were talking to people and people told the police that I had done this murder.

Do you know who told them?

I have my suspicions. I guess I know. It was different people, it was not really the people involved in the scene but the hangers-on who wanted to be inside the scene. Unfortunately they had gotten some very secret information. These people knew stuff that hadn't been written about in the newspapers, so it was easy for the cops to understand that it was true.

What was first visit from the police?

I was arrested when I was drinking, so I don't remember much. It was up in Kvikne, I was outside a local motel drinking with some people. The cops came and wanted to talk to me and they had an arrest order and wanted to go to my apartment and look through my stuff. I woke up at at the police station in Oslo, and understood of course that I had been arrested for this murder.

What happened with your questioning?

I was arrested at night, brought into Oslo in the morning, and that afternoon they questioned me. They asked me if I knew anything about the rumors about me that I killed this man. Of course I said I didn't know anything. Then my lawyer advised me to admit to the murder, which now I understand was not a very good thing to do, because that made me get some more years I think.

He assumed you had done it?

He believed I did it. It was easier for him if I admitted it because then he didn't have to make up a history of what might happened and tell that to the court. It was easier for him to have me admit it. Also when I didn't want to confess to the burning, he immediately came to the police station to talk to me, saying "You have to confess to it." I was not very impressed with the lawyer. He had a very good reputation, but many people have also had very bad experiences with him drinking in court, drunk, and sleeping in court, which he was doing during my case.

Varg Vikernes is disgusted by the fact that while he held fast to a code of silence, others confessed. In his mind, all who testified about the criminal activities are snitches. The trial brought out a who's who of the Black Metal scene, and testimonies flew in all directions, often implicating the witnesses themselves. Numerous documents were introduced before the court: the record contract carried by Vikernes to Oslo, letters written by Vikernes and others, maps and forensic reports, and the now infamous *Bergens Tidende* article.

The resulting statements and police interviews were enough to convict Vikernes of murder and arson and possession of illegal weapons. In his own summation:

> I was sentenced to twenty-one years in prison for three church fires, where they had one witness as the only "evidence" in each of the fires; an attempted torching of a bell tower where two of the same witnesses were the only "evidence"; theft and storage of 100 kilograms of dynamite and 50 kilograms of glynite (slow ignition explosives)—something that I confessed to—and a couple of breaking and enterings into some some cabins in which two books were stolen.[19]

He was 21 years old, ordered to spend that many years again in maximum security prison—the Norwegian equivalent of a life sentence. On the day of Varg's sentencing, two more churches were torched in Norway, presumably as a statement of symbolic support. Bård Eithun received a lesser fourteen-year murder sentence for his crime. Snorre, Vikernes's accomplice to the killing of Øystein Aarseth, received eight years. The rest, people like Samoth and Jørn Inge Tunsberg who had participated in church burnings but confessed to police, received two- to three-year sentences to be served in minimum security institutions. Many of those involved in the church arsons have also had huge fines levied upon them to repay the damages and reconstruction costs caused by their actions.

During the course of the court proceedings, which took place in the spring of 1994, Vikernes quickly became a pariah in the nation's consciousness. He had all the qualities which offered a field day for tabloid journalists. The newspapers and television would train their guns in Varg's direction, and in turn he provided them with all the ammunition they could ever require.

THE OFFICIAL STORY

In 1998, the Norwegian police issued a report entitled *Kirkebranner og satanistisk motiverte skadeverk* (Church Fires and Satanically Motivated Criminal Damage). As a cooperative effort between four different police and judicial officers, one of them a state attorney, and as many investigative agencies, it brings forth a variety of material and reflects a range of experience.

The report details the way in which the Norwegian Black Metal scene was structured around the time the police investigations began, how the police cracked open the subculture, and it offers recommendations of methods for other police departments to deal with similar situations in the future. Even if the report was produced with the benefit of hindsight (which, as the cliché goes, tends to be 20/20), the reader can sense that it is largely written by people whose experience dealing with the dark underbelly of society has given them bullshit detectors in full working order. At the same time, the sheer outlandishness and frequent self-contradictions of the Black Metal scene are bound to bewilder any outside observer—and some of the confusion expressed by the teenage Black Metal rebels is bound to rub off on anyone trying to make sense of them.

The main problems arise when the authors try to place the Norwegian church-burning, Black Metal brand of Satanism into a larger context. It is in these sections of the report, when down-to-earth cops leave their areas of expertise and begin to speculate about fringe religious practices, that the otherwise sober tone gives way to wild exaggerations.

Sadly, some of the material seems to be derived from American Fundamentalist Christian sources. As a result, the police report (which more often reads like a how-to manual for dealing with criminal elements in the Satanic movement) occasionally regurgitates a hodgepodge of Christian Satanic scare propaganda of the sort that fueled the "Satanic panics" which swept across America in the 1980s and Britain and parts of Europe in the 1990s—hysteria-driven panics that almost invariably turned out to be unfounded.

The report also contains factual errors of a nature that anyone familiar with the history of twentieth-century occultism would not make, such as attributing the authorship of Aleister Crowley's famous *Liber al vel Legis* (The Book of the Law) to Michael Aquino, head of the far less influential Temple of Set, a small Church of Satan splinter group.

Especially difficult to take seriously is the alleged calendar of "Satanic holy days" reprinted in the report, with many of the dates involving the sexual molestation of minors—something that is strongly condemned by all established

Satanic organizations. And while it might be argued that fringe religious phe-nomena like Satanism are often so bewildering that it's hard to accurately assess their practices, even complete novices in the study of New Religious Movements should begin to suspect something is wrong when they see references to dates that don't exist, such as April 31. Unless, of course, Satanists are so evil that they fol-low their own calendar.

The only conceivable relevance for printing such a calendar in the report might be if it could alert police officers to possible dates when black-clad young-sters were likely to spark up their cigarette lighters at the portals of their local church. But the pattern of church fires in Norway has been such that the law of averages would be a better thing to study if one wants to predict the next Satanic arson.

When taken too literally, the report is a veritable minefield. But if read with a critical mind, it will give police investigators good ideas of where and how to launch an investigation when the next church goes up in smoke.

Kirkebranner og satanistisk motiverte skadeverk also refers to stories that never really reached the media when the Satanic furor was at its height. Especially inter-esting are two anecdotes about Varg Vikernes that help provide insight into his mentality at the time, and illustrate some of the attitudes which made him such a role model for easily impressionable youths.

At an early point when Vikernes was held for questioning in Bergen in con-nection with the church fire at Fantoft, he intimated that during the next inter-rogation session, he would "lay his cards on the table," and reveal what he knew to the investigators. As he was seated in the interrogation room the following day, he suddenly put a deck of cards down in front of him and stated, "Now I have laid my cards on the table."

But despite his smart-ass remarks and mental capabilities, Vikernes was no match for the seasoned investigators of the Kripos. He sensed that the police net was tightening around him and that he was no longer in control of the situation, especially as the Oslo police dispatched its Church Fire Group to Bergen in 1993 to follow the goose steps of the Count and his subjects around Bergen.

Vikernes knocked on the door of the police investigation's impromptu head-quarters in Room 318 of the Hotel Norge in Bergen, and seems to have virtually forced his way into the suite. Dressed in chain mail, carrying two large knives in his belt, and flanked by the two young men who apparently behaved as if they were his bodyguards or henchmen, Vikernes stated that he was fed up with being harassed by the authorities, and that the police investigation into the Black Metal scene should be stopped.

When the operations leader replied that Vikernes hardly had the judicial weight to be issuing orders to the police, Vikernes took one step back and raised his right arm in a Roman salute, Nazi-style.

While both of these stories come from the police and might have been col-ored by their source, they are not hard to believe. It was, after all, probably

Vikernes's penchant for theatrical display that led him to turn his court proceedings into a media circus, thus setting the stage on which he would play out his role as the cartoonish character "The Count"—a role that later blew up in his face when the courts took his threatening outbursts seriously by giving him the harshest sentence allowed by Norwegian law.

So when Vikernes claims that he is in some way a political prisoner, he has a point. It would be almost impossible for someone of Vikernes's age and lack of prior criminal record to receive a twenty-one year prison sentence. Compared with this, Bård Eithun received a sentence approximately two-thirds as long for a similarly brutal slaying. The differences in sentencing may well be political, for Eithun, despite never expressing much remorse, did not go out of his way to provoke the court as Vikernes did when he used the opportunity to proclaim his adherence to National Socialism.

This, of course, provided a perfect target against whom the courts could set a precedent to demonstrate that this youth phenomenon, this cocktail of the most shocking attitudes imaginable to the status quo of Norwegian society, would simply not be tolerated.

COUNT QUISLING

AS THE CHURCH BURNING AND MURDER TRIALS UNFOLDED IN NORWAY, VARG Vikernes began to take on an almost mythical role. Endless daily tabloid stories spewed forth headlines about his alleged deeds. Varg's artistic pseudonym of "Count Grishnackh" on the early Burzum albums provided the press with a perfect soundbite with which to deliver the nation its first real bogeyman in fifty years. The media tag of *"Greven"* ("The Count") triggered just the right images in the readers' minds: a perverse self-styled aristocrat, outside the law, who enacted his libertine fantasies of destruction with a belief in immunity from punishment for his crimes. "The Count drank my blood!" and other sensational, revelatory headlines bestowed Vikernes with the added compulsions of a sadistic vampire, regardless of the fact that the entire story was probably a complete fabrication.

In truth, by this time Vikernes had disowned his previous "Count Grishnackh" pseudonym. "Varg" was not his birth name either, but he knew it suited his character well. In a magazine interview Vikernes explained the symbolism of his new designation, and his distaste for the one he was born with: "I couldn't stand [the name Kristian] ... which means Christ and Christian. The word *Varg* has a great meaning for me. I could speak about this matter for an hour. Anyway briefly, if you make a diagram of this word, you'll see that it's the combination of the vertical and horizontal of the words *Amor* (the strongest feeling), *Roma* (the center of the world) and *Grav* (grave). Besides, *Varg* derives form an archaic Nordic language and means wolf..."[2] As with his two deceased associates, Dead and Euronymous, Vikernes would be destined to fulfill both the overt and hidden essence of his self-given appellation.

Varg now states he originally adopted the title of "Count" for completely differ-

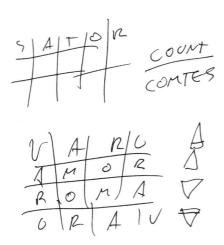

VIKERNES'S NAME DIAGRAMS DRAWN
DURING PRISON INTERVIEWS

ent reasons than the media picked up on. He explains, "Count comes from *Comtes* [sic; in fact, the term is *comes*], a Latin word, which means 'companion, partner' and the idea was that I am the *partner of the people*, but of course nobody realizes that. It was turned into all this Dracula, evil bullshit—typical."[3] The second part of Vikernes's old pseudonym came from his beloved Tolkien books, where Grishnackh is an evil character on the side of Sauron.

Although Varg contributed to the hysteria in his own ways (in a similar manner to some of the contemptuous courtroom behavior by Charles Manson during his infamous trial a quarter-century earlier), he is correct that the portrait painted of him by the newspaper stories is quite at odds with reality. As he explains:

Like my girlfriend says, she hates "The Count" but she likes me. It's something I can say as one of my own feelings as well. I don't like the Count. If I met him I would beat him up, because he seems like a complete idiot. But I know that it's not me. It's like a shadow of mine that's created by the light put on me by these Zionist journalists. The only thing they want is to have a Satan; without that they cannot force people into Christianity.[4]

Varg's contempt of the media's portrayal of his personality is mirrored by his disgust for the court hearings in which he was convicted. He is quick to point out the absurdities and ironies that came to the fore during these proceedings.

VARG VIKERNES

THEY HADN'T FOUND ANY REAL EVIDENCE AGAINST YOU?

They *still* have no evidence. They don't have one single technical proof, nothing. The only reason I'm sentenced is because of those people, who might have done it themselves, *saying that I did it.* That's the only reason I was found guilty. It's all based on testimony, from people who were later found guilty of lying in court! Perjury!

LIKE WHO?

Jørn Inge [Tunsberg, guitarist in the band Hades]. Another zero, an anonymous guy.

How did he know anything?

Because he'd burned it, quite simply! Or he was a part of it. He said that I burned [Åsane Church] in court, and I was found guilty. But he was part of the burning as well, and during his case when he said he was not, they didn't believe him. That's the system.

You would think if people were revealed to have lied about their own actions, that would call their earlier testimony about others into question.

Yeah. And also I had an alibi for one of the churches which I was found guilty of burning. Ironically, I killed the witness—I killed the alibi! But still they had the police interview, he'd told them that in an interview. We should have had that as a proof, but nobody mentioned it. I wasn't allowed to speak to the court.

That's typical trial bullshit. Like my psychiatrists who examined me, one of

6   Lørdag 14. mai 1994

Dagbladet

MOR OG SØNN: Varg Vikernes' mor (45) snakker med Varg etter at hun mot hans vilje gikk i vitneboksen i går for å gi et mer nyansert bilde av sønnen.
(Foto: Jacques Hvistendahl)

– SPRAKK DU I SOLA, VARG?

EGEN SKYLD: Forsvarer Tor Erling Staff mener Varg Vikernes har mye skyld selv for imaget sitt som usosial og dyster.

I bar overkropp spilte Varg «Greven» Vikernes volleyball sammen med andre innsatte i Oslo kretsfengsel Kristi himmelfartsdag. – Du sprakk ikke når sola skinte på deg? spurte Tor Erling Staff sin klient i Eidsivating lagmannsrett i går.

Norwegian Headline: "Did You Burst in the Sun, Varg?" [A play on the idea from Norwegian folklore that trolls burst when exposed to sunlight]

NORWEGIAN HEADLINE: "'I AM THE SON OF
ODIN AND SATAN'—AND HE IS FINANCED BY
THE KU KLUX KLAN"

them was a Jew and a Freemason!
The other was a communist. My
lawyer was a homosexual. The other
lawyer was a Freemason. The one
single Christian faith healer in
Norway was in the jury! Can you
imagine? In other words, a person
who says, "I can look through you
and with the power of Jesus pull out
the evil spirits who make you sick"!

**HOW DO THEY PICK THE JURY?
ISN'T IT RANDOM?**

Officially, but it's quite suspect
when they find "at random" the one
Christian healer in Norway. Also
there were at least two Freemasons in
the jury. All of them were pensioners;
there was only one person who was-
n't elderly. It was just a big act, all of
it bullshit.

The other attorney, for the guy
accused of the same crime [the
Øystein killing], was a Freemason as well, and actually gave evidence against his
own client in court, just to get me sentenced! Snorre had some information, and
it was very important to find out whether he knew it before the police had told
him, or if he learned it from the police. His so-called defense lawyer testified that
he did know it before the police talked to him.

Also I had said the guy had nothing to do with it, and was just in the wrong
place at the wrong time. And he said, "Yes, I had something to do with it, I
accomplished the plan and everything." Very good defense lawyer, who told him
to say that!

HOW DID YOU GET YOUR LAWYER?

Officially he's a very good lawyer, but I'm very dissatisfied with him because
he didn't let me speak. Every time a witness lied, I wasn't allowed to say anything,
even though the judge asked, "Do you want to say anything?" My lawyer told me,
"Don't say anything." Of course you believe your lawyer, right? Especially when
he's supposed to be so goddamned good. So I didn't say anything. But instead, as
they lied, I could have revealed the lie. And punks were testifying against me, from
the Blitz squat [in Oslo]. It was stupid. Also they brought in a Swedish girl who

was insane, and didn't mention that to the jury. Not one single word that she was insane.

CLINICALLY INSANE?

Yeah. She was witnessing against me saying I'd drunk her blood from her neck and everything, and they believed this!

BUT YOU KNEW HER?

Yes, through letters or something; I met her a couple of times.

IS THIS THE PERSON THE MEDIA CLAIMED WAS YOUR SWEDISH GIRLFRIEND, MARIA?

Exactly. I only met her a couple of times.

NORWEGIAN HEADLINE: "THE COUNT WON'T SAY WHO SET THE FIRES: 'I KNEW ABOUT THE CHURCH FIRES'"

For a number of reasons, Vikernes found himself at the center of the Black Metal controversy, both in Norway and the rest of world. In one sense this can be viewed as a result of the massive media coverage he and his *Doppelgänger,* "The Count," received; on the other hand, Varg's status as spokesman or figurehead is fully warranted by his own history, for he does appear to be the personality who gave focus to the ideas welling within the scene, and led people into action. As Vikernes states, "there was *one person* who started it," clearly implying it was he himself. The combination of strong belief in his own role, along with his impressive ability to incitingly voice his opinions, have both ensured Varg's continued influence, even from behind bars.

The fascination with Vikernes on the part of the media and his fans and listeners is not based on mere hype alone. Until the time of the *Bergens Tidende* article and Varg's subsequent arrest, he was admired by most everyone in the scene, and Burzum was considered a band that pioneered the aesthetics and dynamics of the modern wave of Norwegian Black Metal. Even after the killing of Euronymous, when many developed a fierce and abiding hatred for Vikernes, he is still often spoken of with a certain degree of deference.

There is one person who has always stood by Varg's side and spoken out rigorously in his defense: his mother Lene Bore. Not only has she attempted to improve the public perception of her son, she also visits him frequently, helps him deal with correspondence, and assists in business matters relating to Burzum.

A number of Burzum albums have been released since his imprisonment and all have sold admirably well on the worldwide market. Royalties for the record sales are received by Lene Bore, a fact that allegedly allowed for the development of serious trouble in the future. Lene Bore also helped provide the money for recording and releasing the early Burzum releases on Aarseth's Deathlike Silence label, and as a result she had occasion to meet a number of Varg's friends in the Black Metal scene. Her comments are interesting, for she has dealt with an amazing amount of unrest as a result of her son's actions over the years, and some of her impressions of Varg's life are quite different from his own.

LENE BORE

WHAT WAS VARG LIKE AS A CHILD?

Varg was a loving boy. He could be very joyous and happy. Varg had very strong reactions and he was not good at hiding these or adjusting to situations. He never liked organized play or organized sports. He was very good at playing on his own, with a very rich imagination, but as soon as he had to adjust to others in the kindergarten it didn't work so well. He never liked the kindergarten or school.

HOW DID HE GET ALONG WITH HIS FATHER?

His father was very authoritarian and wanted things his way. Their relationship started going bad quite early. His father wanted things his way and Varg had his own ideas about how things should be done. Possibly because he had these problems with his father I had a very close relationship with him. I often felt that it was appropriate to look after him a bit extra because of all the conflicts between Varg and the school, his father, and so on.

YOUR FAMILY SPENT A YEAR IN IRAQ. WHAT WAS THIS LIKE FOR VARG?

I think it might be here that Varg's dislike toward other peoples started. He experienced a very differential treatment. The other children in his class would get slapped by their teachers; he would not be. For example when they were going to the doctor, even when there were other children waiting in line, Varg would be placed first. He reacted very strongly to this. He could not understand why we should go first when there were so many before us. He had a very strongly developed sense of justice. This created a lot of problems, because when he saw students being treated unfairly, he would intervene, and try to sort things out.

DID YOU REALIZE WHAT VARG WAS INVOLVED WITH IN HIS LATER TEENAGE YEARS?

I never knew about the Satanism part of it. I've never seen any signs of it either in his apartment or at home, apart from the way he dressed, which just got worse and worse. I had to see it as a teenage phenomenon, and that he would grow out of it, because all his friends looked almost as bad as him. I felt this as a real blow because when my sons were little, the first punks started to appear, and I wondered what their parents had done. And then my son ended up looking even worse.

WHAT WERE HIS FRIENDS IN THE BLACK METAL SCENE LIKE?

When his friends came home to me, I got to know them a bit. I didn't think they seemed like criminals. They were quite easygoing boys. I was very relieved that there was no nonsense with drinking and drugs or crime.

DID YOU KNOW ØYSTEIN AARSETH?

I met him a couple of times and felt that Varg initially looked up to him a lot. He was very proud that he was the one who had gotten the record contract and not the others. That Øystein, who was five years older, achieved such an enormously strong grip on Varg, made me a little wary. I confronted Varg with this. He said it was nothing to worry about.

Øystein behaved like an alright fellow when he was at our house, even though he might look scary to people in the street. People might think that of my son, too, but I had to relate to them based on how they behaved towards me. I've never seen anyone have such a status with Varg as Øystein did in the beginning. Varg was very disappointed after a while. He lived with Øystein for a few months and then I think he saw things from a completely different angle.

WHAT OCCURRED WHEN VARG LIVED THERE?

I'm not completely sure, but I think Varg was very shocked by things he experienced when he was in Oslo with Øystein. These things were disillusioning toward the image he had of Øystein. He was not the person Varg had thought him to be. I know he was very disappointed that Øystein came forward in the media the way he did after the church fires. He felt let down.

PHOTO: LENE BORE

VARG, AGE 5

Furthermore, I know that Varg no longer wanted to have a record contract with him because Øystein did not follow up on his part of the agreement. He owed Varg a lot of money, but instead of paying it back, he bought himself expensive furniture and spent the money in very unserious ways. The mutual confidence was broken because many of the agreements they had, for example regarding distribution of the records, were not followed up by Øystein.

Thus Varg's confidence was weakened. So when Varg got a record deal with someone else, there developed an enmity between them because Øystein would have to compete. After the church fires, I didn't know what had happened. Øystein had to close his shop because of them. In retrospect, I heard that Øystein had said he could live off selling Burzum records by mail order the rest of his life. He didn't need the shop anymore. If he had counted on living off this, and Varg broke with him, it is clear that his income was disappearing. Therefore, Øystein felt let down, too.

HOW DID VARG DEVELOP HIS CURRENT BELIEFS?

I have no good explanation of how Varg [came to hold such extreme viewpoints]. He had a strong need to rebel, and sometimes chose the paths that would be the most oppositional.

COULD THIS BE MORE OF A GUT REACTION THAN A CONSCIOUS IDEOLOGY? A PROVOCATION?

It usually started with that. But I feel that he now has gotten well into the ideologies he stands for, that he means what he says.

DID HE EVER EXPRESS HIS IDEAS TO YOU?

He liked to talk with people like me who disagreed with him, to have his own opinions confirmed. Very often he would say, "I won't bother to talk with you any more, you're hopeless." But I thought he was even more hopeless than me.

How did you find out about his involvement with the arsons?

I began to have suspicions about the business with the churches when he once told me that he thought the police were quite useless because they couldn't catch the people behind the church burnings.

I reacted when Åsane Church burned. We were in the mountains, but Varg didn't want to come with us. When I talked with him on the phone he asked if I had heard about it. I confirmed that, and said that I thought it was awful. I asked if he agreed. He didn't. He thought it was completely okay. That astonished me. But I didn't really think he had been involved in it.

A Young Varg

Why do you think the churches were burned?

I have tried to ask him why they did it, and I have gotten the impression that it was mostly the excitement he was after. I don't think there was a strong ideological motivation behind it.

The media created the image of "The Count," but didn't Varg also contribute to this himself?

This was all based on the first interview he did. All subsequent media treatment was based on that. He incited it himself by exaggerating and making himself sensationalistic. They would wind each other up in interview situations. It was as if the worse it was, the better. He is stuck with that image. He has tried to reach the media with other points, but they are never heard. It is as if the media wants that twist to it.

What do you recall about Varg's interview in *Bergens Tidende*?

It was very embarrassing, because it was about my son. He had told me about the newspaper interview beforehand, that it was very exaggerated and that I was not going to like it. He said he was considering to contact the journalists because he felt he had exaggerated so much. I had never expected it to look like it did. I think he was quite desperate for publicity around his recording project. I think he expected to get a small piece at the end of the newspaper—instead he got the entire front page.

Did Varg's racism intensify at a certain point?

If he had racist tendencies to begin with, I am sure that they came to the surface when he lived in Oslo.

Varg Vikernes

When did your interests in World War II Germany begin?

It's difficult to say. When I was three years old we moved to a road named *Odinsvei*, "Odin's Walk," and we were playing with the neighbor. He had German toy soldiers, but he always wanted to have the American soldiers, because they were the big heroes in his view. So I ended up with the German soldiers, as he was five years older than I. And I actually came to like them. It developed from soldiers to running around with SS helmets and German hand grenades and a Schmeizer with a swastika on it. In time we tried to figure it out—what the hell does this mean? That's how it really began, and it developed. I was a skinhead when I was 15 or 16. Nobody knows that. People say that suddenly I became a Nazi, but I was actually a skinhead back then. It was in waves—in '91 I was into occultism, in '92 Satanism, in '93 mythology and so on, in waves.

How does your mother feel about your racial views?

You know how fathers tend to be afraid that their daughter might come home with a black guy? Well, my mother was actually afraid that I was going to come home with a black girl! She's very race conscious. She was raised in a very Christian family and when she was 12 or 13 she told her parents, "The Virgin Mary is a bitch who doesn't even know the name of her baby's father!" and a lot of

PHOTO: LENE BORE

Varg as a Teenager

things like that. She could just as well be my friend as she is my mother.

WHAT ABOUT YOUR FATHER?

I have very little contact with him. They're divorced. He left about ten years ago. There wasn't any big impact. I was glad to be rid of him; he was just making a lot of trouble for me, always bugging me. He was in the Navy. We were raised very orderly; it was a good experience. I had a swastika flag at home and he was hysterical about it. He's a hypocrite. He was pissed about all the colored people he saw in town, but then he's worried about me being a Nazi. He's very materialistic, as is my mother really, but that's the only negative thing I can say about her. The positive thing is that she's very efficient, and in business I have to have someone take care of my money and I can trust her fully. I know she will do things in the best way.

NORWEGIAN HEADLINE:
"BLOODY TRIANGLE IN THE SATAN SCENE"

YOU GREW UP IN THE MIDDLE EAST?

Iraq, in Baghdad. I went to school there one year. My father was working for Saddam Hussein! They were developing a computer program to control the economy of Iraq. He brought the family with him when he was working there.

WHAT DO YOU REMEMBER FROM THAT TIME?

A lot of things. I visited Babylon, for example—which doesn't exist anymore because Saddam tore the whole place down—the ruins of Babylon, and a lot of mythological sites. There were a lot of dangerous things that happened, like being chased by dogs with rabies.

WHAT WAS SCHOOL LIKE?

It was an Iraqi elementary school. The English school couldn't take us

VIKERNES PROMO PHOTO, 1993

because they were full. I went to a regular Iraqi school. I could use some basic English. I think it was my mother's idea, because she didn't want us to stay home, bored. We couldn't go out too much because of the rabid dogs and all this, so she put us in school, just to keep us active.

YOU HAVE SIBLINGS?

I have a brother, one and a half years older. He's studying at a technical school. He's a security guard. Actually he was selling alarms to churches—fire alarms! The Police were asking, "Isn't he the brother of *Vikernes?*" Yes! He was making money from it!

WHEN DID YOU BECOME AWARE OF RACIAL MATTERS?

When I was six years old I had a quarrel with a teacher, and I thought, "You monkey!" I called the teacher a monkey in Iraqi elementary school. Of course normally they'd hit the children right then and there, but they didn't dare to hit me because I was white.

The first contact I had with colored people was in Iraq, and after I moved back to Norway it took years before they started to move into the area, upper-class Norwegian society. In Bergen it's a more aristocratic society I was part of, because of my mother mainly. I had very little contact with colored people, really. In Bergen we are still blessed with having a majority of whites—unlike Oslo, which is the biggest sewer in Norway.

DID YOU START TO SEE THINGS CHANGE?

When I was a skinhead there still weren't any colored people, but there were these punks—that was more the reason I went over to the other side. But of course the main reason is weapons: German SS helmets, Schmeizers and Mausers and all these weapons. That's what they shot British and Americans with. Great! We hated British and Americans.

SINCE THE WAR, EVERYTHING GERMAN HAS BEEN TABOO IN NORWAY AND
NORWEGIAN KIDS ARE EXPOSED TO A LOT OF AMERICAN CULTURE AS A RESULT.

And I responded with hate toward American culture! Like when reading the war comic books, it was always the Americans and British shooting the Germans, like one British soldier shooting a whole platoon of Germans. This is bullshit, it wasn't true of course. We didn't like it. We liked the Germans, because they always had better weapons and they looked better, they had discipline. They were like Vikings. The volunteers from America were tall, blond guys, who looked much more like the ones they were attacking than some Dagos who were waving them good luck when they left home. It's pretty absurd. The volunteers, the good men die first.

DID YOU FEEL LIKE YOU FIT INTO BERGEN SOCIETY?

Not really. Although in Bergen we have 90% of all the occultists in Norway. If you go up in the mountains around Bergen every other time you will meet some occultists. There are a lot of occult groups in Bergen—the O.T.O., the Aleister Crowley groups, etc. They have their own large groups at the university. The only real shaman in Norway lives in Bergen.

HOW DID YOU FEEL IN THESE SURROUNDINGS?

I was mostly socializing with weapon-freaks. My hobby was shooting guns, militia training, and playing in the woods with a shotgun.

BUT YOU HUNG OUT WITH SKINHEADS IN BERGEN?

There were no skinheads in Bergen. My brother shaved his head and I cut my hair short. But we were into the weapons, German weapons, and these attitudes like *war means to fight, peace means to degenerate.* Our big hope was to be invaded by Americans so we could shoot them. The hope of war was all we lived for. That was until I was 17, and then I met these guys in Old Funeral.

WHEN DID YOUR INTEREST IN MUSIC BEGIN?

I started playing when I was 14, playing guitar...

WHAT WAS THE BAND YOU PLAYED IN, OLD FUNERAL, LIKE?

These guys were just interested in eating. They didn't care about my sawed-off shotgun or my dynamite, or any of these things. They were just interested in hamburgers and food, they had absolutely no interest in the weapons that I liked.

PHOTO: MICHAEL MOYNIHAN

VARG IN PRISON, 1995

Eventually I also lost interest in my weapons as well. Then came more music, and an interest in occultism developed.

WHAT INFLUENCED YOU TOWARD THAT?

I got interested in occultism through other friends. We played role-playing games, and some of these guys (all older than me) started to buy books on occultism, because they were interested in magic and spell casting. They showed me the books and then I bought similar things. But the music guys weren't interested in that stuff at all, they only cared about food.

WHAT WAS THE MUSIC LIKE?

Originally it was Thrash Metal, and then it became Death-Thrash or Techno-Thrash, and I lost interest. I liked the first Old Funeral demo. It had ridiculous lyrics, but I liked the demo and that was why I joined with them. They developed into this Swedish Death Metal trend; I didn't like that so I dropped out. But I played with them for two years.

WHAT OCCURRED AFTER YOU LEFT?

My own band, Burzum. It really began earlier as Uruk-Hai, and after I left Old Funeral I started calling it Burzum. An Uruk-Hai is the typical berserker in the Tolkien stories. There's a lot of Norse mythology in Tolkien. We were drawn to Sauron and his lot, and not the hobbits, those stupid little dwarves. I hate dwarves and elves. The elves are fair, but typically Jewish—arrogant, saying, "We are the chosen ones." So I don't like them. But you have Barad-dûr, the tower of Sauron, and you have *Hlidhskjálf*, the tower of Odin; you have Sauron's all-seeing-eye, and then Odin's one eye; the ring of power, and Odin's ring *Draupnir*; the trolls are like typical berserkers, big huge guys who went berserk, and the Uruk-Hai are like the *Ulfhedhnar*, the wolfcoats. This wolf element is typically heathen. So I sympathize with Sauron. That's partly why I became interested in occultism, because it was a so-called "dark" thing. I was drawn to Sauron, who was supposedly "dark and evil," so I realized there had to be a connection. That's the reason I liked the book in the first place, because of the veil of hidden mythology.

WHAT IDEAS WERE THERE IN STARTING YOUR OWN PROJECT?

I'm not sure if I really knew what I was going to put into it. I don't think it was that conscious. I wrote the lyrics to "Lost Wisdom," which are very clichéd, about how we don't know everything and the reason why is because the Christians ruined everything, to put it briefly. That's the point, it's like, "There's something more in here."

I also wrote the "Burzum" song, which appears on the *Filosofem* album. Very short, simple lyrics: *When night falls / She cloaks the world in impenetrable darkness / A chill rises from the soil and contaminates the air / Suddenly, life has new meaning.* Quite simple, more mystical really.

Later everyone thinks, "Oh, it's all Satanism." But to answer your question, I don't think I knew what I wanted to do. It was more a matter of seeking, and I was doing a lot of experimenting at that time as well, with magic and runes and making magical weapons—which actually worked as well!

WHAT DOES THE WORD BURZUM MEAN?

It's a fictional word, originally. Tolkien was a professor in Norse mythology and Norse language. When he wrote the fictional language in *The Lord of the Rings* books, it was very much based on Norse. So Burzum—"Burz" means night or dark, and if you take the word in plural it has "um" added, and becomes "Burzum," meaning much night or darkness. Just like democracy claims to be "light" and "good," I reasoned that then we obviously have to be "dark" and "evil."

DEPENDING ON WHO'S CALLING YOU EVIL, IT COULD BE A COMPLIMENT.

Yes. But even though Burzum means darkness, it's really the light of Odin. Darkness is light.

FROM REALITY INTO MYTH

One of Varg Vikernes's most remarkable qualities is his ability to mythicize himself, recasting his own deeds in a new light. This is not to say the he creates outright falsifications, but rather he presents and recounts his actions selectively, amplifying certain aspects or details and ignoring others, presumably with careful deliberation.

As time progressed following his arrest after the murder of Øystein Aarseth in the latter half of 1993, Vikernes began to refer to his own ideology as heathen rather than Satanist. He increasingly downplayed the more childish Black Metal trademarks of "evil for evil's sake" and a simplistic blasphemous attitude toward Christianity, and replaced these with a more thoughtful, encompassing point of view. Instead of being dedicated to Satan as he previously spoke of in older interviews (and most notoriously in the *Bergens Tidende* piece), Varg was now a comrade of the Norse high deity Odin, "the one-eyed enemy of the Christian 'God,'" as he put it. Burzum now existed "exclusively for Odin."[5] It is true, as Vikernes explains, that a certain "Nordic" spirit had always existed within his music, thoroughly infused as it was with Tolkienisms. Whether Vikernes was ever really espousing of any kind of militant heathen outlook in his younger days is another question.

Speaking with a certain indignation to *Terrorizer* magazine a few years ago, Varg explained how the underlying themes of Nordic religion had always existed in his work:

> Take a look at me and Burzum. I have been accused of being a Satanist who suddenly turned Odinic. If the same fucks had the least knowledge about Odinism they would see it in Burzum a long time ago. On the debut we have the song "War," which hails the Odinic idea of dying in battle. "Ea, Lord of the Depths" is the Mesopotamian Aquarius, Odin is the Norse Aquarius. On *Det som engang var* (What Once Was) we start with a track called "Den onde kysten" ("The Coast of Evil") which hails all those who drowned while in Viking [on sea raids]. "En ring til aa herske" ("One Ring to Rule") talks about Germanic people and Draupnir, the ring of Odin. "Lost Wisdom" is obviously heathen, and "Han some reiste" ("He Who Journeyed/Fared") is dedicated to Odin when he hung himself as a sacrifice to himself. On *Aske* (Ashes) the title described Odin's Reich today and "God's" tomorrow. The first track, "Stemmen fra taarnet" ("The Call from the Tower") is about a call from Odin on his throne called Hlidhskjálf, and the newly released album has "Inn i slottet fra droemmen" ("Into the Castle of the Dream"), which is about the [faring] to Valhalla. These are the most obvious Odinic lyrics, written over a period from '90 to '92. The one and only "Satanic" title is "Dominus Sathanas" on the *Aske* album, translated as "The Ruler Adversary" or something similar. So where the hell do they get the impression of my being a Satanist from?[6]

The impression of Vikernes as a Satanist stems largely from his earlier pronouncements, not to mention his deep involvement with Black Metal. As for the latter, he now asserts that he no longer has anything to do with it. He simultaneously downplays the depth or importance of Black Metal, discounting the accuracy of sensational quotes attributed to him in the past, at the same time as he elevates the music as a worthwhile "passageway" for others.

The racial nationalism Vikernes now espouses would seem to be in stark contradiction to some of his prior statements and actions. As a result, his present agenda forces him to justify some of his previous outlandish remarks. Frequently he claims they were distorted or taken out of context—quite possible, given the tactics of many unethical journalists—or he attempts to present them in an entirely new context. Many of his critics accuse him of inventing these justifications for his actions as a form of *ex post facto* revisionism.

Varg Vikernes

Didn't you give Christianity a lot of ammunition, in a sense, through some of your actions?

Sure. But even though they have a lot more people becoming more Christian—if one person becomes Christian, there are also three or four people who become heathen. That's good. It's like a bad thing that has to be followed with good things. And even though some of them go through Satanism, they will eventually end up with Ásatrú. We can see that again and again. We see it with Bathory, I see it in myself. I was interested in Satanism to where I advocated it—all the others as well, with the whole Black Metal community, or the Black Metal disorder—but now there's a growing interest in pan-Germanic heathenism.

If I see some people talk shit about me who claim to be heathens, it doesn't matter because at least they are heathens. I'm not interested in personal glory; the most important thing is to raise attention toward our own culture, our own heritage. With that in mind, it doesn't matter if people become Satanists, because they will eventually arrive at Ásatrú.

Are there real similarities between Satanism and heathenism?

The one thing [the Satanists] lack is honor. When they say "survival of the fittest" they mean survival to the most callous. Survival to the guy who shoots you in the back. Survival to the guy who attacks you ten-on-one, or who cheats and lies. That's Satanism.

How serious is the Satanism in the Black Metal scene?

I wouldn't describe it as serious at all. It's image.

All this obsession with being "evil"...

We were provoking them a lot. We were advocating what we called "true evil." You probably remember some old interviews, where we said: this is evil, that's evil, if you want to play Black Metal you have to be evil. We were just provoking them.

It seems like a lot of statements made by Black Metal people were obvious provocations.

Yeah, but there's a very important thing: I never say anything *to provoke*, but I *provoke* intentionally to say something. Do you understand the difference?

THERE'S A METHOD TO THE MADNESS.

Yes, there's a reason for it, a point.

WHAT ABOUT THE *KERRANG!* ARTICLE?

I *never* said I will become the dictator of Scandinavia myself. I did say that I support Stalin, Hitler, and Ceaucescu, and I even said that Rumania is my favorite country—an area full of Gypsies! But the point is that Rumania is the best example of communism, and when people can realize how ridiculously the whole thing works, they can see what it really is. So in that way it's my *favorite* country. Of course that was misunderstood by the newspapers. The same with Stalin. I said I support Stalin. It may be a provocative way to say it, but if there wasn't Stalin, Hitler would look even worse. Now at least we can say, look at Stalin—he's worse. He killed 26 million.

I wouldn't take *Kerrang!* very seriously. A lot was misquoted. Like that I said "just to walk down the street and kick a boy is stimulating"—that was taken out of context. It sounds like I was trying to be some tough guy, but I was explaining that there was no such thing as blind violence, because even if someone seems to hit another person senselessly, they do actually have a reason—their own pleasure, their own aggression. That's a reason. So it's not blind violence. They took away the point of why I said it and put it in another context.

YOU WOULDN'T DESCRIBE YOURSELF AS A SADIST?

No. I would say I'm quite normal. I can be very brutal but I can also be very kind. The opposites create the energy. On the one hand I can slaughter these idiots with a snap of my fingers, and it doesn't matter at all; on the other side I can play with my daughter. There's no contradiction in that. There's no contradiction in being both total evil and total goodness.

HOW DOES GRAVE DESECRATION FIT INTO YOUR IDEOLOGY?

It's quite simple. [The Christians] desecrated our graves, or burial mounds, so it's revenge. The people who lie in the graves are the ones who built this society, *which we are against*. We show them the respect they deserve. I have absolutely no respect for the people who built this society. [The desecrators] can just smash their graves, piss on them, dance on them.

THERE'S NO POINT WHERE YOU WOULD SAY IT GOES TOO FAR?

No, nothing. Well, there was a T-shirt that Øystein printed which said "Kill the Christians." I think that's ridiculous. What's the logic in that? Why should we kill our own brothers? They're just temporarily asleep, entranced. We have to say, "Hey, wake up!" That's what we have to do, wake them up from the Jewish trance. We don't have to kill them—that would be killing ourselves, because they are part of us.

They just have a Jewish implant in their head which is called Christianity, which we have to get rid of. Once we get rid of that, they will be just as good as us. It's an awakening. Wake them up, they're sleeping. The way to wake them up is to burn the churches, desecrate graves, and all this.

It's very important to let them know why people desecrate graves. The typical public reaction, which I saw in a paper in Bergen, is: "Why do they do it? I don't understand why anyone can have pleasure from doing this." But who the hell says they are doing it for *pleasure?* Of course it's not for pleasure. If they don't think it's for pleasure, they believe it's for fun. It seems to be totally beyond their comprehension that people might do something for another reason besides pleasure. It's not for pleasure. People can act without the motive of enjoyment and pleasure.

IT'S MORE LIKE A POLITICAL TERROR STRATEGY?

Yes.

BUT WITH TERRORISM YOU NEED TO SHOW *WHY* IT'S DONE.

That's why I want to release my book. It explains in detail why people burn churches. People say how it's a tragedy, and how nice our culture is. But at the same time, our culture lies in ruins below the churches. How are we going to know our culture when they build churches on top of it? They say it's not possible to tear down the churches, they're protected, they have historic value. But if we cannot tear away the "historical values" we can never find what lies below them.

Like I mentioned about the Fantoft Church with the *horg* [heathen altar] which the church sits on top of—that's blasphemy, severe blasphemy. There's a natural circle there and you can see the *horg,* and the cross was put on top of it. If that's not blasphemy I don't know what is. This is the case all over the country—absolutely all of our holy sites have been desecrated like this, all of them. That's the point of supporting church burning. When the church is burned we can say, "Now we will go under it and see what lies below." That's another reason for it.

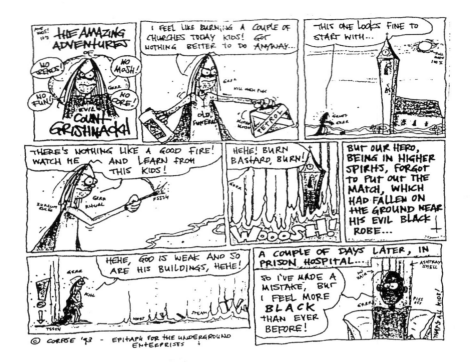

Anti-Grishnackh Cartoon

The World According to Varg

During the first year of his incarceration, Varg Vikernes set about committing his views to paper. He wrote about the Norse gods and tribal practices as he viewed them, and attempted to apply these concepts to the modern world, as archetypal values and behaviors that could be reawakened. He also defended the actions which had landed him in jail with a twenty-one-year sentence. He detailed the killing of Øystein Aarseth, and justified it as an act of self-defense. He rationalized the burning and vandalism of close to fifty churches in Norway, explaining why it was reasonable and even necessary to rescue his fellow Norwegians from their Judeo-Christian slumber.

Varg desired to present his worldview in a systematic manner, although this was made nearly impossible under the circumstances he was experiencing in prison. He was at first allowed a computer, which he used for correspondence and for the preliminary texts which would form his nationalist heathen codex. Some of the essays he composed were forwarded to correspondents and began to appear in underground publications around Europe. Most of these concerned his investigations into the esoterica of Nordic mythology and cosmology. At a certain point, after he had compiled a large portion of his book, the prison authorities decided to take away his computer; presumably they were worried he was somehow employing it for nefarious ends. Varg recalls:

> They confiscated the computer. "Okay," I said, "if I'm not allowed to have the computer, send it out of the prison"—that's my right. But of course the whole book was on the hard disk! So they prevented me from continuing to write the book, but still I got it out, and that's better than nothing. I wrote it in '94 and the second part in early '95. I had to finish it quickly, before they took my computer away, which is the reason so many things are put into it all at once.[7]

Vikernes titled his tome *Vargsmål,* which literally translates to "the speech (or song) of Varg." It is an allusion to certain Old Norse poems of the *Elder Edda,* a collection of skaldic lore and tales originating in the pre-Christian culture of the Germanic peoples. One of the more significant sections of the *Elder Edda* is titled *"Hávamál,"* "The Words of the High One," a poetic monologue by Odin, offering counsel to his folk on *Midhgardh* (earth) in ethics, behavior, and noble aspirations. In it Odin also recounts some of his own deeds and sacrifices, for example how he stole the holy mead of poetic inspiration (which he later bestows to mankind) from the giant Suttung, and his shamanistic trial-by-hanging in which he receives the wisdom and knowledge of the runic symbols. By titling his treatise *Vargsmål,* Vikernes seeks to place himself in mythic lineage as a modern-day figure worthy of the ancient sagas.

The contents of *Vargsmål* are somewhat disorderly, as Vikernes himself is quick to point out. Due to his circumstances, much of this was beyond his control. As a result, he explains:

> Everything is very concentrated; for uninitiated people it's very difficult to grasp the whole with the first reading. I start out with the assumption that the reader already knows something about different mythologies. There's nothing like a bibliography in the book—I'd intended to put something like that in there, but they took my computer away. Also the book suddenly stops, unnaturally. There's also a lot of jumping from one subject to another, it's sort of like different articles I wrote, that day one page, another day another page.[8]

The official publication of *Vargsmål* would only come about years after it was written. With Varg's front-page notoriety there were certain publishers interested in releasing the book, obviously figuring to make a quick buck on the sensationalism that could be generated, but it appears that most backed out when they had a chance to review the actual contents. In addition to mythological commentary, the book brims with volatile statements and racial, anti-Christian, nationalist rhetoric. In Vikernes's words:

Varg in Prison

[*Vargsmål*] contains a lot of Norse mythology, and cosmology in the heathen view, politics, and of course some notes about the murder. It's very controversial. There's a lot of things that really shouldn't be publicized which are in the book. ... It may seem like an attempt to convince everybody that I know a lot, because there's so much in there. It's chronologically written. There's a lot that's directly illegal in the book—defamation of character, severe racism, and incitement to criminal activity. Some books are published and found to not be legal, and they're withdrawn. My book has not even gotten this far. Nobody wants to release it in the first place! That's a big problem. People don't like the truth, and it can be very unpleasant for most people.[9]

Vargsmål contains more than just Vikernes's ideas about mythology and racism—it reveals much about his own psyche. Varg's consciousness of his own role in the world informs the text from beginning to end, and it is impossible to separate this from any "philosophy" or "religion" presented in the book. A brief excerpt provides ample demonstration of this:

To be a Chieftain does not mean having it better than others. It means having to abandon all your personal dreams, most pleasures, and your personal feelings. I would like to find a woman to live with in peace and quiet, far away from the world's problems, but I cannot. It is my duty to sacrifice myself and my personal wishes for the benefit of my tribe. The reason I am Chieftain to begin with is not because I want to be—a Chieftain is condemned to a totally unhappy life without joy or pleasures beyond the absolutely necessities. It is my misfortune to be Chieftain, my dismal fate. It is nothing else than a toil and burden, but it is my duty. The Chieftain is the tribe's greatest thrall. Many will say that this is a heroic presentation of myself. Let them say so. Just such unpleasant assertions I have to bear, it is some of the dishonor I have to bear as Chieftain.[10]

IN THE COMPANY OF HERETICS

Varg Vikernes serves the role of a pariah and heretic to Norwegians, similar on a number of levels to that of Charles Manson in America. Both profess a radical ideology at odds with, and at times unintelligible to the average citizen. Both insist they have done nothing wrong. Both espouse a revolutionary attitude, imbued with strong racial overtones. Both have become media bogeymen in their respective countries, and both knowingly contribute to their own mythicization. Both also understand well the inherent archetypal power of symbols and names—especially those they adopt for themselves. The enigmatic correlations between Varg's name and his unique character will be explored in detail in the next chapter.

Vikernes has continued to amplify and project his heresies from behind bars, and on some level appears to see himself as a heathen avatar for his countrymen, the "Chieftain" of a Nordic resurgence. His stated goal is to awaken the rest of the Norse tribe from a Judeo-Christian, social-democratic slumber. It is unlikely he will achieve this—to the average Norwegian, Varg is a monster at worst, at the very least a demented renegade.

With his increasing nationalism, Vikernes has discovered his predecessor in Vidkun Quisling, the Norwegian political leader who founded a collaborationist pro-German government in the midst of the Second World War. Quisling was tried and executed for treason shortly after the war's end. As a result his name has entered international vernacular as a synonym for "traitor." In Norway, that name is still anathema even today. But what is scorned by the masses is sacred to Varg Vikernes, and he speaks of Quisling with reverent admiration.

Varg Vikernes

I WAS UNDER THE IMPRESSION QUISLING'S RELIGION WASN'T PARTICULARLY PAGAN.

Oh yes, it was. I have a very esoteric book he released in 1929 about "Universism." It's called *That Inhabited Worlds Are To Be Found Outside of the Earth, and the Significance Thereof for Our View of Life.*

But I believe this "Universism" is quite Christian.

No, it's not. In his speech to the court he seemed Christian, but all his ideas were very un-Christian. He criticized Christians for believing that God created the world, because what about all the other worlds out there? This is what the book is all about. It was a very good position he took, very educated. He was far ahead of his time with some of his conclusions, which later, in 1980, scientists have confirmed. He knew all this back then, fifty years earlier. So that was definitely a pagan thing, although there was the image you have to give of being Christian—especially in court!

Quisling's party used the old sunwheel cross, but as a Christian symbol, right?

VIDKUN QUISLING

They said the sun sign was a cross of St. Olav, and therefore they used it. But the youth division of National Union, his party, they were very heathen. They were actually going to open an Ásatrú church in Norway, just like Hitler and Himmler in Germany. But they were suppressed, typically.

Vikernes is correct that Vidkun Quisling did develop his own doctrine of mystical beliefs, which he termed "Universism." In formulating this he drew heavily from ideas ranging from Gnosticism to Taoism, and philosophers from Nietzsche to Kant. The historian Hans Fredrik Dahl, one of Norway's leading experts on Quisling and author of a two-volume biography, states that Quisling was most definitely a Christian—although he considered himself to be a lot more reflective than most of his fellow believers. Many inconclusive suppositions about Quisling's personal philosophy have been advanced, based on the contents of the small volume Vikernes refers to, as this was Quisling's only published essay which touched upon the subject. His philosophical project was to reconcile Christianity with science, and he left behind unfinished manuscripts for what was to become a major spiritual/philosophical work. He had compiled 930 pages of handwritten text but was never able to complete his *opus*. While these manuscripts have been available to researchers, few have actually bothered to look at them until a critical appraisal of the material was published in 1996.

According to another Quisling expert, Oddvar Hoidal, "Universism" would seem to encompass a certain sense of a will to power, à la Nietzsche, upheld and spurred on by a natural oligarchy:

The universe, [Quisling] said, was "the one living and true God" which had been given to the earth, and which would continue to exist long after the world had disappeared, creating new earths and new stars. It was up to man to recognize this, and to work for perfection here on earth. This was the "divine will" as he saw it. This development of the "divine will" would take place in many areas of organized social behavior: "religion, science, art, and practical action—led by an elite."[11]

Despite the fact that Quisling's spiritual system may have paid a certain amount of lip service to Christian cosmology, Vikernes is correct that on one level it could be considered pagan or "pantheistic" in the sense of its dictionary definition as "identifying the Deity with the various forces and workings of nature."[12] His statement that Quisling's organization, *Nasjonal Samling* (National Union), was actively encouraging the development of the old Nordic religion is, however, misleading. Quisling consistently deferred to Christian forces both inside and outside of his political party, long before his trial for treason after the war.

A more fitting role model for Vikernes would be an early National Union activist, Hans S. Jacobsen, who later resigned from the party due to disagreement with Quisling's direction.

WOODCUT OF QUISLING THE "UNIVERSIST"

Jacobsen urged a more strident political outlook and specifically voiced his objections to the National Union's official advocacy of "Christianity's basic values." As Hoidal explains:

[Jacobsen] favored instead the pagan element of German National Socialism, which opposed Christianity because of its Jewish origins, and which stressed the pre-Christian Nordic traditions of the folk. Norway's conversion to Christianity, made possible by St. Olav's death as a martyr at Stiklestad, was described by Jacobsen as the introduction of "something false and unnatural into our folk's life." It was therefore logical for him to condemn Quisling's adoption of the St. Olav's cross as the NS symbol, declaring that the party symbol itself was non-Nordic.[13]

Jacobsen's mouthpiece for his ideas, which he hoped to insinuate into National Union, was a journal he published called *Ragnarok*, named after the Nordic myth of apocalypse and rebirth.

Hans Jacobsen is long forgotten in Norway, and only

QUISLING'S NS PARTY CROSS

Quisling at Work

those reading the more detailed biographies of Quisling will ever hear of his activities. His name commands no attention today —unlike that of Vidkun Quisling, whose specter still looms from the not-so-distant past. Varg Vikernes is well aware of his basic similarities with Quisling, both for their extreme visions of a Norway exclusively for Norwegians, but also in the power of their very names to raise hackles on the necks of the average social-democratic citizen of today. As a result, Vikernes is quick to proclaim his relation to Quisling in both thought and blood.

Varg Vikernes: It's the fifty-year anniversary of [Quisling's] execution on the 24th of October, 1995. I was trying to pay for a wreath, to lay a cross on his grave. It's in Telemark. There will probably be a lot of people gathered there this year. I unfortunately cannot come. I have Quisling blood. Susanne Qisling, she's born 1811 and died 1891, is one of my ancestors. One side of the family spelled their name without the "u." Quisling actually means one who comes from a side branch of the king's lineage. So it's a noble birth, Quisling.

HAVE YOU EVER TALKED TO ANY OF THE ORIGINAL RELATIVES OF QUISLING?

No, they've changed their names, all of them. I'm considering changing my name back to Quisling.

MINISTER OF PROPAGANDA

Confined to prison and unable to record music any longer, Varg now seeks other methods of spreading his message. He lamented not being able to legally register his own religious organization in Norway due to his criminal record. Toward this goal he has, however, formed the Norwegian Heathen Front, a loosely knit operation through which he will issue propaganda. The members of German Black Metal band Absurd, also currently behind bars, are involved with a branch of the organization in their country.

Vikernes explains some of the NHF political outlook, and how he arrived at the name:

> It used to be Norwegian Heathen Undemocratic Front, but we realized that we are not "undemocratic," they are. We're the democrats. What they call democracy has nothing to do with it. It's the rule of the scum. So we left off "undemocratic." The Vikings would choose a Chieftain, and after awhile if you are not pleased with him, you just drop him. Like they tried to drop King Olav, because he was trying to Christianize everyone. And they hail him today as some hero—bloody stupid![14]

Another quote from *Vargsmål* explains his own position as "NHF Chieftain" more fully, imbuing his actions with Odinic significance:

> I am Chieftain of a tribe that has taken the lead in establishing a Norwegian Heathen Front. As Chieftain I have to act like Odin, prostitute myself (as Odin did to get hold of Suttungr's mead), meet dishonor (as Odin did when he learned womanly Seid [sorcery], which is shameful for a man to perform), expose myself to danger (as Odin did to find Mime's well of wisdom), sacrifice myself (as Odin did when he tore out one eye to get to drink from the well of wisdom, and as he did when he hung himself from Yggdrasil), draw knowledge from history (as Odin did when he went to Urdr—the past—to get advice on the future), and a lot more that isn't very fun or relaxing.[15]

Vikernes claims he already has a high degree of support among fellow prisoners. In recruiting from the public at large, he plans to employ his philosophy on the nature of women as a basis for NHF strategy. His awareness of the woman's role in revolutionary activities is not unlike that of Charles Manson before him, although Vikernes claims to have arrived at it from personal observation during his Black Metal period.

Varg Vikernes

What laid the foundation of the mentality of Black Metal?

The groundwork of the Black Metal scene is the will to be different from the masses. That's the main object. Also girls have a very important part in this, because they like mystical things and are attracted to people who are different, who have a mystique. When a girl says "Look how cute he is" when she sees a picture of someone, her male friends will think "She likes him. If I look like him maybe she will like me as well." They turn toward the person she admires. The way to make Norway heathen is to go through the girls, because the males follow the girls.

That's what Charles Manson thought.

Males aren't extreme really. You find females are more to the left or more to the right than the males. Females are more communistic, more extremely Marxist-Leninist, or more extremely rightist than the males. They're predisposed to such extreme things.

It's like S/M, it's a natural thing for women. Pain is a natural thing for women, just like lifting things is a natural thing for males. Females have to give birth, and if they didn't enjoy pain, who the hell would ever lose their virginity? And we wouldn't be able to inflict pain, or ever take the virginity of anybody if they were screaming. It's a very natural thing that males are sadistic and females are masochistic. That's the reason females are also attracted to things like Satan with a big dick, or these macho types. Why else would they be attracted to such things?

Once we're aware of this we can do a lot of other things. We can build a lot out of that.

ARE FEMALES INVOLVED IN BLACK METAL?

I don't know how the scene is today; I have no contact with it. I noticed that there are a lot of females writing to me, something like nine out of every ten letters. It's because of what I just said.

In Oslo everybody fucks everybody in the scene. If one person gets a venereal disease, everyone does. The females I know in the Black Metal scene are not very intelligent, they are basically just whores. That's a typical Oslo phenomenon.

The people I correspond with are not Black Metal girls at all. Some of them were, but they realized that I don't like it and then they realized they didn't really like it either. They were just doing it because they wanted to get in touch with certain people. The way to power is through the women. Hitler knew this as well. Women elected Hitler.

IN HEAVY METAL OR SKINHEAD SCENES THERE ARE USUALLY VERY FEW WOMEN.

I think there are more females than males in Ásatrú, it's mostly girls.

WERE THERE MANY FEMALES AROUND YOU BEFORE?

There were mostly females, and only two or three guys—they were the snitches. Girls never snitch, with the exception of the Rumanian bitch. Girls never snitch, they're quiet.

Recently there have been girls involved in the church burnings in eastern Norway. They weren't caught but they were suspected.

WERE THERE GIRLS WHO KNEW ABOUT YOUR ACTIVITIES WHEN THEY WERE GOING ON?

Yes. They didn't say anything. Like the girl who is the mother of my child— she knew everything but said nothing.

YOU HAVE A DAUGHTER?

I have a daughter with a fair, blonde Aryan woman. She's three years old. I haven't seen her for two years; the mother won't allow me to. She believes the prison would be a bad influence. She's over-protective. The girl is older than me, she's quite extreme in many ways. My mother bought my daughter a sweatshirt which came from America, and her mother was upset because the image on it wasn't Norwegian.

For an upcoming project, Vikernes explains a first step in putting his ideas into action in gaining support:

> My girlfriend is going to have some pictures taken with my chain mail on, with a real Viking sword, and we're going to make a poster that says "Norwegians—Fight for Norway!" with her picture and the address of Norwegian Heathen Front. That's a direct teasing of the male lusts.[16]

Varg has high expectations for the NHF, but the image and ideas he projects are too radical and uncompromising to gain widespread support. Some of his ideological statements are so drastic, it is hard to believe even those on the extremes of the far right would be in agreement.

VARG VIKERNES

WHY AREN'T MORE PEOPLE SAYING WHAT YOU ARE?

The skinheads are like partying Americans, just drunks listening to Viking Rock. It's typical that the guys who are skinheads are the ones with dark hair and dark eyes. A lot of racists have brown eyes. You can ask why, and it's simple. They see that they are getting closer and closer to the aliens, the colored people. They realize that, shit, we have something to lose. The people who really could claim the Nordic heritage, they don't bother. They don't really think about it because it's so obvious to them.

THEY DON'T CARE?

I don't think they're aware of the problem, because when they look in the mirror they see a true Norseman. They don't see a mixture. It's not so easy for them to become aware of it.

NAZIESQUE BURZUM IMAGE

DON'T YOU THINK BY MAKING COMMENTS ABOUT PEOPLE WITH BROWN EYES, YOU'RE ALIENATING MANY WHO MIGHT OTHERWISE SUPPORT YOU?

That's true. In the [*Vargsmål*] I'm alienating them quite a lot, comparing brown eyes to looking into their ass. It's very racial. Look at the sky, it's blue. The sea is blue. The flowers are blue, and my eyes are blue. Behind the heavens are the stars, they are eternal wisdom. The ocean is a sea of wisdom. My eyes are blue—everything is in the blue eyes. But if I look into brown eyes I could just as well be looking up their ass; brown is like shit. Of course that makes an impact!

AND IT WOULD ALIENATE HALF OR MORE OF THE PEOPLE WHO OTHERWISE MIGHT BE ON YOUR SIDE.

That's right, but I also say that people can have brown eyes, and it doesn't matter. They're not any worse than us, but they should not mate with a person of the opposite sex who also has brown eyes. They should mate with someone with blue eyes. Their son or daughter will probably have brown eyes, but when they mate with someone with clear blue eyes, then they will eventually be pure. This also goes for physical height, everything. So I don't rule them out at all. People with brown eyes are just as worthy as we are.

WOULDN'T IT BE BETTER TO WAIT UNTIL YOU'RE IN A POSITION OF INFLUENCE BEFORE MAKING SUCH STATEMENTS?

That is a point, but still what I'm saying is the truth. I don't say that such people are fucked up. We need them as much, but we have to be conscious about who we mate with.

Also by saying that, while I won't get much support myself from people with brown eyes, they will not view others as so extreme. The more extreme I look, the more they will be able to follow, because ten years from now this will not be extreme anymore. They will follow the others who don't say these things, but are still extreme. It's pushing the line out further and further.

One can only wonder if Varg Vikernes has indeed pushed the line out so far in the distance that no one will ever catch up with it. He may realize this himself, and simply not care. He is all too happy to flaunt extremities and fly in the face of decorum without the slightest hesitation. In his role as a modern-day heretic, Varg is always willing to go one step further.

He will remain confined within concrete walls for many years to come, but this cannot stop him from continuing to formulate his political and social strategy. Under the circumstances, he has abundant time for such pursuits. In one of the letters received in subsequent months after the interviews for this book were conducted, Varg related that he had already followed through on at least one of his plans. He had now changed his name to Varg Qisling Larssøn Vikernes.

UNIDENTIFIED FLYING ARYANS

Since the publication of the first edition of *Lords of Chaos,* Didrik Søderlind again interviewed Varg Vikernes for a magazine assignment in March, 2000. Along with Swedish photographer Max Fredrikson, he travelled to the Trondheim prison on the West Coast of Norway, where Vikernes has spent the last few years practically alone. This means that although he is effectively hindered from applying his theories to practical life, the prison environment functions as a hothouse for Vikernes's fertile mind.

Ironically, while Vikernes's name is more or less synonymous with Black Metal, he takes great care to distance himself from that musical milieu. He even now claims the early Burzum releases—records regarded today as milestones of the genre—never were Black Metal music at all, instead classifying them as "standard, bad Heavy Metal." He passionately distances himself from all forms of Rock and Roll, stressing that Rock's roots in Afro-American culture make it alien to white people.

Even while rejecting his Metal past, Vikernes has kept Burzum alive, and taken advantage of the recording equipment he has occasionally been allowed to use during periods of his time spent in jail. Musically, Burzum has developed into a form of somber, ambient Electronica. Appreciated in combination with the mystical imagery of the liner notes, the later Burzum records could even be described as dark New Age music. This artistic direction was, however, effectively silenced when Vikernes's access to recording equipment was cut off. Presently, Vikernes is no longer even permitted to listen to CDs. The only music he is cur-

NORWEGIAN HEADLINE:
"HE RUNS 'HEATHEN FRONT' FROM HIS CELL"

rently allowed to experience must come via MTV—something which, in his case, might be considered a cruel and unusual form of punishment.

Denied a musical outlet, Vikernes has focused his strong creative drive on writing. His output has encompassed political tracts, a book on mythology called *Germansk Mytologi og Verdensanskuelse* (Germanic Mythology and Worldview), and fiction, including a short novel. His fictional works can be compared to the infamous neo-Nazi novels *Hunter* and *The Turner Diaries*, in the sense that much of it functions as a dramatization of National Socialist rhetoric. Vikernes seems to be slightly more aware of his literary limitations than the late author of the aforementioned books, Dr. William Pierce (a former physics professor who became director of the American racialist political group the National Alliance), who makes his characters' tender pillow-talk read like political sermonizing.

The true test of political rhetoric is whether it serves to politicize its readers. Pierce's books have certainly achieved cult status within the radical fringe, and *The Turner Diaries* carries additional prestige after having been publicly dubbed "the most dangerous book in America" by Bill Baker, a high-ranking FBI official. A strange indicator of the popularity of *The Turner Diaries* was the recent development when Pierce sold off his publication rights for the book in their entirety to rabble-rousing publisher Lyle Stuart. The Jewish entrepreneur quickly reissued the novel as a mass-distribution paperback through his Barricade Books imprint, complete with a new introduction offering justification for the edition as an educational tool illustrating the dangers of the radical right.

Vikernes's medium for spreading his ideas has largely involved his initiative the Heathen Front, an organization designed to "promote Heathenism, nationalism and Germanic folkish solidarity on both religious and political levels, as this is the only future for our whole existence" (according to its homepage, <www.heathenfront.org>).

Trying to pinpoint Vikernes's exact role in the organization is difficult, especially since the Heathen Front officially denies that Vikernes is in charge. While this might be true, the claim may also be an attempt to keep Vikernes out of trouble, as it would be illegal for a Norwegian prisoner to lead a political group. In the early days of the Heathen Front, the organization's mailing address was one and the same with Vikernes's private P.O. box prison address. This would, of course, mean that any prospective members would have their letters read and, one presumes, registered by the authorities. And this actually strengthens the Heathen Front's assertion that Vikernes is not the leader: it would be very hard for him to do an effective job of it. Whatever his official role may be, Vikernes certainly has left a strong mark on the Heathen Front. Its program was written by Vikernes, and this is a mix of rather orthodox National Socialist doctrine and neo-Heathen, anti-Christian ideas, along with some emphasis on environmentalism.

Vikernes's chance at influencing the National Socialist world (and perhaps even expanding his readership beyond that cultish environment) will most likely depend on how well his books and writings are circulated. These are currently distributed by the Allgermanische Heidnische Front. The AHF, a more widely-encompassing branch of the Heathen Front, was launched by Vikernes with the ambitious aim of reconstructing Europe as a Heathen National Socialist utopia, cleansed of undesirable elements such as Jews, political dissidents, homosexuals, and bisexual men (bisexual women will, for some reason, be allowed to live—maybe for their potential use in a wholesome National Socialist *menage à trois*?).

The Allgermanische Heidnische Front and its subdivisions in Norway, Sweden, Belgium, Denmark, Holland, Iceland, Germany, and Sweden (with "affiliated subdivisions" in Russia, Finland, and the U.S.A.) are probably little more than Internet tigers. While the AHF's policy of concentrating on producing web pages might be a bid to attract intellectually inclined youthful recruits rather than the streetfighters that make up much of the younger rank-and-file of other European National Socialist organizations, the focus on the Internet may have a more pragmatic motive.

One of the wonders of the Internet is that, in theory, a single person with a little know-how, a modem, and an acceptable computer can create web pages just as impressive as those of any huge organization. And, still theoretically, a loose group of e-mail correspondents across Europe can take on the appearance of a tremendously organized international network. In addition to its functioning as a political equalizer, the added attraction to all this is that Net know-how is mainly the field of younger people—exactly the sort the AHF has aboard. But while Vikernes's network might theoretically consist of one teenage computer nerd per country, each still living in his parents' house, such an estimation would probably be way off the mark. So how real is the AHF?

It is, of course, difficult to estimate the numbers of such an organization. The Heathen Front divisions themselves are not very helpful, and even if they would give out such information, it is a well-established National Socialist sport to exag-

IRMINSÛL

Av Varg Vikernes

<small>Cover of a Doctrinal Booklet By Vikernes</small>

gerate membership figures. On the other hand, history has clearly demonstrated that political groups, especially of the extremist variety, do not need impressive membership rosters to make an impact. And whether the AHF will be noticed in the future probably depends most on if it can succeed at recruiting young Burzum fans (its most realistic recruitment base) into political activism—or at providing a conduit for them into more militant groups and scenes.

Let's take the Swedish division of the AHF as an example. While the various Heathen Fronts are deliberately vague in giving out information, a reasonable scenario would be that the Swedish Heathen Front consists of a handful of core members, along with an outer echelon of somewhat active hangers-on.

Commenting via e-mail from his base in Gothenburg, SHF representative Mattias states that "Our activity consists mostly of educating our members. ... Besides recommending certain books ... we also work to give them the feeling and understanding of the need for ... healthy living and the risks and harmful aspects of contemporary society."

He also explains their recruiting strategy: "We don't approach the great masses, but rather let individuals from the masses approach us instead. This is probably why so many see us as an 'Internet project' or as inactive and passive. We work, but make little noise, and not much of what we do appears on the surface."

Regarding the aims of his group, Mattias states: "We fight not only to secure our existence genetically; this is a struggle for the Germanic spirit, our spirit—for the BLOOD. The driving force is the love of our own people, our culture, and our race; not contempt and hatred towards other races."

This all sounds harmless enough, even if some of the rhetoric implicit in the arguments might carry a threatening undertone. To further underscore this subtext, the SHF has informal links to the hardline National Socialist group the Nationalsocialistisk Front. The latter group rose to infamy in Sweden when three men associated with it killed two policemen during a bank robbery. One should, however, bear in mind that the links might not necessarily mean much. National Socialists in Sweden are as much a minority as they are everywhere else, and young activists are likely to rub brown-shirted shoulders with members of other groups in informal settings like concerts, meetings, and parties. It does definitely mean, however, that the SHF has taken a step into the Swedish Nazi world, which on numerous occasions has demonstrated that it has the will and organization to put its words into action.

How much of a magnet do the various Heathen Fronts around the world serve as for young rebels? This is hard to say. One thing that certainly facilitates any magnetism is the cult of personality that has grown up around Vikernes as a result of his music and notoriety as an underground figure—even among people who do not agree with the former Count in all matters.

A good example of this fandom is the website <www.burzum.com>. Here, a short piece of prose details a young Burzum fan's pilgrimage to the site of the Fantoft church burning in tribute to Varg Vikernes. And while the author of this "Fantoft Report," a young lady who identifies herself only as "Jessica," stressed in a later email message that she does not necessarily agree with Vikernes's politics, she was enthusiastic to pose for a photo inside the re-built Fantoft stave church wearing a Burzum T-shirt.

Another element that clearly adds glamour to Vikernes's public figure is his uncompromising political stance. This *Weltanschauung* has a purity and consequentiality that smacks more of an artistic project than a practical political model. Although Vikernes is in many respects an orthodox National Socialist, he seems far harsher in his policy ideas than even the Third Reich.

For example, while the Third Reich was in some ways a modern welfare state (at least for those whose blood and ideology were in line with NS doctrines), Vikernes asserts that military veterans who are disabled in future wars for the greatness of Germania should commit suicide rather than be a burden on the resources of the Nation. One wonders how a society will fare that expects this of its heroes, even if Vikernes claims they have the comfort of knowing they will be reincarnated.

One of the strangest manifestations to ultimately come out of the black metal subculture must be *Kulturorgan Skadinaujo*. The publication's name means "Cultural Organ Skadinaujo," the latter word being an archaic version of "Scandinavia." It calls itself a "Pan-Scandinavian periodical," which is under-scored by the fact that it prints articles in both Swedish and Danish, although the operation is based in Norway. Its appeals for "greater Scandinavian cooperation" are intermixed with articles about excursions into the great outdoors, etymology,

THE HEATHEN FRONT'S NORDICIST
"CULTURAL ORGAN"

BACK COVER SLOGAN OF THE
KULTURORGAN SKADINAUJO: "THE ORGAN
PROCLAIMS THE [SCANDINAVIAN] TRINITY"

and Norse traditions. The staff claims to be mystified by the attention given to them by antifascists, remarking, "We have no political agenda, least of all a fascist one." Kulturorgan Skadinaujo is also an association that has, according to representative Vegard Chapman, "rather few" members. Chapman claims that the members are "mainly people with an interest in local history. Environmentalism is possibly also a common denominator."

But it seems obvious that the combination of Norse symbolism, blood-and-soil mysticism ("Scandinavia is the trinity we live and breathe for, manifested in rock and earth, flesh and blood," states their website), and reprints from the Norwegian WWII-era radical Nazi magazine *Ragnarok* will gain them attention from antifascists, no matter how unwelcome. Another red flag for the antifascists is the fact that the journal's columns often feature the byline of Varg Vikernes. *Skadinaujo* carries advertisements for Vikernes's Heathen Front organization, and also sells his political tracts. To suspicious outsiders, then, the magazine immediately comes across as an attempt to dress up Varg Vikernes's ideas by trading in the brownshirts for academic tweed.

The journal appears to be the work of young students, some of whom have adopted an academic writing style. Though the fanzine-style musings that occasionally appear in its pages detract from its academic tone, the main reason why *Skadinaujo* seems doomed to fail as a scholarly venture is the fact that it reviews books like the pseudo-archaeology of Graham Hancock side by side with properly executed scholarly works. The end result is hardly something to show your professor.

For all Kulturorgan Skadinaujo's aspirations of being apolitical and academic, it seems very unlikely that anyone would read its magazine, join the association, or contribute to its work who is not already comfortable with its overt connections to Vikernes and to a certain political outlook. It is therefore unlikely to be seen by any-one—apart from its own editors—as anything other than fascism with footnotes.

In addition to advocating hardline Nazi policies and strict racial Odinism, Vikernes has begun to venture into the wild world of UFOs, although he strong-ly stresses that his thoughts on this subject are personal opinions and do not rep-resent an official Heathen Front position. This does not, however, lessen the dra-matic impact of his claims. He has taken to interpreting the Old Norse texts as proof of—or at the very least circumstantial evidence for—contact between humans and extra-terrestrials in ancient times.

VARG VIKERNES

WHAT ARE THESE FLYING SAUCERS THAT PEOPLE ARE TALKING ABOUT?

The UFOs are pre-programmed robots sent out from Sirius. When they dis-covered the earth, they realized that they could create life here. But our planet was too far from the sun. Therefore they set off nuclear explosions to move the earth, something that explains the asteroid belts outside earth and why there are glass sheets in the Sahara desert, something that would have required tremendous heat to create.

As the earth moved, the equator also shifted. And the equator is the Midgard Serpent [the World Serpent of Norse mythology that encircles the world while biting its own tail]. So this corresponds with the myth where Thor fishes the Midgard Serpent. The "Völuspá" [a section of the *Elder Edda*] states that the gods move the celestial bodies, and the Volva seeress who narrates the "Völuspá" tells us that she comes from a world before the present one.

The "world before the present one" is, in Vikernes's opinion, another planet. When the earth reached a suitable climate, the space travellers set about creating life. Through gradual improvement, the gods' robots cultivated terrestrial flora and fauna on the Ur-continent of Lemuria—the crown of their creation being, of course, the race of man.

On the not-yet-lost continent of Atlantis, however, all was not well. The giants—one of the primitive prototypes for what would become *Homo Sapiens*—grew jealous when the gods created the Aryan man.

And in the same way that Hymir sent all his trolls out to wreak revenge on Thor for having gone fishing and catching the Midgard Serpent in one of the most well-known of the Norse myths, a war was waged on Atlantis. After the conflict, the island sank into the ocean and the Aryans sought refuge on other continents, where they eventually mixed with lower races of men. The Atlantean Aryans only survived as a pure race in Northern Europe, where they can produce children like Vikernes: blonde, blue-eyed, and long-skulled.

The UFOs are still here, watching mankind (and, presumably, taking special note of its Aryan contingent), occasionally abducting people and mutilating cows to keep track of our development.

According to Vikernes, the basis for his claims is clearly apparent in the *Eddas* (with assorted tidbits to back it up from the *Vedas* and other Indo-European sources). Vikernes quotes the "Rigsthula," another section of the *Elder Edda*, to recall the time when the alien-gods walked among men:

VARG VIKERNES

IN WHAT WAY DO THE *EDDAS* SUPPORT THE IDEA THAT ALIENS TAMPERED WITH HUMAN DEVELOPMENT?

One example from the myths: Odin says that the humans are useless, and sends Heimdall down to earth to improve them genetically so that they are worthy of entrance into Valhalla. And which bloodline is it that is worthy to enter Valhalla? Not the bloodline of Karl, who has red hair, and not the bloodline of Thrall, who has dark complexion. No, only Jarl's bloodline [the ones with blonde hair] are taught the runes: the Knowledge. The other races are the failed experiments.

Our forefathers possessed knowledge of natural phenomena that they should not otherwise have been aware of. One example is the ozone layer, which the old ones called Svalin and which was a shield between the earth and the sun. If Svalin fell down, the earth would burn. How could our forebears have known this if they had not been in contact with those who were far more advanced?

Thor had red hair, but all our ancestors had blonde hair prior to the degeneration of the Viking Age. But the planet Jupiter is the colour of rust! And Thor protected men against uncontrollable natural forces, just like Jupiter's gravitation protects earth. ... Why does Thor have a belt of strength? Does not Jupiter have a ring around it?

While all this might seem like a mouthful to deal with, little of it is new. There exists a considerable body of literature on the subject, written both by believers and debunkers.

The myth of Atlantis has proven to be an enduring theme running throughout Western occultism. And like so many other esoteric mainstays, the legend of this mysterious sunken island—which once provided a home to advanced, almost Godlike inhabitants—was integrated into National Socialist occultism. The idea that the Atlanteans were somehow more advanced than current civilization was notably promoted in the late nineteenth century by Helena Blavatsky, whose Theosophical movement was a considerable influence on mystically inclined German ariosophists, many of whom who were the proto-National Socialists of

VARG IN PRISON, 2000

the 1920s and '30s. A number of the central tenets of National Socialism were influenced by earlier ariosophic occult groups, and related organizations such as the Thule Gesellschaft were instrumental in developing the NSDAP.

A modern sub-genre in this world of speculative history and pseudo-science is that of Nazi UFOs. The belief in UFOs has been adopted by elements of the Nazi movement with predilections towards the occult. Today, with the idea of National Socialism being shunned by most people on the planet, this mystical branch of the movement may even be the most successful. The world of esoteric Hitlerism intersects in many places with broader New Age phenomena, and UFO theology in particular.

The roots of Nazi preoccupation with flying saucers are complex, and date back to before the Second World War. Clear indications exist that the Third Reich had a program for developing flying saucers as part of its war machine. There is little concrete evidence, however, that the UFO program ever really got off the ground—in any sense—although the stories surrounding this are as contradictory as most UFO evidence in general.

A further complication is the fact that when American fighter pilots started spotting strange flying objects during the end of WWII, dubbing them "foo fighters," a persistent rumor spread among Allied fighter pilots that these were some kind of German secret weapon.

After the war, the UFO myth entered the subconscious of the West, with the rumored UFO crash at Roswell and alien abduction stories becoming standard features in modern folklore. And while many of the contemporary myths dramatized by the tremendously successful TV series *The X-Files* might seem fantastic, the strangest ideas are the ones that people actually seem to believe in. One such notion is that life on earth was to some extent spawned by creatures from another world.

The chief popularizer of the theory that aliens initiated or tampered with human development is the Swiss author Erich Von Däniken. In his opinion, many otherwise inexplicable feats of ancient man (for example, the building of the Pyramids) can be understood by the fact that early men were assisted by extraterrestrial visitors.

While it might be easy to dismiss Von Däniken's theories of UFOs being "Chariots of the Gods" as nonsense (the number of books that criticize his theories rivals his own prolific production), they are in no way obscure. Däniken has sold more than 54 million books worldwide, and the so-called "Ancient Astronaut" field which he made a household phenomenon has grown into a thriving pseudo-scientific subculture, seemingly tailor-made for an audience reared on hippie and New Age ideas and for whom "open-mindedness" seems tantamount to a willingness to accept anything so long as it has a scent of incense or ancient scrolls.

In his 1976 book *The Sirius Mystery,* Robert Temple made the curious claim that an African tribe called the Dogon possessed remarkable astronomical insight

PHOTO: MAX FREDRIKSON

Varg in Prison, 2000

into the brightest star in the sky, Sirius. This included knowledge about Sirius's two companion stars, which are entirely invisible to the only optical instrument possessed by the Dogon—the naked eye. If the Dogon, thoroughly isolated from the centers of modern science in their residence 300 km south of Timbuktu in Mali, West Africa, really knew about such astronomical tidbits, it would indeed be baffling. And combined with revelations about Dogon legends that their forefathers were bestowed with wisdom by the entity Oannes, who descended from the stars, the *The Sirius Mystery* provided a real jolt to the imaginations of its readers. Interest was renewed in 1998 when Temple republished the book, now subtitled "New Scientific Evidence of Alien Contact 5,000 Years Ago."

While the circumstances that led to the creation of the book are convoluted (as any arguments dealing with ancient astronauts invariably are), at the root of the mystery lie the writings of the French anthropologists Marcel Griaule and

Germaine Dieterlen, who did research on the Dogon in the 1930s. Twenty years later, the Frenchmen published their story of how the Dogon had revealed this astronomical knowledge about Sirius (*Sigu Tolo* in the native language) to them.

But other anthropologists who later visited the area have been unable to find the same astronomical knowledge circulating among the Dogon, and the most realistic hypotheses seem to be that the one Dogon informant who divulged the information to the two Frenchmen either learned his Sirius lore from earlier visitors (of the human variety), or indeed from Marcel Griaule himself, a keen astronomy fan who took along star-charts to help extract information. Either wittingly or unconsciously, the Dogon native might have had this knowledge transferred to him from his interviewer—or else Griaule over-emphasized what was passed to him through his interpreter, thus finding exactly what he wanted to. Furthermore, many of the Dogon's astronomical "facts" are just plain wrong.

In the world of the pop esotericism, however, the fact that claims are exposed as lackluster or even fraudulent often has little bearing on their continuing distribution via the myriad magazines and bookshops that cater to alternative ideas. As such, it is hardly surprising that the idea of gods from Sirius also pops up in Varg Vikernes's outlook. It should be noted, too, that such a claim may be con-

PHOTO: MAX FREDRIKSON

VARG IN PRISON, 2000

nected to traditions in various occult circles regarding a preoccupation with Sirius—hardly surprising, since it is the brightest (although not the closest) star in our skies.

The same year the aforementioned *Sirius Mystery* was published, Israeli author Zecharia Sitchin released his book *The Twelfth Planet*. In interviews, Zecharia Sitchin has stated that his "Earth Chronicles" series of books "is based on the premise that mythology is not fanciful but the repository of ancient memories; that the Bible ought to be read literally as a historic/scientific document; and that ancient civilizations—older and greater than assumed—were the product of knowledge brought to earth by the Anunnaki, 'Those Who from Heaven to Earth Came.' I trust that modern science will continue to confirm ancient knowledge."

Sitchin was first attracted to this peculiar field of research because he was puzzled by the Nefilim, who are mentioned in the Old Testament's Book of Genesis, Chapter Six. There, the Nefilim (also spelled Nephilim) are described as the sons of the gods who married the daughters of Man in the days before the great flood, the Deluge. The word Nefilim is often translated as "giants," meaning that the Old Testament asserts there were days when giants walked upon the earth. If this sounds a bit like the occult narrative of Varg Vikernes, it only becomes more so when Sitchin claims that the correct and literal meaning of the word Nefilim is "those who have come down to earth from the heavens." Fallen angels procured the daughters of men as mates, which Sitchin takes to mean that the space-farers mixed their superior DNA with that of primitive mankind, leading to a quantum leap in human genetic and cultural evolution which spawned the blossoming Mesopotamian cultures.

Dr. Michael Rothstein is assistant professor in the Department of History of Religions at the University of Copenhagen. He is an internationally published researcher in the fields of contemporary religions, and is especially interested in the ways people believe in UFOs.

DR. MICHAEL ROTHSTEIN

WHY IS BELIEF IN FLYING SAUCERS SO WIDESPREAD TODAY?

Time changes, and so do humans' ideas about themselves and the world they live in. The UFO myth was conceived as a response to Cold War fears, but gradually it took on other perspectives as well. Today it represents a modern tale of human intercourse with what is non-human or beyond human (either positively or negatively)—a tale which has been told since the dawn of humanity. Thus ideas of UFOs may be considered a modern representation of ancient religious sentiments expressed in a language suitable for a modern, industrial, space-traveling, Sci-Fi—reading society.

In your writings, you have argued that central tenets of the UFO mythos derive from Western esotericism, mainly Theosophy and its idea of "hidden spiritual masters" that enlighten humanity. Does this mean that people with an esoteric *Weltanschauung* are more disposed than others towards an interest in UFOs?

Not necessarily, but it surely means that certain interpretations of the alleged UFOs will appear more frequently or naturally to those involved in esotericism compared to others. Individuals such as George King and George Adamski, for instance, had careers as occultists prior to their UFO interest. This lead them to explicitly theosophically inspired understandings of their new field.

Is there a special connection between National Socialism and UFOs?

In certain ways, yes. Nazism has always had some kind of relation to the occult and certain Nazi groups (often outside the actual Nazi parties) have made a special point out of it. However, this really is fringe stuff. What is more interesting is the fact that UFOs on many occasions have been interpreted as devices developed by Nazi scientists, as German secret weapons. This is, I believe, more interesting than notions of clones of Hitler hiding under Antarctica in huge UFO-related facilities. Nazis are in many ways the demons of the modern world, at least most people find them disgusting and dangerous, and any association between the bewildering UFOs and these groups points to a certain understanding of UFOs as sinister or demonic.

In the eyes of most mildly skeptical people, Von Däniken's work has long been discredited, but this doesn't seem to shake the faith of his supporters. Why is that, and is it something peculiar to people that dabble in "far out" phenomena, or is it a common human trait?

The phenomenon is known throughout history, not least of all in the history of religions. What is important to note is that leaders, ideologists, prophets, etc., actually can do very little to elevate themselves and claim authority unless people are willing to bestow this kind of authority upon them. As long as people wish to believe, they will readily accept authorities that support their beliefs. The phenomenon is *not* that Von Däniken is able to persuade people of anything. The phenomenon is that people *want* Von Däniken to provide material for them to believe in. Furthermore, this is not in itself a "far-out" belief. Any belief in things out of the ordinary could be considered "far out": God, for instance, or the Resurrection of Christ, flying yogis, whatever. People's minds operate in this way, and it lets them develop coherent worldviews that make the world approachable and intelligible.

VARG VIKERNES SEEMS TO READ THE *EDDAS* LIKE VON DÄNIKEN READS THE
BIBLE, INTERPRETING IT AS MEMORIES IN MYTHOLOGICAL FORM OF HUMAN
CONTACT WITH ALIEN GODS. WOULD SUCH A READING BE POSSIBLE WITH MANY
OLDER RELIGIOUS TEXTS? FOR INSTANCE, THE VEDIC TEXTS OF ANCIENT INDIA
MENTION THINGS THAT CAN BE INTERPRETED AS FLYING VESSELS.

Surely any, and I do mean any, ancient text could be interpreted along such lines. Historically speaking it is nonsense—but most, if not all, religious representations could be termed nonsense when considered from a scholarly point of view. What we see is contemporary interpretations, a radically new exegesis. Religious texts do not carry a complete meaning. Rather, their meaning is created through the process of interpretation, and interpretations vary over the years.

As hinted by Rothstein, one of the most unusual marriages of UFO lore and National Socialism is the idea that the Third Reich is alive and well under the Antarctic ice-cap, keeping watch over the world by means of its flying saucers and waiting for the day to return and free the world from Zionist bankers, communists, and other enemies of the Aryan race. This particular theory fits snugly with a popular older belief alleged to have been held by some Nazis, namely that the earth is hollow.

The most eloquent spiritual representative of such ideas in the present day is the Chilean dignitary and author Miguel Serrano, a former diplomat (to India, Yugoslavia and Austria) who counted both Carl Jung and Herman Hesse among his circle of friends. Serrano authored a number of books in the 1960s and '70s concerning his yogic pilgrimages across India and personal accounts of magical love rooted in alchemy and allegory. In the late 1970s he began writing a series of texts to delineate his faith of "Esoteric Hitlerism," which encompasses beliefs regarding the hollow earth and the existence of secret Nazi UFO bases in Antarctica. His book *Das goldene Band* (The Golden Band) addresses these topics specifically, but since publication in German in 1987 it has been banned as illegal Nazi propaganda by the democratic government of that country. Nevertheless, the book continues to circulate, primarily as a downloadable text file via Internet sites like the "Thule-Netz." While some commentators might try to dismiss Serrano's ideas as simply a recruiting technique for more overt political initiatives, they are undoubtedly a sincere expression of his mystical outlook.

Mattias Gardell is a lecturer in religious anthropology at the University of Stockholm. He has studied radical religions extensively, and is the author of a book on the Nation of Islam, *Countdown to Armageddon*.

His latest research project has involved a year of travelling around North

America and interviewing figures involved in the neo-Nazi and Ásatru movements, two milieus that sometimes overlap—and especially so in the case of Varg Vikernes.

MATTIAS GARDELL

SOME ANTIFASCIST COMMENTATORS SEE THE NAZI PREOCCUPATION WITH UFOs AS A TACTICAL MOVE TO SPREAD THEIR POLITICAL MESSAGE INTO CIRCLES THAT SEEM TO SWALLOW VIRTUALLY ANYTHING. HOW CORRECT DO YOU THINK THAT IS?

That is hard to estimate. I know that some propagators of NS ideology, such as Ernst Zündel, would fit that description. His main drive is Holocaust revisionism. He reasons that most people believe the Holocaust took place because the Jewish control over media and education is almost total. To find an audience (outside the National Socialist scene) receptive to his ideas of a "Holohoax" he would need to find free-thinkers who are willing to accept as true knowledge things that most others would reject. And when he finds people who willingly accept as credible the idea that the earth is hollow and populated by a superior race with a high-tech culture that now and then visits the outer-earthers in its flying saucers, then he knows he has found such an audience.

WHY DOES UFO THEOLOGY, IF THAT IS THE RIGHT WORD FOR IT, STRIKE A CHORD WITH PARTS OF THE NAZI OR RACIALIST MOVEMENT, AND HOW COMMON IS UFO THINKING IN THOSE CIRCLES TODAY?

It's getting more and more common. Fascination with UFOs and theories about extraterrestrial links and/or Aryan extraterrestrial origins date back to the 1940s and 1950s, but they have really made a breakthrough on the scene today.

I think that part of the reason why Aryan revolutionaries are so receptive to these theories is related to the fact that both UFO theologians and white National Socialist racists hold as valid knowledge what is rejected or ridiculed by mainstream society. A believer in one kind of stigmatized knowledge tends to be receptive or open to other kinds of stigmatized knowledge—the fact that it is not accepted as true by the universities and mainstream media is interpreted to mean that it must be something to it. This might—in part—explain why white racists tend to be open to all kinds of alternative medicine, ideas of lost worlds, parapsychology, alternative religions and alternative science, including UFO theologies.

The UFO theories put forth by Varg Vikernes, even if they might seem novel when taken in a heathen and National Socialist context, are nothing new.

Vikernes, however, claims that his ideas have developed primarily through what he calls "deep intuition"—literally from the "blood." Such ideas of blood as a carrier of hereditary information are common in Nazi circles, and can in some way be compared to Carl Jung's theory of the collective unconscious. Whether one believes this or not is irrelevant, as it is hard to imagine that Vikernes arrived at his "flying saucers from Sirius" conclusion as the result of some racial genetic memory when the UFOs are flying all around him.

One example of how the UFO myth permeates Vikernes's immediate environment is in the Norwegian orthodox Hitlerite organization Zorn 88, recently renamed Norges Nasjonalsosialistiske Bevegelse (The Norwegian National Socialist Movement), whose magazine, *Gjallarhorn*, Vikernes has occasionally contributed to. Erik Rune Hansen, *Gjallarhorn*'s editor and the secretary of the NNSB, has publicly claimed to have seen a UFO and *Gjallarhorn* has carried a number of articles with an esoteric slant.

Dabbling in UFO lore has a long tradition in Norwegian right-wing and Nationalist thinking. One reason for this might be found in the continuing influence of Vidkun Quisling's philosophy of Universism, which included speculations about the existence of life on other planets. For some of the political activists who stepped into the vacuum left after Quisling's execution for treason, the post-war preoccupation with UFOs melded perfectly with elements of Universism.

One prominent figure in this confusing landscape—although he can in no way be seen as a direct successor of Quisling—was Anders Lange. He was secretary of the ultra-patriotic and staunchly anti-communist Fedrelandslaget (Fatherland League) in the 1930s. The most prominent personality involved with the Fedrelandslaget was Fridtjof Nansen, a Norwegian national icon who was famous for his daring exploits in the polar regions and his relief work in the famine-stricken Soviet Union. During the latter period, Vidkun Quisling served as one of his most trusted helpers.

Anders Lange seems to have been considerably more radical than Nansen and most of his comrades in Fedrelandslaget. In his younger days in the 1930s, Lange said he considered himself a fascist and supporter of Mussolini. But as with many others, the war caused him to distance himself from totalitarian opinions, and in the post-war era he emerged as a fierce opponent of state intervention in private affairs, although his politics still retained a racial slant.

Lange was an avid dog enthusiast. As an extension of running his own kennel, in 1948 he began publishing *Hundebladet* (loosely translated: Dog News). The newsletter soon came to deal with matters far beyond the canine realm. Anders Lange was a firm believer in a tolerant editorial policy, which led to his publication becoming a rallying point for all sorts of alternative perspectives.

One such avenue of thought that manifested itself in *Hundebladet* was UFO speculation. The newsletter regularly published articles and items relating to flying saucers. Lange might have seen this as a logical extension of his interest in Quisling's Universism theories, but regardless it certainly attracted readers who were far more interested in extraterrestrial spacecraft than politics.

The apex of Anders Lange's political career came in 1973, when he formed Anders Langes Parti for sterk nedsettelse av skatter, avgifter og offentlige inngrep. This mouthful translates to "Anders Lange's Party for a Drastic Reduction in Taxes, Rates, and State Intervention," and the name encapsulated the crux of the party's platform. After a television debate in which Lange posed with a sword, the ALP (as it was known for short) won five percent of the vote and Lange entered parliament as its representative, where he made quite an impression with his flamboyant personality, no doubt assisted by his ever-present glass of egg liqueur. The egg liqueur not only served as a tonic for Lange's voice (in the ALP's heyday, Lange would give speeches almost daily), but also became a political protest in its own right. Enjoying a glass during television debates had a strong symbolic value in a country with strict alcohol restrictions—precisely the kind of "State Intervention" that the ALP staunchly opposed.

Per Bangsund is a respected Norwegian journalist, editor and publisher who has written extensively on Norwegian post-war radical right politics.

PER BANGSUND

WHY DO YOU THINK ANDERS LANGE WAS SO INTERESTED IN UFOs?

I guess it's easy to understand why people with extreme ideas about the purity and nobility of Nature easily fall for quasi-philosophies about the Universe and see UFOs as a manifestation of something "out there." As far as I can remember, UFOs were not a big issue in *Hundebladet*. The fight against fluoridated water was far more important!

The ALP would never really make the transition into mainstream politics. The year after establishing the party, Lange passed away. However, his legacy has been stronger than anyone could foresee, as the ALP later mutated into what became known as Fremskrittspartiet (The Progress Party), which grew huge in the 1980s as it rode on the same neo-conservative tidal wave that dumped Ronald Reagan and Margaret Thatcher into office. In recent years, Fremskrittspartiet has become one of Norway's biggest parliamentary presences, although by its very nature the party tends to bounce up and down in opinion polls.

One figure who has followed the party from its inception to its present state is attorney Eivind Eckbo. He assumed the post as leader of the ALP when its founder passed away, and retained the position for six months afterward. He has also held posts for Fremskrittspartiet.

Eivind Eckbo

How did Anders Lange's Party work?

The ALP was based more on coincidences than conscious action. It was really more of a protest movement than a party, but it grew the way it did because it struck a chord with many people. Anders Lange was a dynamic character; in his time with Fedrelandslaget in the 1930s he would drive his truck around the countryside holding political rallies. You can say what you want about Anders Lange, but he was the only Norwegian of the twentieth century to whip up a political party from nothing; all other new parties have been splinter factions of already-established parties.

While UFOs hardly seem to have been a major point in Lange's worldview, or that of the people that surrounded him, he remains a highly visible figure that certainly helped to introduce notions of extraterrestrial visits into radical political circles. Because the circle around Lange was very informal and political distinctions appear to have been secondary, some of the rebellious types who surrounded him later emerged as more moderate politicians, while others moved into nationalism and National Socialism.

It is possible that Varg Vikernes may have arrived at his Aryans in Space theories on his own, but in light of the long-standing connection between UFOlogy and the Norwegian radical right, it is hard to imagine such a voracious and informed reader as Vikernes re-inventing the wheel—or, in this case, the saucer.

Depending on which way the prison authorities decide to calculate the remainder of his sentence, Vikernes will be released from prison on August 22, 2005 or 2007. Vikernes claims to have taken the lengthy prison sentence well so far, joking that "time flies when you're having fun," and comparing his life to that of a monk or hermit who chooses isolation from outside distractions to better focus on his work and studies.

When asked whether he now regrets having killed Øystein Aarseth, he sticks to his old explanation that it was a pre-emptive strike because Øystein had planned to kill him. "To regret killing Øystein would be to regret being alive," he says.

Varg Vikernes

Do you think that your worldview would be different if you had not been locked up?

To be honest, I think I would have been dead if I wasn't arrested. Let me put it like this: when the police caught me, I had 150 kilos of dynamite, and I was waiting to have some machine pistols delivered. I suppose it would have gone awry.

It would appear that everything you say is diametrically opposed to what established society stands for.

We even count the weekdays differently, so it clashes there, too. But the purpose of all this isn't to do contrary things to what society is doing. And it cannot be explained as youthful rebellion either—I'm too old for that. Unless you say that I've been in jail so long that I'm still mentally a teenager. For prison is a closed environment, and many people don't develop when they socialize with junkies.

resurge - 1. to rise again, as from death or from virtual extinction. **resurgent.** adj. rising or tending to rise again; reviving.

atavism - 1. *Biology.* the reappearance in an individual of characteristics of some remote ancestor that have been absent in intervening generations. 2. reversion to an earlier type.

—*Random House Dictionary of the English Language* [1]

ARCHETYPES ARE LIKE RIVERBEDS WHICH DRY UP WHEN THE WATER DESERTS THEM, BUT WHICH IT CAN FIND AGAIN AT ANY TIME.

—C.G. JUNG, "WOTAN" [2]

RESURGENT ATAVISM:
THE METAPHYSICS OF HEATHEN BLACK METAL

A WAVE OF VIOLENCE ERUPTS ACROSS AN OTHERWISE TRANQUIL LANDSCAPE, a conservative but humanistic society which has always ensured that its citizens are well fed and finely educated. Whatever their future station in life, they can count on comfort, security, and all the other benefits of a country with one of the highest standards of living in the world... yet the young dream of murder, blood sacrifice, revenge.

The Christian religion plays no great part in their lives, though its secular counterpart, the system of social democracy, offers them great opportunity. They reward such benefaction with a curse of fire, basking in the glory of destruction. Nothing excites more than the thought of chapel and vicarage ablaze, illuminating the womb of the night sky with darting flames, dancing and thrusting upward. The beauty is in ruins; a temple laid to waste becomes an aesthetic victory.

Their law of the strong scorns pity as a four-letter word; they await the day it is banished from the dictionaries. They despise doctrines of humility. Christ's Sermon on the Mount is even worse poison to their ears. War is their ideal, and they romanticize the grim glory of older epochs where it was a fact of life.

Where is the source for such a river of animosity and primal urges? Did torrents of hatred arise simply from the amplification of a phonograph needle vibrating through the spiralled grooves of a Venom album? Is Black Metal music possessed of the inherent power to impregnate destructive messages into the minds of the impressionable, laying a fertile seed destined to sprout into deed? To an enlightened mind it would seem unlikely.

If there is no clear, rational explanation for why Black Metal went to such hellish extremes, an investigation of the genre's more irrational or visionary aspects is in order. The following two chapters investigate the metaphysical and spiritual underpinnings of Black Metal, and how they have manifested in the real world.

Black Metal is primarily seen as a musical movement tied to Satanism, and the varying implications of this will be touched upon in Chapter 10. Many principal figures in Black Metal—Varg Vikernes especially—have also pledged a dedication to what they claim are heathen ideals. Scandinavia was one of the last European cultures to convert to Christianity. The explosion of Black Metal there warrants a look at possible correlations between ancient Norse heathenism and modern musical extremism.

AORTA JOURNAL

THE WILD HUNT DRAWS NIGH

In one of many articles detailing his interpretations of Nordic heathen cosmology written from prison, Varg Vikernes elaborates at length on his fascination for the folklore of the *Oskorei:*

The demonic-Odhinnic deathcult is one of the nuclei of Germanic volk-culture; connecting the living with the dead. Oskoreien—the "Ride of the Dead" during the Holy twelve or thirteen nights of Yule and at time of fasting—or Åsgardsreien (as it is also known) originate from the martial/mystical mystery-society of

"Werewolf-warriors" selected and initiated after severe rules and regulations. Oskoreien/Åsgardsreien will be wearing black shields and warpaint on their bodies, symbolizing dæmonic/lycanthropic transformation... Such a so-called Varulv Orden [Werewolf Order] will rush forward at night with wonderful wildness.[3]

Vikernes goes on to describe various permutations of this Odinic death cult, explaining that a ritual-initiation will lead to a higher spiritual state, culminating in a joint ascension with one's ancestral spirits of something he calls the "Transcendental Pillar of Singularity"—also referred to in a Burzum song title. Before this is dismissed as nothing more than mindless verbiage on Vikernes's behalf, it deserves a closer examination.

After reading a number of similar texts by Varg Vikernes, the Austrian artist and occult researcher named Kadmon was inspired to investigate in detail what enigmatic connections might exist between the phenomena of modern Black Metal and the ancient myths of the *Oskorei*. The *Oskorei* is the Norse name for the legion of dead souls who are witnessed flying, *en masse*, across the night sky on certain occasions. They are rumored to sometimes swoop down from the dark heavens and whisk a living person away with them. This army of the dead is often led by Odin or another of the heathen deities. Throughout the centuries, there are many reports from people who claim to have experienced the terrifying phenomenon—they attest to having seen and heard the *Oskorei* with their own eyes and ears. The tales of the *Oskorei* also refer to real-life folk customs which were still prevalent a few hundred years ago in rural parts of Northern Europe. They normally occurred at Yule time, when groups of rowdy young men would ride by night in groups on horseback, often frightening the villagers with the sound and

NINETEENTH-CENTURY ENGRAVING OF THE WILD HUNT

fury of their arrival. Folklorists have attempted to
explain the legends in different ways. Kadmon's essay on
the *Oskorei* and Black Metal is
reproduced as Appendix II. It
is a fascinating comparison of
details in the recorded folk
tales of the *Oskorei* and
uncanny similarities to many
of the traits which are distinct
facets of modern Black
Metal—noise, corpsepaint,
ghoulish appearances, the
adoption of pseudonyms,
high-pitched singing, and
even arson. Kadmon discovers
further correspondences with
the old tradition of the haunting and costumed *Perchten*
parades which still take place
in Austrian towns on certain
festival days. These winter
folk traditions may have roots
in the older worship of the Germanic winter/sky goddess Perchta. Today they
comprise processions of both the benign or beautiful looking *Perchten,* as well as
their sinister and demonically-masked counterparts the *Schiachperchten.*

Certain general connotations and correlations of the *Oskorei* legends are significant. The phenomenon appears particularly potent in Norway, although it has
manifested in all the Scandinavian lands in differing forms. In German folklore,
stories of the *Oskorei* correspond directly to the "Wild Hunt," also termed
"Wotan's Host." Wotan (alternately spelled Wodan) is the continental German
title for Odin, Varg Vikernes's "patron deity," thus he might feel an obvious affinity to the stories of the *Oskorei* due to their "demonic-Odhinnic deathcult" connection, as he terms it. In a number of the legends, the spirits of the *Oskorei* take
on a sinister air, and are treated as if demons. Crosses are employed, à la Dracula,
to ward them off. Aschehoug and Gyldendal's *Store Norske Leksikon* (The Large
Norse Encyclopedia) states the name *Oskorei* can be interpreted as "the terrible
ride," and describes it in detail:

There were often fights and killings at those places Oskoreia stopped. They could drink the yule
ale and eat the food, but also carry people away if they were out in the dark. One could protect against
the ride by gesturing in the shape of a cross or by throwing oneself to the ground with the arms

stretched out like a cross. The best way was to place a cross above all the doors. Steel above the stalls was effective as well. The Oskorei was probably regarded as a riding company of dead people, perhaps those who deserved neither Heaven nor Hell. One must take into account the midwinter darkness and the common belief that the dead return at yuletide.[4]

THE LURE AND LORE OF ARCHETYPES

Given the dark, ghoulish, and quasi-diabolical nature of the *Oskorei*, it is not surprising that Vikernes and others in the Black Metal scene might develop a visceral fascination for it. Images of the frenzied hunt across the night sky were not unfamiliar to the music scene; the cover of Bathory's first "Viking" album, *Blood Fire Death*, features a haunting depiction of the *Oskorei* in action. The remarkable development is how so many of the minute details of the legends would inadvertently or coincidentally resurface in unique traits of the Norwegian Black Metal adherents. This behavior had already become prominent years before the scene acquired its current attraction toward Nordic mythological themes, and before Vikernes ever began writing commentaries on such topics.

When Norwegian Black Metal sparked its initial flurries of mainstream publicity, it was generally portrayed as a neo-fascistic or despotic strain of Satanism. At the same time, there were always elements present which harkened back to the Viking age, or at least displayed a superficial identification with Viking strength and barbarism. The basis for such attitudes was rarely explained with any degree of depth until recently, when previously peripheral elements became driving forces for many of the bands and personalities.

Varg Vikernes is today the most overt of all the heathen advocates within Black Metal, but he is far from alone in his interests and sources of inspiration. Many of the "Satanic" bands even evince a strong fascination for native folklore and tradition, seeing them as vital allegories which represent primal energies within man. This type of viewpoint is expressed well by Erik Lancelot of the band Ulver:

> The theme of Ulver has always been the exploration of the dark sides of Norwegian folklore, which is strongly tied to the close relationship our ancestors had to the forests, mountains, and sea. The dark side of our folklore therefore has a different outlook from the traditional Satanism using cosmic symbolism from Hebraic mythology, but the essence remains the same: the "demons" represent the violent, ruthless forces feared and disclaimed by ordinary men, but without whom the world would lose the impetus which is the fundamental basis of evolution.
>
> Our use of old Norwegian imagery is not an end in itself, but rather a manner to symbolize our own thoughts with pictures close to our own traditions. ... We believe that the underlying, metaphysical source of life is essentially what "white light" religions have regarded as "evil" because it is ruthlessly and aggressively vital, untamed by any restrictions lest they be the morals imposed by "reason" or "culture" in order to subjugate the expansion of force.[5]

FOREST ENGRAVING FROM A NORWEGIAN BOOK OF FOLKTALES

Varg Vikernes speaks of Burzum as a resurrection of primordial forces. In explaining his justification for the church burnings he states it was to "Show Odin to the people and Odin will be lit in their souls," imbuing his actions with an atavistic motive.[6] When asked of his attitude toward the Norse gods in an interview with *Descent* magazine, Varg elaborated:

They're not "gods," but Áses. They're the archetypes of the Northern race. Thus within me. They're the names we gave to what once was, during what once was so that our posterity should never forget. Alas, only a few of us remember, and we always will. I will never forsake my forefathers, my nature, or myself. And truly this is what heathendom is—our nature.

We all learn about the Christian interpretation of heathendom, making it "mythology." More and more are waking up from the sleep of idiocy and following their nature. By showing my interpretation to the people, I light the heathen fire in their souls. It's inevitable, because they are our archetypes. Odin wins.[7]

Varg's statements may sound irrational, but they are not unique. The renowned psychologist Carl Gustav Jung developed his own theories of the collective unconscious, which may manifest in different groups of people based on the archaic archetypes of their culture. He explains this in terms of "primordial images" in his 1928 work *Two Essays on Analytical Psychology:*

There are present in every individual, besides his personal memories, the great "primordial"

ICY NORWAY

images, as Jacob Burckhardt once aptly called them, the inherited powers of human imagination as it was from time immemorial. The fact of this inheritance explains the truly amazing phenomena that certain motifs from myths and legends repeat themselves ... It also explains why it is that our mental patients can reproduce exactly the same images and associations that are known to us from the old texts.

The primordial images are the most ancient and the most universal "thought-forms" of humanity. They are as much feelings as thoughts; indeed they lead their own independent life...[8]

As Kadmon's essay illustrates, similarities between aspects of Norwegian Black Metal and the furious, Wild Hunt of the dead are startling. Can this be explained as a Jungian "primordial image" resurfacing in a modern generation of youth? Kadmon also points out a few strong contrasts between the rural folklore and Black Metal, which he sees as an urban phenomena. He is not entirely correct in this assertion, however, as many of the Norwegian Black Metal musicians do not come cities such as Oslo, Bergen, or Trondheim, but live in small villages in the countryside. And Varg Vikernes, too, is proud to make the distinction that he is originally from a rural area some distance outside of Bergen, rather than the city itself. Further examples can be found with the members of Emperor, Enslaved, and a number of other bands. Considering the intriguing parallels drawn in Kadmon's essay, the subject of the relationship between heathen metaphysics and Black Metal—and whether some sort of resurgent atavism may be at their root—is worth investigating in detail.

There is no doubt that a vast number of those involved in Black Metal emulate a barbaric image in their appearance and demeanor, statements and

COUNTRYSIDE OF TELEMARK

lyrics. The music could certainly be similarly described as barbarous by an unwary listener, although it is often complex and beautiful as well.

Beyond drawing inspiration for such an outlook from Heavy Metal's long tradition of masculine motifs, and more specifically from the "Viking trilogy" of influential Bathory albums, many in the scene appear to take things more seriously than simply erecting a façade of fantasy imagery. Besides Bathory, one other early Scandinavian Metal band had also extolled the religion and lifestyle of the

NORWEGIAN MOUNTAIN RANGE

Vikings in their music, a group
from the '80s called Heavy Load.
Possibly they also inspired some
of the kids later involved in
Black Metal, and indeed they
have been mentioned with
appreciation by some close to
the scene, like Metalion.

Among the Death Metal
bands, we have noted the presence of Sweden's Unleashed,
who stand quite apart from the
rest of their peers in terms of
their lyrical and spiritual inspiration. Unleashed have always
made clear their admiration for
the pre-Christian Norse religion
of Ásatrú. Singer and bassist
Johnny Hedlund explained the
source for his impulse toward
these themes:

JOHNNY HEDLUND

> The influences that I have are actually from my ancestors and from sitting in the countryside and
> feeling the power of nature—just by sitting there knowing that my grandfather's, father's father was
> standing here with his sword ... by knowing that you are influenced from it.[9]

Similar sentiments are often voiced by many of the Black Metal bands, who
speak of the Norwegian landscape and countryside in tones of reverence. In
explaining one of his personal sources of inspiration, Vikernes once commented
to a journalist at *Terrorizer* magazine, "I strongly recommend you to try and walk
in the middle of a winter night in a Norwegian forest all alone, and you will
understand what I mean: it actually speaks."[10] Obviously Vikernes is not the only
one who feels this attraction, since nearly every single Black Metal band has had
themselves photographed amongst snow and trees.

The group Immortal even went so far as to make a professional video clip
with every band member shirtless in the midst of a freezing winter snowscape,
furiously playing one of their songs. A video for the Burzum song "Darkness"
goes much further, leaving out any human traces whatsoever—the entire eight
minute clip is based on images of runic stone carvings, over which shots flash of
rushing storm clouds, sunsets, rocks, and woods. Co-directed by Vikernes from
prison via written instructions, the result is impressively evocative despite the
absence of any storyline or drama.

WOTAN *REDIVIVUS*

The end of the twentieth century has witnessed attempts by contemporary men and women to resurrect a wide array of pre-Christian religions. The instinctual or atavistic nature of heathen religion itself is nothing new, and many of these "revivalists" have experienced its magnetic allure. The gods of the North seem particularly prone to stirring feelings which may unexpectedly resurge among the descendants of those who once worshiped them.

According to Carl Jung, it is not always modern man who actively seeks to consciously revive a pre-Christian worldview, but rather he may become involuntarily possessed by the archetypes of the gods in question. In March, 1936, Jung published a remarkable essay in the *Neue Schweizer Rundschau,* which remains highly controversial to the present day. Originally written only a few years after the National Socialists came to power in Germany, it is entitled "Wotan."

Jung states in no uncertain terms his conviction that the Nazi movement is a result of "possession" by the god Wotan on a massive scale. He traces elements of the heathen revival back to various German writers, Nietzsche especially, who he feels were "seized" by Wotan and became transmitters for aspects of the god's archetypal nature. He states, "It is curious, to say the least of it ... that an old god of storm and frenzy, the long quiescent Wotan, should awake, like an extinct volcano, to a new activity, in a country that had long been supposed to have outgrown the Middle Ages."[11]

Jung would some years later reveal his conviction that both Nietzsche and he himself had experienced personal visits in their dreams from the ghostly procession of the "Wild Hunt," the German equivalent of the *Oskorei.*

In the "Wotan" essay he goes on to describe *Jugendbewegung* (Youth Movement) sacrifices of sheep to Wotan on the solstice, and explains in detail his belief that Germany is being led away from Christianity via "possession" by the ancient deity. Jung concludes his explication with the prediction that while Germany in the '30s may be under the specific sway of Wotan's more furious attributes, in the "course of the next few years or decades" other, more "ecstatic and mantic" sides of the god's archetype will also manifest themselves.[12]

This belief in the atavistic power of the old Norse religion is shared by Stephen McNallen, who is generally credited with sparking the current day revival of Ásatrú or Odinism in the English-speaking world. In the late '60s, McNallen felt powerfully drawn to investigate the religion of the heathen Norsemen, and what he discovered so inspired him that he composed rituals of worship for the

Norse/Germanic gods and set about to find others on a similar spiritual path. After founding a small group, the Viking Brotherhood (which evolved into the Ásatrú Free Assembly), McNallen discovered that a number of people in distant parts of the Western world had also felt an identical "Odinic" pull at the same point in time as he had. Without having any knowledge of one another, groups dedicated to the worship of the gods of Northern Europe simultaneously sprung up in England, Iceland, and on the East Coast of the U.S., along with McNallen's efforts in Texas. Why this revival would occur in such an "organic" and synchronistic manner is difficult to say—the Jungian explanation of Wotan *redivivus* is as reasonable as any.

In Norway and Sweden there has also been growing general interest in the indigenous religion of their forefathers, to the point that at least one heathen group, Draupnir, has been recognized as a legitimate religious organization by the Norwegian government. Along with them, other Ásatrú organizations such as Bifrost also hold regular gatherings where they offer *blot*, or symbolic sacrifice, to the deities of old.

There is absolutely no specific connection between these Nordic religious practitioners and the Black Metal scene. In fact, public assumptions that such a link would exist have been a severe liability to these groups. Dispelling negative public impressions of their religion is made considerably more difficult with characters like Vikernes speaking so frequently of his own heathen beliefs to the press.

When told of Draupnir's irritation at constantly having to publicly state their lack of any common ground with Black Metal and Satanism, Vikernes appears to naively misunderstand that his own declarations are what caused such difficulties in the first place:

This situation with the Christians is like a new Inquisition. People like Draupnir would have been burned at the stake as Devil worshippers. But today they put us in prison. If any Ásatrú group does not stress that they are not Satanists, then they are accused of being that, anyway. So they have to stress that we are not this or that. It must be quite annoying. It's annoying for me as well, because I'm being called a Satanist all the time.[13]

"THE WILD HUNT"
BY GERMAN ARTIST FRANZ VON STUCK

THOR (DETAIL FROM A PAINTING BY M.E. WINGE)

Ásatrú has no central body to decide who or who isn't part of it, and of course no one can stop Vikernes from explaining his own heathen worldview as he sees fit—or making his bold assertions that the church burnings, grave desecrations, and other crimes were done in order to "show Odin to the people."[14] Vikernes's extreme and bloody interpretation of indigenous Norse religion is just as problematic to the neo-heathen groups as was his flaming-stave-church and brimstone variety of Satanism a few years earlier to organizations like the Church of Satan. When contemporary figures sought to revive the old religion of Northern Europe, they had not intended to bring back uncontrollable barbarism and lawlessness with it.

One can see a clear shift amongst the Black Metal bands toward a heathen outlook, although few, if any, of them appear to have been influenced by any outside group such as Draupnir or Bifrost. Many of the more Satanic bands have altered their focus, removing explicit reference to the Devil and replacing it with more vague allusions to the "old gods." Thor's Hammer amulets can be seen around the necks of just about every band member of any Scandinavian group in promo photos.

Burzum, Enslaved, and Einherjar are just a few of the dozens of groups who play music that is unequivocally focused towards Norse religious themes. These obsessions (exemplified in some of Vikernes's more far-fetched statements, or musically in Enslaved's recording an entire album sung in Old Icelandic language) clearly go beyond the point of simple, passing interest. But it remains to be seen where such a road, stretching as it does from the farthest reaches of Nordic heritage and into the vast realm of *Skuld*, the future, will finally lead.

In Jung's "Wotan" essay, he states in his conclusion that in addition to its bloodier manifestation, he also believes the "prophetic" aspect of Wotan will become apparent in future. Did elements of the *Oskorei*, linked so strongly as they are to Odin/Wotan, in some tiny way serve as premonitions which would re-manifest in the centuries of "civilized" behavior that followed? There is another obscure old fable of the *Oskorei*, where they fetch a dead man up from the ground, rather than their usual choice of someone among the living. It was collected by Kjetil A. Flatin in the book *Tussar og trolldom* (Goblins and Witchcraft) in 1930. If the folkloristic and heathen impulses of Norwegian Black Metal are in fact some untempered form of resurgent atavism, then this short tale is even more surprising in its ominously allegorical portents of events to come over sixty years later with Grishnackh, Euronymous, and the fiery deeds that swirled around them:

On Aase in Flatdal, they were drinking and carousing one evening around Christmas time. Two men strapped themselves together with a belt and fought with knives. One of the men was stabbed and lay dead on the floor. Then the Oskorei came riding in through the door, took the dead man with them, and threw a burning torch on the floor...[15]

IN THE SHADOW OF WOLVES

While researching the possible similarities between Nordic cosmology and elements of Black Metal, other intriguing material came to light. Just as Euronymous and Dead fulfilled the grim destinies of their adopted names, this can be seen in other cases as well. An investigation into the old Nordic connotations of the name taken on by Vikernes unearthed some startling correspondences which would appear to indicate the most obscure and archaic meanings of the word itself were destined to make themselves manifest.

Originally bestowed with "Kristian" for his first name, Vikernes found this increasingly intolerable in his late teenage years. When he first introduced himself to the Black Metal scene it was still his forename. Sometime in 1991–92 he legally changed his name to "Varg." His choice of a new title is curious in light of the actions he would later commit, and the legend that would surround him— although he claims to have adopted it mainly for its common meaning of "wolf." If one understands the etymology and usage of the word *varg* in the various ancient Germanic cultures (and there is no evidence that Vikernes did at the time of his name change), his decision becomes downright ominous.

A fascinating dissertation exists entitled *Wargus, Vargr—'Criminal' 'Wolf': A Linguistic and Legal Historical Investigation* by Michael Jacoby, published in Uppsala, Sweden, but written in German. It is a highly detailed, heavily referenced exploration of the Germanic word *Warg*, or *vargr* in Norse.

The paper begins with a section "The Term *Warg* as a Designation for the Criminal in Ancient Germanic Sources," discussing the connotations of the root word among the various Northern European cultures. It appears in the different language dialects, but always with a negative implication when descriptive of men, conveying the sense of "criminal," "outlaw," "outcast," "thief," "malefactor," "evil being," "the damned one," and indeed, even "Devil."

The designation was used in the oldest written laws of Northern Europe, often with a prefix to add a specific legal meaning, such as *gorvargher* ("cattle thief") or *morthvargr* ("killer"). Comparative mythology researcher Mary Gerstein, author of the essay "Germanic *Warg*: The Outlaw as Werewolf," notes that in the old Icelandic legal text, the *Grágás*, "one finds *morthvarg* 'murder-*varg*' as a term for a particular subclass of outlaw ... [which] implies killing furtively ... as well as the attempt to conceal the crime. It is the crime of a skulking werwolf."[16] The term also appears in the ancient Norwegian legal context, to designate the

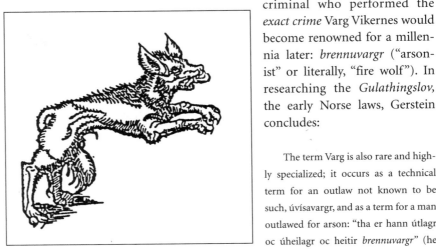

criminal who performed the *exact crime* Varg Vikernes would become renowned for a millennia later: *brennuvargr* ("arsonist" or literally, "fire wolf"). In researching the *Gulathingslov*, the early Norse laws, Gerstein concludes:

The term Varg is also rare and highly specialized; it occurs as a technical term for an outlaw not known to be such, *úvísavargr*, and as a term for a man outlawed for arson: "tha er hann útlagr oc úheilagr oc heitir *brennuvargr*" (he

WEREWOLF   shall be outlawed and deprived of all

ULVER *THE MADRIGAL OF NIGHT*

rights and shall be called "fire-*varg*") ... *varg* as it occurs in the earliest Old Norse codes is an item of petrified legal vocabulary, retained in expressions involving oral pronouncement of outcast status for especially odious crimes, such as arson, oath breaking, and secret slaying.[17]

Jacoby's research continues with an investigation and examination of the most noteworthy crimes which were strongly connected to the word. These are: grave robbery, treason, theft, and manslaughter. A case can be made that Varg Vikernes fulfilled each one of these specific connotations in some respect. Describing the first of the crimes, there is clause in another ancient Germanic legal text, the Salic Law, which states: "If any one shall have dug up or despoiled an already buried corpse, let him be a *varg*."[18] Vikernes's advocacy of, and participation in, grave desecrations surely qualifies him for this designation. As regards treason, Varg proudly states a desire to see the current government of Norway overthrown, and he identifies with the man whose name has become synonymous with treason in the international vocabulary, Vidkun Quisling. Vikernes has also often been called a "traitor" by others in the Black Metal scene for killing Øystein Aarseth. Vikernes was found guilty of theft—he stole 150 kilos of explosives and had this stored in his apartment at the time of his arrest. The old

Germanic laws do not appear to make a distinction between first-degree murder and manslaughter, and refer only to the latter. Vikernes was convicted of murdering Euronymous, although he insists this was only manslaughter, done in self-defense. It is eerie and uncanny that someone could live up to their name so well, even down to the subtleties of its earliest etymological essence. As a result of his actions, he has truly become an "outlaw" and "outcast" in the eyes of society.

The Rev. Sabine Baring-Gould, in his *Book of Werewolves,* writes of the other meanings inherent to Vikernes's chosen namesake:

> The word vargr, a wolf, had a double significance, which would be the means of originating many a were-wolf story. Vargr is the same as u-argr, restless; argr being the same as the Anglo-Saxon earg. Vargr had its double signification in Norse. It signified a wolf, and also a godless man. [...] The Anglo Saxons regarded him as an evil man: wearg, a scoundrel; Gothic vargs, a fiend. ... the ancient Norman laws said of the criminals condemned to outlawry for certain offenses, Wargus esto: be an outlaw! [be a varg!] ... among the Anglo Saxons an utlagh, or out-law, was said to have the head of a wolf. If then the term vargr was applied at one time to a wolf, at another to an outlaw who lived the life of a wild beast, away from the haunts of men—"he shall be driven away as a wolf, and chased so far as men chase wolves farthest," was the legal form of sentence—it is certainly no matter of wonder that stories of outlaws should have become surrounded with mythical accounts of their transformation into wolves.[19]

FRODELOVENS TYVSSTRAF

ILLUSTRATION OF A THIEF HUNG WITH A WOLF FROM A 1907 EDITION OF SAXO'S *HISTORY OF THE DANES*

The above elucidation reveals a few further elements which reflect Vikernes's character and circumstances. He is by nature an extremely restless person, brimming with energy and possessed of a defiant gleam in his eye. His position of "outlaw" goes beyond just his status with everyday society, since a number of people in the Black Metal subculture have also sworn they plan to kill him if given the chance. This is much like the position of the outlaw in older times, banished from society and fair game for anyone who would deem to destroy him.

There are a number of other associations which come to light upon closer consideration of the statements and actions of Vikernes, in his persona as the heathen "Varg." As can be seen from the Baring-Gould quote above, the wolf connotation of the term later became associated with werewolves, and in certain sources the Devil himself is referred to as a werewolf. However, this negative outlook on wolves appears to surface after the onset of the Christian period of Europe; the pre-Christian heathens had a quite different perception.

A number of Black Metal bands display a fascination for the wolf. The most obvious example is Ulver, whose name itself means "wolves" in Norwegian. Their most recent recordings have been based entirely on wolf-lore. The band's guitarist Erik Lancelot states:

> The mythical wolf is a Satanic character. He is often pictured as a solitary antagonist, a representative of animalism appearing before humans to promote values of selfishness and brute force, as for instance in the tale of "Little Red Riding Hood" and certain tales of La Fontaine. The wolf lives in the forest, symbol of the demonic world outside the control of human civilization, and serves thus as a link between the demonic and the cultural, chaos and order, light and dark, subconscious and conscious. Still I do not by this mean to say that the wolf represents the balance point between good and evil—rather he is the promoter of "evil" in a culture which has focused too much on the light side and disowned the animalistic. He symbolizes the forces which human civilization does not like to recognize, and is therefore looked upon with suspicion and awe.[20]

In the older Viking times, wolves were totem animals for certain cults of warriors, the Berserkers. A specific group is mentioned in the sagas, the *Ulfhethnar* or "wolf-coats," who donned the skin of wolves. Baring-Gould recounts the behavior of the Berserks who, wearing these special vestments, reached an altered state of consciousness:

> They acquired superhuman force ... No sword would wound them, no fire burn them, a club alone could destroy them, by breaking their bones, or crushing their skulls. Their eyes glared as though a flame burned in the sockets, they ground their teeth, and frothed at the mouth; they gnawed at their shield rims, and are said to have sometimes bitten them through, and as they rushed into conflict they yelped as dogs or howled as wolves.[21]

The Berserks were described in the old chronicles as "men of Odin," the god to whom Vikernes also claims exclusive dedication. Wolves are sacred to Odin, the

"Allfather," who is usually accompanied by his own two wolf-elementals, Geri and Freki. Many Germanic personal first names can be traced back to another root word for wolf, *ulv* or *ulf*, so this was clearly not an ignoble or derisive connotation, except in its *varg* form.

THE MASKS OF ODIN

Odin himself is a challenging deity, providing an archetype for the Faustian seeker: he who makes a dangerous pact in return for increasing knowledge and experience. Some of the more notable attributes of the character of Odin and the cult that surrounded him in ancient Scandinavian tribal society are exceedingly sinister. In the old sagas he is bestowed with myriad names and titles, some of which include Herjan ("War God"), Yggr ("the Terrible One"), Bölverkr, ("The Evil Doer"), Boleyg ("Fiery Eyed"), and Grímnir ("the Masked One").

Odin is mentioned in the *Elder Edda* as first having brought battle to the cosmos: *"On his host his spear did Odin hurl / Then in the world did war first come,"*[22] states the Eddic poem "Voluspá." His early worship demanded the sacrifice of innocent men. Odin is often referred to as a great "stirrer of strife." Comparative mythologist Georges Dumézil remarks:

The character of Odin is complex and not very reassuring. His face hidden under his hood, in his somber blue cloak, he goes out about the world, simultaneously master and spy. It happens that he betrays his believers and his protégés, and he sometimes seems to take pleasure in sowing the seeds of fatal discord...[23]

ODIN CARVING FOUND IN HEGGE STAVE CHURCH

It is not difficult to see the appeal of the Odin archetype for those who assume the role of the heretic, pariah, or outsider. Varg Vikernes is all these things, and his long-standing obsessions with weapons, warfare, struggle, and death also fit into an Odinic paradigm. In her essay on the word *Warg*, Mary Gerstein also discusses comparative symbolism between Odin, who hung on the world tree Yggdrasil for nine nights in order to gain wisdom, and Christ, who was hung on the cross as an outlaw, only to be reborn as an empowered heavenly deity. Vikernes, despite his heathenism, has in certain respects set himself up as both avatar and Christ-like martyr for his cause, willing to suffer in prison for his sacrifice. Gerstein also draws parallels between Odin in his mythological role as the binder of foes, and his relationship to those who are deemed a criminal *varg*:

> Odin differs ideologically from other [Indo-European] binder gods in his essential amorality: he delights in strife between kinsmen and urges men to break their vows. The strangled *warg* belongs to him more from a sense of "like seeking like" than in punishment. His very name indicates his nature; Adam of Bremen's "Wodan, id est furor" ["Wodan, that means fury"] stands fast: Odin is the embodiment of every form of frenzy, from the insane bloodlust that characterized the werwolf warriors who dedicated themselves to him, to erotic and poetic madness.[24]

Odin was intrinsically connected to death itself. In the *Ynglingsaga* it is stated, "at times [Odin] would call to life dead men out of the ground, or he would sit down under men that were hanged. On this account he was called the Lord of Ghouls or of the Hanged."[25] Odin is related in function to a psychopomp, as he receives the souls of dead warriors into his "hall of the chosen," Valhalla. His hall is distinguished from those of the other gods by a unique and foreboding display, as Gerstein notes: "The putrefying corpse of a *varg* on the gallows is the emblem of Odin's power and the sign of his presence."[26] She then quotes the passage of the "Grímnismál" which states, "Odin's hall is easy to recognize: a *varg* hangs before the western door, an eagle droops above."[27]

Vikernes often now downplays his former interest in Satanism by claiming that Odin himself is the "adversary" of the Christian God, and therefore can be seen as Satanic. He points out that after the conversion, the old heathen gods of the North were demonized by the Christian missionaries and leaders. In this he is correct, and a perfect example survives in the "renunciation oath" which was enforced under Boniface among the Saxons and Thuringians, who were ordered to repeat: "I forsake all the Devil's works and words, and Thunær [Thor] and Woden [Odin] and Saxnôt [the tribal deity of the Saxons] and all the monsters who are their companions."[28]

In contrast to the historical precedent where the old heathen gods were transmogrified into Satanic monsters and demons, many of the denizens of Black Metal music pledged allegiance to these same demonic spirits of Christianity, only later to recast them as heathen forces. Even so, much of the culture of Black

Metal will always remain rooted in concepts of the Devil and Satanism. In order to fully understand why a music genre could help to spawn as much vehemently anti-Christian destruction as has been linked to Black Metal, one must also explore its starting point in the realm of the diabolical.

EVIL PERSONIFIED APPEARS AT FIRST SIGHT REPULSIVE. BUT THE MORE WE STUDY THE
PERSONALITY OF THE DEVIL, THE MORE FASCINATING HE BECOMES. IN THE BEGINNING
OF EXISTENCE THE EVIL ONE IS THE EMBODIMENT OF EVERYTHING UNPLEASANT, THEN
OF EVERYTHING BAD, EVIL, AND IMMORAL. HE IS HATRED, DESTRUCTION, AND ANNIHI-
LATION INCARNATE, AND AS SUCH HE IS THE ADVERSARY OF EXISTENCE, OF THE
CREATOR, OF GOD. THE DEVIL IS THE REBEL OF THE COSMOS, THE INDEPENDENT IN THE
EMPIRE OF A TYRANT, THE OPPOSITION TO UNIFORMITY, THE DISSONANCE IN UNIVERSAL
HARMONY, THE EXCEPTION TO THE RULE, THE PARTICULAR IN THE UNIVERSAL, THE
UNFORESEEN CHANCE THAT BREAKS THE LAW; HE IS THE INDIVIDUALIZING TENDENCY,
THE CRAVING FOR ORIGINALITY, WHICH BODILY UPSETS THE ORDINANCES OF GOD THAT
ENFORCE A DEFINITE KIND OF CONDUCT; HE OVERTURNS THE MONOTONY THAT WOULD
PERMEATE THE COSMIC SPHERES IF EVERY ATOM IN UNCONSCIOUS RIGHTEOUSNESS
AND WITH PIOUS OBEDIENCE SLAVISHLY FOLLOWED A GENERALLY PRESCRIBED COURSE.

—PAUL CARUS, *THE HISTORY OF THE DEVIL AND THE IDEA OF EVIL*[1]

THEIR SATANIC MAJESTIES

THE IDEOLOGY WHICH DRIVES BLACK METAL IS COMMONLY REFERRED TO AS "Satanism," but what does this mean in practice? In Norway it has become equated with violence and church burning, but this is a distinction peculiar to that country. Satanism—like its antithesis, Christianity—means a good many things to a myriad of people. Nor is there is a strict consensus on defining Satanism within the Black Metal scene, beyond a basic "opposition to Christianity." From that starting point a number of quite distinct strains of thought issue forth.

Some central personalities—Varg Vikernes, most prominently—dismiss the importance of Satanism altogether, seeing it merely as an introduction to more indigenous heathen beliefs. Others were never involved deeply in any kind of Satanic outlook at all, managing to avoid it completely as a reference point. Ivar

Bjørnsson, of the Norwegian "Viking Metal" band Enslaved, explains, "Satanism is as remote for us as Christianity. It's just something that doesn't interest us. We listened to all the Satanist stuff, but we were always only interested in the music."[2] Enslaved are closely associated with Black Metal circles, although their lyrics and approach are more thoroughly rooted in Viking Age culture than any form of Satanism. Their steadfast use of explicitly Nordic iconography is far less ambiguous than even that of a project such as Burzum.

There are those who see Satanism and Black Metal as essentially intertwined, and a number of important bands have attempted to formulate a coherent philosophy centering around this. But in general, Satanism has been for show only, following in the footsteps of Venom and Bathory, and concerned solely with cartoonish efforts to assume "evil" poses in promotional photographs or make outlandishly uninformed statements in interviews. As Metalion comments:

ENSLAVED

I don't think that Satanism has been that important besides being a flirtation with the occult symbols and as a concept for the lyrics. ... I think very few Black Metal musicians are involved in the secrets of the Black Arts. Of course some are, but they keep it to themselves. I've met people who are into rituals, etc., and are deeply into the Black Metal scene as well, but they are not necessarily in a band.[3]

Similar thoughts regarding the superficiality of much of the Satanism are echoed and elaborated upon by M.W. Daoloth of the respected Greek Black Metal band Necromantia:

They used it for its shock value—sex, Satan, and violence sell well. A lot of bands still do this, but there are musicians who've adopted Satanism as a lifestyle and the key point here is that these musicians were members of the most influential bands. So other people started to copy their music and ideas no matter if they believed in them or not! Satanism inevitably adopted a more intellectual profile. Still, the musicians that are seriously involved in the dark side are few— compared to the existing number of bands—but they are in major bands and that is what counts.[4]

Much of the Satanism found in Black Metal is little more than a given band employing the simplest catchphrases and symbology, often merely in imitation of other groups they admire. This might be augmented by bits and pieces of additional material garnered from a stray occult text, or more likely, exposure to horror novels and films. There are some publications that circulate through the Black Metal underground which attempt to inspire the musicians to a greater depth of knowledge and a focus for their efforts. One of these is *The Nexus,* published from New Zealand by Kerry Bolton. He has long been active within the wider Satanic underground, and is well qualified to comment on the attitudes of Black Metal bands and fans:

M.W. DAOLOTH OF NECROMANTIA

Observing other magazines, especially those of a specifically Metal nature, it is true that many of them, and many bands, are childish. They see Satanism as nothing more than a means of blaspheming Christianity, and Jesus specifically—although I've often wondered how it's possible to "blaspheme" something unless one actually believes in it to start with! I used to read a lot of this some years ago. At first I thought it extremely funny and would laugh out loud; eventually it became boring, predictable, and eventually annoying.

The "medieval" style of Satanism or Devil worship is what's most easily accessible to the average youth in search of Satan, since this is the type perpetrated by the mass media and entertainment industry.[5]

For every rule there are exceptions, and this is true of the prevalence of "medieval" Devil worship and other primitive views in the realm of Black Metal. While most of the musicians come from this background, certain key personalities have evolved significantly. They are also, as Daoloth states, the more influential people in the scene. One such figure is Ihsahn, singer in Emperor—one of the most popular, and arguably the most majestic sounding, of all Black Metal bands. Ihsahn's philosophy is far advanced beyond many of his contemporaries in the scene, and in actuality bears strong resemblance to the original outline of Satanism which Anton LaVey summarized in his *Satanic Bible* in 1969. Due to his long-standing involvement with Black Metal, Ihsahn is familiar with the various Satanic veins running through the scene, and the ways in which they have progressed since the beginning of the decade.

IHSAHN

WHAT WERE YOU LIKE WHEN YOU FIRST BECAME INVOLVED IN BLACK METAL?

When I was younger, I was much more extreme. I dressed more extreme, and I think it was more important for me to show everyone else around that I was different from them and had very strong points of view. It was to get a reaction back that would prove my identity. Then I became older and I developed more rational views. Now it's not important for me to prove myself, to prove that I have these views, or that I'm a Satanist. I'm so aware of it now, and I'm very comfortable with my beliefs, so it's not important to get a response.

HOW WOULD YOU DESCRIBE THE IDEOLOGY OF EARLY BLACK METAL IN NORWAY?

I think Black Metal tried to concentrate more on just being "evil" than having a real Satanic philosophy. Everyone took it very seriously, but it's hard to live up to those ideals. It's hard for anyone to be as "evil" and as hateful as the ideals the Black Metal scene had. All of us tried in a way...

WHAT IS THE APPEAL OF BLACK METAL?

Black Metal wanted to be in opposition to society, a confrontation to all the normal stuff. Everybody needs some excitement, and if you look at youth today, they're all very boring.

In my town all they do is have their cars and they drive up and down the one main street. They have nothing else to do—it's a kind of competition for who has the finest car and the loudest stereo. They basically live in their cars. Those who are younger, who don't have a car—they sit at the side of the road and look at the cars. Their lives are extremely boring, and I can see that some people want more out of existence, they want to have their own personality and expression which makes it impossible to be associated with all those meaningless humans who walk around everywhere.

I think like that now—they're only "human." Shit, I don't want to be a human. Those are the people you see everyday when you walk in the street, the junkies, suffering starving African children—they're all "human," and I don't like them. There are sayings like, "It's human to fail"—I hate failure. People who think like me don't want to be associated with that, so you have something that makes you different.

Satanic philosophy has changed my whole way of thinking—you think in

IHSAHN

different ways, through the philosophy you have. People say Satanism and Black Metal is a very destructive thing, but it's the opposite. It's creative because it's all about yourself, you on your own, and those you care about. To get into that state you have to break down what you had before, to create space for all the new impressions. Jumping into Black Metal, there are so many impressions at one time, that it might be difficult to handle all at once. Many people won't make it through that stage because there is too much pressure. That tests who will be left after a period of time.

The Black Metal scene has matured a lot, and now people are much more aware of their own thoughts. I remember a year ago everybody was very obsessed by being "true" or "not true"—"true Black Metal" and all that. We got very tired of it, because who is true? We will know in the end; it's not very important. The weak will perish by themselves.

WHAT INSPIRED THE INITIAL FORM OF BLACK METAL?

A lot of the earlier Black Metal bands, like Venom, expressed very primitive, hateful views. It was very Satanic music. It also started up with the whole "anti-LaVey" attitude that was common within the scene, because his form of Satanism is very humane. No one wanted a humane Satanism; you should almost be Satan himself.

People wanted to be dead serious—and you should take such matters seriously—but I think people misunderstood the whole thing, because they made themselves miserable by being like that. You're not alive if you don't enjoy yourself, if you're miserable. I think Satanism has nothing to do with being a loser.

WHY DID THE ANTAGONISM TOWARD LAVEY'S IDEAS DEVELOP IN THE SCENE?

Many people turned against LaVey, and wanted it to be more extreme. I can also understand that, because for many people it was also about not being like everyone else. When LaVey says that the simplest housewife can be a Satanist, which it seems like he does in the *Satanic Bible*, I guess some were terrified that he had views that would take the special thing they had away from them.

HOW DID THE SCENE BECOME SO EXTREME?

It just came with the whole imagery of the Black Metal scene as it evolved in Norway. It was Satanic, and very dark and very evil. Christianity was the opposite. When people entered the scene they were not necessarily very hateful against Christianity; their hate against Christianity built up together with getting into Black Metal.

We were very inspired by what everybody else said. The emotions and atmosphere around it were very "evil." Many people did not laugh; they were very

EMPEROR

serious all the time. Nothing should be "good." Everybody was very grim looking. Everyone wanted to be like that, and I guess there are some who are that way still.

I probably piss many people off because I'm not like that; I'm not a miserable person. I'm actually having quite a good time and I laugh and enjoy myself. I must admit I was inspired by those other things earlier, but I don't think to the same degree. Of course you were affected by the whole atmosphere, that you don't sit and laugh in this Helvete place, and you have respect for the known figures in the scene, and were careful what to say to Euronymous in the beginning, before you got to know him. Everything was very serious all the time.

WAS IT A REACTION AGAINST STRICT CHRISTIANITY IN NORWAY?

The Norwegian State Church is not strict at all. I think it's quite funny, we have female Bishops and priests, and we have homosexual priests and homosexual marriages, which is very much against what's said in the Bible. The State Church in Norway is very liberal.

OR A REBELLION AGAINST CHRISTIAN UPBRINGING?

My parents are not religious at all. Normal people assume, "Oh, people into Black Metal must have had a terrible childhood and have been molested. They're weak and come from terrible backgrounds." But as far as I'm concerned, many people I know in the scene actually come from good families, non-religious families, and had a great childhood with very nice parents and no pressure at all. Quite wealthy families, really.

WHY WERE SUCH OVERTLY EXTREME STATEMENTS MADE BY PEOPLE LIKE EURONYMOUS TO THE PRESS?

I think that was very much to create fear among people. But I know people who believe in things like burning in hell, and have quite primitive Satanic views. I respect that.

WAS ANTON LAVEY'S *SATANIC BIBLE* A SIGNIFICANT INFLUENCE ON YOU?

I bought the *Satanic Bible* and read it, and was of course very fascinated by it, because it's a book that's very easy to agree with. Most people can associate with what it says. I also got excited by the Satanic imagery, which was very special. That inspired me very much. You've got to start at one point, then you get to other influences, other impressions... I was then much influenced by the Black Metal scene and more extreme stuff. After awhile you go back and forth and create your own thoughts out of it, as you mature. Now I don't agree with anybody; I don't have similar views to anyone in the scene.

For some, LaVey has been quite influential. He has been important just to get a word like "Satanism" out, because I don't think it was very much known in that manner before he started the Church of Satan. He made more of a name for it that people recognize. And in Norway because of the Black Metal thing, now everyone here knows what Black Metal is and everyone has heard the word Satanism.

HOW WOULD YOU DESCRIBE YOU OWN VIEWS ON SATANISM?

My form of Satanism has very little to do with ritual; it's much more a philosophy—you come to logical explanations for anti-Christian behavior. The *Satanic Bible* describes how most people live and how most people react; it describes ordinary stuff in Satanic imagery. If someone hits you, most people would hit back, but it's not necessarily Satanic. So I think there's also more to Satanism besides the philosophy. There are very many emotional elements as well. I try to give very much of myself, and my emotions, to the music which I create. That's as important to me as the philosophy. It's as much a spiritual life and it gets stronger and stronger the more you know about it.

CAN ANY AVERAGE PERSON FOLLOW A SATANIC PHILOSOPHY?

I don't feel like a normal person. Not everyone can be a Satanist. LaVey has done a very good job getting people interested in anti-Christian thinking and Satanic imagery. I also believe that he is much more serious and spiritually into this kind of Satan than he describes in his books. Picturing things in Satanic imagery, you have to have feelings for that kind of imagery, that way of thinking.

Do you agree with LaVey's statement that "Satanists are born, not made"?

I have turned now to become a Satanist, but I feel I could not be anything else. Even if I was raised in a different environment I would still have turned out to be a Satanist. I couldn't be anything else. It's very important to me, and has affected my whole life and my way of thinking.

Sometimes it can be also hard; you get a lot of trouble for being a Satanist. But I would never give that up for anything else. Sometimes I think it would be great to be more anonymous—it's a small town that I live in, everyone knows who I am. People look at me even though I don't dress particularly extremely, just because everybody knows what I am. Also with where I work, people are very skeptical towards me, and sometimes it would be easier if no one knew. But it's so important, it's not a thing that you can give up just because it's difficult.

Another band who have distinguished themselves from many of their contemporaries in terms of sound and vision is Ulver. The music of Ulver is impossible to easily categorize—although it is firmly rooted in Black Metal—and they have even released one album, *Kveldssanger* ("Evening Songs"), recorded solely with acoustic instruments. The result is a collection of haunting, baroque songs which lie somewhere between traditional Norse Folk music and Classical. Ulver are equally competent at creating blinding and aggressive electrified Black Metal. They also strongly identify with Satanism.

Ulver

Do you consider yourselves to be aligned with Black Metal in music and ideology?

Erik: Ulver was born out of the Black Metal scene, and on all of our releases so far except *Kveldssanger,* there can be no question about our alignment with Black Metal music. Our statements have also born evidence of related attitudes. However, bearing in mind the way Ulver has developed over the years both musically, lyrically, and philosophically, the label is becoming too limiting.

But what is behind Black Metal "ideology"? The source of Black Metal is Venom: beer-drinking, base-minded rabble, icons of Heavy Metal idiocy. The essence of Black Metal is Heavy Metal culture, not Satanic philosophy. Just look at our audience. The average Black Metal record buyer is a stereotypical loser: a good-for-nothing who was teased as a child, got bad grades at school, lives on social welfare and seeks compensation for his inferiority complexes and lack of identity by feeling part of an exclusive gang of outcasts uniting against a society which has turned them down. And with Heavy Metal as a cultural and intellectual foundation, these dependents on social altruism proclaim themselves the "elite"! Hah! Could it be more pathetic?

Garm: In certain ways I still cherish Black Metal as it was definitely the decisive factor for both my interests in music and the dark side. But since the early days I have matured quite a bit, and find it difficult to see myself as a part of this movement because a lot of Black Metal people follow very fallacious and narrow concepts of life. I seek to be impeccable, and this can only be achieved through open-mindedness. This implies interests outside what is common in the above circles.

A lot of abominable developments have happened in the scene since I was truly involved, and I am sad to say that most of the people who now dominate this milieu are but a bunch of conformist alcoholic losers with no genuine feeling for the concept and searching for an easy way to feel initiated into something eccentric and special. Black Metal now makes ignorant and unconfident young people feel warm and cozy, and functions more as a crutch for individual weakness than anything else. Now isn't that cute!

Is Christianity in Norway something that should be battled against?

Erik: Christianity is but one expression of herd mentality, and to battle against it is like battling against the nature of society. For as long as organized human societies exist, there will always be a division between the unconscious masses and conscious individuals. The Christian religion may wither and die, but only to be replaced by another philosophy glorifying the qualities of the herd. It lies not in the nature of the herd to live according to elitist ideals—their nature is to be cogwheels in the machinery of society, and the fact they follow a philosophy which glorifies this quality is aesthetically nauseating to the heretic, but still necessary for society to function.

The Satanist is an observer of society—to him, the world is like a stage, in relation to which he chooses sometimes to be a spectator, other times a participant, according to his will. He can watch from the outside and laugh, cry, sigh, or applaud depending on the effect the scenery has on his emotions; or he can throw himself into the game for the thrill; but his nature is always that of the watcher, the artist. He is not overly concerned with changing society, for his commitment to humanity is minimal.

So no, I do not bother to battle against Christianity. In what ways does it affect me? It fills me with disgust. But I feel no urge to take the role of a Messiah, teaching the blind how they should live.

ULVER

Garm: There is no logic in actively pursuing Christianity for a Satanist because this in no way benefits him. The "Christlings" legislate for the weak and worthless with humility, charity, subordination, guilt, and the taking of the world's burdens upon one's shoulders as their agenda. This is extremely easy for one of the Devil's party to take advantage of. The fact that they preach such degenerate morals prevents them, with a few unimportant exceptions, from being able to put out the emancipated spiritual fire in him. Instead they try by foolish means to talk him into changing his mind. Hah!

The cold, calculating scrupulousness of the heretic mind has infinite possibilities in such a society, and can but revel in cruel, selfish ecstasy. In this picture the "Christlings" are masochists, whilst he is the sadist holding the whip. If he was to set out and convert everyone to his line of thought, his world would look quite different, and we would no longer be able to touch the stars undisturbed. In my eyes this is nothing to strive for.

An appropriate example of how such futile aspirations may end is the case of Varg Vikernes: a neo-Viking martyr. A prophet of the ego who paradoxically enough chose to be the Jesus of his ideals, and now must suffer for it behind the walls of spleen. I have much respect for this man's conviction and courage, but not his sense of reality.

The picture of perhaps a hundred militant "Satanists" believing they can start a war against Christianity with Heavy Metal as their spiritual banner is pathetic. I choose to oppose Christianity by growing in my knowledge rather than waste my life on illusive dreams of a righteous world returning to the laws of nature. In our age the human brain is too complex to work after such systems anyway, and I see it as our destiny to be separated from them. Mankind has taken temporary control over these powers by means of technical intelligence, but soon enough this is what will blow us all into oblivion—and the reckless force behind this evolution is the triumphant mark of Satan.

All this said, I mind in no way attacks on Christianity, but I believe it is killing itself more rapidly than any church burner could ever dream of doing. After all, we live in the end of the second millennium and most people are enlightened to such a degree that they are capable of smelling rotten fish.

OUTSIDERS LOOKING IN

As the most influential form of music to have ever openly called itself "Satanic," Norwegian Black Metal is unique. In an effort to understand some of the philosophical and spiritual qualities inherent to this peculiarly Scandinavian manifestation, we spoke to two outside observers who wrote thoughtful commentaries on the subject in the press—commentaries which went beyond the scandalized headlines of the tabloid papers. Both men are contributors to Norway's cultural newspaper *Morgenbladet*.

Simen Midgaard is a freelance writer and author with a Master's Degree in the Humanities. Midgaard also founded the Oslo branch of the Ordo Templi Orientis, the occult order of Aleister Crowley, in 1984. He resigned from the leadership in 1993. Midgaard has kindly allowed us to print an English translation of his essay on Black Metal Satanism that appeared in *Morgenbladet* as Appendix III of this book. It is one of the most astute commentaries on the subject that has been published in Norway.

A number of Black Metal bands pay homage to Crowley in their imagery, and a few members of the Norwegian scene contacted the O.T.O. between 1992–93 seeking information. Simen Midgaard became more familiar with the Black Metal scene when he conducted an interview with Ihsahn of Emperor for *Morgenbladet*. In the course of our discussion with him, Midgaard presented an intriguing theory which traced the "medieval-style Satanism" of early Norwegian Black Metal back to a series of lurid newspaper exposés written about the O.T.O. and Satanism in 1990–91. This was shortly before Black Metal began to coalesce as a viable music genre in Norway. As our research progressed, we found that other observers besides Midgaard had arrived at similar theories regarding a possible link between sensationalist press coverage and the Norwegian Black Metal attitudes which would follow.

The conversation with Simen Midgaard is followed by an interview with Pål Mathiesen, a writer on theological issues for *Morgenbladet*, and a professed

Christian. As one would expect, the official response of the Church in Norway to the arsons and attacks perpetrated by Black Metallers was a negative one, but it consisted of little more than outraged statements about the "shocking rise of Satanism among youth." Mathiesen, as a bit of outsider, is able to forsake such simplistic rhetoric in his comments, and his thoughtful conclusions may surprise even the ardent Satanists.

SIMEN MIDGAARD

WHAT IS THE CONNECTION BETWEEN BLACK METAL AND SATANISM?

I don't see a very strong relation to any tradition of the world when it comes to Black Metal and Satanism; I don't see any real heritage. All this Satanism among the youths began some time after there was a "revelation" of Satanists in the O.T.O. It began in *Dagbladet* [one of Norway's leading tabloids], and they were speaking about cannibalism and sacrificing babies and all this medieval nonsense.

THEY LAUNCHED AN EXPOSÉ CAMPAIGN AGAINST THE O.T.O.?

Yes, they did. It was completely unfounded. This campaign was not only directed against the O.T.O., but also against some imagined Satanists. It was started by a policeman in around 1990 or '91. His name was Kobbhaug.

It was a Christian fundamentalist scare?

Yes—and this is the source of most of this youth Satanism we see in Norway; they have no other ideology. They may have also heard something of Satanism from LaVey; I know his book sold fairly well in Oslo. Now they have stopped the sale of it [the *Satanic Bible*], because of this thing with the Count. It's a little childish, if you ask me, because I think LaVey is quite contradictory to everything the Count stands for. This [LaVeyan Satanism] is the real Satanism, this sort of humanism under a black mask. They are standing up for individual freedom towards religious preference, and still trying to maintain a sort of religious context in their lives. I can't see anything "evil" about it.

WAS THERE ANYTHING GOING ON WITH SATANISM IN NORWAY BEFORE THE EXPOSÉ YOU REFER TO?

This kind of Satanism which the Count stands for resembles so much the kind of Satanism that was propagated in the newspapers a few years before he came out into the light, and I think he was influenced by it, and the whole Black Metal community was also influenced by that kind of propaganda.

IS THERE ANY SERIOUS TRADITION OF SATANISM IN NORWAY?

A kind of tradition of Satanism does in fact exist in Norway. You had it in the 1890's with Przybyszewski and Dagny Juel, and the clique around Edvard Munch, the painter, and around August Strindberg. I do think you had small groups in the western part of Scandinavia which practiced a form of Satanism; at least you had it in Denmark. It was a sort of Satanism, but nothing resembling the status of this "propaganda."

WHAT DID THIS CIRCLE AROUND MUNCH DO?

They practiced Black Masses, very oriented towards sex of course. It was in the fringe; I don't think Munch was really involved. But Dagny Juel was—she was a remarkable female feature in the *fin de siècle* of the Norwegian milieu. In the Symbolist tradition you find a rather civilized Satanist, a sort of Satanist with refinement.

WERE THERE ANY OTHER MORE RECENT EUROPEAN SATANIC TRADITIONS?

The German tradition is something in itself. After the O.T.O. they had these people—not exactly Satanists, but in some ways they are remotely the same—in these societies, who sacrificed humans. They were not really Satanists but rather some sort of paramilitary pagans.

THE BLACK METAL PEOPLE COULD BE SEEN TO HAVE ACTED OUT IN A SIMILAR WAY.

There is a difference between cultivating sinister ideas and acting them out. This is a very important distinction. I think Ihsahn of Emperor likes these sinister ideas, and meditates upon them, but he would never kill someone or burn a church. He has declared his opposition to that sort of anti-Christianity. He said to me he would support church burning if it was a new, ugly church. Not the old churches. He doesn't really condemn that, but he thinks it's *unsophisticated.*

IS IHSAHN ONE OF THE BLACK METAL PEOPLE WHO CONTACTED THE O.T.O.?

No, he wasn't. But he's one of the few people I would have let in.

PEOPLE LIKE BÅRD "FAUST" YOU WOULD NOT LET IN?

A murderer would not be allowed into the O.T.O., according to its rules.

BUT BEFORE HE'D DONE THAT?

I think he wrote us a rather primitive letter, just two lines about "I'm a boy of 18 who is interested in Satanism," or something.

WERE BLACK METAL PEOPLE CONTACTING THE O.T.O. BECAUSE OF THE IMAGE THEY HAD OF IT FROM THE NEWSPAPERS?

Exactly, this was the case.

THE PROPAGANDA FROM THESE NEWSPAPER STORIES SOUNDS HARD TO BELIEVE.

Yes, and the juridical establishment didn't believe it as well. The leading figures in the police in Oslo were astonished by it, and they didn't believe it at all.

YOU WERE CONTACTED BY THEM?

No... well, after two years, after all this church burning they came. They were standing down in the courtyard. I didn't open the door when I saw it was the police. They came to some friends of mine, the same thing. I had no interest in talking to them. As a matter of principle I never let officials into my home—never. They are another *tribe*.

HOW WOULD YOU DESCRIBE IHSAHN'S BELIEFS?

I would classify him as an intellectual, civilized, and intelligent kind of Satanist. A positive Satanist, who is not predominantly anti-Christian. He is not interested in anti-Christianity but rather a kind of creative Satanism—a romantic, Gothic Satanist. He is strongly revolting against all these new and ugly things which we find in the modern world. He's a sort of aesthetic Satanist.

MORE IN THE TRADITION OF LORD BYRON, OR SUCH PEOPLE?

Yes.

WHAT CAN YOU SAY ABOUT ØYSTEIN AARSETH?

I don't know much about Øystein. I spoke with a journalist who had interviewed him some years ago, and he had been at Helvete, this shop he had, and Øystein wouldn't open the shop because his grandmother had forbidden him to speak to the media!

MANY OF THE BLACK METAL PEOPLE SEEM TO BE MORE BARK THAN BITE, AND RATHER TAME IN PERSON.

Yes, most of them—but not only. We have had at least two murders, and one disappearance. A son of a priest in Tønsberg. He's disappeared in connection with Satanism. But they haven't found him dead or alive.

DO YOU KNOW ANY DETAILS ABOUT THIS DISAPPEARANCE?

He wasn't a Satanist himself but he may have met someone who was. He was a part of a role-playing group, so maybe he met some of them there, I don't know.

IT SEEMS THAT ROLE-PLAYING GAMES MAY HAVE BEEN AN INFLUENCE ON THE BLACK METAL PHENOMENON. THERE'S A PHOTO OF GRISHNACKH IN HIS ROOM WITH A BIG MAP OF MIDDLE-EARTH ON THE WALL, TAKEN FROM A ROLE-PLAYING MANUAL.

The name "Grishnackh" is taken from Tolkien anyway.

DO YOU THINK A LOT OF THEIR INSPIRATION COMES FROM SUCH ROLE-PLAYING IMAGERY?

It may be that their range of study is somewhat limited. I think many of them have grown up with the Bible and phone book as the only books in the house. We should also pay regard to the long Christian tradition in Norway—that's very important. I think it's a very sound revolt against that kind of education and culture, if you can give Christianity those attributes.

CAN YOU SEE BLACK METAL AS A CONTINUATION OF THE PARTICULAR NORWEGIAN PIETIST TRADITION OF CHRISTIANITY THAT EXISTS ON THE WESTERN AND SOUTHERN COAST?

Yes, it continues it because of its fanaticism, and it's a simple standard of truth, which is sort of positivistic in an extremely primitive way. There is no kind of irony, for instance. They believe in the book without any reference to the world. They are not able to see things without it. They have no concept of relativism. It is just like Fascism in Italy or Nazism in Germany. You have this low church culture which predominates in the small communities.

DO YOU SEE ANY REASON WHY BLACK METAL BANDS WOULD HAVE A ROMANTICIZED NATIONALIST IDEA ABOUT NORWAY?

Yes, if they can connect it to the paganism, then you have a romantic affinity. Without that I don't think it would play a very important part. But I don't think they are particularly educated in this aspect of nationalism itself, really.

WHAT DO SEE AS THE CONNECTION BETWEEN SATANISM AND PAGANISM?

Just the anti-Christianity. That's the connection.

THERE SEEMS TO BE A GENERAL SHIFT FROM THE MORE MEDIEVAL-STYLE SATANISM TO AN INTEREST IN PAGANISM, AND A DARK OBSESSION WITH NATURE. DO YOU THINK THEY UNDERSTAND WHAT THE HEATHEN WORLDVIEW MIGHT BE?

I don't think they understand very much, in general! But of course Satan is a Judeo-Christian person, and if they are going to get rid of Judeo-Christianity, they will have to get rid of Satan as well, as a matter of fact. He is a sort of Trotsky in the revolution, when it comes down to it. Satan is useful in the Christian world. It's a point to consider, because it's logical—if you are going to be consequently anti-Christian, then is Satan just a mediating figure?

SOME OF THE HEATHEN BANDS HAVE REJECTED SATANISM COMPLETELY, LIKE ENSLAVED.

I don't think the romantic Satanists are going to creep over into this, because these people have managed to make a positive thing out of Satan. Those Satanists whose only motive is to revolt against Christianity will have to get rid of Satan, because he's a part of Christianity. The other ones who seek a positive Satan, will of course not have any need to.

WHAT ARE YOUR OWN VIEWS TOWARD CHRISTIANITY IN NORWAY?

I do think Christianity makes people more stupid. That is a consequence, in many ways, of a disgusting religion. I don't think it's very honest, with their ideas of sacrifice, and of pain, all this nonsense, all this masochistic view of life. They are subjected to the power as a metaphysical principle, and are creeping before their god. I wouldn't call it good morals. And they have the propagating view that half the world is going to end in eternal pain because they don't sub-mit to it. I find it disgusting in that sense—completely disgusting.

SO YOU CAN SYMPATHIZE WITH BLACK METAL PEOPLE REACTING AGAINST IT?

Yes, yes—that's quite to the point. But I mean, I'm not a teenager any-more.

CAN YOU SEE ANY VALUE TO WHAT THEY DID?

With the burning of churches? Well, of course there is a certain value in it because it causes the Christianity community to wonder. It's a strong reaction, but I myself wouldn't want to react against something as weak as an individual church, something as feeble as that. But I can see a certain value in it as a revolt and to make people consider a few religious questions.

Do you think this has made the Norwegian church stronger?

Of course it has, and therefore I do think it is outrageous to burn churches!

Yet there is a certain symbolic value as a reaction against Christianity?

Yes, but those who are really reacting toward Christianity are all these people now going to church. This is the mentality of people in the cities, at least when it comes to the official Norwegian church. I'm rather indifferent to the State Church. I'm *not* indifferent to these terrible small sects who teach their people with fear from the day they are able to talk. I support any revolt, however strong it is, against that kind of Christianity because I think it makes people into neurotics. It should be forbidden by law because they torture their own children. I do see they had fairly good reasons for their revolt. I wouldn't burn a church myself, but I can understand why they are burning churches.

Do you think it has potential to develop any more?

Yes, it has a lot of potential. And *it will develop.*

You don't think that it will die out when the public loses interest in the music, which is bound to happen?

No, it will go into new forms. Because now one has already seen a polarity, and this polarity will not dispose of itself at all.

Do you see these people maturing into a more sophisticated form of occultism or anti-Christianity?

Yes, and I think that will happen, or already is happening. For certain parts of it—at least one out of ten.

Is there a more intelligent place for these people to go at that point?

I think the O.T.O. would be such a place, indeed—although the O.T.O. is not very much for revolting. It's a Masonic organization, as a matter of fact. It's not a movement.

Pål Mathiesen

What has been the after-effect of the church burnings in Norway?

The congregations that have been affected by the church burnings have had a huge new interest in the community from people who might baptise their children and so on, but don't actually go to church themselves. Where there have been church burnings and rebuilding of the churches, there has been a huge interest in the congregations, so they have experienced a kind of "Christianization" during this process, but it hasn't affected Christianity in Norway as such. I don't think more people have become Christians in Norway because of Norwegian Satanism, but the specific congregations have been affected by it.

How Christian is the average Norwegian?

It depends on what you mean by "being a Christian." This is a big discussion in Norway right now. I think we have a rather deep Christian culture here. The belief in the rituals—I don't think that's very strong. It's a cultural phenomenon, you feel related to a true culture. In that sense I would say Norway is a Christian country with strong Christian culture, but not with a strong Christian life for the people living there, if you can understand the distinction.

Is the hatred of Christianity here reasonable?

I don't think it has much to do with reason. If they hate Christianity that's not a very reasonable thing to do. It's emotional. As for *why* they hate it—when I was 15 or 16 years old I hated Christianity. I wasn't brought up with Sunday School, going to church, reading the Bible, saying prayers, etc., and I really hated it at the

same age as many people who become Satanists.

Opposition toward Christianity is very strong among the youth in Norway. You'll find very few Norwegian youngsters that have a relationship to Christianity; if they have it, they have a very extreme relationship towards it, and are involved with very extreme charismatic movements. But most people actually hate it.

Fifteen years later I look upon it and I think *that was a Christian thing*, to be in opposition to the religion. To hate God, or to hate the Church, meant that I actually *felt* something for it and had a relationship with it. The hatred shows that you have love, that you have a concern. You wouldn't be able to put many emotions and hatred into it if you didn't have a strong feeling of what I would call love.

It's interesting when you come to Satanism, and look upon it as a religious phenomenon. I would maybe define some of these people as Christians today, because I think the hatred they have is actually showing that maybe in their heart they're loving God, or have a relationship to Jesus. I think it's possible. It's an extreme form of what happens when people are jealous—they kill their lover. It's not an unchristian thing to hate the Church. A lot of good Christians have done that. I'm not saying this is the truth, but it's an interesting way to look upon the Satanists as a Christian movement to some extent...

It think it's important to differentiate between the opportunistic side of Satanism and the serious side. The leaders have a deliberate view upon religion as such, and I would say they are not opportunists. In its heart Norwegian Satanism has a very close relationship to Norwegian Christianity.

Is there a tradition of Satanism in Norway?

238

We definitely have an occult tradition in the Nordic religion, that's obvious. We also have occult traditions within Christianity both through the medieval age and after the Protestant reformation. There is a very long and continuous religious tradition of occult phenomena. I would call the medieval tradition of burning witches something which is based in the occult, and that's rather close to the Church today. It's a verdict on the immoral aspect.

When I was talking to Ihsahn, he was saying that what he hates most about the Church is that it's really weak. It doesn't have a morality. It's immoral and he would look upon that as one of the things he hated most about it. If the Christian Church would actually lower a verdict on people, to judge and be hard with that, he would have much more respect for it. That's a pretty Christian thought to me.

Satanism is really just another expression of occult phenomena in Christianity. Freemasonry, for example, is a Christian occult tradition. There are many movements on the fringe of the Christian religion that still have a relation to occultism. All these occult phenomena that we have been seeing, including people like August Strindberg and things that we have seen in the last two centuries, have a relation to Christianity. I have a rather broad definition of Christianity.

How would you define occultism?

Occultism has something to do with the dark aspect of human nature. It's based on undogmatic thinking—you take your own personal experience as a basis for what you do. You don't use religious laws or anything of that nature. It's an extreme form of subjective religious experience. This could be almost anything. With this definition I would have to say that some of the charismatic Christian movement is also "occult." They have no law, they have no government, they are just experiencing, choosing whatever aspects they feel like, and experiencing dark aspects by going through that.

Is the Christian mass an occult rite?

It has aspects of the occult. The communion, in the Catholic and Greco-Roman tradition, has occultic aspects, but I wouldn't say it *is* occult.

Also the sacrifice of something which has this love—the killing of it—has occult aspects, but I wouldn't say it is occult. These phenomena are related and it's a typical historically unaware thing that we do today when we look upon Satanism as something very new and different, wondering, "What is this?" It's in a long, long tradition of religiosity which is based on human experience and rituals. It's not anything new at all. If you look at the Old Testament, God also did this, he was burning down cities and killing people when he was dissatisfied with them. This aspect in religion is not new.

I have a reason for making this analysis of it, and the motivation is to make it human in some way. In the postmodern way of thinking, you see one phenomenon which is extreme and then you say that you have to judge all these people. These are bad people and we just have to hate them and isolate them. I don't like that mentality and I think it's wrong.

If you look at Satanism as a reflection of the spiritual life and spiritual tradition that we are standing in, I feel that it makes the Satanists more human. It makes them moral people who actually have a cause, and who are trying to say something to us. If you see some of the leaders, they are bright and reflective people, they are people with integrity. I would look upon them as moral people, and we have to take seriously what they are saying. If I thought of them just an extreme example of disobedient youngsters, I wouldn't have to listen to them.

That's what the Church is doing; they just try to isolate the Satanists and say it's not serious, it's just violence and brutality, it's just revenge they're after. They don't define them as part of their own tradition, and I do. We have to listen to what they're saying.

THE FACT THAT THEY'VE KILLED SOMEONE DOESN'T COMPROMISE WHAT THEY HAVE TO SAY?

How many Christian people have killed for the beliefs of their own religion? Killing people is an extremely human thing and doesn't exclude them from being sincere and having a message. The Baader-Meinhof [German terrorist group] has a message which I think we should take seriously—although they did dreadful things. Doing criminal things and killing people doesn't exclude you from having an opinion that is important.

WHAT'S THEIR REAL MESSAGE?

My motivation is to understand what they're saying, and to take that message seriously. The violence in Satanism is not particular in any way, it's not more severe than other violence in this society, and maybe it's less if you compare it with football hooligans or whatever. The Satanists have a religious message, and that is the interesting thing, that they have something to say to our religious tradition and they are definitely saying it. Being violent in a religious tradition is not a very strange thing—it's normal in that context. The Satanists are killing each other—many have been doing that in the Christian tradition for thousands of years. They're only killing people when they disagree with them, there's nothing new about it. It's historically unaware to look upon this as something specific and "Satanic," the fact they are killing each other when they have a conflict among themselves.

Look at the church fires. If their primary motive was just violence, they would burn the church down when there was a funeral or a baptism there, if they really wanted to make hell for people and show that violence is the most important thing. Why burn it in the middle of the night? Of course it's dark, but in many parts of Norway it's dark in the daytime too. So they could burn a church in the north of Norway on a Sunday and still get the aesthetic side of it, and kill a hundred people at the same time by blocking the doors and burning it up. Why don't they do that? Because violence isn't the basic message. It's extremely obvious to me.

When we look at pictures of the bands, they look very violent. I think some of that is just the visual trappings of violence more than the actual thing. Are these really violent people going around? I don't think so; I think they're quite normal, when it comes to being violent people or not. It's part of the cult to make a violent statement, to visually show off something violent, but it's not a violent culture as I see it.

WHAT IS UNIQUE ABOUT NORWEGIAN SATANISM?

There is Satanism and occultism in a lot of places in this world, but the reason why the Norwegian Satanism has become so strong and interesting compared to other countries is because it has been so intense. There is sense of a Satanism here that is very judgmental. You have this LaVey sort of thing with enjoying life, but at its best Norwegian Satanism is the total opposite of that. It's an aesthetic movement with strong beliefs not to enjoy life, but only to dedicate yourself to destroying the church and Christianity. As Ihsahn was talking about, destroy it because it's weak, because it doesn't have a right to live anymore, because it's just good to everybody. It doesn't have the power to judge anymore. It's just some sort of social-democratic Christianity, and these people despise that kind of weakness. Satanism in Norway has become strong because it's a despotic form of Satanism, but that is also why it's going to fade so fast—because people are not able to live like that for a very long period of time. Also our Christian tradition is moving away from this more despotic side.

HOW WOULD YOU DEFINE SATANISM?

Satanism in its basis is a protest against civilization as such, whether you consider it the Greek or Christian civilization. It is against the fact that you have moral laws: how you should be, what you can't do, that you can't kill people, that you are supposed to be nice to people that are different from you, etc.

The Satanists say—to put it brutally—that we are animals. The animal culture is the most important one, and we are losing that part of us. This is broad in the culture today, with the "wild women," etc., this whole thing of going back to nature. Being part of nature instead of spirit or morals is very strong now.

I think Satanism has been an expression of that, and was one of the earliest things to do so. If you hate somebody, kill them. Just do it, there's nothing immoral about that. Animals do that. If you hate somebody there's no reason against doing that.

ISN'T THAT STRIVING TOWARD NATURE AKIN TO THE HEATHEN RELIGION?

The interesting thing about the old Nordic religion is that the current justice system in Norway comes from there. They had written laws, meeting places, judges. Everybody thinks that these people were just living out in nature, but it was just another religious system, with laws, with civilization in a different manner.

This dark aspect of human nature—to kill someone if you don't like them, to rape someone if you feel like it and to not feel bad about it—goes back much further and is older than the Nordic religion, definitely. They didn't accept that. They built societies and civilizations on different standards, but the ideal was the same that you have to respect the collective norms and laws of society.

Satanism says something totally different: do what you like to do, don't ask anybody else what they think about it. Just do what you think is right. That is something different, and if they try to mix that with Nordic traditions, that is very unhistorical—and it becomes extremely explosive because you can take the violent aspects of the Nordic tradition and legitimize it through this new thing. You legitimize it through the symbols of that time, which is totally incorrect, and then use it in our time as an expression of extreme individualism.

That struck me when I was talking to Ihsahn, the symbols he was using of three or four-thousand-year-old Eastern symbols of different religions, and at the same to say that it's only Norway for me and only the Nordic religion that counts. It's not rational on that point at all. It doesn't relate to history as something rational—you just use it.

WHAT DO THINK THE MESSAGE OF SOMEONE LIKE VIKERNES IS?

I should say that I don't look upon Vikernes as being the most representative of the Satanists in Norway. He is a very special personality; he is not a conformist in any way. If he was a supporter of a football club he wouldn't wear the same clothing as they do, he would always want to be individualistic toward any trend.

It would be dangerous to define Vikernes as simply a Norwegian Satanist, because I don't think he is that. He has become a leader or a spokesperson because of his extreme individualism and because he's so strange as a person. He could be that kind of a leader to very, very many different groups. For him being a Satanist, I think that just may be the most extreme thing going down, to some extent. I would question whether Satanism actually is important for Vikernes.

The leaders are moving in a new direction. The basic Satanism is about to leave and change. I think they will be moving more towards classical occultic things, magic, and so on. There you have the weakness of this movement: you have strong leaders, reflective kinds of people, and they couldn't stay Satanists for twenty or thirty years. For a reflective person that's an impossibility. It is very natural that it moves on.

DO YOU THINK VIKERNES IS TRUTHFUL CLAIMING THAT THERE WAS A WHOLE STRATEGY BEHIND THE CHURCH BURNINGS?

I think he's bragging about his own influence. I don't think he has been that conscious about his own purpose. That's an advanced thought which he comes up with afterwards to justify his own intentions. Any intellectual will do that, any person with the ability to reason does that with their own history, because you have the extremely strong need as a thinking person to make meaning of what you have done, and feel that it leads forward to the point where you are standing now. It's an interesting statement, but I wouldn't trust it and I think in five years he will say something different about it again.

VIKERNES HAS NOW TAKEN UP A MILITANT ADVOCACY OF HEATHENISM AS HIS CAUSE.

I think Vikernes has been analyzing our times and thinking, what can we do to achieve something? But I also think that over the years he will find out that for us to go back to the heathen religion is very, very unrealistic. It's not going to happen if you look at the religious aspect of it. We're not going to go back to that kind of religious ritual. That is not going to happen.

They have had a very romantic notion about the extremely individualistic aspects of it—and what that does to our society—which is absolutely not accurate. What it's leading to, as I see it, is just the legitimizing of violence, lawlessness, immoral acts of any kind, and that is going to affect our culture, because a lot of movements and people think it's good to break the foundation of our society. They are capable of achieving some of that because there are many forces in our time that want to break down Christianity. The Norwegian Labor Party has been doing it for forty years, it's nothing new! It's just accelerating. That is what they are going to achieve, to break down culture, but they are not going to get back any of the heathen religion or rituals or anything else that they want to have.

HAS THERE BEEN ANY WIDESPREAD REVIVAL OF INTEREST IN HEATHENISM?

There is general interest in the Nordic religion which has been growing rapidly here over the last five years. Now we have amusement parks with whole areas devoted to just the Norwegian old religion. That's a big movement in the spiritual life of Norway, much bigger than Satanism.

THE HEATHEN IDEAS OF VIKERNES ARE TIED IN WITH QUITE A STRONG RACIAL BELIEF AS WELL.

Racism, and to legitimize racism, is becoming a big issue in our culture today—definitely the Satanists are doing that too. What they actually do is say it's okay to hate, it's a good thing, a natural thing, to hate. That is true, it *is* natural for human beings to hate.

If you look at Yugoslavia or wherever a war is going down, if you emphasize and legitimize hatred, then you get the brutal aspects of human life, like ethnic cleansing. When you legitimize hatred, then you get killing. You get people not helping each other. It's rather simple in that way.

They look upon it that we have been false, by saying we can be good or moral. They look upon that as being untruthful to human nature, and that's correct. The whole Christian project of civilization tries to say that human nature has to be put a little bit to the side—we can't build civilization if we just base it on human nature. We have to say that human nature is something bad; it's not just good things. The effect of Satanism today, to legitimize people being evil, to legitimize people hating each other—that cannot and will not help anything. That can't be good. I understand the motivations for it and the psychological aspects of it, but if they understood anything about the effects of what they are doing, they would stop doing it very fast. It's because they are naive about the effects of that mentality. I think to legitimize hatred is the most dangerous thing human beings can do, if you look at Hitler or someone similar. That's what he said—"It's okay to hate." It's okay to hate Jews. And the Serbs say it's okay to hate the Muslims. When you say that it's okay to hate someone, then you step over a borderline in your own psyche and everybody knows what happens afterward. It's not good. I think Satanism in that aspect is definitely evil in any society.

You have to believe that society as such is something very stupid which we should get away from as soon as possible, to think that Satanism can be constructive in any way. It can't be because it's not a collective thought at all. It doesn't have any concern for anything but itself... it's even worse than America!

ARE THESE SATANISTS IRREDEEMABLE?

I think in a Christian context, I would say that these Satanists are committing sins, that they do sinful actions, but I don't look upon them completely as sinners. In our culture you have a strong tradition of condemning people, and when they are condemned, then they're finished—they're out. They don't have a chance—it's not like Catholicism when you can be forgiven for what you've done. If you are declared a "Satanist" or "Nazi" in Norway, then you are that for the rest of your life, there's not a question about it. You will be condemned for the rest of your life. I hate that aspect of our culture, I really think it's a bad thing, because if we don't have an opening for forgiveness it becomes very alien to me.

I would say that's the Church to some extent, but the Satanists do it too, in the way that they condemn people and don't give them a second chance. That is not a Christian thing. Christianity is *forgiveness and mercy,* as I look upon it, based on Christian thinking. That you do one thing, but you have a second chance, a third chance, a fourth chance... That's why I look upon Satanism this way, that there are sinful actions, but there is room for forgiveness within the Church, or there should be room for forgiveness for these people and their sinful actions.

I think that's very important, the Christian foundation of looking upon them as humans and also people we should listen to instead of just saying these are shitty guys and let's just freeze them out.

CAN YOU ELABORATE MORE ON THE SPECIFIC REACTION TOWARD THEM BY THE CHURCH AND THE MEDIA?

The Church was definitely shocked and didn't expect anything like this to happen at all. When it happened, and they found out that there were Satanists behind it, they just condemned it right away and were starting to talk about the Devil, that we must be aware the Devil is always lurking in this world and that he looks for new members all the time, and that this is an act of the Devil. That was the basic Christian reaction from the Bishops.

I think in society when something like that happens it's a very good opportunity for the media. They like it because they can start a lasting soap opera with strong characters, and these Satanic groups. The media embraced it to a certain extent, and made it really big in Norway. Of course it *was* big, but I would say that the media capitalized on it, because it was something extreme, new, and specifically Norwegian. For them to sell newspapers, they treat it as extremely as possible. Very early on the media started to define them as total extremists, the same way they might look upon the neo-Nazi movement. They defined them as that right away; then they had them there and they can look upon them like animals doing strange things, and they can report it like something that is very different from the rest of our society. I think it's untrue to view them that way, but that is the mechanism that the media and society make, because it's a shock for them. They don't understand where the Satanists are coming from, they don't understand what they want, and then they isolate them as a group. But of course that doesn't help them in any way—it has the opposite effect, that many youngsters find it a taboo and it becomes extremely interesting.

They are resourceful people, many of them—Vikernes is a good example of that, Ihsahn is also an example. Black Metal is not like the neo-Nazis, either, who have a kind of magnetic effect on the weak people, the outsiders. It's not like that.

WHY DOES BLACK METAL ATTRACT THESE MORE RESOURCEFUL TYPES OF YOUTH?

I think there is a culture in Norway around the collective dream of society. Everything is a collective dream, which is quite reminiscent of the foundation of communism. I think in Ihsahn's case he didn't like this at all.

This is something that's important—individualism in Norway has been held down. That has happened. If you are different in school, or very good for example, or very intelligent, that becomes a problem for you. We don't accept people with exceptional gifts or anything like that. In England or the U.S., you have schools for these kind of youngsters, you send them somewhere else, and say, "You are different, go over there." We don't have that. Everything is supposed to fit in, in a classroom of twenty-five or thirty people. If you are too weak or too healthy, or if you're too good, you're supposed to shut up. It's mediocrity.

Satanism then, for these people, starts as a purpose against this pattern. It's the exceptional people who actually feel this the most! People with great resources and intellectual strength who actually feel that the system has been holding them down. They've been oppressed because they have special gifts, and that's true. We have been doing that. We don't like people like that in Norway. That's one important aspect in Norwegian society, and because of that when it boils over it becomes very extreme because the hatred toward the mediocrity is so strong that when it breaks free then the results are that much more extreme.

Then they run into what we have with nature. We have a very special relationship to nature, a very close one. And during the Christian period this thing with nature has been suppressed—nature is not good, nature is "evil," so to speak. Norwegians interact with nature and are very closely connected to it, just due to the way the country itself is formed. So they go to nature and start to get these kinds of powerful emotions and relationships.

I think if they had done strategic and really bright analysis they could have learned something much greater about this, about Norwegians having a special relationship to nature. The Satanists could have done this much better, if their

goal was to create a broad movement for going back to nature and also back to the heathen religion. If these deep-souled figures of strength like Vikernes had done that at that time they could have made something really big in Norwegian society. But I don't think that was what they wanted.

DID THEIR ACTIONS MANAGE TO HAVE ANY EFFECT ON SOCIETY?

In 1995 in Norway you had a very strong movement toward religion—towards Christianity and towards the New Age kinds of things—everybody is going into religion now. I was just writing an article about the Labor Party, which actually has just now become positive toward having more Christianity in schools. They've spent fifty years after the war bringing down Christianity, and for the first time they're saying now that we need more Christianity in the schools. It shows the times have changed. Maybe we have become conscious to some extent about the Christian culture when people start to burn down our churches—maybe, you can't rule that out. It's possible that when we see that in this country people are burning churches down then we have to make a statement against that.

I'm doubtful that the Satanism has had any great affect on society, but I could be wrong. I don't know what people actually do or think all the time...

DO YOU THINK IT WILL CONTINUE? IS THERE AN IMPETUS FOR IT TO KEEP HAPPENING?

It's not going to succeed in any way in Norwegian society, but it's definitely going to go on for some years. That's possible. I think they're going to need strength, mostly because it has become somewhat normal now. When you burn down churches it's not a big sensation anymore, we're kind of used to it that they burn down churches sometimes.

I don't think it's going to get stronger; I think it will get weaker, and it's going to move from Satanism into magic or these kind of things. The New Age religious movement is growing in Norway, and it becomes kind of linked together with those kinds of powers and occultic interests. I think they can grow in that way but then they won't be Satanists anymore, they'll be something else. That's where the strong people are going to go, and you will get some mutated expressions of Satanism in the future.

If you are talking about what can survive from Satanism, I think the dramatic part will—the very interesting visual aspects, the drama. That aspect, as we see it now, that people make these huge performances, that they have roles they play. This drama aspect is going to survive as a religious phenomenon, it's going to go on and I think it could be extreme and very interesting, but it's not going to remain as Satanism.

IS THERE A SPECIFIC REASON FOR THAT?

The reason Satanism eventually will not last is because it doesn't bring any-thing, or give anything back. Destruction doesn't give anything back. It kind of wears itself out, because what do you get back from thinking or being like that?

GIVING THE DEVIL MORE THAN HIS DUE

Asbjørn Dyrendal is a Research Fellow at the Department of Cultural Studies at the University in Oslo. He has been primarily researching the new and emergent religions, especially Wicca. He has also done considerable investigation into the hysteria that has been running rampant in the Norwegian and foreign media about a Satanic conspiracy. Dyrendal has summarized his findings in a fas-cinating article entitled "Media Constructions of 'Satanism' in Norway (1988–1997)" where he offers a chronology of the shifting manner in which the Satan scare was presented there by the press.

According to Dyrendal, the horrifying tales of cult conspiracies and Satanic ritual abuse arrived in Norway a few years after their explosion in the tabloid press of America and Britain. The Norwegian State Church had addressed Satanism as a problem in its annual Bishops' Conferences dating back to the late '70s, but it was generally considered a small aspect of the general growth of New Age and occult trends in spirituality. Satanism per se was not a grave threat.

Satanism hit the newspaper headlines in the summer of 1988, beginning with a few oddball stories of alleged groups of Satanists gathering in small towns. In one case a pair of brothers stole items from a church, threat-ened people, and engaged in "worshipping Satan at midnight dances."[6] In another case a small Satanic ritual site was discovered dur-ing a drug bust. Concern was expressed by journalists and Christian commentators over the availability of Anton LaVey's *Satanic Bible* in Norwegian bookstores (the book had been published in Danish, and the English edition also had international distribution), a theme which would resurface during the Black Metal hysteria years later.

In 1990 reports of Satanic ritual abuse exploded in the press. The hoopla was bolstered by statements from Willy Kobbhaug, a police lieutenant on the Oslo Vice Squad, who told the press he had evidence indicating criminal Satanic activity was becoming prevalent in Norway and was the object of serious investigation by the police. These revelations were met with skepticism from certain quarters (the "Satanic abuse conspiracy" tales having been widely debunked in America by that time), but regardless the media continued to describe disparate "Satanic" crimes in the context of an organized movement. In the heat of the hysteria about Satanic groups operating in Norway, the occult society the Ordo Templi Orientis was also accused of involvement in sacrifices and other criminal activity, but none of these allegations were ever proven, nor were they taken seriously by most in the police departments.

In his article, Dyrendal explains how the Satanic ritual abuse stories eventually dissipated, only to be replaced by the arrival of Black Metal to the headlines in 1993. He writes:

> The main image of and debate on Satanism was being made by the sudden, high visibility of teenagers, mostly aged 15-18 years old (but ranging from 14 to 25), who were playing with the identity of being evil. Sometimes they would claim to be Nazis, sometimes Satanists, sometimes Odinists, and at other points they would refuse any label other than "evil," spouting statements such as: "We're not Nazis. The Nazis only hated the Jews, we hate everyone." "We're not racists, we want all people to suffer." "If our music causes people to commit suicide, that's good. It weeds out the weak." The reason they got the opportunity to go on the record with this philosophy, was that some of them also acted: some attacked people, most attacked property—by desecrating graveyards and burning churches. ... During the period of 1991-1993, several people were beaten, some stabbed, at least one girl (15) was raped, allegedly by two 17-year-old arsonists, of which one was convicted of a lesser charge), and two people were murdered.[7]

Dyrendal notes the media served to create the impression of a large-scale Satanic assault on Christians in Norway. It is no surprise that this in turn sparked a fearful response from both the police and the Church, which in many instances may have been warranted:

> In some places the interest in alleged ritual sites approached panic reactions, where anything unusual could be interpreted as signs of Satanist activity. The drive towards action was even larger among some churchgoers. Police and congregations several times kept nightly watch over their churches—with variable success. Some of these churches were burned down at later dates, when watchfulness was down. Not all were as conscientious as 67-year-old Victor Andersson, priest in the Trinity Church in Oslo. According to Aftenposten (6/8/93), he armed himself with an axe and kept watch in the sacristy at night: "If we are to survive as a cultured nation, society has to strike back at these plebeians (pøbelveldet)," said Andersson...[8]

After a period of sensationalist coverage, the media approached the Black Metal phenomenon in a more serious manner. A few different theories have been advanced as to why it took hold in Norway, some of which have already been presented in the interviews in this book. These theories range from negative cultural influences via music, role-playing games, and occultism, to criticisms leveled at the Church for its inability to reach out to youth in a manner capable of sustaining their attention. Some in the Church believed they must become more aggressive in their dealings with young people, and Dyrendal even mentions one conservative priest who wanted to bring back the practice of exorcism. Despite the varying proposed solutions to the problem, there was no doubt of the consensus that something was gravely wrong.

What is particularly fascinating about Dyrendal's study is how it implicates the media. By printing lurid stories which highlighted gruesome (and undocumented) allegations about Satanic practices, the tabloid papers may have helped create the atmosphere for real-life criminal behavior that would later unfold. Dyrendal's research would seem to partially vindicate Simen Midgaard's theory that the original exposés on Satanic cults in 1990–91 provided the blueprint for the ideology of Norwegian Satanism that would develop in the Black Metal scene.

ASBJØRN DYRENDAL

HAS NORWAY IMPORTED AMERICAN STEREOTYPES ABOUT SATANISM?

If you look at the Norwegian media, there is not much written about Satanism before 1988 or '89. Then some reports started turning up, almost exclusively about youth Satanists. There was a police raid on a nest of Satanists in Halden in which some rather down-and-out people were arrested.

[The "nest" Dyrendal refers to was uncovered during a drug raid that took place in southeast Norway. It contained an altar adorned with a picture of Baphomet, "ritual" knives, a skull, and tarot cards. The group consisted of people 16–30 years of age. Some of them were arrested for possession of marijuana.]

BUT THESE PEOPLE IN HALDEN HAD NOTHING TO DO WITH BLACK METAL, CORRECT? THEY SEEMED TO BE MORE INTERESTED IN DRUGS.

Yes, and one of them, a girl who claimed to have had the name "Lucifer" within the group, later turned up in the conservative Christian newspaper *Dagen*. She came out as having been born again. A year later, she was in the same paper again, saying that Satanists pray to Satan to crush the powerful

Evangelical awakening in the border areas near to Sweden. These rumors seem to come from Evangelical circles in that country. And even though all of this really has nothing to do with Black Metal, it is interesting to note that the Black Metal culture later grew very strong in these parts of the country.

Apart from this rather sad coven, there were only some teenagers out in the countryside that were involved in Satanism. Then in 1990 and 1991, figures like Fred Harrison and Dianne Core came into the picture. Fred Harrison is a free-lance journalist for the major Norwegian tabloid *Dagbladet*. He interviewed some English psychologists, psychiatrists, and "child-rescuers" about Satanism. As a result, on August 11, 1990, *Dagbladet* had a headline about Satanists eating babies and doing other abominable things. The year after, all this was repeated in the media by Willy Kobbhaug. Kobbhaug claimed to have seen similar cases in Norway. I have been told that he had recently come from a police seminar in the Netherlands where he had heard these stories.

Many of the Satanic survivor stories in Norway come from Christian sub-cultures. In Harrison and Core's book *Chasing Satan* there is an abortion scenario that is reinterpreted, within a very Christian framework, as a sacrifice to Satan.

THIS SOUNDS LIKE WHAT IS CALLED A "BREEDER" STORY, IN WHICH THE SINISTER SATANIC CONSPIRATORS IMPREGNATE WOMEN TO PRODUCE BABIES WHO WILL LATER BE SACRIFICED TO THE DEVIL.

Yes, and it is part of an older myth, which dates back to the '60s and early '70s. In Sweden there was a "Satanic survivor" story in the '70s. A woman claimed to have been a victim of a Satanic cult, and have been forced to participate in child sacrifice. The police didn't find anything back then either.

After being supplied with these stories, the police and media started looking for Satanic cults that would fit this image. In typical fashion, the Ordo Templi Orientis was singled out, simply because they were visible. The O.T.O. is estab-lished in Norway, unlike the Church of Satan, Temple of Set, or other real Satanic organizations.

The police and press didn't find the cults they were looking for. What they did eventually find, though, were caves with inverted crosses, stolen tombstones, and so on. In other words: Black Metal culture. They then tried to project this cult stereotype that they got from Kobbhaug onto what they found. It didn't work.

WILLY KOBBHAUG [INTERVIEWED IN AUGUST, 1997—NO LONGER WORKING IN THE VICE DIVISION OF THE OSLO POLICE]

How did you first discover these stories?

I was involved with building up the child section of the Oslo Police Department. As a result, I got into contact with specialists working with children, some of them on seminars abroad. I wrote an article in the Oslo Police Dept.'s internal magazine in 1989 about these things. *Dagbladet* newspaper used some of this material and the ensuing rabble made me not write any more on the subject.

But police abroad like the Scotland Yard, that have been investigating similar allegations, have not come up with any evidence.

The problem with finding witnesses in these kinds of cases is that many of them have difficulty distinguishing fantasy and reality. Most of them are psychiatric cases. One might ask why they are so—is it because they have been subjected to quite horrible things?

Do you think an organized network of Satanists who sacrifice children exists?

I intended to have evidence for this back then. I haven't followed it in the later years, so I don't know exactly how things are now. There is an organized Satanic network. But I don't think they sacrifice children. Norway is a country with few people, and they are easy to keep track of. Children just don't disappear like they would have to for this to be true.

Asbjørn Dyrendal

Did the Black Metal scene mimic the images of Satanism that were presented by the media?

This is an interesting phenomenon where people try to emulate the stories that are circulating. There you had a lot of young people who wanted to be Satanists. Where could they hear about what you do when you're a Satanist? They had to get it through the media and Christian sources. They got the myths, and they tried as best as they could, by their rather modest means, to live up to them. You can see that in the early interviews with Varg Vikernes. There were situations where the journalists were trying to see this in light of the stories supplied by Kobbhaug, and where Vikernes played the appropriate role. He was hinting that many people disappear each year, that these might have been killed, and then said that he cannot comment on who was doing the killings. When asked if he has killed anyone: "I can't talk about that." He was building up to get the question of whether he had killed anyone, and then denying it in a manner which implied the opposite.

WHAT ABOUT THE CASE OF THE TEENAGER THAT DISAPPEARED IN TØNSBERG?

There is a lot of exaggeration in this case. That is understandable, given the fact that he was a priest's son and obsessed with the occult. According to one story, he checked the number on the electricity meter in his home and discovered that it had three sixes in it. That would suggest a certain interest. The police don't know what happened. He may have killed himself, which seems the most probable given how kids that age behave. But since it is an unsolved case, it remains open for speculation. His family tried to resolve it by hiring a private investigator, but the investigator didn't come up with much.

WHERE DID THE BLACK METAL WORLDVIEW, IF YOU CAN CALL IT THAT, COME FROM?

You draw from the cultural resources that are at your disposal. Vikernes was very fond of telling people that he read LaVey and Crowley. However, what he has come out with in interviews indicates that he hasn't understood it all very well.

Inverting cultural values seems to be the easiest way out in devising a rebellious ideology. Quotes like: "We are not racists, we hate everyone," "We are not Nazis—Hitler only wanted to kill the Jews, we want everyone to suffer," indicate both a need for opposition and use of the resources that are present. I wouldn't call it a worldview, but more a relative self-identity, very dependent on the situation. There is little to indicate, judging from interviews with their parents, families, etc., that this is an identity they have taken with them into everything they have done.

This group identity seems to have been internal from an early stage. It was directed towards the other members of the inner circle. It was not aimed at the rest of society before Vikernes. He was the one that actively solicited the media, the great publicity whore.

SOME OF THESE PEOPLE SEEM TO HAVE LIVED A KIND OF DOUBLE LIFE. ONE MOMENT THEY HAVE BEEN HAVING A NICE DINNER WITH THEIR MOTHERS, THE NEXT THEY ARE OUT BURNING CHURCHES AND KILLING PEOPLE...

To immerse yourself into a total lifestyle takes a lot of time. Most of the Black Metal people were young, still in their teens. Much of the criminal activity has been spontaneous, which is typical of juvenile delinquency. People have to remember that if you are as shoplifter or are violent, it isn't necessarily apparent that you are a criminal. Crime is something that you do on the side, unless you have a career based around it.

Do you think that the media has been fanning the flames in the case of the Black Metal crimewave?

I didn't think so initially. After talking to a good amount of journalists and people that have been working with Vikernes's trial, I have changed my mind. "Street cred" is very important in youth subcultures. The mass media was invaluable for Vikernes in building his street cred. The media allowed him to build a near-mythological image of himself.

You can also see it in statements from people in the Black Metal scene itself where they say that everything got really wild after the mass media had started focusing on this. The media then threw gasoline on the fire, in that the coverage intensified the internal struggle for being the dominant personality. It is true that subcultures like the Black Metal scene have an internal dynamic that will operate without regard for the outside world. In this case, I think media may have played a larger role than is usual because the attention these people got was so massive.

Why have young people been attracted to this?

It has elements of dark mysticism in the music, it has a mythological dimension in the link to the Viking Age, and so on. The music has a very aggressive force, and in the wake of listening to it you experience the feeling of identifying with it. That is a very powerful thing. If you are an adolescent, you are in a period of your life where it is impossible for you to exert influence upon your surroundings. Being able to hate and feel strong can be very liberating. This is much of the same power that lay in other forms of Metal and in Punk.

The Black Metal image is also appealing to people who are a bit of an outcast, or feel like outsiders. The Black Metal uniform sends very strong signals, especially after people have started associating these outfits with very powerful and scary things. It has passed the point where people point at you and laugh, and reached the point where people shy away from you.

Let's not forget the biological dimension either, with hormones running amok.

There have been two major theories among the people that have been working with the Black Metal thing in the media. One has been that modern, secular society has created an atmosphere where all moral and ethical limits have been destroyed. Now that things have gone so far that it has produced Black Metal, it is time to draw some lines. The other has been that Black Metal is the result of all other symbols of rebellion having been used up. Almost every form of shocking behavior will only make your parents say, "Well, we did that when we were young too." So, to get a shock effect, you have to go much further in your symbolism. Personally, I think these explanations are a bit simplistic.

A LOT OF THIS HAS FUNCTIONED ON A MYTHOLOGICAL LEVEL, AS WELL.

I think Vikernes is interesting in that he has been able to create a myth around himself, a myth that has made other people try to emulate his actions. I don't think he is very interesting as a person.

HE SEEMS TO HAVE BEEN ABLE TO SET HIMSELF UP AS A SYMBOL FOR SOME-THING THAT IS FAR GREATER THAN HIMSELF, AND ALMOST EVERYTHING THAT NORWEGIAN SOCIETY FINDS ABHORRENT: SATANISM, RACISM, NAZISM, MURDER, BURNING SACRED OBJECTS, ETC.

I am of the opinion that most people see Vikernes as a rather pathetic figure—someone with delusions of grandeur who is only able to function within this self-created image.

Kjetil Wiedswang is a Norwegian journalist who is also very skeptical of the way the media handled the Satanic hysteria that was imported to Norway in the early 1990s. He also argues that sensationalist media coverage conceivably made Satanism look glamorous and far more important than it really was, thereby attracting people to it:

> There is obviously an interaction between the media and people who do things. This is especially clear in the case of terrorism. In many cases the whole point of the terrorist act is to get media coverage—if nobody wrote about it, there wouldn't be a point in doing it.
>
> It is hard to prove that people were attracted to the Black Metal scene because of Satanic scare headlines, especially so because the models for how people are affected by the media get more and more complicated each time they are revised. One no longer believes that people automatically emulate whatever they see in movies and read in books, but still, the idea that media has some level of influence over people seems reasonable.

Wiedswang realizes the dilemma inherent to news coverage of sensational activities, especially those which are based on mere hearsay. As he explains:

Journalists cannot be forced to always take into account the consequences of their stories when they write, because the alternative to an unrestricted press—censorship—would be much worse. The problem with the Satanism coverage in the '90s wasn't that the newspapers were writing about it, it was the way they were writing about it. They should have had a much better guard against urban legends slipping into their material, especially since the big Satanic scares in England and the U.S. were so recent.

As a journalist, you can never really know, and this was the case with the Satanic stories too. People do a lot of weird things. But the stories, and the way they were presented, should've smacked too much of the story of the "Evil Brotherhood" for a good journalist. The myth of the outwardly respectable, even upstanding, citizens that go out at night to do terrible things to children has been around for thousands of years and has been levelled at Christians, Jews, Catholics, Protestants, heretics, Freemasons, and lots of other groups. It was then recycled by horror writers, who fictionalized the material. It now seems to be influencing reality again. One account of "ritual abuse" I have read seems to have been lifted directly from *Rosemary's Baby,* one of the great horror classics.

Another issue is that people who present these kind of "victim" stories maybe should be protected from themselves. One such story that was printed concerned a woman, an obvious mental case, who described having had a forced abortion in Oslo in the '60s. The atrocity took place in an open back yard centrally located in Oslo, as she was surrounded by men in black robes. But when people started checking the date, it turned out that this coincided with a bombing spree in which a mysterious bomber left grenades with tripwires in public places. As a result, the city was in a state of panic, with everyone looking out for suspicious activity. So it doesn't seem very credible.

BÅRD EITHUN

HOW SERIOUS WAS THE SATANISM FOR YOU?

For a few people it was bloody serious, but to a lot of them it was all a big hype. I had been interested in Satanism but there are other things as well. Basically, I don't give a shit.

DIDN'T YOU TRY TO CONTACT THE O.T.O.?

Yes, that's true. I contacted them once, just to check out what it was. But I doubt it was anything for me. They are beyond this good/evil shit, I like that, but it becomes a little too obscure for me.

SIMEN MIDGAARD HAS A THEORY THAT SENSATIONALISTIC NEWSPAPER ARTICLES ABOUT THE O.T.O. INFLUENCED THE BLACK METAL SCENE.

That might be true. I remember in the late '80s there was much writing about this in the Norwegian newspapers, about secret cults and sacrifices. I thought that people might have been influenced by this, because it creates a very mysterious atmosphere and people want be the ones who the papers are writing about.

THE *KERRANG!* ARTICLE DID THE SAME THING.

After this issue was released the other guys got really enthusiastic about it, because it meant that we got a lot of attention.

IT SEEMS TO ME *KERRANG!* CREATED A LOT OF THE PROBLEM, WITH KIDS IN ENGLAND BEING INSPIRED TO COMMIT CRIMES AFTER THAT FIRST ARTICLE.

That's true. Actually this happened in Norway as well, because after our arrests, and the media mentioning this, we saw there were many kids attracted to the scene. Most of the churches that are burned today are done by kids who got into it after our arrests. You could say that the media is making all this so big.

HOW CONNECTED DO YOU STILL FEEL TO EVERYTHING?

I'm part of the underground scene which existed when I was free. I'm not part of the one that exists now.

In the end of October, 1997, Willy Kobbhaug was charged with exposing himself to a 15-year-old, and therefore underage, neighboring girl. He had been standing in his own garden while the girl's parents videotaped what was going on. The 52-year-old Kobbhaug confessed to the affair, and was suspended from his position. Ironically, Kobbhaug lives in Kløfta, the same town where Bård "Faust" is incarcerated.

In the years that passed since the Satanic scare in the media, Kobbhaug had built up a considerable reputation as an expert on sexual abuse, both in Norway and abroad. In a strange twist, the police confiscated around ten firearms in a closet in his house. These guns could be linked to criminal activities; one was stolen in Oslo, and another was stolen from the Kripos headquarters in 1977.

The police claim to be able to document that Kobbhaug exposed himself to the teenage girl on five or six occasions. The documentation is exceptionally good on the last occasion, the act having been captured on videotape. Some debate was sparked when his attorney speculated in the media that it was his work with abused children which may have turned him on to such activities. This caused an outcry from other policemen, who felt that these speculations stigmatized them as well.

Kobbhaug is also charged with a separate case of indecent exposure against another even younger girl in 1995. These cases have triggered a series of assertions from people in his neighborhood alleging that Kobbhaug exposed himself on other occasions, with some of the incidents dating as far back as twenty years. If that is true, then it is hard to take seriously the explanation that Kobbhaug's behavior was caused by trauma at work since these cases then would predate his involvement in this type of crime.

If convicted, Kobbhaug will probably get off with a moderate fine. But Whether Kobbhaug is guilty or not, it seems reasonable to think that he has his own demons to fight against.

THE HIGH PRIEST SPEAKS

In uncovering the expressions of Satanism in Black Metal, evidence reveals two quite distinct viewpoints. Many of those involved have also shifted their outlook over time from one to the other, as they gained insight and maturity. The crude Satanism is found in the caricatures of "Devil worship," black magic, and occultism presented by bands like Venom and Bathory, which is still perpetuated by the lower-brow echelon of music groups and fans. This is the ideology that may have been actively fostered and unwittingly encouraged by the media hysteria about Satanic cults and ritual sacrifices which entered Norwegian headlines in the nascent days of Black Metal.

There is a stark contrast between these views and the comments of musicians like Ihsahn or the members of Ulver. It is possible they may have started out in the "Devil worship" camp, but if so they have progressed far beyond those views. The ideas they express now are quite in line with the "official" Satanic doctrines as promulgated by Anton Szandor LaVey, the notorious founder and High Priest of the Church of Satan, who died in October, 1997.

There have only been a handful of Metal groups with direct ties to LaVey's church over the years (King Diamond being one of the more outspoken), although in recent times this has begun to change. LaVey was himself a musician, specializing in lost or obscure songs of ages past, but he often mentioned a personal distaste for Rock and other modern music in interviews. This might have alienated some musicians—who otherwise exemplify LaVey's philosophy—from any public allegiance with the Church of Satan. In reality, LaVey understood fully why a genre like Black Metal has appeal for youth, though he may not had have much interest in the cacophony of the music itself.

As Ihsahn mentions, members of the Scandinavian Black Metal crowd attacked LaVey's philosophy in the past, although this was more common a few years ago. The standard reason for their dislike of the Church of Satan was its alleged "humanist" values. This seems to have been rooted primarily in ignorance, and a desire to draw attention for themselves as being more extreme than the recognized "official

Satanists." The Black Metalers are also quite mistaken if they believe LaVey is merely a humanist. Even a cursory study of LaVey's actual writings will uncover his
unabashed misanthropy and derisive scorn for the follies of humankind.

To understand LaVey's genuine opinions—both regarding his definition of
Satanism, as well as his views on music such as Black Metal—we spoke with him
directly. The following comments are compiled from interviews done with LaVey
and his Secretary/Biographer Blanche Barton in 1994 and 1996. They form a fitting conclusion for our analysis of Satanism, particularly in relation to the phenomenon of Black Metal. LaVey dispels many erroneous notions about Satanism
which have arisen in the wake of events in Norway and elsewhere, but by the same
token his conclusions and predictions paint an ominous future role for music to
pave the way toward a Satanic society.

Anton Szandor LaVey and Blanche Barton

What are your feelings about Black Metal and how some of the people involved may have misrepresented Satanism?

LaVey: I don't know to what extent they misrepresent Satanism, since I only
hear a limited amount of news about them. But as far the philosophy of genuine
Satanism is concerned, all I did was write a book that explains it primitively. If
someone wants to understand Satanism, they can get the book through a friend,
or track a copy down themselves—it's been available for almost thirty years
now!—or find a spokesman of the Church of Satan to enlighten them. But really
you need the book, it's a primer which codifies contemporary Satanism. Many of
the so-called Black Metal "Satanists" appear to me as essentially Christians—
they're defining Satanism by Christian standards.

Barton: They buy into the Christian definition of Satanism which Doctor
LaVey smashed in 1966.

LaVey: That was the first time it had been demonstrated in such a way. A lot
of people had tried to give it exposure, as Devil's advocates—writers like Twain
and Nietzsche—but none had codified it as a religion, a belief system.

How much was your interpretation of Satanism influenced by the Zeitgeist of the '60s?

LaVey: The hippies lit a fire under me, because it was so close at hand, the
last straw. Everyone was trying to get me to drop acid and join in. Push came to
shove and I decided there had to be an alternative.

They were championing "Jesus Christ Superstar," love and peace, while exalt-
ing the lowest classes of humanity. I interpreted it as the last burp, the last days of

COLLAGE OF ANTON LAVEY BY PETER H. GILMORE

Christianity. I didn't do anything consciously, it just developed. But I saw there were enough people out there to marshal it into something that was to become the Church of Satan, and the tracts I was writing at the time evolved into the *Satanic Bible.*

HOW DID YOU FORMULATE THE IDEAS THAT BECAME THE TENETS OF SATANISM?

LAVEY: In the case of the "Nine Satanic Statements," it took me twenty minutes to write them out. I was listening to Chopin being played in the next room and I was so moved I just wrote them out on a pad of paper lying next to me. The crux of the philosophy of Satanism can be found in the "Satanic Rules of the Earth," "Pentagonal Revisionism," and the "Nine Satanic Sins," of which of course "stupidity" is tantamount, closely followed by "pretentiousness." Often pretentiousness comes in the form of so-called "independent thinkers" that have a knee-jerk reaction to any association with us.

As far as Satanists are concerned, taking the way things are and taking what suits you best and dwelling on it—that's what it is all about. Religion should be about what's most important in your life and recognizing that. For example, today I just wrote something about my favorite cars. Satanism is above all concerned with earthly indulgence. These Black Metal guys want to concentrate on death and destroying themselves—there's nothing self-indulgent about that!

BARTON: For some people Satanism is their life, their fetish, but the real Satanists *use and apply it* to what they enjoy.

LAVEY: It sounds like there's a lot of stupid people in Norway too, like any country. But the intelligent people are capable of responding if they receive the right information—again, it's all about communication. We get more mail from Russia than ever, now that the Soviet Union is gone. They've been under atheist control for so long and the new religious "freedom" is pushing bullshit they can't swallow. They almost yearn for the good old days of Soviet atheism... like "the South will rise again!"

WOULD YOU CONCEDE THE BLACK METAL CROWD JUST REPRESENT A DIFFERENT BRAND OF SATANISM?

LAVEY: That's not the way it's intended, but they're entitled to their own opinions. But if they say theirs is the *right* way, then they are acting even more like Christians.

BARTON: You have to keep all this in perspective—there simply was no legitimate, codified form of Satanism before the Church of Satan was formed.

LAVEY: Generally when one these "self-styled Satanists" actually finds out what the Church of Satan is all about, they change over and ally themselves with us. A lot of them are kids and they like the name Satan just as they might be attracted to a swastika and the colors red and black. The whole thing can be summed up by Occam's Razor. Communication is the key. They simply don't have the proper medium to find out what Satanism is all about.

HAS TELEVISION SENSATIONALISM DONE A LOT TO SPREAD FALSE CONCEPTIONS ABOUT SATANISM?

LaVey: Well, if you see one of these tabloid talkshows, they'll have someone on who's screaming about their kids being sacrificed, going on for twenty minutes about it, and one of our people will have forty seconds of airtime to counter that. Now, if a representative of the Church of Satan had just one entire hour on national TV to say what we want to say, Christianity would be finished. But as it is you've got academics on the one hand who dismiss us, and then the hysterics on the other who claim we're taking over everything.

MANY FEAR A STRONG CONNECTION BETWEEN SATANISM AND SOME FORMS OF FASCISM. IS THERE ANY TRUTH TO THIS?

BARTON: It's an unholy alliance. Many different types of such people have made contact with us in the past. The anti-Christian strength of National Socialist Germany is part of the appeal to Satanists—the drama, the lighting, the choreography with which they moved millions of people. However, the Satanic attitude is that people should be judged by their own merit—in every race there are leaders and followers. Satanists are the "Others," who will push the pendulum in the direction it needs to go to reset the balance—depending on circumstances, this could be toward fascism or in the opposite direction. Satanism is a very brutal, realistic way of looking at things sometimes. Let it stand or fall on its own merit as Doctor LaVey wrote it.

LaVey: Aesthetics more than anything else are the common ground between Satanism and fascism. The aesthetics of National Socialism and Satanism dovetail.

BARTON: They were aware of pomp, drama, fear...

LaVey: The aesthetics of Satanism are those of National Socialism. There's the power of romance and drama. The National Socialists had that drama, coupled with the romance of overcoming such incredible odds. Satan is a standard to fight under, you're flying the colors. I believe in Satanism as colors you're fighting under. *Esprit d'Corps.* Mayakovsky did a beautiful poem about reactions to a Soviet passport—you know you represent something that's feared. There's awe, it's controversial, like the SS experienced when going into a cabaret—everyone shuts up. There's something magical about the concept—frightening evil and taking pride in being that. It's a hard act to follow, in a sense that *calm self-recognition of one's own nature* is the ultimate evil.

BARTON: In every culture there's the Prometheus figure—that's essential in the human spirit. Those who are on the borderlands, the magicians.

LaVey: I get gut reactions to the stupid bravado of assholes. It's fear—they're threatened. I realize it's wonderful, that I should upset them that much.

Are hatred or anger important emotions to a Satanist?

BARTON: Satanists have the posture of true anger against a god that allows tragedy. We would stand in eternal defiance to such a "god."

LaVey: I can empathize with Varg Vikernes burning a church down. People's prejudices get the best of them—I'll plead guilty to feeling that way at times. There are a lot of people whose greatest purpose is for target practice—moving targets.

What is your response to Black Metal types who would accuse you of forsaking any real occultism or "black magic" in your philosophy of Satanism?

LaVey: The Church of Satan acknowledges the potential of ritual magic and its practice, but there is also something else besides this. These people obsessed with occultism—who I call "occultniks"—can't conceive of pragmatism being hand-in-hand with magic. We're too practical for people who are looking for "the key." This is where these types are missing the boat. There's no rationalism, no grounding. We are the ones wielding the power—Satan has become ruler of the earth. Our image of Satan demands not worship but skepticism and rational inquiry.

In our personal practice of Satanism, there is no limit to the supernatural you can put into it. You can do anything you want. Some can consider their performance on stage a ritual—a very powerful one—for whatever purpose. I advocate that. An emotionally-charged Rock concert performed by dedicated Satanists is today's rally, ritual, and call to arms.

BARTON: The occultniks want supernaturalism to be their fetish. We certainly believe in elements of the supernatural. We're tapping into these forces everyday.

From some of your writings it appears that you're not too fond of the Rock and Roll genre. Why is that?

LaVey: First you need to tell me what it is. How can someone say, "I don't like Rock and Roll", because *what is it?* It's never been defined. There's so much that's fallen under that general heading, but I guess it then evolved into what we have now, which I've described as being like a linear metronome, i.e., music without *music.* They've just run out of ideas, really.

Is Rock, as it stands today, a hopeless form as far as you're concerned?

LaVey: The biggest point I'm stressing is that kids are being born into a default situation where there are no good alternatives. They don't know about any other form of music *besides* Rock. All music for young people emanates from that particular culture. But I would say it's not hopeless because it does still have impact to those who don't know about any other form of music.

IN WHAT WAY?

LaVey: I believe it's really the visuals that are what matters now. Not MTV images but rather the record sleeves. There's a visual identification. Just like if it were Nazi-oriented music and the artwork has a swastika on the jacket, if it's Satanic there's going to be Satanic imagery on the package. And you can clearly see a tendency toward the Satanic, especially within the Heavy Metal genre of Rock. That creates a strong differentiation between something like Black Metal and other Rock music, and it's an alternative for these kids. They're going to opt for the Satanic whether it's the lyrics or the visuals; they want to tap into that option. That's what matters. So kids who don't know anything besides Rock music can still gain strength and motivation from Black Metal, Death Metal, and so forth.

THE CHURCH OF SATAN DOESN'T DISCOURAGE THESE PEOPLE FROM JOINING?

LaVey: No, not at all. From our correspondence we know there are a lot of people who are stimulated by this kind of music and after that they want to explore Satanism more seriously, as a philosophy.

In a strong sense the enemy, Christianity, has created a Frankenstein monster by drawing so much attention to this music, because the kids will go for the dark stuff every time! There are entire fanzines dedicated to Satanic Black Metal, exclusively. It follows that if the market is moving towards Satanic Rock then you'll have two camps emerging—those who are just stimulated and then those who decide they want to pursue the ideas we're promoting. Just as there are those who will raise the sign of the horns at a Metal concert not knowing why they're doing it, there are many who do it and *understand...*

SOME MUSIC GROUPS HAVE OPENLY ENDORSED THE CHURCH OF SATAN. ARE THEY REACHING AN AUDIENCE THAT'S POTENTIALLY VALUABLE TO YOU?

LaVey: The majority of their audience are not just numbskulls, and the reason they go for these bands is because they're the *real thing*. There's a whole camp who want that. We hear every day from people who are only devoted to the groups who *practice what they preach*.

Barton: And these letters are so fervent... they want the music to be more blasphemous, more violent against Christianity, with no compromise and no holding back. You could say the music is almost an updated version of the "Horst

Wessel Lied" for them—it's providing that sort of motivation and focus. So many kids write and say, "I got into Satanism because of this music—it makes me feel powerful."

LaVey: It's the sound of the world for them. That's their threshold—if they don't go anywhere with it then it's just noise but if they go to the next step... these are their tools. What else do they have to work with? Pride is a part of it too; they don't want to be ostracized from their colleagues.

What are the essential ingredients that make a piece of music Satanic?

LaVey: The key element of Satanic music can be revealed in the question, will it appeal to you on an individual rather than herd basis? It's evocative, emotionally charged. It evokes something which wasn't previously hyped and it's done without forcing the cards. There's no group or collective identity which it merely confers on the listener. It shouldn't be a secondary device to tap into an identity associated with the music. Satanic music stands on its own merit without one knowing who wrote it or where and when it came from. Simplistically speaking, it's the kind of music you can walk away whistling or humming—thematic.

Why is the Satanic music you're defining dangerous?

LaVey: Because Satanic music will cause introspection and get someone to think, and even worse—*to feel*. The more they think and feel the more dangerous they are to a system dependent on consumerism and mass conformity.

Most kids would probably tell you the only Satanic music is Heavy Metal, or Black Metal.

LaVey: This is the real horror of it all: they're listening to something akin to a jet blasting off and are motivated by what it *says*, spelled out loud and clear. They're moved by it, and they're truly militant. Now comes the real threat: supposing we drop the megaton bomb, and they hear—and listen to—music hyped as Satanic that has the sound of Wagner or Liszt or Beethoven? Suppose they're bombarded with that kind of stirring sound, packaged as Satanic music? That will be like putting guns in the savages' hands, like giving them AK-47's! It's just like what Hitler did—he came along during the Weimar Republic, which was producing the most *banal* music. When you hear this sort of thing [*LaVey begins playing a 1920's era march on his organ, bubbly and monotonous. Without warning he transforms it into the opening lines of the "Horst Wessel Lied," electrifying the room.*] Now that's pretty heady stuff after that first bit! That's a demonstration of what I'm getting at.

DESCRIBE HOW THIS PROCESS WILL HAPPEN IN REAL LIFE.

LAVEY: Picture an assembly of kids—who aren't under the influence of any mind-numbing drugs—who've listened to a whole evening of Black Metal and then hear a roll on some kettle drums and trumpet fanfare. It'll be like that scene in *Samson*, or in *Cabaret*, with thousands of right arms going up into the air. God help the Christians then!

These kids are being primed right now with the Satanic Metal and when that moment comes and they hear the sounds of drums and trumpets it will be like an epiphany, a religious experience. The time is right. It's approaching D-Day and the apocalypse is at hand. They've created a musical mood that's made the homogenized din, this wash of omnipresent sound, so that any drastic violent change in the format is going to have impact that's unbelievable—it'll drop 'em in their tracks. It doesn't take much—it's just the right timing. It's happening right around them and they don't even know it. Like the flock of birds all flying out of the trees at the sound of the first thunderclap of a storm, it's going to happen at one given moment.

SELLING SATAN

One of the most remarkable features of consumer society is its ability to turn any kind of rebellious expression into a commodity. This is especially prominent and predictable in regard to youth culture. In the period of vociferous musical protest in the Sixties, one of the major record labels ran an advertising campaign that proudly proclaimed "all the revolutionaries are on CBS." This trend has continued ever since, and each time a youthful attempt is made to construct an angry identity or voice a radical opinion, there is a huge commercial apparatus already positioned to pick up, mass-produce, shrink-wrap, and sell that very same angst back to other youngsters.

It would only be a matter of time before this happened to Black Metal, especially since the early bands like Venom had already demonstrated that such rebelliousness could easily be turned into hard cash. When the Black Metal underground became manifest toward the end of the Eighties, the black-clad musicians increasingly excelled at low-budget marketing, eventually using the shock value of their criminal acts as PR for their records. As a result, Black Metal turned into a thriving cottage industry with a monumentally high public profile. It was inevitable that larger record companies would wake up and smell the money.

The biggest success story in Norwegian Black Metal—measured in chart positions, magazine coverage, and gaudy magazine posters—is Dimmu Borgir, a

Invitert
til Spellemann-showet

Vil bruke blod og liksminke

Black metal-bandet Dimmu Borgir er invitert til å opptre under Spellemannsprisen den 19. februar. – En fin sjanse for å få spredd vårt satanistiske budskap, kommenterer bandet.

Av HÅKON MOSLET

[...]

Blod og liksminke

[...]

PROVOSERER: Black metal-bandet Dimmu Borgir er nominert til Spellemann i klassen for hardrock-band. I Vlegg er de invitert til å opptre under showet på NRK 1. Hva innslaget skal inneholde, ber det store spørsmålet.

NORWEGIAN HEADLINE: "INVITED TO THE
SPELLEMANNSPRIS [NORWEGIAN GRAMMY AWARDS]
SHOW: WANT TO USE BLOOD AND CORPSEPAINT"

band which boasts of six-figure CD sales on the German label Nuclear Blast. Dimmu Borgir were not part of the initial waves of Norwegian Black Metal, and therefore they have neither blood nor soot on their hands. But they have been very adept at capitalizing on the shocking image of their predecessors in the genre, while at the same time carefully distancing themselves from the worst excesses so as not to lose record sales or gigs. A typical example can be seen in the promo pictures of Dimmu Borgir engaging in the mock sacrifice of a virgin—pictures that were produced in versions ranging from "softcore" (less gore) to "hardcore" (very bloody), so that different media could pick the version most suited to their audience. In other words, it seemed as if Dimmu Borgir wanted to be provocative enough to make the kids think they were cool, but not so provocative that the kids couldn't get their parents to buy them the album for Christmas.

Walking a tightrope between credibility and commercial success, Dimmu Borgir are the pathfinders for an growing trend in which the leading figures of the Black Metal scene concentrate on making a living from music instead rather than plotting to burn churches. This is easy to understand. Most of the veterans of the scene have grown older (and, presumably, wiser), running up increasingly larger bills in the process.

Asbjørn Slettemark is the editor of the Norwegian music business weekly *Faro-Journalen,* which counts the Scandinavian correspondent for *Billboard* magazine among its staff.

ASBJØRN SLETTEMARK

HOW POPULAR IS NORWEGIAN BLACK METAL?

Two or three years ago it was on the verge of becoming really, really big, and the international press was interested in Black Metal. If there had been more bands like Dimmu Borgir and The Kovenant that could have made it big in the mainstream, Black Metal could have been another example of an underground that stepped up to the major league. But strong forces in the scene suddenly became very introverted and reverted to an older, harder style of Black Metal.

Three years ago you would be signed if you were a Black Metal band from Norway, because the record companies knew that a Norwegian release would sell at least 5,000 copies. Of course, that led to a lot of Norwegian rubbish being released on German and Dutch labels. The audience proved faithful, and probably will be so for a while longer. But today it is quality that counts, and it is the veterans that sell.

How much do they sell?

For a while, it was popular among Black Metal bands to brag about sales figures. People have stopped doing that now. There is a handful of bands that sell well, about 10,000 to 20,000 copies of each release. But sales figures are hard to confirm, because labels tend to exaggerate; and on the other hand, many of the retailers for Black Metal records don't register their sales.

What happens when bigger labels such as Nuclear Blast start signing bands like Dimmu Borgir?

It is my impression that Nuclear Blast realized their stable of Death Metal and Speed Metal artists were starting to lag behind. It seems to me like they picked Dimmu Borgir more or less by chance, because the records that got them the contract weren't really that special. But Dimmu Borgir were still developing as a band, and they were willing to do the image and magazine poster thing. It wouldn't be possible to sell a more established band like Mayhem or Darkthrone the same way. I guess Dimmu Borgir have the good old Pop Star ambition, the standing in front of the mirror singing into the toothbrush thing.

In Europe, there is a marked divide between those that are into mainstream metal like Korn and Metallica, and the Black Metal audience. If you can bridge that chasm then you can triple your sales figures. And this is what Dimmu Borgir tried to do. For example, they were promoted toward the mainstream press, something that almost never happens to Black Metal bands.

The level of promotion was largely what separated Dimmu Borgir from their colleagues and competitors in the scene. With a professional record company behind them they were aggressively marketed. Record shops were provided with generous amounts of promotional material and eye-catching posters. The only things missing are the glossy cardboard display-stands for the store aisles.

Compared to the multinational record companies, Nuclear Blast Records is like a hot dog stand. But the German label has its home base in the world's biggest market for heavy metal, and is serious enough to have an American distribution deal with Warner Records. And Nuclear Blast know how to "move units," in record business parlance. The Marketing Director of Nuclear Blast, Yorck Eysel, says Dimmu Borgir has sold 150,000 copies of their last album and 400,000 discs in all during the time they have been with his label. These numbers are repeated like a mantra by everyone that works with the band, but should be taken with a pinch of salt, as exaggerating sales figures is the oldest trick in the book for vinyl and CD pushers. They know that it is easier to sell you a record that has been in the charts than one which has only been coveted by a few obsessive collectors. Even if the sales figures might be inflated, Dimmu Borgir has sold an impressive amount of records, and Eysel thinks that is due to the band's merit.

YORCK EYSEL

HAVE YOU HAD ANY SPECIFIC MARKETING STRATEGY FOR THAT BAND? HOW DO YOU SELL A BLACK METAL BAND TO A WIDER AUDIENCE?

You cannot call the promotional and public relations work, or the marketing, a "strategy." We just work with the tools that we get from the band, for example the photos and the artwork, or the video, and finally the music, the records. The promotion and marketing can only be as effective as these tools are in getting the interest of people, but again, it is ultimately the music or the current album that determines whether people will buy it or not, or whether the press will love the album or not.

With the last studio album it was also the print media that gave the band a lot of lead stories, making them more popular than before. What I want to say is that the simple question is not an easy one to answer, and you cannot reduce the success of a band just to the marketing—it is much more complicated.

DO YOU FEEL THAT THE "SHOCK VALUE" BLACK METAL MUSIC USED TO HAVE BECAUSE OF THE CRIMINAL BEHAVIOR HAS HELPED TO SELL DIMMU BORGIR RECORDS OR TO GIVE THE BAND CREDIBILITY?

As far as I know the band was never involved in making bullshit comments to the press where they claimed responsibility for anything stupid and brutal.

In Poland, where a Black Metal fan did commit a murder, or in Sweden, where Dissection was actually involved in a murder, it did not help to sell records at all. In those places we had no increase of sales and we won't use those facts for any kind of slogan on advertisements. It would simply be ridiculous.

BLACKLISTING

Arvid Skancke-Knudsen was the editor of Norway's leading Rock magazine, *Rock Furore*, when the Black Metal wave first hit the small, but active Norwegian music scene. He is regarded as a senior music writer, and has a long track record following the developments of various strands of Norwegian Rock culture.

Skancke-Knudsen explains that at first he saw Black Metal as an exciting new stylistic development in Rock music, and recruited writers from the scene for his magazine in an attempt to give it accurate coverage. Later, he felt compelled to withdraw from contact with the scene after some of the leading figures made statements in the media that gave a distinctly racist impression. One must assume that the crimes which ensued didn't make Skancke-Knudsen any more keen to deal with Black Metal, and his attitude was shared by many others who were writing about music at the time.

As the subculture grew more extreme, the music press withdrew and the crime journalists took over. The Norwegian mainstream media found a milieu that would say and do things to justify any headline. Interestingly, during Varg Vikernes's trial a Burzum album was reviewed in the news section of *Dagbladet*, one of Norway's most important tabloids; this was at a time when his band was being treated with contempt by the Rock press.

As the sensationalist accounts of Black Metal excesses led to fame and brisk sales for the bands abroad (at least by Norway's standards, since Pop music there generally has been difficult to export and the Metal bands regularly outsell the "commercial" Norwegian bands), the press would eventually have to acknowledge that the Black Metal scene was primarily about music. Thus Sigurd Wongraven of Satyricon, who had earlier starred in a *Rock Furore* exposé about racism in Black Metal, later received the full Rock star treatment in mainstream tabloid *Dagbladet* for a two-page article which focussed on the fact that Wongraven liked Italian designer clothes. Black Metal had become popular enough, and house-trained enough, for the mainstream press to dispense with the barge pole when touching it, even if the specters of racism and Satanism still surfaced often enough to make the bands seem somewhat scary.

SMOLDERING PR STUNTS

Ketil Sveen, a co-founder of the record label and distributor Voices of Wonder, was one of the first people to sell Norwegian Black Metal records on a bigger scale. He ended his cooperation with Burzum after Varg Vikernes stated that he was a National Socialist. Today there is a racism clause in the contracts which prospective artists have to sign in order to work with Voices of Wonder.

KETIL SVEEN

HOW MUCH DID THE SHOCK EFFECT
HELP THE SALES OF BLACK METAL?

Black Metal sold long before the
church fires and murders came along
around 1993. Øystein Aarseth had
been doing this since the mid-'80s,
and the first Mayhem record came
out five years before anything criminal emerged from the scene. On the
other hand, the fact that this was in
the news the world over probably
made people aware of Black Metal.
We sell Black Metal in 25 countries—
there's not a lot of other music that
we get out to so many.

NOW THAT SOME BLACK METAL
BANDS HAVE REACHED A CERTAIN STATURE, WILL THERE BE A POINT WHEN REAL
MAJOR LABELS START TO SNIFF THEM OUT?

I think that might happen, but not if you are talking about the first genera-
tion of bands, like Burzum or Dark Throne. But with the new generation of bands
I certainly think it is possible. I heard recently that the French division of
Polygram was interested in The Kovenant.

VOICES OF WONDER ALSO MADE THE INFAMOUS PROMOTIONAL LIGHTERS
FOR BURZUM'S ASKE ALBUM WITH THE IMAGE OF THE SMOLDERING RUINS OF
FANTOFT STAVE CHURCH.

I've done a few stupid things in my life, and that lighter was one of the stu-
pidest. In my defense I want to say that none of us suspected Vikernes had really
done anything like that [burning churches]. We figured that if he was crazy
enough to torch a church he would not be crazy enough to go around bragging
about it. So the lighter was supposed to be a take on all the exposure he got in the
media. Under the circumstances at the time I thought [making the lighter] was
okay; in retrospect I would prefer not to have done it.

GERMANY DESERVES SPECIAL TREATMENT... I LOVE GERMANY AND THE GERMAN FOLK...
THERE IS NO PEOPLE IN THE WORLD WHO HAVE BEEN TREATED MORE UNJUST THAN THE
GERMAN FOLK; THE LEAST I CAN DO IS TO SHOW ... BURZUM FAVORS DEUTSCHLAND
TO THE REST OF THE WORLD. RISE DEUTSCHLAND, TAKE BACK YOUR GLORY.
WOTAN IS WITH US.

—VARG VIKERNES[1]

FUROR TEUTONICUS

I N THE FALL OF 1994, THE UBIQUITOUS GERMAN WEEKLY *DER SPIEGEL*, THAT country's left-leaning equivalent of *Time* magazine, published an article in its national pages under the "Youth" subsection. "Infernus and Sacrificial Blood,"[2] the headline screamed. In the center of the page the reader encounters an illustration from the fanzine *Infernus*—an image of corpses in battle gear juxtaposed with a xeroxed picture of an SS ceremony from the Third Reich. A statement adjacent to the pictures is also legible:

The pope himself should be raped by thirty Satanist sisters and I also would like to desecrate his lovely asshole. There is no punishment cruel enough to let him suffer for his mistakes and lies but I guess it would be nice to shred him.[3]

Welcome to the world of German Black Metal. Less well known than its Norwegian counterpart, the German scene remains genuinely underground, an obscure exit off the darkened *Autobahn* of extreme Rock. That changed briefly following the night of April 29, 1993, however, when the members of the Black Metal band Absurd followed the example set by Bård Eithun and Varg Vikernes and replaced thought with crime. The exploits of Absurd lacked the grand drama and notoriety which surrounded the "Grishnackh-Euronymous affair" later that year, but the violence was just as intense. They demonstrated that while fewer in number, the Teutonic wing of Black Metal was willing to live up to its Nordic cousin in terms of making a point without fear of the consequences—be they derision or prison time.

DER SPIEGEL 41/1994   91

DER SPIEGEL ARTICLE

The article in the normally staid *Der Spiegel* begins in a manner more befitting a pulp tabloid:

By night the clique meets for macabre rituals in an old quarry. The leader, dressed in black, praises the angel Lucifer with outstretched arms. Then, according to a 17-year-old who was present, he grips the hand of the one to be baptized, draws a knife, and makes a cut in the arm of the initiate. The Master slurps the blood and licks the knife. He then declares the ceremony has ended.[4]

The article continues, explaining that the Satanic baptism which took place in Sondershausen was only a prelude to a more gruesome event to come in April, 1993. On that day, members of the group of high school students who allegedly called themselves the "Children of Satan" engineered the murder of a 15-year-old classmate. The murderers were later found to all be members of a macabre fledgling music group named Absurd.

The *Spiegel* piece was one of dozens in a media frenzy that brought national attention to the nondescript town of Sondershausen, located in the state of Thuringia in former East Germany. The research of two journalists from Berlin, Lianne von Billerbeck and Frank Nordhausen, culminated in the book *Satanskinder* ("Satan's Children"), published in 1994. The subtitle of the book is "The Murder Case of Sandro B.," which refers to the name of the victim, Sandro Beyer. Written in a straightforward manner, *Satanskinder* attempts to unravel what really happened within the youth milieu surrounding Absurd, and what influences may have contributed to the murderers' behavior.

According to the authors' findings, a small subculture had emerged amongst a few young high school students who shared a growing fascination with extreme Heavy Metal, the occult, violence, and horror films. Such curiosities were difficult to satisfy until the Wall fell in 1989 and East Germany was opened to the West. At this point previously forbidden or impossible-to-obtain records and videos steadily came within reach. The three 17-year-olds Hendrik Möbus, Sebastian Schauscheill, and Andreas Kirchner began to draw attention to themselves with their Satanic obsessions and penchant for Black Metal. They were antagonized for their interests by many of the other kids in town—both left-wing punks and right-wing skinheads—but developed a group of admirers among the local schoolgirls.

As their imaginations were increasingly stimulated, they began to meet with a small circle of adherents in the rock quarry where they supposedly held Satanic "baptism" ceremonies like the one so dramatically described in *Der Spiegel.* At a certain point in 1992, a younger student, a 14-year-old named Sandro, also developed a fascination for the members of this sinister band and their associates.

The descriptions of Sandro Beyer in *Satanskinder* make it is hard to sympathize with his personality. Widely disliked due to his irritating manners, he had almost no real friends. He quickly began to adopt the style and interests of the "Satanists" and desperately tried to ingratiate himself into their circle. He would ask to attend band rehearsals and began corresponding with them and the others in the clique around Absurd. *Satanskinder* describes a peculiar "letter writing culture" that thrived among all of these youths. Opinions, concerns, and demands were sent back and forth among the penpals, even though they lived within walking distance of one another and met frequently at locations such at the Youth Center, where Absurd rehearsed for a time. Heated arguments also took place there between them and members of the Christian Youth

Satanskinder Book Cover

ABSURD LOGO

Club, which met regularly at the Center as well.

Sandro's parents, both Christians, frowned upon his new clique and refused to tolerate the accouterments that had come with it. On one occasion they burned one of his T-shirts, which bore a pentagram, after his father exclaimed it was a "symbol of the Devil."[5] Only a short time passed before Sandro himself realized such things were not his cup of tea, anyway. The boys of Absurd had never accepted Sandro into their fold, and visibly displayed their dislike towards him. In response to their constant insults, he began to argue and taunt them in return—further provoking their wrath. At one point he promised his mother, "Mommy, don't worry, I won't hang around with these people, they're too brutal to me," and threw away all the Satanic items in his room.[6]

Despite his claims that he had broken all ties with the Absurd crowd, he still felt drawn to them. His attraction was now soured but consuming, like that of a

SANDRO BEYER

spurned secret admirer. Together with a young girl named Rita, Sandro began to plot actions against Sebastian and Hendrik, hoping to make a mockery of them in Sondershausen. He began a campaign of writing slander letters and spreading unpleasant rumors. He was also aware of an ongoing affair between Sebastian and an older married woman named Heidegrit Goldhardt, now pregnant with Sebastian's child. Sandro threatened to reveal the clandestine adultery to the rest of the town. Upon receiving word of this, Sebastian replied to Sandro in writing, issuing the threat: "Primitive violence is not our thing. Sorcery is more effective."[7] He sent a further message, partially in English: "The hell come to your home. You will die. Sathan awaits! Stay away from us you whimp and poser! Sathan be my guard [sic]."[8]

All the while—if the statements in *Satanskinder* are to be believed—emotions were tense among Hendrik, Sebastian, and their close friends. Intrigues and jealousies arose over new allegiances and preoccupations. Sebastian's romantic relationship with Heidegrit, who oddly enough was an evangelical Christian schoolteacher, had produced some unexpected results. He had joined in with her pet projects for environmentalism and animal rights, and now spent time writing polemical letters to the newspapers about such issues. He developed a double life between these activities and nights spent with Absurd, rehearsing their Luciferian hymns and drinking. The parties occasionally led to wild outbreaks; one night they invaded a deserted house and destroyed much of the contents in a drunken fury.

SEBASTIAN SCHAUSCHEILL

The biggest problem for the group—one that they all agreed needed to be dealt with—was Sandro. Sebastian later told the police, "It was only just that lately Sandro had gotten on our nerves with his appearance. He had such a tactless manner ... and because we were slightly fixated upon him, this caused an idea to form."[9]

In a bizarre interview done with a high school fanzine in late 1992, Hendrik broadcast an array of vehement unpleasantries and exaggerated claims, much in the same spirit as some of Varg Vikernes's grandiose early statements to the Norwegian press. When asked who Absurd considered their allies, he took pains to specify by name that "Sandro B." had *nothing* to do with them—he was the type of person they abhorred. Undoubtedly the publication of this interview slammed another thorn in the side of the disgruntled Sandro, increasing his resolve to embarrass Hendrik and Sebastian.

Absurd no longer rehearsed at the Youth Center, but had moved their equipment to a small cottage built by Hendrik's father in the nearby woods. Through the guise of a female friend, "Juliane," a letter was sent to Sandro in which she confided her hatred of Absurd. She asked Sandro to meet her one evening at the Rondell, a WWI memorial in the forest above the town, in order to discuss how she could contribute to Sandro's campaign against the Satanists.

HENDRIK AND SEBASTIAN

Sandro arrived at the Rondell as scheduled. It was 8 P.M. on the evening of April 29th, the night before the heathen and Satanic holiday of *Walpurgisnacht.* "Juliane" didn't appear, but the members of Absurd did instead. Sandro must have been confused, but dismissed any idea that he had been set up. They then somehow convinced him to accompany them elsewhere so that they could all discuss an important matter.

They led him through the woods to the bungalow belonging to Hendrik's father. At approximately 8:30 the group of youths entered the cottage. Once inside they invited Sandro to take a seat, giving the impression that they now would undertake their discussion. Sandro was unsure what was going on, and stated, "It's getting to be too much for me."[10] He was ready to leave. Suddenly Andreas grabbed an electrical cord and wrapped it around Sandro's neck. A struggle ensued, Sandro tried to scream for help. At this point, Hendrik is alleged to have pulled a knife and cut Sandro. They tied his hands behind his back. Sandro begged to be let free, promising to never speak about anything that had just happened. They could even have his life savings—500 German Marks (approximately $325). The boys considered the idea of letting him go free in the woods, but feared he would not keep his promise of silence about the abduction, especially now that he had been wounded.

Sandro began screaming for help again and struggling to break free. The boys leapt upon him, Hendrik grabbing his legs. Andreas and Sebastian threw a piece of the electrical cord around his neck and tightened it from both sides with all their might. They held it in determined tautness until certain that Sandro's heart had come to a standstill.

When the reality of the preceding frenzied few minutes sunk in, Andreas is alleged to have remarked, "Oh shit—now I've completely ruined my life."[11] The other two convinced him there might be a way they could get away with the crime; they simply needed to dispose of the body. The three hauled the corpse about a hundred yards away from the cottage, where they hid it in a dilapidated shed by a creek. They went home for the night.

It was only a matter of hours before Sandro's parents and the police were looking into the disappearance. On May 1st the three members of Absurd returned to the scene of the crime and dragged Sandro's corpse, wrapped in a blanket, to a nearby excavation pit, where they quickly buried him.

The corpse was found almost immediately, and the trail of the strangled 15-year-old quickly led to Sebastian, Hendrik, and Andreas. Once caught, they were tried for murder and convicted. The case elicited a steady stream of excited headlines from journalists determined to present it as some kind of "Satanic sacrifice." During the initial police interviews and on the stand in the court hearings, Sebastian only provided ambiguous justifications for the killing, none of which had anything to do with Satanism. "It could not have happened any other way. It was simply inside of us, like a compulsion," he explained. He admitted that the idea of killing Sandro had been come up a week before the deed, but maintained the murder had been "relatively spontaneous," and there was "no logical motive." In Sebastian's words, "the guy simply had to go."[12]

Asked whether the violent imagery of Black Metal music had provided a

SEBASTIAN AND HENDRIK

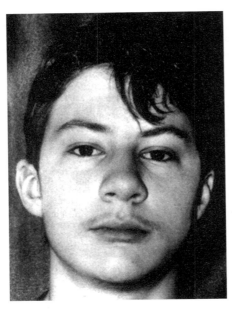

THE LAST PHOTO EVER TAKEN OF SANDRO BEYER

motivation for their behavior, Sebastian conceded it may have been a slight influence, but he was reluctant to blame Heavy Metal. Despite the brutal lyrics, the music was not a main factor in what they had done. Sebastian related a strange personal anecdote: about six months before the murder he heard a voice in his head. It was difficult to understand; he thought it uttered the nonsensical phrase *"Küster Maier."* Later he decided it probably must have said *"töte Beyer"* ("Kill Beyer!"). He added, "It sounds crazy, I know, but I can't really say what I have experienced."[13]

Hendrik and Sebastian were clearly the real forces behind the ideology and imagery of Absurd. Andreas appears to have been mainly an impressionable follower. All of them have refused interviews for years and would not speak to the press about the action they took. The story detailed above follows the chronology presented in *Satanskinder,* although the book embellishes it with endless psychological speculation. The descriptions of the authors are based entirely on comments by disgruntled ex-friends and hangers-on who had interacted with the killers, since the latter refused to speak to them. The picture painted is one of an outsider group of youths whose fantasies got the best of them. Increasingly driven by melodrama, they finally crossed over the line to where the horror and violence turned real.

How much of a resemblance the *Satanskinder* account bears to reality is hard to say. If one speaks to the killers directly, it becomes apparent that there was clearly more going on in their minds than the book would have you believe. The following interview is derived from correspondence that took place during 1997–2002 between Hendrik Möbus and the authors of this book. It was the first time he had agreed to speak about the murder of Sandro Beyer since the killing took place. The reader should keep in mind that his answers come with the hindsight of a number of years which have passed since Sandro Beyer fulfilled his date with "death from the forest." Hendrik's replies also illustrate well the extent that strains of esoteric racialist mysticism have permeated some aspects of Black Metal. For the present edition of *Lords of Chaos,* some answers in the earlier interview have been revised or expanded upon, and Hendrik also discusses events that took place after his release from juvenile incarceration. In a number of instances he appears to have tempered some of his earlier rhetoric. Those wishing to read his previous responses may consult the first edition of this book.

Hendrik Möbus

What were the primary influences when you were younger?

THE SECOND BLASPHEMY

I guess we always felt linked to some kind of "counter-reality," to the things that were "absurd" to society. Certainly this link must be seen in reference to our life in the Soviet Occupation Zone of East Germany, where we grew up for our first fourteen years. The East German government was a totalitarian one—the dictatorship of the workers and peasants. People raised in the "Free World" will never wholly understand these kinds of social structures. Besides, it was never anything but a satellite of "Big Brother" Moscow, totally oriented toward and dependent on the U.S.S.R. Thus we were taught to love everything Russian, but to hate our own nationality. But nobody can deny his origin, and this contradiction-in-terms displeased us, making us look for something beyond the Communists' agitprop.

Infernus Fanzine, with Absurd on Cover

What subjects were you interested in?

At home, I learned quite a bit about ancestral research, German history, about folklore and fairytales, and of the love for untouched nature. As a kid back then there was much less of a possibility for wasting away one's day in front of the TV, and so a lot of time was enjoyably spent outside. At church—keep in mind, though, that the East German society was almost wholly atheistic—I learned to deal with religious topics, but unfortunately I also learned all the Semitic fairy-tales from the Old Testament. But at least through this I got an insight into the Christian mindset. However, Sebastian and my big brother and I all felt the same way, and like certain others our age, we tried to escape the dull and indoctrinated society by affiliating with some kind of youth culture.

How did you first become interested in extreme music, and later Black Metal?

To listen to any other music than the "politically correct" was of course frowned upon, and thus, it became a special form of protest. We used to listen to British and German Punk Rock, British Oi, as well as Thrash Metal. It was rather hard to get any releases; mostly we obtained Polish or Hungarian bootlegs, or recorded stuff from the West German radio. We developed more and more of a preference for the "sinister" Metal stuff (both in terms of music and attitude)— for example Slayer, Destruction, Sodom, Morbid Angel, Possessed. We felt this music best fit our attitude and point of view.

DID YOU HAVE A DIFFERENT PERSPECTIVE, OR DIFFERENT ACCESS TO THESE THINGS SINCE YOU LIVED IN WHAT WAS A PART OF EASTERN GERMANY?

In late '89 the East German government fell apart, fading away like a flame without fuel. We had realized that this system couldn't survive without Soviet support, even if the Communist Party tried to teach us that Communism would one day achieve worldwide victory. Now we have seen that a system that wants to equalize people by oppressing national feelings holds no great future.

All that we learned from the East German experience is that we must remain linked to our origins, as a condition for vital development. To sever the roots leads to disadvantage in every way, and that is true in individual circumstances as well. The Communists wanted to teach us *Strength and Honor* about being part of their "World Revolution," but they revealed weakness and dishonor—we loathe them and their utopia. Nevertheless, from the ruins of East Germany we followed our trail for strength and honor, and I guess it was just a question of time before we became aware of splendid bands like Deicide, Beherit, Sarcofago, Bathory, Mayhem, and Darkthrone...

WHEN DID YOU FORM ABSURD, AND WHAT IS THE EARLY HISTORY OF THE BAND?

We didn't choose the bandname on a whim, but rather because to our minds "absurd" was a very fitting description for the attitude held by the wider masses toward those things which we did at that time and which were dear to us. We were never actually understood. Our thought and behavior was seen as being in conjunction with manifestations that were wild, bewildering, destructive and subversive. This chaos, which we apparently represented for many people, was seized upon and manifested by us.

Though we started the band on January 2, 1992, we had played music together before, but more just for fun and without serious intentions. Up to this time, Sebastian already played guitar for many years, and I attended a local music school; thus we always listened to music as well as created it.

Nevertheless, after Darkthrone released their awe-inspiring *A Blaze in the Northern Sky* album in 1991, we felt the urge to express our very own "sinister attitude" in music as well, namely the reborn Black Metal. And even though we were quite impressed by Norwegian Black Metal, we didn't want to copy their style of music.

WHAT ELSE INSPIRED YOU?

The Black Metal we play is influenced by Oi and R.A.C. [Rock Against Communism, a Nazi skinhead music organization] as well, and our inspiration came from various bands like Der Fluch, Mercyful Fate/King Diamond, Manowar, Danzig—this probably explains why our own music is so "un-Nordic" in sound. The classic movies of Bela Lugosi, Fritz Lang, Vincent Price (mostly the Hammer films), and Leni Riefenstahl influenced our ambience due to their own atmosphere and aesthetics (especially in regards to Riefenstahl). Almost the same goes for modern films by Dario Argento, Sam Raimi, and such. The biggest inspiration, though, came from the *Conan the Barbarian* film (and its soundtrack). Unjustly this film has been deemed a B-movie. The direction was done by John Milius, who among other things wrote the screenplay for *Apocalypse Now*. For *Conan* he wrote the screenplay as well, together with Oliver Stone. The result was a very multileveled and powerful film, the theme of which is probably obvious: the confrontation between the man of the North, adorned with a sunwheel, and the high priest of the Semitic snake cult. The movie is fantastic and, for us, possibly the best motion picture made since 1945. There have been many inspirations we tried to drop into our music, but the most important ones came from our inner self.

DID YOU PLAY CONCERTS?

Even when we had the chance to play live in our local Youth Center, we cancelled our participation, because we didn't want to be onstage alongside the leftist morons of various Punk bands, or the faggots of a Blues band.

GERMAN HEADLINE: "HIGHSCHOOLER (15) STRANGLED WITH CORD. SATAN CULT IN SONDERSHAUSEN. CHRONICLE OF AN ANNOUNCED MURDER"

HENDRIK IN PRISON

WHERE DID MOST OF THE FANS OF ABSURD COME FROM?

Our strongest supporters come from Germany, mainly central Germany (the former East German territories), but from the western part as well. Besides this we have fans in many other Black-Metal-compatible countries around the globe. We praise everyone who really feels attracted to our music, and who supports us. It is also observable that many of the fans don't originally come from the Black Metal scene at all. Among our fans we have skinheads and people into Industrial and Ambient music as well.

And inevitably just as there are many fans, there are also some enemies. The latter mostly turn up in those circles where Black Metal is just one of the musical genres they listen to. They level the incensed, jealous accusation against us that Absurd just want to drag Black Metal into the dirt.

WERE THE NORWEGIAN BLACK METAL BANDS AN INFLUENCE ON YOU?

As far as the music is concerned, we received less influence from Norway, but considering their "way of life," we still are rather fond of them. The Svarte Sirkel

SEBASTIAN (FAR RIGHT) IN PRISON BAND

[Black Circle] exactly expressed an attitude similar to ours: fierceness, darkness, cruelty, somber mysteries, and extreme denial of the "Christianized modern world." The behavior of the Svarte Sirkel bands/musicians towards the music biz impressed us quite a lot, and we were glad to see Black Metal boycotted by the major labels due to the "shocking and entangling" image the Norwegians had outlined for themselves. Reviewing these glory days of '92 and early '93, I doubt there will ever be such splendid feelings toward Black Metal again. Reminiscing about it brings on nostalgia.

DID YOU HAVE CONTACT WITH PEOPLE FROM NORWAY?

We have had and still have a strong relationship with the Norwegians. Before he "moved to the beyond," Øystein Aarseth wanted to sign Absurd to Deathlike Silence, since our *Death from the Forest* demo appealed to him quite a bit.

WHICH GROUPS DID YOU FIND THE MOST IMPORTANT FROM THIS TIME?

Actually all of the Deathlike Silence bands, such as Mayhem, Burzum, Emperor, Enslaved, and of course Immortal and Darkthrone. Especially Count Grishnackh, Varg's alter ego, projected a very grim, somber, and eerie image of Norwegian Black Metal. But as far as the music is concerned, Mayhem (with their furious *De Mysteriis Dom Sathanas* album) and Darkthrone are the most influential.

Norway will stay the source of supreme Black Metal. Without Øystein the Black Metal revival is unthinkable, but without Varg, neither is its transformation from music into action.

WHEN YOU FIRST HEARD OF THE CHURCH BURNINGS IN SCANDINAVIA, WHAT WAS YOUR REACTION?

HENDRIK MÖBUS AFTER HIS INITIAL RELEASE

We heard about the arsons rather quickly; I guess shortly after Varg burned the Fantoft Church near Bergen on the 6th of June, 1992. We were electrified by the wave of fire that struck Scandinavia from that point on.

WERE YOU INFLUENCED BY THE FACT THAT THE NORWEGIANS MOVED FROM MUSIC INTO ACTION?

I wouldn't say it "influenced" our attitude, since from our very core we always support everything that contributes to the rotting of, and which weakens and undermines the Judeo-Christian regime.

If an artist really believes in the art he/she is creating and performing, then they must also draw the conclusions and transform this art into action. That's exactly what the Svarte Sirkel has done, and we truly appreciate these heroes of the anti-Jewish/anti-Christian resistance, for their participation in the overcoming of western Christendom.

If I am correct, then from the first beginnings until today, more than 100 churches have been burned (or damaged), and I'm sure IT WON'T STOP!!! Before our incarceration we also had made plans to become similarly active, but didn't achieve any concrete results.

Many people declare such arsons as "foolish," because the churches will be rebuilt sooner or later, and the popular solidarity that it generates for the congregations affected is very large. But I'll reply to that with the essence of a statement from Mao: "Burn one—threaten hundreds!" Be aware it's not an economic form of warfare but a psychological one.

ABSURD HAS CALLED ITSELF "LUCIFERIAN PAGANS" AND MUCH OF THE EARLY IMAGERY IS A COMBINATION OF SATANIC/LUCIFERIAN INSPIRATION AND THEN GERMANIC HEATHEN INSPIRATION. FROM WHERE DID THESE INSPIRATIONS DEVELOP?

You can use the terms "Luciferian," "Promethean," and "Faustian" to describe one and the same principle: reaching out toward a higher stage of existence and awareness by facing and overcoming the limiting circumstances. That is the trail we are on. However, a "Luciferian will" on its own would fall into hedonism and egomania. For that reason we need heathenism; on the one hand for expression of free will, but also for its channeling toward the greater good. In other words, a person of this sort should not operate only according to self-interest, but rather should serve his ethnic community and be the "light bringer" for it.

WHAT ARE YOUR VIEWS TODAY?

Our comprehension of philosophy/religion/mythology is far-reaching, but we try to avoid Judeo-Christian areas. We are deeply rooted within a "Blood and Soil" cosmology. We are fascinated by blood mysticism and through this developed an interest in genetics and eugenics. "Blood and Soil" was of course a slogan associated with the Third Reich. It is much deeper and more encompassing than a short-sighted interpretation would have you believe. On the cosmic scale every human being is only a single molecule. If you do not want to lose your way, you have to sense and recognize your nature—that despite your singular vanity, you are thoroughly important through history, and even can become immortal as a component of a long chain of ancestors. For such a realization one must naturally look beyond the horizon of the individual and understand that the "molecule man" exists in an organic unity with others who are of the same kind. The greater races of mankind are one such type of organic configuration. Every race has a specific genepool, and the DNA is the source for physique and appearance as well as the collective subconscious, with its archetypal symbolism and instinctive behavior. With the human being and the differences in races and subraces nature has created such a wondrous work of art, one that only the really ignorant would be unable to recognize and would want to destroy. It has nothing to do with "racism" when I mention that the "White," i.e., Indo-Germanic race, was and is, from its natural potentiality, chosen for developing superior civilization and for imperialism. The world history bequeathed to us is that of the White Ones conquering the earth.

When the Cro-Magnon archetype of our race appeared in prehistoric times, he conquered Europe with supreme skills and abilities, wiping out the competing race of the Neanderthals. That was the first known example of genocide—and does it not say something significant about the ambivalent nature of the White Man?

In any case, I believe that the origin of our race lay in ancient Sumer, and as we know, Sumer was the first urban civilization. From there, the White Man spread out in every attainable direction on the earth, and among other things founded the "super-civilization" of Thule/Atlantis which was, however, destroyed in the antediluvian age. The survivors of the flood then had a decided influence upon the Mayan, Incan, and Aztec civilizations of Central and South America, as well as others.

"Folkdom" is not only made up of those with common blood. The landscape where the folk live also exerts a large influence on the character of their culture, religion, and civilization. People are molded by the landscape; at the same time there are naturally significant regional differences. Only through this confluence of blood and landscape do a specific "folkdom" and folk customs arise. Of course, the primary aspects of this process are religious and cultural. Although substantial differences can be observed amongst the Indo-Germanic peoples, a correspondence exists between their religious conceptions and their form of writing (which was originally only used for religious purposes). Through these their kinship and "rank" can be known.

Therefore we feel related to every ancient culture that is illuminated by "Thulean" awareness and aesthetics. Certainly we are very fascinated by martial cultures, such as the Spartan and of course the Germanic ones. The law of the

CREDITS FROM ABSURD'S *OUT OF THE DUNGEON* DEMO, 1994

strong operates throughout nature and also among men. We are very proud of our pure German descent. Perhaps the Germans were not the most civilized branch of the White Race, but they were the most honorable and virtuous.

We recognize DNA as the seat of the (collective) subconscious, and the subconscious shelters everlasting archetypes. We could also be wrong and there is a sort of "eternal force-field," which houses the collective archetypes and projects them into our souls. But that is not important. I guess we are too secularized to believe in deities as "supernatural beings," but we view them as archetypes of course, and, as far as it concerns our race, as Germanic ideals. For example, Donar [the German name for Thor], the Thunderer, is the ideal of the armed German peasant: diligent, brave, sincere. He is responsible for fertility and for fighting the hostile-minded Ice-giants (symbols for uncontrollable natural forces). Another example is Wotan, who represents the Sorcerer-King; he is interwoven with every secret of an occult nature—communication with the birds/animals, use of necromancy, bringing the dead back to life, as well as being the leader of the "wild hunt." He is a gracious and just ruler for the Aesir, as well as for man. It is not for nothing that German aristocratic families have been eager to trace their ancestry back to Wotan. Perhaps the mythology even springs from our shadowy memory of antediluvian times, when our gods in Thule really existed?

For certain the background of Germanic mythology is of an esoteric/occult nature (such as the world-tree Yggdrasil, the Runes, Valhalla). But more importantly, we are of the opinion that these myths bring us closer to an ethic and desire to show us a way of life. In any event, German mythology is a heritage given to us that we can't deny, and we are fascinated with every expression of the Germanic being.

It goes without saying that National Socialism is likewise such an expression. If one looks at the Black Order of the SS without preconceptions, then one sees mostly people who believed in their vision with devotion and fanaticism and who were taken up with their mission. Finally in this regard one can no longer explain the dynamic of National Socialism as "Machiavellianism" or the like, but instead one has to agree with C.G. Jung that a primordial power had newly possessed the people: the archetype of Wotan. As Hermann Rauschning said, "The deepest roots of Nazism lay hidden in secret places."

We are convinced that the will of the White Man is actually constructive. Even in cases where he destroys, he does so only to build what is—in his view—a better and more beautiful world. All his endeavors aim for refinement and ennoblement. But wherever there is so much light, there must also be a great shadow. The adversary of the "Aryan" will is the "Semitic" will. Whenever the reflection of Thule fades, the Semite gains a foothold there and begins his destructive work.

The Germans used to banish negative influence by purifying themselves, i.e., the tribe, from it. Everyone who harmed their natural ethics (deserters, traitors, homosexuals, adulterers, "black magicians," etc.) was executed and drowned in the bog, in order to incarcerate the "ill spirit." This concept naturally had to be rejected when whole tribes converted to Christianity. Christianity finds no correspondence with "Thulean" consciousness. It is completely alien to our nature.

We cannot come to terms with the fact that this anti-spirit, Christianity, which is so diametrically opposed to our true nature, still holds hostage the sacred shrines of our ancestors and that it should determine our history—and not just in terms of the individual.

From this reason we support every idea or concept that is subversive to the status quo, and which swings the pendulum to our side. Personally I'm rather fond of the "political heathendom" concept developed by Varg Vikernes. He discovered the way for combining *Realpolitik* and heathenism. Therefore Absurd also supports the "Pan-Germanic Heathen Front" program!

MANY OF THE MORE WELL-KNOWN BLACK METAL BANDS SHIFTED IN FOCUS FROM SATANISM TO HEATHENISM. WAS THIS ALSO TRUE FOR ABSURD?

In a way I can concur, although while emphasizing that our worldview never changed in its orientation. But naturally we developed and came to new realizations. We always placed great value on our origins and therefore explicitly labeled our music as German Black Metal. We have never been truly ardent Satanists; instead we dealt with the matter at that time in an overly superficial way. Classical Satanism—which seems to be as popular as ever in the Black Metal scene—is just an invention of the medieval Inquisition. The heathens and heretics had to be dealt with somewhere in the Catholic catechism; this was best accomplished by demonizing them. The *Malleus Malificarum* bears testament to it.

There is no way we could identify with that, and the nihilistic glorification of violence, war, and extermination no longer holds any spectacular importance to us. I mean, these "shadow sides" of humanity are all too familiar to us, and we know that every human being possesses innate "sinister" tendencies. It is exactly the greatest saints who are the worst devils. There is nothing exceptional about this; it's only "all too human."

WHAT LED TO THE MURDER OF SANDRO BEYER?

There are many rumors, some of them hair-raising, about what lead to Sandro's death and how it transpired. Now is probably the time to at least describe how things really played out in the background of what happened. Sandro was a very odd young man, who obviously had managed to repeatedly bring down the wrath and ridicule of his peers upon himself. I didn't know him well enough to be able to come to any clear assessments of his character. But I do know that from the start that I found him very disagreeable—not just because of the things he said or did, but because of the manner in which he said or did them. And it was not only me who was repulsed by this. He had such an unpleasant, arrogant disposition. In any event, in the summer of 1992 he wanted to join our clique, after a girl—with whom Sebastian had a relationship and a child—put him on our scent, so to speak. On account of his manner, we wanted nothing to do with him. Also why we would we, who had so arrogantly and "elitely" distanced ourselves from our peers, welcome Sandro the "loser" with open arms? Nevertheless, in the subsequent period a quite normal relationship developed between Sebastian and Sandro since both were close to the above-mentioned girl and Sandro also let Sebastian tape a lot of music from his record collection. If this situation could have actually continued, a disagreement between Sandro and us would never have occurred. What we didn't know, and only first learned from the court record, was that Sandro was bisexual. With a likelihood bordering on certainty, Sandro had fallen in love with Sebastian. That is also not astonishing, as in those days Sebastian had a certain "sex appeal" among the youths.

So Sandro discovered the relationship between Sebastian and his lover, who was married and eight years older than him, while Sebastian was also considered the leader of the local Satanists. If this relationship were to become public—which did indeed happen after the arrests—then it would have caused a significant fuss in the small town of Sondershausen, the result being that the girl would have been expelled from her congregation.

Sandro recognized the explosive nature of this situation and used it for his own ends. He wrote anonymous letters to Sebastian in which he let it be known that he was aware of the affair. At the same time he threatened to make his knowledge public if Sebastian did not leave the woman. Above and beyond that, he spread rumors about our clique and pretended to be a member of Absurd. All in all it was a mixture of jealousy, envy, and vengeful feelings which motivated his actions. However, I suppose it was fate that Sandro wanted to start his trouble at a point when our clique and the band were already experiencing problems. As a result we paid quite a lot more attention to Sandro's silly game than we would have under normal circumstances. If Sandro had actually made good on his threat, then Sebastian would have—as he said back then—left Sondershausen with the mother of his child. The clique and Absurd would have been broken up. For me personally at the time, it was a very shocking realization.

Therefore we decided to solve the "Sandro problem" short and quick, by forcing him to abandon his plans. There could be no lengthy discussion with him. If need be, we would put pressure on him. Unfortunately we overestimated our capabilities for conflict solving and underestimated Sandro's rebelliousness. The rest of the story is known.

THE MEDIA TRIED TO SAY THIS WAS SOME KIND OF "SATANIC SACRIFICE"...

Countless people still hold this view, all the way up to the present. But it is fundamentally wrong! The conflict between Sandro and Sebastian (representing the clique) was of a purely personal nature. Religious and ideological motives played no role before, or during, the deed. I must also deny the assumption that it was a sacrificial ritual, although I know that this simple attempt at an explanation is the favorite interpretation of the death for many people. It sounds, however, too much like a cheap horror film. Such "satanic sacrifices" only take place in and for the media. The reality is much different. If one wants to find a religious component in Sandro's death at all, then one has to really make a stretch. The manner and the course of his injuries could be seen in conjunction with ancient Germanic sacrificial rites in which the victim was killed by stabbing and strangulation and then sunk into the bog. But that is very far-fetched. At the time of the deed we had not *consciously* celebrated any ritual. To do so under these circumstances would not have even occurred to us. Instead of imaginary religious or

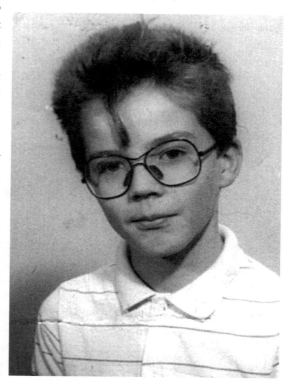

HENDRIK MÖBUS

ideological aspects it would be better if more attention were paid to the psychological situation at the time of the deed. I am thoroughly convinced that Sandro's death would have never come about if he had just behaved somewhat differently. Thus it was a classic "lock and key" situation, one which opened up the possibility for escalation of events. Nevertheless this theme is very complex and also of a very private nature. For this reason I do not wish to say very much publicly. Besides, every passing second a human dies, so there's no need to make a big fuss of this one kill. The seemingly "exceptional" nature of our deed was something entirely fabricated by the media.

WHAT HAPPENED AFTER THE MURDER?

Due to blind confidence on the part of Sebastian, he told a girlfriend we were in contact with about what happened. She told others about this event, and eventually the parents of our victim became aware of it. They scoured the forest, without knowing their son was buried there, and discovered his damaged shirt. They alarmed the cops once again, who questioned us, among other pupils, about where Sandro could be. A person who did know about our involvement in Sandro's disappearance, and who disliked us, told the cops what he knew, and thus they arrested us the same day, one week after our deed. I was at home when they came—school was just over this day—and I tried to contact Sebastian and Andreas in order to create some kind of alibi. But the cops were quicker (and I did not know they were already informed, otherwise I would have tried to be even quicker myself!) and arrested me and, a few hours later, my two accomplices.

WHAT WERE YOU EACH FOUND GUILTY OF?

Due to our age of 17, they had to use the youth laws for punishment, which meant a maximum of ten years in detention, no matter if even for mass-murder. At the start of 1994 our trial took place, which was a giant media spectacle. Among other things, the court found us guilty of first degree murder, deprivation of liberty, threat and duress, and bodily injury.

WHAT WERE THE JAIL SENTENCES YOU RECEIVED?

Sebastian and myself were each sentenced to eight years of detention, and Andreas received six years. Now, taking into account the usual punishment for murder—life in prison—we got off relatively lightly. Lastly none of us had to serve the full sentences that we were given; we all were granted early release.

Ironically, the section we were sentenced under is one of the few pieces of legislation that remains today from National Socialist jurisprudence. Apparently something from the Third Reich held good for modern German "democracy"!

Wenn Liebe könnte Wunder tun
und Tränen Tote wecken,
dann würde dich lieber Sandro
nicht so jung die kühle Erde decken.

Durch einen grausamen Gewaltakt wurde unser geliebter Sohn und Bruder aus seiner
blühenden Jugend gerissen.

Sandro Beyer
geb. 12. 04. 1978   gest. 29. 04. 1993

In unsagbarem Schmerz
Peter Beyer und Frau Cornelia geb. Bauerschmidt
Bruder Christian
Joachim Beyer
Bernhardt Bauerschmidt und Frau Eva
Günther Beyer
Helmut Beyer und Frau Grudrun
Andreas Bauerschmidt und Frau Ursula
Franz von Oppenkowski und Frau Sylvia
geb. Bauerschmidt
Lothar Schulz und Frau Rita geb. Bauerschmidt
Volker Beyer und Frau Gabriele
sowie Hartmut, Mathias, Tanja, Christina,
Jens, Claudia, Carolin, Marcus und Johannes

Sondershausen, Bischofferode, Elgersburg, Menden, Auma, Ebeleben, im April 1993
Die Trauerfeier findet am Mittwoch, dem 12. 05. 1993, um 15.00 Uhr auf dem Hauptfriedhof Sondershausen statt.
Von Beileidsbesuchen bitten wir Abstand zu nehmen.
– Bestattungsinstitut "Pietät" Hettler –

BEYER FUNERAL ANNOUNCEMENT

HOW DO YOU LOOK BACK ON THE MURDER NOW, SEVERAL YEARS LATER?

Basically all of us regret the terrible situation that we brought to our families. This familial liability was and is a fact that we can't come to terms with. Although what happened with Sandro was not planned, it can absolutely be seen as the *ultima ratio* in the disagreement between him and us. On a societal level death and murder are so mundane, but individually they are extremely archaic and consciousness-altering experiences. Through a deed of this sort one breaks through borders and reaches regions that play no role in ordinary reality. In this sense it actually has to do with the human "twilight zone" and one becomes a stranger to this "normal" world. Nobody who has not experienced something similar can understand that. I also do not wish to ever explain it to anybody, and with this I should always justify it to myself. Indeed, regarding the deed itself there is nothing that can be changed. *"Den Tod geben und den Tod empfangen"* ["To give death and to welcome death"]—this was once the motto of the Waffen SS and says much about the original and Germanic relationship to such things. Someone was dealt death by my hand; sometime I may be in his place. *Amor fati?*

HOW DO YOU FEEL ABOUT HOW YOUR CASE HAS BEEN PRESENTED IN THE PRESS?

Totenburg

Our case was publicized throughout the entire German media, both TV and print, quite a lot from May '93 to May '94, and even in the following years. Besides the trashy book *Satanskinder*, at least three other books feature our case. However, this book is certainly wrong with its version (although several phrases sound familiar...), due to the fact we refused to cooperate. A TV-film has also been made based on the events in Sonders-hausen. We have become "Satan murderers" and "Children of Satan" for all time. One could laugh about these stories, which are eternally the same old thing, if only they hadn't led to such dire consequences. Apart from the media's self interest for an ongoing story, there are also circles of people that have utilized the media for engaging in personal conflicts with, for example, my parents. It has long since ceased to have anything to do with "discovering the truth" (if that ever had even played a role) or "informing the public." It has to do with chicanery, with calculated slander. It can further be asserted in my case that I turn more and more into the archetype of the scapegoat. I am the modern Loki, whom the gods punished for their own sins. That sounds now like tragic self-aggrandizement and self-pity, yet the process of my demonization does actually go on. In the mean-time you only hear about me in connection with the murder, as if I were the lone killer of Sandro. Besides, to me alone is attributed the leading role in all of the incidents, which perhaps have only the farthest thing to do with my crime. Through the constant propaganda against me such a poisoned climate has been created in public that barely anyone desires to be made aware of the truth, in oth-ers words, to pay attention to the factual relationships. The people say, "Some of it must be true," for they cannot imagine that they have been duped with an incessant brainwashing propaganda from the side of the media. But I've also got-ten the accusation that this constant reporting was something desired and encouraged by us. For my part, I would like to deny this. I could have meanwhile appeared on nearly every TV station and in every magazine and expressed my opinions, but I have nearly always refused those offers. It is unpleasant and even embarrassing to me when I read my name in the paper and see my picture. I don't wish to be a "public figure."

How has it been for all of you since you were released from jail?

Andreas was released a year before Sebastian and I. After getting reacquainted with the scene for a half-year (among other things, he attended a Mayhem reunion concert in Bischofs-werda), he retreated completely back into his private life. He broke off all contacts, lives with his girl-friend, and has a good job. Even if I was unhappy about his "depar-ture," I nevertheless wish him all the best. Sebastian has totally devoted himself to a folkish world of ideas. He is married and has made a small circle of friends and acquaintances in which he actual-ly plays the same role as he once did in our clique in Sonders-hausen. In the meantime he has

ABSURD CASSETTE COVER
WITH BEYER TOMBSTONE

also recorded and released new Absurd material. In addition he sings with Halgadom, a joint project with the band Stahlgewitter who are friends of his. He has only a peripheral contact with the scene, a situation that has probably kept him out of the media's sights. It is different with me, for I have always had and main-tained numerous contacts in the scene. In addition, I worked at Darker Than Black Records, through which I naturally was in a more prominent situation than my two former accomplices. Since then the media has decided to put me in the stocks and clothe me as their new scapegoat. Because I also nurtured an association with nationalistically inclined people, I have been charged severely. Nobody was inter-ested in the facts anymore, the only thing that counted was sensationalism. This spectacle left me with no possibility of gaining a foothold in society again.

Since my release I have not hurt anyone or destroyed anything. But it has long since had anything more to do with what I did, but rather with what people think about me and do to me. Through the efforts of the leftist opinion cartel, my behavior—which in other countries would be of no consequence—was ultimate-ly depicted as if I had committed the worst crimes against humanity. This process can no longer be halted; it goes beyond my destruction. It was my undoing that I had willingly guided not only my life but that of Andreas and Sebastian— I am a quasi-"missing link" between the two of them.

Do you feel Black Metal is still an important form of music?

If you're talking about the Black Metal underground, then I would agree it's important, but if you're talking about the fashionable music biz, then I have to point out that we don't care about it. If "musicians" feel the urge to prostitute themselves to the business, then let them do so. They will perish, along with the Judeo-capitalistic system they are a part of.

Black Metal from its very core is very important and influential—especially now, at the dawn of the New Aeon, when Christendom will perish and a neo-heathen state will arise. "Herr Wolf" once declared: "A violently active, dominating, intrepid, brutal youth—that is what I am after. Youth must be all those things. It must be insensitive to pain. There must be nothing weak and tender about it. I want to see once more in its eyes the gleam of pride and independence of the splendid beast of prey. I want my youth strong and handsome. They shall overcome mortal dread in the most difficult trials. That is the stage of heroic youth." The youth influenced by Black Metal and other ideologically related music corresponds to "Herr Wolf's" description almost wholly. A youth without false scruples, discarding altruism and morality, the youth of the New Aeon, the new Reich.

We really appreciate the sinister art of Black Metal, and will never change our style, because we became aware of Black Metal as the sound of the forthcoming Aeon of Horus, and the return of Wotan: still absurd, undreamt of by the narrow-minded, but nevertheless the soon-to-be reality, our reality, beyond all doubt! The sun is rising over Europe—will it destroy us or give us light?!

ABSURD *ASGARDSREI*

The harshness of the rhetoric behind Absurd has intensified immeasurably since their early days among the high school students of Sondershausen, as has their music. Beginning meagerly with hymns to demons discovered in Satanic horror films, the early demo cassettes of the band are low-fi chunks of adolescent noise, soaked with distortion and offering unintentionally humorous spoken introductions to the songs. Their music is more akin to '60s garage Punk than some of the well-produced Black Metal of their contemporaries—but what they lacked by way of musical execution they were more than willing to make up for with the real-life execution of the sad figure of Sandro Beyer.

Lyrically they have always sung the praises of revenge against one's enemies, and a number of their earlier songs appear to refer to—or portend, depending on when they were written—their killing, through a recurring leitmotif of murder in the forest. Pushing the limits of poor taste a step further, one of the Absurd cassettes released since their incarceration employed a photo of Sandro Beyer's tombstone for its cover art.

If there is any clear spiritual mentor behind Absurd's transformation over the years, it is Varg Vikernes. Varg himself seems to be aware of this, and smiles when talking of recent events inspired by what happened in Norway: "In Germany some churches have burned. And there are the Absurd guys, who have also turned neo-Nazi...."[14] Judging from the interviews conducted with Hendrik above, Varg's remark about the ideological transformation of Absurd is correct. The long quotation Hendrik attributes to "Herr Wolf" at the end of the interview is in actuality the words of Adolph Hitler, speaking of the new prototype of hardened, pitiless youth which Nazi Germany would produce.

Similarly to how Varg once brazenly put a picture of the burnt remains of Fantoft Stave Church on the cover of Burzum's *Aske* mini-LP, Absurd's *Facta Loquuntur* disc also prominently features a photo of the charred framework of the Frogn church, which was torched in Norway in 1995. The title of the album is Latin for "deeds speak for themselves," and the liner notes exhort the listener to "Remember your pagan origins and follow always the honorable way of your pagan ancestors!" A few sentences further they state, "This release is dedicated in everlasting worship to our martyrs who died or have to suffer in one way or another in order to set a flaming sign for our movement. Our kingdom will come."[15] Such sentiments would make Varg Vikernes proud. Absurd's own tiny record label, Burznazg, takes its name from a term Varg once planned to use for his own operations, and

Kapelle in Brand gesteckt

Die 350 Jahre alte Wallfahrtskapelle auf dem Gehilfersberg bei Rasdorf (Kreis Fulda) ist von Brandstiftern angesteckt worden. In dem Gebäude, in dem sich wertvolle Heiligenfiguren und andere Kunstschätze befanden, brannte in der Nacht zum Samstag bis auf die Grundmauern nieder. Die Polizei bezifferte gestern den Schaden auf rund zwei Millionen Mark. Ein technischer Defekt scheide aus. —FOTO: DPA

GERMAN HEADLINE: "CHAPEL WAS IN FLAMES"

the most infamous criminal in Norway was surely proud to know of the "Tribute to Burzum" compilation CD project initiated by Hendrik Möbus and friends. The band still continues despite their jail sentences, although they have encountered numerous obstacles. Originally incarcerated together in the Erfurt prison, after a period of time the media made a scandal of the fact that the three killers had regular contact with one another inside the prison walls and were being treated much too nicely in light of their crime. Hendrik explains:

In March of '95 the self-declared "Grand Inquisitor," an evangelical parson named Jürgen Hauskeller, together with a member of German parliament, Vera Wollenberger, visited the jail in Erfurt. Although the warden of the jail refused to let them inside, Wollenberger enforced the right for this visit with the help of the Thuringian ministry of justice, and thus they came to look at what was going on with us. Certainly they expected to see us suffering with only bread and water, and were badly surprised to find the opposite was true—we lived together on the same floor, made music together, and so forth. After this visit, they managed to start a hostile campaign against us via the yellow press, by telling how "good" we had it behind bars. The mother of our victim then declared her son had died all over again, and she demanded they stop our alleged "holiday" and start the punishment. The consequences were that each of us has been moved to a different jail, and the warden at Erfurt lost his job, due to the alleged "privileges" he gave us.[16]

GERMAN HEADLINE:
"ENORMOUS BLAZE DESTROYS BELFRY"

The trademark Black Metal pseudonyms of Absurd's personnel have changed since their first recordings, and by '94 they had adopted titles from dark aspects of Germanic mythology, recasting themselves as "Surt," the fire giant who ignites the earth at *Ragnarök;* Nidhögg (literally "the one striking full of hatred" in Old Norse), the dragon who gnaws at the roots of the world-tree and drinks the blood of corpses; while Sebastian, formerly known as "Werwolf Dark Mark Doom," has now shortened his appellation to simply "Doom."

Like Vikernes, Hendrik is of considerable intelligence, and has spent his time behind bars delving deep into the legends and romanticism not only of heathen Germany, but the history and esoterica of the Third Reich as well. While the status of Absurd is certainly limited to the far reaches of the underground, their records have continued to appear and find an audience. The band demonstrated they could engage in the acts they sang about, thereby endowing themselves with a unique aura of "authenticity." The fact they were willing to spend nearly a decade in jail for the experience of committing murder gives them a perverse form of credibility over the bands who merely sing and dream of empty morbid fantasies. By their actions they also set a grim example—as Bård Eithun and Varg Vikernes did before them—which others may feel compelled to live up to.

Möbus also reveals the existence of a Germanic "Black Circle" which he claims the members of Absurd are also connected to, called *Die Teutsche Brüderschaft* (Teutonic Brotherhood). The *Brüderschaft* is mentioned prominently in the dedication list on Absurd's debut CD. Still, Hendrik wonders, "Considering the effects Black Metal is causing, I'd expect something to spread like a wild fire across Europe. It's difficult to say why this has yet failed to appear."[17] It may be that the contemporary German environment is somehow lacking the ingredients that allowed Black Metal to take the extreme turn it did in Norway, but there is evidence that the potential exists.

As an aside during an interview we conducted with Dani, the driving force behind British gothic Black Metal band Cradle of Filth, he mentioned a fleeting encounter they had during one of their early tours with a knife-wielding German youth who claimed to be part of a "Satanic Gestapo." Whether this is the same as the "Teutonic Brotherhood" spoken of by Hendrik is unknown.

DANI — SINGER OF ENGLISH BAND CRADLE OF FILTH

HAVE YOU HAD ANY PROBLEMS WHILE ON TOUR?

We have abroad. Some German guy from the "Satanic Gestapo," I think they were called, who jumped on stage with a carving knife. This was on the Anathema/At the Gates/Cradle of Filth tour, and I was looking the other way when the bouncers grabbed him, and basically beat the crap out of him and threw him on the floor. But he came up afterwards and apologized, and just said, "Oh, sorry," really innocently. I think he just said the knife was a prop, but we were getting threats from people all over Germany. There was a band called Pyogenesis, and these kids who were the mouthpiece of the lower rank of this supposed "Gestapo" were telling people that the girlfriend of a guy in Pyogenesis had been stolen from him and abducted, and they'd been repeatedly raping her.

PHOTO: NIHIL ARCHIVES

CRADLE OF FILTH

THEY ACTUALLY DID THIS?

No, they didn't do it at all. It was bullshit. We saw the guy in Pyogenesis and he said it was absolute rubbish. But we'd heard it from people at a concert saying, "Beware, they mean it," and it was frightening if you put it in context, that people would *make* threats like that.

In other communications, Hendrik reported that in Germany a number of churches and chapels have burned, or were attempted to be torched, under suspicious circumstances. He elaborates:

From late '93 until early '97 there have been around around a dozen church arsons (including attempted ones and/or desecrations inside the church) throughout Germany. Almost all of them have a proven link to Satanism or Black Metal, due to unequivocal symbolism at the scene of the crime. Most of the important events (countless small and large cemetery desecrations, a couple of damaged or burned churches and chapels) took place in Thuringia and Saxony. Some examples: a church desecration in the town of Greiz during the spring of '94, a series of cemetery desecrations along with a burned chapel around

Leipzig during '95–'96 (those "criminals" have been caught already), and a church burned to the ground in Riethnordhausen during the spring of '97. The most recent church fires happened in Lübeck, Hamburg, and Husum (all in north Gemany) during four weeks in April and May '97, but the police, who once again caught all the "criminals," said almost nothing about their background except for that of a link to the right-wing scene.[18]

Churches have also been set alight in nearby Poland—or "Eastern Germany" as Hendrik terms it, recalling Hitler's "Großdeutsches Reich." About the church attacks he elaborates, "Many more were damaged and profaned, and even count- less cemeteries desecrated likewise—but all this I can sum up as 'after-pains' of the Norwegian events."[19] Overall in Europe as of 2002, Hendrik claims to now be aware of more than 100 acts of anti-Christian arson, although it impossible to know on what he bases this figure—presumably rumors circulating in the under- ground he is a part of.

The atavistic element of Black Metal can be seen in the evolving efforts of Absurd, who are beginning to employ more recent and incendiary paradigms from the tumultuous Germanic legacy in their worldview. How many others may be awakened to follow in their halting footsteps? In their song "The Gates of Heaven," written some months before they dispatched Sandro Beyer from earth- ly existence, Absurd demand in slightly broken English: *"Straight on through the gates of heaven, Evil will destroy the souls—Where's your saviour, where hides Jesus? Why isn't he at war against us?"*[20] Unhindered even by temporary confinement to prison, their question is a mocking one.

"HEATHEN HORROR"

It is difficult to document how many of the church arsons and attacks in Germany that occurred in the late 1990s actually emanated from the Black Metal scene, but there is no doubt that in many instances a connection exists. As evi- dence of one minor such incident we can quote from an anonymous communi- cation that was received by the authors in the Autumn of 2000. A two-page letter accompanied by two blurry photos, the missive was entitled "Heathen Horror" and related various accounts of church desecration before signing off with the exhortation "Kill for Wotan!" We are unable to verify any details of this account (including whether or not the "Surt" mentioned here is also the member of Absurd who uses this stage name), but the photographs, despite their poor qual- ity, would lend a degree of veracity to the story. We offer a section of it here in translation to provide a glimpse into the moonlight activities—in all their earnest incompetence—of a militant segment of the German Black Metal scene.

On a cold November night in 1999 "Surt" and "Tyrann" traveled through towns in the countryside in order to find a remote church that could be set on fire. After some hours of searching we found a secluded House of God in a small village, situated far enough from the town that we would not be heard. We had prepared for our project with torches, kerosene, a crowbar, and a sledgehammer. We parked the car about a half-kilometer away, so that possibly no one might connect it to the action. Were someone to in fact notice us at the church and call the police, we would hear it immediately over a police scanner, and still have time enough to disappear undetected since the closest police station was in the next town many kilometers away. Besides, nothing usually goes on in little towns. After a long trek we reached our goal. We made it over a low fence to the cemetery where the church was also located. It was quite a sight—the church lit by moonlight and the red glow of the graveside candle lamps. After trying unsuccessfully to get the main door open with the crowbar, we crept around the church to find another way in. At the vestry, we finally managed it. We were very nervous and just wanted to hurry. Without looking around us much, we stormed into the main part of the church—by the light of our torches—to lay waste to it and spread the flames. Surt took the kerosene out of his backpack and poured it over the pews as Tyrann held his torch to it and… nothing happened! Shit! It can't be true! All that energy for nothing? We tried to get the fire going with the kerosene; this looked especially good by night inside the church. Again we poured kerosene on the pews, now more than before. Again Tyrann held his torch to the wet pews, and again nothing happened! In a hurry and mad rush we lay candles, seat pillows and whatever else we could find on the pews and lit it. Smashing the window panes, we took off at that moment since we were too nervous and just wanted to get out as quickly as we could. So, okay—the church wasn't burnt down. But it was still a decent desecration, since all the church pews were ruined with fire damage, so that no church services would be taking place there anytime soon.

RADICAL RIGHT-WING ASYLUM SEEKERS?

After serving the court-ordained portion of their jail sentences, the youths convicted in the slaying of Sandro Beyer were all released on parole. As Hendrik mentions in the previous interview, only he and Sebastian carried forth with the musical endeavors of Absurd. The band's reconfigured record label, now called Darker Than Black, also began to develop a higher profile. Hendrik renewed his contacts in the music scene and appeared in a few Black Metal fanzines. In July of 1999 announcements circulated about the release of Absurd's new 4-song CD entitled *Asgardsrei*. The CD featured a more aesthetic presentation and an evolved sound, although with much of Absurd's garage-band ambience still intact. Guests on the release included Graveland's Rob Darken and well as an "ex-member of the German mainstream band Weissglut." The end of the advertisement advised interested customers to "ORDER IT NOW before ZOG²¹ take YOUR copy."

This warning about the confiscation of CDs by governmental authorities was not overly paranoid, however, as just a few months later on October 6, 1999, the German police raided a number of homes across the country, in particular the residences of the Darker Than Black and No Colours record labels. The initial charges consisted of "distribution of National Socialistic, anti-Semitic, racist, and violent releases." Hendrik commented at the time, "This is the first time that the Black Metal scene has experienced the same kind of charges as the White Power scene." He later noted that the government's actions failed to result in any legal proceedings against those who were subject to the raids, meaning that the items found in the raids—with Absurd records prominent among them—were not sufficiently in violation of the law to make for a strong court case.

But the governmental crackdown on the record labels was the least of Hendrik's problems. The public prosecutor had now decided to launch an effort to revoke Hendrik's parole on the basis of alleged political crimes he had committed since his release from juvenile prison. These consisted of displaying banned political emblems and also giving a "Hitler salute" at a concert.

In September of 1999 the court ruled against Hendrik, and he immediately tried to appeal the decision. Attempting to remain stoic in the face of these new developments and the resulting media furor, he commented: "Narrow-minded people even claim that I want to be the German counterpart of Varg Vikernes, but honestly speaking, I have never wanted to experience the 'Vikernes-effect' on myself at all. However, there is no point lamenting about my fate. I have to accept this burden and must try to make the best out of it."

It was around this time that Hendrik disappeared from public view, leaving the musical demimonde behind, and went truly underground. Rumors have abounded concerning the details of his subsequent actions, but it is certain that he managed to eventually fly to America and arrived in Seattle, Washington toward the end of 1999. Travelling across the U.S.A., Hendrik passed through a string of ill-fated liaisons with racists upon whom he depended for safehousing, culminating with two of them violently threatening him. Following this incident, he eventually made his way to the state of West Virginia and to the headquarters of William Pierce's racialist group the National Alliance. All was relatively quiet for a number of weeks until Hendrik was arrested in late August, 2000 by U.S. federal agents acting on an international warrant. The German government had requested to have Hendrik extradited to face his charges of parole violation.

The press treatment of the case was unusual, with Hendrik being elevated from a "Satanic murderer" to a "neo-Nazi fugitive." He became an international *cause célèbre*—garnering headlines in *U.S. News and World Report*, as well as major papers like the *Los Angeles Times* and the *Washington Post*—and his case raised many serious issues about the way in which modern democratic states handle persons who they deem as threats to democracy itself. Soon after his arrest, Hendrik wrote a letter to U.S. President William Clinton and Attorney General Janet Reno and requested status as a political refugee, stating that if he were extradited back to Germany he would be persecuted on account of his political beliefs.

Hendrik was supported in his legal defense by the National Alliance, with William Pierce soliciting donations to help offset the cost of lawyers. A "Free Hendrik Möbus" campaign was also launched on the Internet, and William Pierce produced episodes of his radio program *American Dissident Voices* in which he addressed the topic of Möbus's case in detail. In the first major ruling, the U.S. magistrate decided that Hendrik was not eligible for political asylum as he was a "convicted felon" in Germany. Hendrik then attempted to appeal the decision. In their commentaries on the case, both he and William Pierce attempted to make the fundamental issue one of free speech, since the actions which resulted in the original parole revocation were not of a violent nature, but rather "political" misdeeds (which would be perfectly legal according to U.S. laws). Both the U.S. and German governments tried to avoid this thorny issue and confine the legal proceedings to the logistical issues of Hendrik's parole violation itself, rather than debating the validity of the charges that led to the violation.

Hendrik's support website <www.hendrikmoebus.com> raises similar issues. Alongside a wealth of newspaper articles about the case, the site contains a number of essays and articles, written by Möbus himself, which question the Federal Republic of Germany's behavior toward political dissidents. In one article, an "Open Letter to the German Nationalists," Hendrik explains why he hopes they will stand on his side:

> The louder and more publicly this and other questions are discussed in Federal Republic of Germany and in the USA, the more the authorities will claim that a state of emergency exists. They will try to hush up my case and try to distort and cover up the facts.
>
> You, however, can help prevent this. I urgently request that you do not let this opportunity pass by. If the national resistance in Germany does not use my case for its purposes, the system will abuse my case to damage all German Nationalists.

Police catch up with neo-Nazi in Lewisburg

Convicted murderer Moebus wanted by German government for parole violations

By Tom Searls
tomsearls@wvgazette.com

A neo-Nazi German murderer wanted for parole violations was arrested over the weekend after leaving the mountaintop compound of William Pierce, a neo-Nazi leader who resides in Poca-

ginia, said Tuesday.
Moebus was being held in Central Regional Jail, Flatwoods, pending a Sept. 7 hearing. He was convicted in Germany in 1994 of luring a "non-Aryan" teen-ager into an apartment and strangling him.

After his release on parole in

the German media saying he would avoid arrest and fled to the United States last December.
Marshals had been watching Pierce's 200-acre compound at Mill Point for at least two weeks, said Claxton. Pierce heads the National Alliance, a neo-Nazi organization, from the compound.

lar to one described in the novel.
"We really don't know what brought [Moebus] to West Virginia, other than the [National Alliance] and the white supremacist ties there, and that's pure speculation," Claxton said.

When marshals went to Poca-

I do not make this request so that I can be the center of attention. I do not want to play a role in your organizations. But I know how serious and dramatic our situation in Germany is. This situation requires unusual and detailed commitment. My case provides an opportunity for this. Who knows, perhaps a US court will grant me asylum. This would be an impressive demonstration of what we have known for a long time: the Federal Republic of Germany is not a democracy, but rather a criminal state!

When Hendrik Möbus arrived at William Pierce's compound, Pierce was in the process of building up his Resistance Records music label and hoping to expand its horizons outside the skinhead genre. Hendrik was eager to get involved, for he had already tried to bridge the gap between skinheads and Black Metal youths in Germany. In an

HENDRIK MÖBUS SHORTLY BEFORE HIS ARREST IN WEST VIRGINIA

effort to make Black Metal more palatable to the other radical elements of the racial movement, Hendrik has also written about the genre for Pierce's magazine (under the pseudonym "Hagen von Tronje," a reference to the dark figure of the medieval German epic *The Nibelungenlied*). One of the main obstacles toward Black Metal's acceptance in the arena of radical politics stems from its Satanic and frenziedly destructive past. Along with Varg Vikernes, Hendrik Möbus is therefore endeavoring to present the musical movement he is connected with in a wholly militant heathen light, now devoid of the old Satanic imagery. This may ultimately be a futile cause, for Black Metal has been defined by its Satanic tendency from the earliest beginning, and old perceptions die hard.

In stark contrast to his stated desire "not to be a public figure," Hendrik Möbus inadvertently became a subject for international news headlines. His strategy for avoiding extradition created a further paradox: he was forced to seek the mercy of liberal democratic political asylum laws—exactly the sort of laws which a strident German nationalist would vehemently oppose in their own country for anti-immigration reasons. Ultimately his ploy was unsuccessful, and on July 29, 2001 Hendrik was extradited back to his *Vaterland* and into the custory of the Thuringian Justice Department, who decreed that he serve the three-year remainder of his original sentence. Two further court judgments against him, one for public display of the Hitler salute and the other for mocking his victim in published statements, have added more than two years of additional incarceration to the time he will serve in jail. It quickly became clear that Hendrik's personal goal of collaborating with William Pierce in a venture to promote radical Black Metal through the racial music underground would be impossible to realize from a German prison cell. An equally significant obstacle arose exactly one year later when William Pierce died suddenly from cancer on July 23, 2002. Whether the organization and record label he leaves behind will still endeavor to capitalize on the Black Metal market remains to be seen.

LORDS OF CHAOS

IN THE CONSCIOUSNESS OF FANS OF INTENSE, CUTTING-EDGE MUSIC, "BLACK METAL"
has become synonymous with Norway. This is understandable, as the events
there received a significant amount of media attention through articles in
Kerrang!, *Spin*, *Fortean Times*, the *Manchester Guardian*, and other papers and
magazines around the world. What few commentators realize—except those
immersed in the Black Metal underworld—is that Norway is far from unique.
Black Metal is a worldwide phenomenon, and in many parts of the globe it is just
now gaining popularity and momentum. Like an unquenchable forest fire, spreading beneath a cover of leaves and underbrush, the smoking embers in Norway created by the loosely-knit "Black Circle" began to surface in faraway places.

It has been demonstrated how the desolate soil of East Germany provided a
paradoxically fecund womb for Black Metal ideology to blossom into Absurdist
crimes—all that was needed was fertilization by way of an example set by
Scandinavia. They are not the only ones. Restless youth around the world long for
a symbolic identity to join with, one that provides catharsis for their rebellious
impulses. The manifestation of such energies often produces jolting results. What
follows is a selective, country-by-country scorecard of the unfolding mayhem
related to Black Metal, either in actuality or in spirit.

SWEDEN

A considerable cooperation and cross-pollination occurred between the
Swedish and Norwegian Black Metal scenes. Most of this centered around the

activities of Øystein Aarseth and his Deathlike Silence record label. Various key players from Sweden would visit Oslo on occasion, hang around the Helvete shop, and thus an alleged Swedish "Black Circle" eventually developed in a parallel fashion with their neighbors to the west.

The first documented Black Metal transgression in Sweden took place under the direction of Varg Vikernes when the 18-year-old future mental patient Suvi Mariotta Puurunen attempted to burn down the house of Christopher Jonsson on July 26, 1992. While the crime didn't amount to much, her demented diary provided ample fodder for the media's later portrayal of Vikernes as the perverse persona "The Count." Puurunen was later brought in to testify during the trials in Norway of Vikernes and others.

A few short months later, on Halloween night in the town of Finspång, a party took place. All Hallow's Eve is considered one of the more important Satanic holidays, and the celebration was allegedly attended by members of two of the most well-known Swedish Black Metal music groups, Dissection (who in fact predate the modern wave of Scandinavian Black Metal by a few years) and Abruptum. The latter group consists of the bizarre duo "Evil" and his accomplice "It," a dwarf who asserts he adopted his pseudonym because he was so evil he could no longer be considered human. Both bands are often referred to as central forces in the Swedish Black Circle. During the course of the night's merry-making, an 18-year-old in attendance named Linus Åkerlund was instructed that he should prove to the others he was capable of killing without compunction. Attempting to fulfill the direc-

"IT": THE EVIL DWARF OF ABRUPTUM

tive, he attacked an innocent 63-year-old man, stabbing him repeatedly in the neck. The elderly man nearly died from blood loss; his attacker received a four-year prison sentence. Åkerlund served two years of his sentence and was released. He claims today he never committed the crime. In a separate incident, one member of Dissection was ordered to serve four months in jail for the desecration of 250 graves.

In early December of 1992, Deicide, the Satanic Death Metal band from America, was on tour in Europe. They played in Oslo and shortly afterward in Stockholm, Sweden, at the Fryshuset club. Before they had taken the stage, an explosion went off by the fire exit of the venue, knocking out an entire wall and effecting major structural damage. A number of people were injured,

PHOTO: MICHAEL MOYNIHAN

DEICIDE LIVE

though no one seriously so. It was first speculated that the Swedish Black Circle might have been behind the bombing, either as an attack against Deicide, who they may have considered rival Satanists, but more likely directed at the opening band Gorefest, an antiracist and politically correct Death Metal group. Further investigation of the matter raised serious doubts whether the bomb could have been placed by anyone connected to the Black Circle. When Deicide played in Oslo a few nights earlier, many in the Black Metal scene attended, and Øystein Aarseth was even the DJ at the concert. The Norwegians, at least, approved of Deicide's Satanism and got along well with lead singer Glen Benton. The clue to the Stockholm bombing may have come shortly afterward, when death threats were made against Deicide prior to their U.K. appearances by an organization calling itself "Animal Militia"—a radical anti-vivisectionist group. Their threats were specifically aimed at Benton himself, who had previously advocated the torture and sacrifice of animals in Satanic rituals, and claimed to regularly take part in such activities himself. In the death threat sent by their "Manchester cell" to Benton, they began it with the sentence: "Stockholm was just a taste of what is to come."[2] Given this evidence, and the fact that bombings have not been the usual *modus operandi* of Scandinavian Black Metalers (although Vikernes later did steal

RE: DEICIDE.

STOCKHOLM WAS JUST A TASTE OF WHAT IS TO COME.
BENTON IS LIVING HIS SCHOOLBOY FANTASY BUT THIS IS REAL LIFE - WISE UP!
HES PARANOID ABOUT CHRISTIANS FOLLOWING HIM, BENTON, THERE IS NO GOD, THERE IS NO SATAN,
AS YOU ARE ABOUT TO DISCOVER, THE HARD WAY.
YOU AMUSE US WITH YOUR 'RAMBOESQUE' THREATS OF VIOLENCE, AND 'MODEL BOY' POSING NEXT TO
INVERTED CROSSES, HOW DANGEROUS, HOW DESPERATE.
YOU ARE THE IRRITATING PIECE OF SHIT HE MUST SCRAPE OFF THE SOLE OF THE WORLD'S
SHOE.
YOU ARE THE MAN IN THE SPOTLIGHT, WE ARE THE INVISIBLE, WE HAVE OUR CONTACTS AND
WE CAN BE WHOEVER WE CHOOSE TO BE. THE PASSENGER AT THE AIRPORT, THE VAN ON THE
ROADWAY, ROOM SERVICE AT THE HOTEL, THE FAN AT THE GIG, OR THE SECURITY!
THIS CITY IS RULED BY THE GUN - ANYTHING'S POSSIBLE.
BENTON, THE VENUES AND THE PRESS HAVE ALL BEEN WARNED, IF INNOCENT PEOPLE SUFFER THEIR
BLOOD WILL BE ON THE HANDS OF THE PEOPLE BEHIND THE GIGS, WE WILL NOT BE HELD
RESPONSIBLE.
HELL, THIS IS GOING TO BE OUR EASIEST TARGET TO DATE, OUR ONLY REGRET IS THAT
BENTON WON'T SUFFER ENOUGH, WE'LL TRY OUR BEST!
WEDNESDAY 16th DECEMBER AT A VENUE WE KNOW INSIDE OUT, THIS IS GOING TO BE
ARMAGEDDON.
THIS IS THE FINAL WARNING, SHIT, IF SALMAN RUSHTIE HAD BENTONS BRAIN HE WOULD HAVE
BEEN DEAD YEARS AGO.

WE THANK YOU FOR YOUR TIME

ANIMAL MILITIA DEATH THREAT

150 kilos of dynamite and other explosives, which were found in his apartment at the time of his second arrest), the likely suspects for the Deicide show detonation would be allies of the Animal Militia.

The Swedes did, however, quickly take up their own firebrands after the example set by Vikernes and others in Norway. About a month after Vikernes had publicly revealed the connection between Black Metal and church burning in the mass media, on February 7, 1993, the Lundby New Church in Sweden erupted into flames. Built in Gothenburg in 1886, the giant church was famous for its stellar acoustics and the many recordings made there. Ironically, an obsessive strain of music fan would attempt to destroy it. Three males, all about 18 years of age, eventually received two- to three-year sentences for arson. The same night also witnessed the vandalization of another Christian building not far from the Lundby New Church.

Later that year, on the 3rd of July, another church was attacked. The Salabacke Church was a wooden building erected in 1957, approximately forty-five feet high. A fire was started from solvent-soaked papers placed against the outside of the church. Due to the wood construction and the building's height, the blaze raged out of control, completely destroying the church organ and much of the building's contents. The church silver, pulpit, and altarpieces were blessed enough to survive. Two 15-year-old girls were arrested, but their young age meant they would only be confined to youth homes by the state. The arsonists declared they had committed their act as a salute to Varg Vikernes and to hail Satan. They had planned to continue burning churches and to threaten priests. Beyond having to pay a joint fine of 75,000 Swedish Kronor (approximately $9,400), one of the girls, Alexandra Jansson, clearly received no rehabilitation during her time as a ward of the state. She was later implicated in grave desecrations, death threats, and violence against civil officials in 1995 and '96.

Another antique house of worship, Föllinge Church, had served the Christian community since 1815—until drunk and drugged-out Death Metal musician Stefan Dahlberg set the wood building alight on July 17, 1994. The 19-year-old youth was ordered to pay 50,000 Kronor ($6,200) in damages and confined to a mental institution. Besides the arson, Dahlberg was also found guilty of thirty grave desecrations.

Others directly involved in Swedish Satanic bands have attempted to cause disruption with varying degrees of violence. One of the members of Black Metal band Algaion, singer Mårten Björkman, was convicted with a one-month sentence for setting an old building on fire. Far more terrifying was the action which took place on February 22, 1995 in the city of Linköping, when three youths between 16 and 18 years old went on what they termed a "niggerhunt." Wielding an axe and two machetes, they terrorized a black man. Two of them had also attempted to burn down a church a few weeks earlier, but were unsuccessful and caught by the police. Involved in both crimes was "Belfagor," a member of the Black Metal band Nefandus.

The racist attack of Belfagor and friends was not unprecedented, although it was crudely and haphazardly executed. A few years earlier Sweden had experienced the campaign of the so-called "Laserman," a clandestine assassin armed with a laser-scoped firearm who perpetrated at least ten murders or serious woundings of male immigrants and non-white citizens.

The most recent crime report from Sweden which received media attention occurred in mid-1996. In late July of that year, two males burglarized the sepulchral chapel in the town of Köping. Once inside the chambers, they found the room for the dead awaiting burial and managed to lift off one of the coffin lids, at which point they proceeded to paint Satanic symbols on the corpse. They also stumbled upon the clever notion of switching the names on two of the coffins awaiting interment. The authorities only figured out about the name swap later— after this small detail had caused the burial of the wrong person at a funeral.

Though the number of serious offenses may be lower, Sweden rivals Norway in the scope of atrocities related to Black Metal. While most of the Norwegian bands have now evolved past their earliest primitive obsessions with exemplify-

SWEDISH HEADLINE: "DEVIL WORSHIPPER
BURNED DOWN THE CHURCH?"

ing "pure evil," their Swedish cousins appear to remain attracted to such concepts. The main personality in Abruptum, "It," even claims to have personally conceived the entire idea for the "True Satanist Horde," which in turn inspired the formation of the Norwegian Black Circle. "It" insists that he and his allies will carry on in the original spirit of such efforts.

Beyond those who actively take part in it, the Swedish police seem to be the only others who know what the Black Circle really is about in practice. The mayhem in Sweden has not abated over time, and may even overtake that of Norway in terms of sheer violence. On December 18, 1997, a 20-year-old Swedish "Satanist" was arrested in connection with several murders. According to the media (the police are reluctant to give out information), this might be the beginning of an internal "housecleaning" of the Swedish underground in a similar way to what occurred in Norway. Varg Vikernes is seen as a probable influence.

The police originally raided the home of the man for suspicion of abusing his girlfriend. In his apartment in the south of Stockholm, the police found a pistol with live ammunition and a human skull. They also found a so-called "ritual room" with an altar, skeletal remains, and "Satanic symbols."

In connection with the raid, the police learned that the

SWEDISH HEADLINE: "CHASED BY THREE IN AXE DRAMA"

man had "claimed responsibility" for a murder committed in Gothenburg (or more likely boasted of it, given the behavior of other Black Metal criminals). According to the Swedish tabloid *Expressen*, the murder in question is an unsolved case concerning a teenage girl who was found undressed and dead in a graveyard in the summer of 1994.

Furthermore, the young man is now under suspicion of having killed a 37-year-old man from Algeria. The man was killed in a park in Gothenburg in July, 1997. The police believe that the 20-year-old might have killed more people. They later charged him with the suspected murder of a 16-year-old girl,

SWEDISH HEADLINE: "THE CHURCH IN ASHES"

Malin Olsson, killed on July 23, 1994—the exact same month and day of the murder in 1997.

The young man had been in trouble with the law before. A few weeks before his arrest, he was charged with assaulting two men and a woman outside a restaurant in Gothenburg. The woman recalls that the man screamed: "Sieg Heil! Shall we slaughter people?" She also described him as a leader for a group of other young people. "They were like trained dogs. He pointed and told them to stand to attention, and they obeyed," she said. Other witnesses describe the man as a "Satanist," and say that he made Hitler salutes. The 20-year-old himself says he was too drunk to remember anything.

A second man has been charged in relation to the crimes, a 22-year-old who was alleged by the Swedish media to have been a close friend of Varg Vikernes. He is described as a "star in a Satanic rock band" by the press. This is, in fact, Jon Nödtveidt of the group Dissection, who may well be the source of the following quote from *Slayer* magazine in 1995, which was attributed to an anonymous member of the band:

...there are far more evil things to do than just bragging about church fires! Wait and see... Our empire seeks its senses in the darkest depths of mankind's senses. What is hidden, but nevertheless existing. It cannot die! I don't think that the Black Circle should be a fan club for Black Metal, it's not about that...[5]

ON RECHERCHE
POUR CRIME
CONTRE L'
HUMANITE

JESUS (dit le Christ)

Il est accusé d' être l'
initiateur de persécutions et
de meurtres de millions de
personnes
Il est le fondateur du
christianisme, une religion de
fanatiques qui promet la vie
éternelle mais a comme
finalité l' esclavage.

ATTENTION

Les partisans de Jésus (dit le
Christ) ont pris le contrôle de
dizaines de nations et de
millions d' esprits.
Ils sont armés et dangereux,
à la fois politiquement et
idéologiquement.

NAPALM ROCK N° 4

WANTED: JESUS

FRANCE

There are no reports of church burnings in France—yet. If the swelling interest in Satanism and Black Metal continues there unabated, anything is possible. The music received mention in a spate of newspaper articles which appeared in early 1997, focusing on connections between Satanic youth groups, Black Metal, and extreme factions of the right wing. While the accelerating media coverage resulted in a typical overreaction and a tendency to draw correspondences and conclusions that may have been unwarranted, there is no doubt that a number of bizarre actions did take place.

On the night of June 8, 1996, a desecration took place in the cemetery of Toulon. According to L'Express magazine, four youths exhumed the cadaver of Yvonne Foin. After liberating the body from its twenty-year rest beneath the earth, they rudely planted a cross in the center of her heart. Two of the desecrators, Anthony and Christophe Mignoni, both age 20, were known fans of Black Metal. Police soon raided Antony Mignoni's apartment and discovered certain tracts and pamphlets among his belongings. L'Express drew particular attention to a leaflet with a unflattering portrait of Christ and the caption: "Wanted for Crimes Against Humanity: Jesus (AKA the Christ). He is accused of initiating the persecutions and murder of millions..."[4] The leaflet is a publication of Napalm Rock, an underground magazine dedicated to heathen and revolutionary music groups opposed to the current political system. Napalm Rock is connected with the Nouvelle Résistance (New Resistance), a political group founded by Christian Bouchet.

In "another unsettling discovery," the magazine reports that desecrator Anthony

Mignoni is also a member of the French Black Metal band Funeral, in which he uses the pseudonym "Hades."[5] Interviewed in an alleged neo-Nazi fanzine, *Deo Occidi*, he is reported as stating:

> I have created Funeral in order to spread my ideas based on the destruction of the Jewish, Christian, and Muslim religions, and on the purity and supremacy of the true Aryan race. ... The spirit of Heinrich Himmler will not die. We are the elite of the superior race. Under the sign of the SS, we will triumph. Loyalty and Honor. Sieg Heil![6]

FRENCH GRAVE DESECRATORS

Later in the interview, he claims to be involved with an occult group calling itself "The Sacred Order of the Emerald." Supposedly dedicated to Lucifer, the group was created by someone named "Antitheos," who turns out to be none other than fellow desecrator Christophe Mignoni, operating the "Order" out of his parent's home. The fanzine also provides evidence that the Mignoni boys paid regular visits to the graveyard. The interview is illustrated with a poorly reproduced photograph of two males in corpsepaint makeup, standing before a cemetery tomb with a Nazi armband in clear view.

A follow-up article in *L'Express* reveals further evidence which "confirms the ideological references of the young 'devils.'"[7] Some months after the original despoilment of Yvonne Foin's corpse and subsequent raid of Mignoni's apartment, groundskeepers at a military area on nearby Saint Madrier peninsula discov-

ORDER OF THE EMERALD

ered an odd sack under a pile of rocks. Upon
closer examination, the contents of the sack
were found to be photos of youths dressed in
trenchcoats and wearing sinister face paint,
manuscripts from the Sacred Order of the
Emerald, and a number of neo-Nazi publications. The bag was later traced back to
Christophe Mignoni. Police theorize the
sack was hidden by his brother David, in a
panic after the arrest of his sibling and
friends. *L'Express* then goes on to imply
the desecrators must have been involved
with all the groups whose literature was
found in the sack, including the
Charlemagne Hammer Skinheads, the
French Nationalist Party, and the inner circle
of Nouvelle Résistance. Such speculations
seem unfounded. The citizens of Toulon should
be more worried that some of the tracts previously
in the hands of the "little devils" also included
instructions on homemade bombs, Molotov
cocktails, and explosive lightbulbs. If no one else, at

FATHER UHL

least the youths' patron deity Lucifer (the "light bringer") would be impressed.

Sensational tales in the press didn't stop with the Toulon affair. In an act
recalling the brutality of the Norwegian killings a few years earlier, on Christmas
eve, 1996, a 19-year-old in Mulhouse paid an unexpected visit to an elderly priest
in the town. The youth, David Oberdorf, had professed his faith before the same
clergyman in the Saint Adelphe Church some years earlier. Wielding a recently
purchased dagger with a twenty-centimeter blade, Oberdorf appeared at the residence of Father Jean Uhl. Once face-to-face with the priest he declared, "I am
possessed by the demon—I must annihilate men of religion!"[8] Father Uhl tried in
vain to dissuade him from committing an irreparable act, but Oberdorf would
not be deterred from his unholy mission. The body of the Church Father was later
found dead, stabbed thirty-three times. Prosecutors speculated the killing was
done as an attempt "to symbolize the death of Christ."[9] Whatever the motive,
Oberdorf inflicted a number of wounds on the body after it was dead, including
peculiar incisions on the insides of the priest's palms in the shape of a "V," or what
may have been unsuccessful attempts to carve a pentagram. A legal official noted,
"It's not a matter of defense wounds—these are scarifications made *after* the
death."[10]

The report in the *France-Soir* paper describes Oberdorf as an "impressionable youth of modest intelligence," who had previously attempted suicide.[11] He
had also placed numerous anonymous harassing phone calls to Father Uhl prior

to the murder. The teenager's room was described as quite ordinary, except for a collection of disturbing compact discs. His neighbors had often noticed sounds blaring from his room, "gnawing music, hard and stressful, which one would hear late at night"—not a bad description of standard Black Metal from an unfamiliar listener.[12] Other media reports referred to the youth as a fan of "Viking music." Oberdorf had no girlfriends, but spent time with a few other male teens. One, 18-year-old Stephane Fest, was later arrested after police found he had hidden the murder weapon for Oberdorf. Both youths routinely dressed in black. Investigators also found links between Oberdorf and Toulon grave desecrator Anthony Mignoni, who

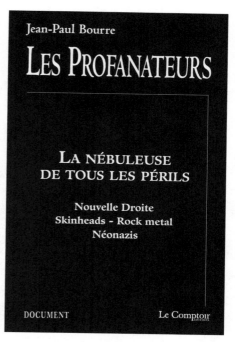

Jean-Paul Bourre

LES PROFANATEURS

LA NÉBULEUSE DE TOUS LES PÉRILS

Nouvelle Droite
Skinheads - Rock metal
Néonazis

DOCUMENT   Le Comptoir

FRENCH ALARMIST BOOK

was thought to be the "initiator of David Oberdorf."[13] Mignoni, having served the sentence he received for the corpse defilement of the previous summer, could not be directly implicated in the murder of Father Uhl as he had a sound alibi. He had been at the home of his grandmother that evening.

The *France-Soir* piece on the Mulhouse killing also mentions the right-wing influences which pop up in Black Metal, and on the same page of the paper one finds an article titled "From Lucifer to the Extreme Right: The Skins" describing a recent French book by Jean-Paul Bourre, *Les Profanateurs* (The Desecrators). This 200-page exposé, by the previous author of *The Luciferian Sects,* spins tales of a dubious web joining skinheads, Black Metalers, drug use, neo-heathenism, and the right-leaning cultural intellectuals of the "Research Group on European Civilization." The fascination surrounding the grave of Jim Morrison of the Doors (buried in Paris' famous Pere La Chaise cemetery) and those of other notable personalities is also inexplicably discussed in one chapter. *Les Profanateurs* desperately attempts to pull all these disparate elements into a sinister scenario in hopes of alarming its readers. It makes the questionable assumption that anyone interested in vaguely similar ideas—even when of the broadest sort, such as "neo-heathenism"—must therefore be part of a *de facto* hidden conspiracy. Such grand conspiracies may make good fodder for the front pages of tabloids, but the reality of the situation is far less organized and interconnected than such journalists argue. The same was certainly true in Norway.

VARG VIKERNES (main pic), and the saga as shown in the pages of Kerrang!...

CHRONOLOGY OF *KERRANG!* ARTICLES

ENGLAND

Black Metal in the United Kingdom erupted in two different realms. Underground fans of the music inaugurated a series of church attacks in emulation of their Norwegian hero Varg Vikernes, and almost caused Black Metal music

'This music must be banned'

Cover of
normality
hid evil
beliefs

Whitsun's orgy of desecration was to cause churchgoers maximum distress

BRITISH HEADLINES

to be banned in Britain as a result. On the other hand, homegrown English Black Metal achieved far greater popularity than the genre had anywhere else in the world, entirely due to the success of one band. Both strata in the U.K. scene had a small bit of common ground.

By the spring of 1994, reverberations of the church burning epidemic in Scandinavia had been heavily covered in the British press, from *Kerrang!* magazine to the *Manchester Guardian* newspaper. *Kerrang!* in particular had devoted steady, melodramatic coverage to the Norwegian scene, regaling its readers with the latest shocking actions and pronouncements from Øystein Aarseth, Varg Vikernes, Fenriz of Darkthrone, and others. As a result, young fans were excited by Black Metal and well aware of the harsh ideological rhetoric that came with it. Vikernes's statements—in particular, his claim the church arsons were acts of heathen terrorism—made a strong impact on a small clique of teenagers from the town of Tunbridge Wells in Kent, England.

PAUL TIMMS

The group of friends, led by 18-year-old Paul Timms, formed the nucleus of an underground Black Metal band dubbed Necropolis. Other members included Dave Wharton, a 22-year-old postman, Mark Reeves, also 22, and Kevin Mooney, a 21-year-old engineer for British Airways. Timms's girlfriend later stated that the band was created after inspiration from the Norwegians. *Kerrang!* also believes that the group's campaign of "attacking the church, with whatever means possible, was to earn respect and notoriety from their idols."[14] It certainly gained more attention than they would ever receive for their music, as Necropolis does not appear to have recorded a note.

Beginning in April, '94, members of Necropolis carried their impulses to fruition, and began a desecratory assault against churches and cemeteries in their area. They would knock over or break as many as sixty headstones in a single night. Graveyards in Rusthall and Tunbridge Wells were hit first. On Easter the assaults accelerated with the desecrations of St. Peter's Church in Southborough and St. Mark's Church in their hometown. In the latter instance windows were shattered, the altar destroyed, prayer books shredded, and artifacts upturned. Timms later commented, "We wished we had burnt it afterwards."[15] He also claimed the group would have targeted larger churches if they'd only had access to explosives. Desecrator David Wharton said the actions were carried out in the early hours of the morning with the group outfitted in camouflage clothing. Timms stated he felt nothing for those buried in the cemeteries or their living relatives, and justified himself: "We are Satanists. We believe it is revenge against Christians. They destroyed pagan boundaries and built their churches on top of them."[16] Such words demonstrate an obvious emulation of Varg Vikernes. Vikernes is quoted in the same *Kerrang!* feature as saying, "No one can stop the church burning. And if these people claim to be influenced by me, then that's fine."[17]

Following the initial graveyard and cemetery ransackings, a week later the group again attacked the church in Southborough along with St. Peter's Church in Fordcombe. Their final assault, called "an orgy of desecration" by one U.K. paper, resulted in the vandalization of graves in Speldhurst, Groombridge, and Frant.[18] Not only were headstones toppled over, but those which were in the shape of crosses were ripped up, inverted, and left standing upside-down. Timms and his fellow musicians were finally arrested in simultaneous police raids on May 27th. The authorities were acting on an anonymous tip, which may have resulted from someone overhearing Timms talk of the crimes to his girlfriend in a pub. At first police only brought in Wharton, Reeve, and Mooney, unaware of Timms's connection to the group. However, in the raids on their homes, investigators found a homemade poster of Necropolis depicting the four members. Based on this they quickly realized one of the criminals was still probably at large. They arrested Timms two days later.

During one of the court hearings, presided over by a Catholic judge, Timms donned a T-shirt from the English band Cradle of Filth which featured the slo-

gan "JESUS IS A CUNT" across its back. The youths expected to receive assign-
ments of community service for their actions, but ended up with two-and-a-half
year jail sentences. When initially in custody and asked by the jail wardens what
he wanted to eat, Timms replied: "A bible!"[19] He starved himself for four days
before relenting with his dietary request. Damage for the crimes was assessed at a
minimum of £100,000 ($160,000), possibly much higher.

Timms's girlfriend, 16-year-old Justine Turnbull, described how he would
talk to her about the plans of defiling the churches:

> He used to say that if he didn't do it, then he would be a hypocrite. Cradle of Filth talk about
> doing all this stuff against Christianity but they haven't actually done it, whereas Paul put what he
> believed into practice. I admired that in him. I still do.[20]

When asked if she thinks he and his bandmates took it too far, she states simply: "No."[21] The Reverend John Banner of Tunbridge Wells, a former exorcist and
friend of Timms's mother, was vociferous in his outrage at the acts of destruction:

> This is the first time I have come across a group who have seen, by virtue of a cult, what they have
> to do and go and do it like a military operation. Their acts were committed to cause the most horrif-
> ic offence to innocent people, arriving at their churches for Pentecost.[22]

Rev. Banner subsequently used the example of the desecrations as justification for attempting to ban Black Metal music in the U.K. altogether. "I have no

CRADLE OF FILTH

doubt the Black Metal and Death Music and its teachings is 95 percent to blame for this. It has to be stopped...”[23]

The *Kerrang!* article points out that Timms was allegedly in regular contact with U.K. Black Metal bands Gomorrah and Cradle of Filth. The media excitement over the Tunbridge Wells vandalism soon developed into feature articles on the horrors of Black Metal music itself, and Cradle of Filth was generally singled out for attention. In reality, the band had no connection to Paul Timms whatsoever, although he had spoken to them on one occasion after a concert. Cradle's singer Dani recalls:

I met the guy once and he was really polite. It was quite weird because he was in awe of the band. We're quite down-to-earth people, there's no façade there, but he was like that, in awe of us. He came up to us at a show, and you knew he was peculiar and that there was something wrong there. I didn't pay much attention to it, really. When I was young and not appreciative of places like graveyards, etc., I remember being drunk with punks in the middle of a town and—it was a childish and immature thing to do—spray painting tombstones and kicking them over. This is all they did. They got pissed and destroyed a few graveyards and subsequently they were in prison for it. The hoo-hah died down pretty quickly over it, and that sort of thing isn't good for a band of our stature anyway because people get the whole ideology wrong straight away. This is why we kind of branched off from the Norwegian thing because as soon as you've got the Black Metal tag, people assume you are a fascist and you're into Devil worship, which can be linked to child abuse.[24]

Cradle of Filth began to make some waves in the Black Metal scene after the release of their first album *The Principle of Evil Made Flesh*. It was at this time that Paul Timms was allegedly in "awe" of them. The band began fairly quickly to distance themselves from their musical peers in Scandinavia by employing evocative aesthetics in the album artwork, and covering more romanticized themes drawn from nineteenth century literature and poetry. They wore the requisite Black Metal corpsepaint, but began to cultivate an atmosphere befitting of Hammer horror films rather

Satanist CDs on sale to children

'Pagan lyrics spur attacks on churches'

Adrian Swift, 13, with the Black Metal CD he bought from HMV

SATANIC heavy metal music blamed for brainwashing youngsters into wrecking gravestones is freely available in Maidstone.

Albums by several Black Metal bands, who preach devil worship and the destruction of Christianity, are on sale in the HMV Shop. Albums by Deicide are also available in Richards Records in the High Street.

by ROBERT BARMAN

The records can be easily bought by children and do not carry parental advisory stickers, which are common on albums containing strong language or material likely to cause offence.

The shop has defended its position, claiming it is not in a position to impose censorship on record buyers and that any restrictions should be left to the Government.

Black Metal music has been blamed for brainwashing four young men who attacked churches and desecrated dozens of graves in the Tunbridge Wells area, causing £100,000 worth of damage.

David Wharton, 22, and Mark Reeve, 22, from Tunbridge Wells, and Kevin Mooney, 21, from Eynsford, were jailed for 2½ years for the vandalism by Maidstone Crown Court. A fourth man, Paul Timms, 18, also from Tunbridge Wells, was given 2½ years in a young offenders' institution.

The case has prompted calls from David Wharton's parents and Tunbridge Wells' vicar the Rev John Banner to ban music which encouraged devil worship and letters have been sent to Kent MPs calling for action.

Maidstone MP Ann Widdecombe claimed the case was clear proof that impressionable youngsters were corrupted by certain types of music.

She said: "I think it goes to show that people who dismiss the influence of this kind of thing are wrong.

"I would rather that material were not on sale, but there should also be more responsibility on the part of parents and the people who make these records."

Fans of Black Metal are encouraged through the Satanic message of songs to desecrate graves and churches and to pursue "true evil".

A member of one band, Darkthrone, is a self-confessed grave destroyer,

according to *Select* magazine.

He is quoted as saying: "We want to see a return to the Dark Ages, when Christianity and Satanism fought it out for supremacy."

"I like nothing better than spreading hatred from the stage. We want to incite the audience to go out and do our dirty work for us."

The lead singer of Deicide has an inverted crucifix burned on his forehead and throws blood at fans, according to the report.

A Cradle of Filth album, also bought from the shop, features a pentacle design, often associated with devil worship, and speaks of "clawing at the grave of the dead nazarine".

A spokesman for HMV said: "We would certainly not condone any behaviour like this and regret what has happened.

"We do not generally restrict the sales of any titles in our stores because we do not want to be in the position of censor.

"If anything is banned because of the Obscene Publications Act, we react accordingly. Otherwise it is difficult to draw the line."

● TO SHOW how easily Black Metal music can be bought by a schoolboy to buy a Deicide album.

Adrian Swift, 13, was served at the HMV Shop in Maidstone, unaccompanied by an adult.

The compact disc he purchased, Feasting the Beast, featured song titles such as *Sacrificial Suicide*, and *Carnage in the Temple of the Damned*.

FULL STORY ON PAGES 16 AND 49

THE BRITISH MEDIA REACTS

than the one-dimensional "evilness" projected by other groups. Later releases *Vempire* and *Dusk and Her Embrace* brought the group to a exponentially increasing audience.

Cradle of Filth has many critics in the Black Metal scene who consider them "fakes" or "sell-outs," and it is true some of their publicity efforts have made them look silly. The band is not a necessarily a harmless theater troupe, however, and comments made by Dani and his bandmates in glossy U.K. Rock mags put things in a different light. "Think of all the people like Countess Bathory and [mass child murderer Gilles] de Rais and the Marquis de Sade. All these people had money, and that's what allowed them to do what they did. Don't think for one minute, if we had access to those opportunities, we'd all do whatever occurred to us. We'd do worse."[25] A few paragraphs later he elaborates on such urges, "Put it this way, if I was in control of the world, I would wipe out half of it instantly and indiscriminately without any remorse ... I'd nerve-gas half the world."[26] Combining such misanthropic visions with alluring graphics and sensual music, Cradle of Filth is reaching many more listeners beyond the typical Black Metal audience with its message. They wield considerable influence over the next generation of young musicians, writers, and artists. Guardians of morality are upset by the sounds and statements of groups like Cradle of Filth, but there is no end in sight. The future is destined to bear even more ominous fruit.

EASTERN EUROPE—RUSSIA & POLAND

Along with every other Western pop culture phenomenon, Heavy Metal made its way east, achieving added impetus from its forbidden allure in a totalitarian state. The belief in extreme music as "anti-system" has already been attested to by the members of Black Metal band Absurd, who reside in the territory that was once East Germany. Similar feelings must be commonplace in Poland, Russia, and other areas formerly under the communist yoke. Contemporaneous with its development in Europe and America, Death Metal rose to prominence amongst Russian youth by the the first half of this decade. Not as musically extreme as its Western counterpart, it more than compensated by courting the forbidden in other respects. News of the new wave of Russian Metal first reached Western readers in a *Wall Street Journal* article on February 18, 1993. Titled "Mayor of Moscow: Spider the Metalhead is Ready to Serve," the piece revealed the strange, newfound allegiance between violent metalheads and the radical political parties of the right wing, or as the article describes, "nationalistic former Soviet Communists, in their cheap polyester suits, and Russia's trash rockers, in black leather and chains."[27]

In a strange political twist, an extremist racial group, the National Radical

KORROZIA METALLA

Party, nominated the singer of Metal band Korrozia Metalla as a mayoral candidate in Moscow. His name is Sergei Troitsky, AKA "Spider," and he normally dresses in black T-shirts, jeans, and jackboots. Korrozia Metalla's most popular song among fans is called "Kill the *Sunarefa*," a slang term for darkly hued minorities from the south. Fans call out for the song at concerts, which are frenzied spectacles of more than just amplified cacophony from the bands. Additional titillation

KORROZIA IN CONCERT [NOTE EFFIGIES ON SIDES OF STAGE]

regularly comes from naked females dancers who prance and masturbate on stage beside the musicians. After one such show, kids in attendance swarmed outside, set fire to kiosks operated by minorities, and turned over parked cars.

A September, '93, feature in *Penthouse* magazine included not only photos of sleazy live Metal shows (memorably exemplified by a shot of the dwarf singer of one band, onstage in his underwear, cavorting with a naked stripper) but also translations of the liner notes to the *"Sunarefa"* number: "We dedicate this song to all patriots who wage war against the southern Asiatic animals who poison our lives with their rotten fruits and

vegetables and rape our women. Death to the *Sunarefa* is our anthem."[28]

Sergei Zharikov, youth advisor to the National Radical Party and publisher of a paper called *Raise the Axe,* believes a magnetic figure like Spider may have serious chances in the political world. "[He] is charismatic, and he knows the mood of the street. Two million listen to his records."[29] Zharikov's beliefs are probably similar to many of those few million who buy the albums: "We respect might and power, and we do not like all the Western pop that has clogged the airwaves."[30] He also admits concern for the edge the Party straddles in courting the energies of the angry Metal audience: "Our greatest difficulty is to keep the young from extremism and violence ... it could all end in anarchy..."[31]

The political parties cultivating the Russian bands eschew any kind of Satanism, due to the Christian nature of their overall constituency. Nevertheless, an examination of record covers by Korrozia Metalla and other groups reveals occult symbolism and upside-down crosses alongside Nazi banners, hooded Klansmen, and gratuitous illustrations of bloodthirsty violence.

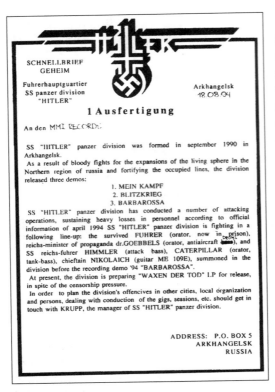

HITLERIAN PRESS RELEASE

The union of these strange bedfellows is demonstrated in the right-wing newspaper *Den* ("Day"), which runs a music column alongside its standard political commentary and photos of prisoners of war being marched to internment camps with the caption "This is what we will do to the democrats."[32] The back page feature dubbed "Rock—The Russian Resistance" tries to bring in a younger readership, hyping the music of bands such as Korrozia Metalla, Exorcist, and Death Vomit. The Deputy Chief Editor of the paper, Vladimir Bondarenko, explained, "I'm not exactly a big fan of Heavy Metal, but you can't deny that it's an intrinsic part of Russian culture. ... We're opposition and they're opposition. We need them; they need us."[33]

Neo-paganism and occultism have crept into certain areas of the Russian

GRAVELAND *FOLLOWING THE VOICE OF BLOOD*

far right, although the large majority remain loyal to the beliefs of the Orthodox church. However, books on runes and Nordic history have begun to appear from right-wing imprints, and the youth in particular are ripe for an appeal cloaked in barbaric Viking imagery. The name Russia itself, after all, comes from the predominantly Swedish Viking tribe of the Rus who settled the region in the year 852 C.E.

It is difficult to gauge how the situation in Moscow and

elsewhere has evolved since 1993. Things take longer to seep into Eastern Europe and take hold, although there is a rabid underground waiting to swallow up anything exciting from the West. The cassette kiosks which sell bootleg music tapes have been providing Black Metal for years, and undoubtedly the disenchanted there find much in it to rally around. When Russian bands—already happily using the stage as a platform for racism and calls to arms—decide to integrate the uncompromised grim outlook of Black Metal into their oeuvre, the results could be volatile. A Russian Rock critic already commented in 1993 that "an atmosphere of pogroms"[34] was increasing among the youth. Flyers have circulated in 1994 for one band calling itself "SS Hitler Panzer Division." The members have adopted pseudonyms in typical Black Metal style,

GRAVELAND

although with a German twist: "Fuhrer" is the lead singer (or "orator" as their press release claims), "Dr. Goebbels" plays "anti-aircraft drums," and Himmler is present on "attack bass." The number of even more extreme bands incubating in the fertile and fetid post-communist Russian underground is anyone's guess.

Outside observers might dismiss the images of these Metal bands as nothing more than exotic attempts to attract attention. But Russian bands like Korrozia Metalla feel they are involved in something much more serious than mere hedonism or entertainment. Spider matter-of-factly states, "U.S. Rock is a tea party. Here the fight is for real."[35] In a style similar to some of the pretentious exclamations of Norwegian Black Metal that would be heard a few years later, he calls on his audience to "join forces and rebuild the empire. We have a great task ahead of us."[36]

Russia is not the only place on the eastern edges of Europe where such ideas have taken root. Poland, too, has a rapidly growing Black Metal scene which is closely linked to the rise of extreme right-wing activity there. The most visible band from that country is Graveland, led by the outspoken frontman Robert Fudali, AKA "Darken." Musically Graveland has received rave reviews from Black Metal fans worldwide, but their political statements have engendered some neg-

ative reactions. In published interviews, Darken explains his goals in terms similar to Spider of Korrozia Metalla: "I prophesy the coming era of the great rebirth
of paganism, the rebirth of the Aryan Pagan Empire, stronger because of the
experiences of the last two thousand years."[37]

He is also unequivocal in his support of Adolf Hitler, stating, "Without a
doubt, I belong to those who think Adolf Hitler is the biggest figure in European
history... His ideas stir in us great admiration."[38]

Graveland releases its music on a German label, No Colours Records, which
also produced the album by Absurd. And like their German and Norwegian counterparts, the Polish Black Metalers appear to be moving from the realm of music
into one of action. Reports of church burnings in Poland are filtering to the West,
no doubt fueled by the anti-Christian statements of bands like Graveland. As
Darken warns, "I would like to teach people to search for their true pagan personality and identity. The pagan spirit sleeps in every one of us; it is very strong
but dormant. Once awakened, it shall resent and destroy that which denied it life
all these centuries."[39]

UNITED STATES

The popularity of Black Metal in America has not yet reached the levels evident in Europe. There are far fewer bands, extremely infrequent concerts, and the

AMERICAN BLACK METAL FANZINE *PETRIFIED*

genre has remained under-
ground. There are a number of
record labels attempting to
change that, including Century
Black (a division of Century
Media Records), Necropolis, and
a U.S. division of the French label
Osmose. Century Black has
released some of the more noteworthy Norwegian bands, including Mayhem's legendary full-
length *De Mysteriis Dom Sathanas.* Necropolis Records, run by
Paul "Typhon" Thind, released
Nordic Metal, a CD compilation
dedicated to the late Euronymous. Thind claims close ties
to the Swedish Black Circle or
"True Satanist Horde," and the
label's releases are almost univer-

sally of a vehement Satanic or anti-Christian nature. Their business appears to be thriving, despite a dearth of coverage in music magazines or any widespread store distribution.

An allusion to a more organized U.S. Black Metal movement appears in an old copy of the Florida fanzine *Petrified*, which glorifies the more notorious members of the scene from Norway. A 1994 issue includes interviews with both Bård "Faust" Eithun, who states that homosexuals "are nice to put knives into," and Varg Vikernes, who extols readers to follow the example he has set and "lay waste the Jews' world."[40] In the interview with Bård, the editor asks his opinion of the "new American Black Metal Circle," to which Eithun replies: "I have to admit that I haven't heard about this circle, but if it leads to any form of death or human suffering, I think it's worthy."[41]

GLEN BENTON OF DEICIDE

For the most part, there is little evidence any such American Black Circle exists, unless they have simply managed to thus far operate unnoticed. Fans of extreme Metal in this country are often far less intelligent than their Norwegian or European counterparts. The primary American interests outside of music include drugs and alcohol, neither of which played any significant part in the Norwegian Black Metal milieu. As a result, any antisocial actions are likely to be misdirected at best. The attempts to interrelate them into any kind of grand Satanic conspiracy are fruitless; the main similitude of these crimes lies in their irrational confusion.

Florida is also the home of Death Metal band Deicide, who have always projected a staunch image that is not far off from the "medieval" Satanism glorified by the early Norwegian scene. Singer Glen Benton branded an upside-down cross into his forehead years ago, and (to the obvious irritation of groups like Animal Militia) often advocates animal sacrifice in interviews. Allegedly the band's albums have sold hundreds of thousands of copies worldwide.

In January of 1993, two 15-year-old boys in Vernon, New Jersey abducted and then sacrificed "Princess," a neighbor's dog. They ripped the animal's tongue out and impaled the mangled creature on a large metal hook before hanging it in

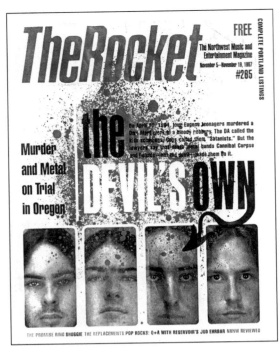

COVERAGE OF THE EUGENE MURDER

another neighbor's tree. The youths later told police that their fascination with Deicide led them to kill the dog, and that they were listening to the band's music prior to the act. One of the boys described the sacrifice to his lawyer as an "out-of-body experience." Benton was quoted as stating he would not take any responsibility for the killing, but was not opposed to it. "I enjoy killing," he told a New Jersey newspaper.[42]

Another crime related to Satanic Metal, and Deicide specifically, took place on April 10, 1994 in the city of Eugene, Oregon. A few minutes before midnight four teenagers, Michael Hayward, Johl Brock, Jason Brumwell, and Daniel Paul Rabago arrived at a run-down Dari Mart convenience store and initiated a robbery at the cash register using a 1.7 lb. metal bar as the weapon.

While Rabago and Brumwell stood guard, Hayward went into the rear cooler room, where a second store employee was restocking beverages. In a matter of seconds the female employee was lying on the ground, fatally beaten and stabbed to death. Before leaving the store the group brutally attacked another woman behind the front counter, although she survived the violent assault.

The youths were caught a few months later when detectives realized that a roll of Lotto tickets had been stolen from the store on the night of the murder, and these were later cashed in with the culprit's name on them. There was ample evidence to convict the boys of their crime, and Hayward received the death penalty from the jury.

Civil lawsuits followed, wherein both the surviving store clerk and the family of the deceased claimed that the criminal's behavior had been heavily influenced by the music of Deicide and Cannibal Corpse. Rabago had been recorded during his police interrogation as stating of the crime, "I did it in essence of Glen Benton and Chris Barnes [the lead singer of Cannibal Corpse]."[43] The youths had also allegedly been listening to Deicide music in a church parking lot shortly before the convenience store bloodbath. The civil suits were levelled mainly at the record labels of the bands, Roadrunner and Metal Blade. CDs, T-shirts, band photos, and "Satanic literature" seized at the youths' homes were entered into evidence. The cases were settled out of court, with the record labels paying substantial sums while "expressly not admitting guilt."

There are human deaths tenuously linked to Satanic Metal as well. In early 1996 in Arroyo Grande, California, a group of youths murdered another teenager, allegedly as a Satanic sacrifice done to receive blessings of power and success from the deity. The youths were fanatical Slayer fans. The drummer for Slayer at the time, Paul Bostaph, resigned from the band shortly after news of the murder made headlines. His reasons for leaving revolved mainly around artistic differences, but he was also uncomfortable with the band's dark image. Not long after his departing Slayer, Bostaph made a remark about the teenage murderers in an interview: "I guess these guys were total Slayer fans. After hearing that, it totally made me glad I left the band. I don't want the music I'm involved with, or I create, to influence anyone like that."[44]

The propagation of anti-Christian sentiments goes beyond the Heavy Metal genre in the case of Wisconsin band The Electric Hellfire Club. Their music is a blend of Industrial electronics, Psychedelic keyboards, and Metal guitar riffs. Since their 1993 debut album, *Burn, Baby, Burn!* (the cover of which featured a painting of a church consumed in flames), the band has extolled acts of Satanic crime by teenage psychopaths in their lyrics and offered exhortations to their listeners to continue such activity. One of their early anthems is "Age of Fire," now a staple crowd-pleaser at their concerts. The lyrics ask:

THOMAS THORN OF THE ELECTRIC HELLFIRE CLUB

Synagogues and churches burning
Can't you see the tide is turning?
How many fires will it take?
Before you realize your god is dead...[45]

In light of the band's underground popularity, it may not come as a surprise that some fans of the group have begun vandalizing churches. Singer and lyricist Thomas Thorn is obviously untroubled by such behavior. In a recent interview where he was asked about the church burnings in Norway, he stated:

I'm all for it. It's certainly no coincidence that we had a picture of a burning church on the first album. A lot of people will say, "That's a horrible thing to say! There's a history behind the architecture, if nothing else." Nobody said that when they were blowing up the Nazi eagles on the top of the Reichstag at the end of World War II. The missionaries who came and took away the Nordic gods and Scandinavian culture weren't all nice guys who said, "Just come over to Jesus." A lot of these people were doing it at sword point and saying, "Renounce your gods and attend this church—which we're going to build on the holy place where we knocked down your temple." There is a new generation reclaiming its ethnic spirituality. Part of reclaiming that is the recognition of centuries of oppression. For them, it's a revolutionary act, it's not an act of vandalism. It's a statement. The church is the legacy of the people that stole their heritage. By all means—burn, baby, burn![46]

Asked whether he would advocate Norway-style church burnings in America, he replied:

I wouldn't condemn them, I'll say that. I'm not going to jail because somebody says I told them to go out and burn a church. Somebody called me up and said, "You're not going to believe this but two little kids were taken into custody in Jacksonville, Florida for spray-painting a church and they cited a band called The Electric Hellfire Club and a song called "Book of Lies" that says, '*There's a church across the street / Let's spray paint the walls*.'" I'll say that brought a smile to my face and I certainly had pleasant dreams that night. There's some people whose station in life is to do something stupid and rot in prison for it. Quite honestly, I'd rather have them burn down a church than kill their girlfriend. If people are bound to fuck up and be incarcerated for a stretch

CALEB FAIRLEY

of time, they might as well do something worthwhile. Why not burn down a church rather than shoot a convenience store clerk? That's my message to the youth of today.[47]

Not all of the band's fans are content to concern themselves with mere vandalism. The most disturbing crime connected to The Electric Hellfire Club concerns the case of Caleb Fairley, a teenager from King of Prussia, Pennsylvania, with a history of minor sexual misconduct. Fairley was employed at Your Kidz and Mine, a children's clothing store owned by his parents. On September 10, 1995, he was the only one at the store, except for a woman and her young daughter who arrived to shop just before closing time. Fairley proceeded to lock the customers into the store, murder them, and allegedly violated their corpses before dumping them somewhere outside. He then immediately headed off to his scheduled entertainment for the evening—a concert of The Electric Hellfire Club. At the venue, Fairley approached Shane Lassen, the band's keyboardist, and demanded plaintively, "Can you help me?" Lassen was slightly bewildered, and asked Fairley to explain. "I need help in establishing a more personal relationship with Satan," he elaborated, and told Lassen how he had tried utilizing books like the *Necronomicon* and the *Satanic Bible* to no avail. Lassen would realize the fan's attempts to please the Prince of Darkness had entailed much more than reciting spells when he read of Fairley's pre-concert activities in the subsequent newspaper headlines. Fairley was charged with two counts of murder, robbery, two counts of aggravated assault, and "abuse of a corpse."

Far more dramatic than any of the above scenarios is another story with roots in Florida. In the spring of 1996, a series of crimes began to take place in the city of Fort Myers. On April 13th, a group of male teenagers commenced a campaign of mayhem and terror with startling similarities in spirit to the Norse eruption in 1992–93. Calling themselves the "Lords of Chaos," the cabal of six began their crusade by burning down a supermarket construction trailer. They followed this with the arson of a Baptist church. The terror spree escalated in perversity when the youths spread gasoline around a tropical aviary cage adjacent to a theme restaurant, then ignited the thatched-roof structure and watched the blaze exterminate the entire collection of exotic birds.

Things were just getting underway for the self-styled militia. The next attack was on a deserted former Coca-Cola bottling plant, where they arranged explosive propane tanks inside before retreating and tossing a molotov cocktail into the building. The structure was nearly obliterated while they observed the ensuing detonations from across the street. Only six days passed before they moved into action again, carrying out a masked armed robbery and carjacking in front of another restaurant.

The finale came on April 30th, which the astute reader will also recognize as the Satanic holiday of *Walpurgisnacht*. At 11 P.M. that night, the marching band director of their high school, Mark Schwebes, caught the boys on school grounds and confiscated the cans of peaches they were preparing to lob through the school windows. Halting them from an apparent act of surrealist vandalism, Schwebes ordered the boys to go home and warned them they would receive a visit from the school's deputy the next day.

A few hours later that night, Mark Schwebes answered a knock at the front door of his home. Seconds after he had pulled open the door, a 12-gauge shotgun was blasted into his face. Three days later after the execution of Schwebes, police arrested key members of the group. At the time of the arrest they were headed out to rob a restaurant at gunpoint where two of the boys worked. The police stated they planned to kidnap the restaurant's manager and shoot anyone who tried to interfere.

After jailing those involved in the Lords of Chaos, investigators discovered more about the group. It consisted of Derek Shields, Peter Magnotti, Christopher Black, Christopher Burnett, and Thomas Torrone. The leader of the self-styled militia was Kevin Foster, an 18-year-old whom the others allegedly referred to as "God." They each had reserves of weapons in their cars and houses. For the murder of Schwebes, Derek Shields had been the one to knock on the door—he was

a member of the Riverdale school band and therefore could make sure it was his teacher who answered. As soon as Schwebes had opened his door, Shields gave Foster a signal to pull the trigger of the shotgun. Foster then allegedly unloaded a second shot into Schwebes's buttocks because it was believed he was a homosexual. When Schwebes had caught them on the school grounds earlier that evening, it turned out they were in fact preparing to burn down the building (the canned peaches remain a mystery). Shields recently pleaded guilty to murder and will testify against two co-defendants in exchange for a life sentence without parole. In doing so he avoids the death penalty which his former associates are certain to receive.

Had they not been interrupted by the authorities, the "Lords" had more ambitious plans. They already decided upon their "ultimate crime of chaos," a sinister strategy for their upcoming graduation night party at Walt

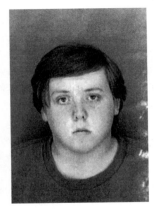

TOP: THOMAS TORRONE BOTTOM LEFT: CHRIS BURNETT,
BOTTOM RIGHT: CHRISTOPHER BLACK

Disney World.[48] Once inside the park they would steal life-sized cartoon character costumes. Thus disguised, they would stroll around the theme park, randomly murdering black tourists with silencer-equipped handguns. Ft. Myers Sheriff John McDougall stated he doesn't believe the plan would have gone smoothly due to the strict security at Disney World, but that the Lords of Chaos would have reacted violently if anyone attempted to stop them. "They were going to make a strong statement at Disney. It would have been a bloodbath," he said.[49] Sociologists might secretly hope the unexpected brutality of the Lords of Chaos could be traced to poverty or lack of edu-

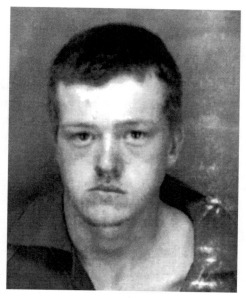

KEVIN FOSTER, "GOD"

cation, but such explanations were futile. One of the boys charged in the murder of Schwebes was even a straight A student, recently awarded with a full college scholarship, and another had scored 158 on an IQ test.

LARRY KING, FORT MYERS SHERIFF'S DEPARTMENT

WERE THERE JUST THE SIX PEOPLE INVOLVED?

There really wasn't any more than that. They were very much at their beginning stages. You had Kevin Foster, who was basically the ring-leader, and he had access to weapons and things of that nature through his stepfather's pawn shop. He was familiar with weapons and their use. A lot of weapons were recovered later. You can't typify them as a gang; you couldn't

LEFT: PETER MAGNOTTI, RIGHT: DEREK SHIELDS

typify them as a "militia group" or anything like that. They had certain characteristics from those types of things which all combined into the Lords of Chaos. That's why they called themselves that—they were intent on creating chaos for a period of time. When we captured them at the Hardee's restaurant they were in the process of conducting an armed robbery in order to get funds to go to Disney World. Once they got there they were going to shoot African-Americans and things like that, supposedly after getting into character costumes. They were going to go out and wreak havoc in the park itself.

DID THEY CONFESS TO THIS?

It was information that was revealed out of evidence we gathered. At this point everyone either pleaded guilty or plea-bargained, with the exception of Foster. They've basically all agreed to testify against him. Magnotti and Shields were the last two to make plea agreements.

DID MORE PEOPLE OUTSIDE THE GROUP KNOW WHAT WAS GOING ON?

There were a couple of others on the fringe, that weren't on the inside as far as knowing what was going on. There were dabblers that the group was looking at recruiting, so to speak. But it was very close-knit.

We did receive some tips from other juveniles, so they had been talking or bragging about it to some degree. Once we were aware of the situation, we were able to act on it. We basically diverted all our manpower into it. We had them under surveillance, and that was how we were able to make the arrests as they were on the way to pull off the robbery at Hardee's.

HOW WOULD YOU DESCRIBE THEIR BACKGROUND?

Magnotti and Shields and the rest were bright students; in fact I've heard some typify them as more of the nerd type, because they were intelligent. Shields had a band scholarship.

THEY WEREN'T RUN-OF-THE-MILL DELINQUENTS?

Certainly not in that sense, but they did gravitate towards one person—Kevin Foster.

HOW WOULD YOU DESCRIBE HIM?

He's certainly more of a cold and calculating individual, one that could be described as having a "dark side" to him. He's got the attraction to weapons and how to make bombs—that's what kind of took control. He was certainly cold and calculating in the murder of Schwebes; the witnesses have said it was something he didn't bat an eye about.

DO YOU KNOW WHERE THEY GOT THEIR NAME FROM?

They had made a pact, so to speak, and written what their primary goals and objectives were, what they called a "declaration of war." It was found in an envelope addressed to the county's traffic violations bureau.

PETER MAGNOTTI'S ARTWORK: "BRILLIANT"
—*FORT MYERS NEWS-PRESS*

IS IT TRUE THEY CALLED FOSTER "GOD"?

It seems so. They were a close-knit group of individuals, as I mentioned—a second family so to speak. That's what Foster was developing. He had a cult-like control over the other individuals. Part of it is intimidation. So it had that cult aspect. Whether this was just kids dabbling or they were really serious about that is still up in the air. I wouldn't call Foster a particularly charismatic person, but to this group of individuals he apparently was. To the average person probably not.

ARE THERE ANY OTHER STORIES REGARDING THE CASE THAT WEREN'T IN THE INITIAL MEDIA REPORTS?

Not that I'm aware of, but we're still limited in what we can say because there's the pending trial of Foster.

WAS THERE ANY UNIQUE SYMBOLISM THEY WERE USING?

They had their logo and drawings and things that could have called more attention to them. There were a bunch of things that would lend to thinking of them as a little bit different.

AND THEY EXHIBITED A DEGREE OF RACISM?

I think it was pretty clear what their intent was when they went to Disney World. It might have more to do with the area and their upbringing might have had some impact on that. It's more of a rural background.

The Lords of Chaos did not display any signs of overt Satanism, although they clearly held no respect for Christianity. They drafted a statement of purpose which is written in a similarly grandiose and antagonistic manner to many of the pronouncements from Varg Vikernes, Fenriz, and others in the Norwegian Black Metal scene. They share a similarly apocalyptic frame of mind, and they even use the same terminology as Vikernes when they glory in the idea of "laying waste" to the world. And like the Black Circle of Norway, they felt compelled to take credit for their actions and taunt the public with threats of worse atrocities to come. This is the text of their manifesto which was recovered by the police during the arrests:

DECLARATION OF WAR:
FORMAL INTRODUCTION TO THE LORDS OF CHAOS

This is not a confession. This is a claim to criminal acts committed against society by the militant, anarchist group LORDS OF CHAOS (L.O.C.). During the night of April 12, L.O.C. began its campaign against the world. A few juvenile acts of theft and vandalism began in the night, which in a span of a few hours escalated to massive proportions. [It all began] in downtown Fort Myers with the theft from and subsequent destruction of various county-owned vehicles (we shall not dwell on lesser acts such as broken windows, the torched cross...). After innumerable smaller acts of random violence, the L.O.C.'s night of terror took a turn in a new direction—ARSON. After gleefully torching The Hut, the L.O.C. successfully determined the response time of the fire department (which was all but disappointing). In contrast to media reports, the construction site, not the church, was destroyed next. The L.O.C. would like to convey the infinite amount of joy they received from watching the aforementioned inferno. Finally the L.O.C. descended upon the church. Using nothing but an ordinary cigarette lighter, your friendly neighborhood arsonists torched trailer and bus. Though very excited and giddy, the L.O.C. decided to call it a night, being very tired and dirty from a hard night's work. In conclusion, the L.O.C. would like to deliver a message to officials and employees of the city—WE ARE NOT PLAYING ANYMORE! The activities of April 12 were random and spur of the moment, but the L.O.C. is scheming future "Terror Nights" and are planning greater endeavors. Lee County is dealing with a formidable foe, with high caliber intelligence, balls of titanium alloy, and a wicked destructive streak. Their ranks are growing, and they are developing a well organized militia. Anyone doubting the sheer power and connections of the L.O.C. should rest well that their day SHALL come and that the L.O.C. is a force to be reckoned with. Lee County has not felt pain the likes of what is to come. Be prepared for destruction of biblical proportions, for this is the coming of a NEW GOD, whose fiery hand shall lay waste to the populace.

THE GAMES HAVE JUST BEGUN, AND TERROR SHALL ENSUE...

Signed, the LORDS OF CHAOS[50]

The manifesto was not the only example of the kind of mindset operating behind the Lords of Chaos. After making arrests, authorities sifted through the members' notebooks and computer files, only to find numerous stories and autobiographical statements. Peter Magnotti wrote about himself, "I am a sociopath-paranoid-pyromaniac. Another quality of mine is that I can draw good and I can make friends easily."[51] Indeed, he had recently been voted by his fellow senior class students as the best artist at Riverdale High School. An article from the local paper described Magnotti's artwork: "His drawings, often brilliant and highly detailed, are in the comic book style, full of mind control, suicide, death, and diabolical plots. He loved explosives."[52]

Both Magnotti and Kevin Foster wrote morbid stories of destruction for their own amusement. Foster's tales feature him and his friends as central characters. They are full of typographical and grammatical mistakes, written in a terse, violent style. One story paints the Lords of Chaos as local heroes:

> pete and kevin were vigilanties taking out bad guy's ... cop's were great full to them, wrong doers feared them and noone knew them. pete was known only as death. kevin was known as saint nic, because just like santa he knew if you were bad or good. if bad you DIE. the two man team made the streets safe to walk, made most of the populus white and took care of most of society problems [sic].[53]

In one of Magnotti's stories called "How I Killed the Earth," his words sound like an eerie prophecy of the consequences of the later crimes they would commit. The protagonist in the tale laments: "I don't know who I am anymore. I stumbled in a daze toward the light and found myself here. There's blood on my hands and on my head."[54]

Assessing the trail of mayhem left by the Lords of Chaos, Sheriff John McDougall said, "It was like a vortex of bloodlust and arson. It was consuming them. They couldn't get enough."[55] Identical observations would be fitting for the actions of the Norwegian and Swedish Black Circles. A Christian commentator, Tom Ascoll, writes of the Florida savagery: "Thank God that the Lords of Chaos stand out because they are exceptions and not the norm. But do not be deceived about why this is so. It is not because of poverty, lack of education, or any other social ill. Their actions are the consistent outworking of sin—rebellion against God."[56]

LUKE WOODHAM

In a more recent and similarly bizarre chain of events, a group of high-schoolers in Pearl, Mississipi banded together with a pact for sowing destruction in their small Bible Belt town. After killing his 50-year-old mother with repeated stab wounds early in the morning on October 1, 1997, Luke Woodham arrived at 7:55 A.M. to the Commons Room of the town high school and proceeded to open fire with a .30-30 rifle on the crowd of fellow students in the building, methodically executing two girls and wounding two others during the shooting spree. According to Joel Myrick, an assistant principal who later caught him, Woodham calmly walked down the hall "like he was out on a Sunday stroll."[57] After tackling him outside after he left the building, Myrick demanded of the boy, "Why did you do that?" Woodham, who held a job as a delivery boy, replied, "I'm the one who gave you the discount on the pizza the other night."[58] He later stated, "The world wronged me and I couldn't take it any more."[59] As it turned out, Woodham's attack at Pearl High School was not his the first explosion of violence from the otherwise quiet and introverted student. A diary/manifesto was later found which detailed previous actions: "On Saturday of last week, I made my first kill. The victim was a loved one, my dear dog Sparkle. ... I will never forget the howl she made. It sounded almost human."[60] Woodham and another accomplice sprayed solvent down the dog's throat, stuffed it in a sack before dousing the bag with lighter fluid, lit it, and drowned the creature in a pond. Describing the sack sinking into the water, Woodham wrote, "It was true beauty."[61]

Police later discovered that Woodham was part of a group of boys led by Grant Boyette, an 18-year-old the others referred to as "Father." Allegedly he prayed to Satan and admired Hitler and the philosophy of Friedrich Nietzsche. The watchword of the group was: "We can't move forward until all our enemies are gone."[62]

Another boy involved in the group, Allen Shaw, claimed that in addition to talking about killing, Boyette and his followers worshipped demons and attempted to summon them to do their bidding. Supposedly the ultimate goals for the seven-member group of outcasts were money and power. Conspiratorial plans for mayhem had been concocted where they would cut the phone lines before utilizing homemade napalm to torch the high school. The boys would eventually escape to Cuba via Louisiana and Mexico after slaughtering their enemies.

In the aftermath of the killings and subsequent discovery of the group, the townspeople of Pearl desperately attempted to make sense of the carnage in their midst. With no clear rationale for the behavior of Boyette and his disciples, it was easy for the predominantly Christian community to arrive at supernatural explanations. As the father of a 15-year-old in the town told the *Los Angeles Times*, "It's the grip of evil is what it is."[63]

FINLAND

In Norway, the Black Metal crime wave reached a low ebb when the most active members landed in jail following the police crackdown. With the majority of the trend setters either dead or growing too old to play with matches, the blaze of church burnings flickered out, although sporadic attacks do still occur.

Nevertheless, the scene continues to grow internationally and the grotesque glamour of Black Metal finds new legions of adherents. Such is the case in Finland, which has had a small but thriving Black Metal scene of its own for many years. Finnish groups like Beherit and Impaled Nazarene have enjoyed considerable success worldwide, paving the way for many fans to form their own bands and follow in their footsteps. And just as in Norway, segments of the Black Metal subculture also wed themselves to an especially virulent strain of teenaged Satanism.

Ari Soronen, an officer connected with the Finnish Criminal Police, estimates that there are about 200 Satanists in Finland. It seems likely that the word "Black Metal fans" could be substituted for "Satanists" here, for even though Finland also has a small contingent of law-abiding black magicians (Finland's most famous public Satanist actually holds a job as a customs official), the teenage Satanists comprise the majority. They wear the distinctive Black Metal make-up, which gives cause for some Finns to call them "penguins," and they flock to music festivals where their favorite bands play. Most of them do nothing illegal, but that does not mean they shouldn't be taken seriously. Soronen is especially concerned about the young girls in the scene. "I have spoken with girls as young as 12 that have been sexually abused," he says.

Merja Hermonen, a researcher with a clerical background, more or less agrees with Soronen's assess-

BEHERIT

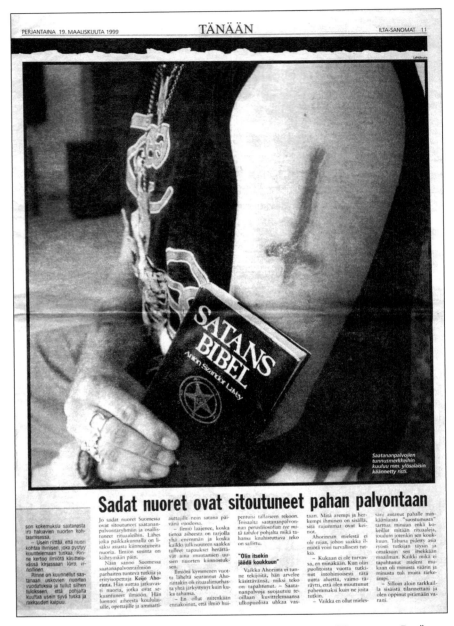

PERJANTAINA 19. MAALISKUUTA 1999   TÄNÄÄN   ILTA-SANOMAT 11

Sadat nuoret ovat sitoutuneet pahan palvontaan

Finnish Headline: "Hundreds of Teenagers Are Committed to Worshipping Evil"

ment of the situation: "I have no reason to doubt that the stories about sexual abuse are true, but I don't think things like that had anything to do with rituals as such. These kids are more into graveyard vandalism, and in a few cases some of them tried to dig up human bones. But there are just a few cases, and I think the scene is stabilizing at the moment."

Sami Tenetz writes about Black Metal for the Finnish Heavy Metal magazine *Suomi Finland Perkele*. He also plays in the band Thy Serpent. Despite the fact that it isn't a Black Metal band, Thy Serpent still attracts some of the corpse-painted crowd to its shows. "There aren't many true Black Metalers around. Most of them only follow the trend because it has criminal associations. Their mental state is really bad, but that is usually because of problems at home, and not because of Black Metal or Satanism," he says.

Unlike the scene in Norway, the crimes connected with Black Metal in Finland emanate from the fans, not the prominent artists. Despite its small size, this confused scene has produced one of the grisliest events to arise anywhere out of the Black Metal phenomenon. In one of the most notable cases in Finnish court history, four young Black Metalers murdered a friend in a scenario which featured overtones of Satanic sacrifice, cannibalism, and necrophilia.

At the time of this writing, the court case is not yet resolved, with some sentences (including a life sentence for the main defendant) being appealed. Therefore, those that could shed some light on the subject are politely but firmly refusing to give any comment. Reporting on the case is further complicated by the fact that the court has implemented a forty-year secrecy act on the entire legal proceedings. This means that many details will unavoidably remain sketchy. It is possible to piece some elements together, but the result is hardly a complete picture.

Hyvinkää is typical of the small towns that exist as satellites around larger cities, a commuter-friendly train ride away from the capital of Helsinki. Like other

FINNISH HEADLINE: "JARNO ELG EVEN TORTURED HIS DOG TO DEATH"

towns in the south of Finland, where the Swedish influence has been the strongest, it also has a Swedish name: Hyvinge. On November 24, 1998, a severely mutilated male human leg was found at a garbage dump in the town. Subsequent discoveries of other body parts in similarly inappropriate places made it possible to eventually identify the body of a young Black Metal enthusiast. After investigating the affair, the police finally arrested four of the victim's closest friends, some of whom had even lived with him, who were charged with murder.

A bizarre tale began to unfold in the Finnish media. On November 21, 1998, a gang of five black-clad youths visited a mobile Christian teahouse. Having become agitated after arguing with the Christians, they returned to the dreary apartment in Hyvinkää where a couple of them lived. Their apartment building is situated in a block that is perhaps the closest to a slum that the town has to offer, an area well known to the police as the source of many a domestic disturbance call. The locals sarcastically refer to this depressing section of Torikatu

Street as "Luotikuja" (bullet alley). After arriving at the shabby apartment, the five youngsters listened to Black Metal records and drank heavily. The quintet were notorious imbibers of a drink called "Kilju," a beverage brewed by adding yeast to orange juice and letting it ferment. Kilju smells bad and tastes worse, and, as can be imagined, this moonshine is only popular with those who demand nothing more than high octane from their liquor. To satisfy the thirst of the Black Metalers, there was usually a vat of Kilju going in the apartment.

As the party got wilder, the details become hazy. The little information that is available to the public is contained in the application for a summons, a document penned by the District Attorney of Hyvinkää. It should be kept in mind that this is a statement from the prosecutor, and as such represents only one side of an ongoing court case.

For reasons that are unclear, the group turned against the fifth member, subjecting him to a series of punishments and humiliations. As the situation escalated, the apartment became the scene of what the application for a summons calls *"...sadomasochistic acts requiring the subjugation of the victim, such as burning the victim with hot metal and leading him on all fours like a dog around the apartment."* The victim was also urinated upon. Alternately fainting and regaining consciousness, the victim was stabbed with scissors and *"...his mouth was shut with a piece of duct tape, which the victim however was able to tear off. He begged the subjugators for mercy and promised them not to tell anybody about their acts. [...] As he went on moaning, his whole head, including the mouth and the nose, was taped."* (When visiting the building, we found that sound easily carries through the doors and walls of the apartments, so forcing the victim to keep quiet would be very important.) He was then stabbed to death.

After the victim died, the group "...*started to carry out the rituals of Satanic worship known to them. They mutilated the corpse with scissors, dug out the inner organs, especially the heart out of the chest, cut off the genitals, as well as practiced cannibalism, necrophilia, and the disgracing of the victim's sawn-off head by drilling the eyes, and other acts included in Satan worship.*" (It should be mentioned that the District Attorney, Erkki Koivusilta, feels that the murder was not a ritual in itself, but was an emulation of things the gang had picked up in books and horror films.) After they finished their grisly business, the youths sawed the remains of the victim to pieces and then spread them to dustbins and garbage dumps around the area—where they were eventually found, leading to the arrest of the four killers. The man unanimously pointed to as the leader of the quartet was 23-year-old Jarno Elg, who apparently wielded considerable influence over his 17-year-old girlfriend and two male friends, respectively 20 and 16 years old.

The police have stated to the media that the murderers bragged about their acts to friends. The rumors supposedly spread like wildfire through the little scene, but were kept within it, partly due to fear of the killers but also because of a code of silence similar to the one found in biker gangs or the *Omerta* code of the Mafia. All the participants in the crime were deeply involved in Black Metal. This as also true for the victim, who had played in a Black Metal band called Utuk Xul. He had an unsavory reputation in the Black Metal scene, and yet was apparently admired by several others—some say simply because he was old enough to be looked up to by younger kids.

Finnish society reacted to the crime in a similar manner to how Norway did when first confronted with the criminal excesses of its own Black Metal scene more than five years earlier. Finnish newspapers screamed out headlines full of phrases like "Ritualistic Murder" and "Satan Told Me To Do It." Jarno Elg was described by a journalist at the influential *Hufvudstadsbladet* newspaper as one of the two most hated men in Finland. This was probably not an exaggeration.

On the road that led Jarno Elg to the apartment in Hyvinkää, his life seems to have taken a serious detour. His career as a glue-sniffer and aspiring alcoholic led to psychiatric care at the young age of 11. He tried hashish the following year. By the time he was 16, young Jarno was drinking daily and devouring books on Satanism. This diet of Kilju, psychoactive chemicals, and teenaged Satanism was bound to go awry. In 1992, Elg and a friend decided to set fire to a medieval church in his neighborhood. The church was made of stone, so they set fire to the altar, the organ, and whatever else they could get to burn. When the fire department arrived, Elg did not try to escape, but instead cheered at the firemen.

Jarno Elg has been described as a bully type, but he seems to have been charismatic enough to gather a small circle of alienated youngsters around him. The clique were outsiders even to the Black Metal scene, and in the Hyvinkää apartment they cooked up their own version of Satanism, stirring various Wiccan and New Age flavors into the pot, and acting out rituals on a nearby hill. Money was made by shoplifting, and Elg seems to have had plenty of time to construct a world of his own and gradually slip into it.

In a side story that did little to help his image, it turned out that Jarno Elg had killed his dog in the same apartment on Halloween, twenty-one days before he turned on his friend. The killing of his unfortunate canine companion followed a similar pattern to that of the later murder: its head was taped before it was abused and stabbed with scissors. It is difficult not to see the killing as a rehearsal for bigger, badder things.

The researcher Merja Hermonen observed the actual court proceedings for a week. While she is careful to point out that she never talked to the perpetrators herself, and thus can only offer her personal opinions, she kindly agreed to relate some of her impressions of the murderers. "They were seeking something, like young people often do. I even had the feeling that they were changing their statements along the way. It seems like they are very lonely people. They are emotional outsiders, some of them in very profound ways," Hermonen explains.

Since those who could shed some light on the motive for the murder are unable to talk due to the court's gag order, Finland is rife with rumors. Speculations regarding the motive range from jealousy over Jarno's girlfriend, to drug debt or just downright sadism. Some say that the killing might have been the result of a game that got out of hand as a blood-frenzy overtook the participants. All these theories are impossible to prove or disprove and, seeing as some of them even contradict each other, they should all be taken with liberal doses of skepticism.

In a surprise development in the case, Jarno Elg gave an interview to the Finnish magazine *Hymy* in its October 1999 issue. In the interview he tries to explain the murder more as a result of drunkenness than of Satanism. He also denies eating part of his victim's remains, claiming that the cannibalism was something that his group bragged about to his friends. And while it is nearly impossible to discern a motive for this sort of murder, it is almost as difficult to understand why someone would go around bragging about eating part of his friend. Unless, perhaps, the parallels to the suicide of Dead can provide some clue. And if that theory is taken one step further, the case begins to look like a peculiar form of Norwegian cultural export.

A chain of reasoning might be as follows: Black Metal bands like Venom intended their Satanic image as a joke, but the music they created was imported to Norway and picked up by teenagers who were inclined to take this form of showbiz Satanism at face value. Then the Norwegian bands upped the ante by creating a reality out of Venom's weird fantasy world—a reality which commanded international respect in a youth culture that venerates not only those who "talk the talk," but those who "walk the walk" as well. Thus Norway in turn exported something that was one step even further toward the extreme. And if the

Finnish killers are indeed the spiritual children of the Norwegian scene, they seem to have been intent, consciously or not, upon doing their Norwegian models one better—or worse.

If the description provided by the District Attorney is accurate, the murder itself appears so violent that it borders on a horror fantasy, almost as if it were the most puerile and excessive Black Metal lyric made flesh. This point was not lost on the media either, who claimed that the murder was directly inspired by a song by the band Ancient.

Even with her clerical background, Merja Hermonen warns against emphasizing the Black Metal connection too strongly when making observations about the defendants from the Hyvinkää case: "They have the same problems as all other young people. Problems that aren't resolved continue to pile up until something goes wrong. To blame Satanism is scapegoating. If you focus on Satan, you don't see the real reasons—and then you can't do anything about them."

Whether or not Mrs. Hermonen is right will perhaps become clear in the year 2038.

RAGNARÖK

THE SIGNS OF CHRISTIANITY'S INFLUENCE ON WESTERN CULTURE ARE EVERY-
where. God is regularly invoked in the speeches of the politicians, and
references to his name flow throughout the streams of secular society.
God is impossible to avoid. It is thus not surprising that those who proclaim
themselves "fists in the face of God" (to borrow a phrase from Fenriz of Darkthrone), would end up attacking society as a whole.[2] It is also not surprising that
in their desire to crush Christianity they should adopt a new belief—real or
symbolic—in other deities and demons. Spirituality is innate to the human
psyche, and has a way of rearing its head even in the most rational and atheistic
of people. The same person who rids himself of one theology may well harbor a
desire for a new faith—one full of mighty and unforgiving gods, capable of
smashing away the ruins of the old.

Black Metal provides all of this. Whether it is centered on Satanic or heathen
symbolism matters not. In both instances the iconography and the music fuse
together into an *odium theologicum* directed at the faith and lifestyle of the status
quo. It is essentially intolerant, uncompromising, and absolutist in its worldview.

The messages of Black Metal are varied, but isolation, struggle, and confrontation rank among the more prominent ones. These are united with a strong belief in
pride and warfare against the "enemy," be it in the form of religion or mortal men.
Sociologist Jeffrey Arnett has described Heavy Metal music as the "sensory equiva-

FENRIZ

lent of war."[3] Black Metal takes such a notion literally, and is definitely unwilling to engage in any peace talks with its declared enemies.

The average Black Metal fan is someone who is alienated from society. The prime movers and strong personalities of the genre are undeniably intelligent, and in light of some of the statements they've made, an impressionable fanbase is to their benefit. Fenriz, drummer of the seminal Darkthrone, is notorious for once stating, "I like nothing better than spreading hatred from the stage. We want to incite the audience to go out and do our dirty work for us."[4]

Many of those who participated in the first wave of church burnings no longer advocate such measures. They believe they are futile, or that there are more effective means of propagating anti-Christian beliefs without spending time in jail. But their fans don't seem to be listening, and prefer to commit their acts of terror regardless. The die has been cast. The concept of Black Metal representing an actual, violent attack on society is reality. It now has a life of its own, and does not appear likely to vanish anytime soon.

Black Metal is apocalyptic, with its calls to arms and declarations of Satanic or heathen holy wars. By its nature it should not be assimilable into the mainstream; it will always remain isolated in its hatred. The early behavior of the music's proponents had an air of impending cataclysm, driven by a determination to up the ante until it would go no higher. If the various instigators in Norway had not been jailed or killed, where would it

DARKTHRONE *TRANSYLVANIAN HUNGER*

have led? Varg Vikernes has never been one to put his actions in check, and not long before his final arrest he had stolen approximately 330 lbs. of dynamite. There are conflicting claims that he planned to detonate a cathedral in Trondheim or an anarchist squat in Oslo, but either way his restless nature would have been compelled to find a grandiose use for the explosives.

With its militant bravado, "warrior nature," and fantasies of ideological conflagration, the violent wing of Black Metal displays a number of similar traits to the far reaches of the radical right. Both share belief in an ultimate day of judgement for their enemies. Both revel in, and are spurred on by, a vision of their ultimate victory, despite the overwhelming obstacle of public opinion which staunchly opposes their views, behavior, and interests. Both share a strong fascination and identification with symbolism and myth. These two strains of alienated subculture bear many significant differences as well, but due to their relative proximity in the subterranean world beneath society, the question becomes one of their attitude toward one another.

BLACK METAL BLACKSHIRTS

From the earliest mainstream press coverage of Black Metal, journalists have worried over the alleged "fascism" espoused in the genre. In some respects this has probably been exaggerated in such articles, although there is no doubt that a figure like Varg Vikernes inspires obvious fears on the issue. His statements have been echoed by those of others. How prevalent are such beliefs, and how serious is the likelihood of the apocalyptic forces of Black Metal and the revolutionary right uniting on a common front?

Tracing the exact entry of fascism into Black Metal is difficult. Many in the scene accuse Vikernes of adopting extreme right-wing views opportunistically after he was tired of Satanism, or after the latter ideology had lost some of its shock value. Varg insists his racial/nationalist feelings have been present since childhood. The *Bergens Tidende* article on Varg from January, 1993 (a time when he did not have a particularly racist image within the Black Metal scene), does mention his apartment containing Nazi memorabilia, and a photo taken at the time of the interview shows an SS war helmet in plain view atop a bookcase in his living room. The *Kerrang!* article which followed some months later refers to the Black Circle as "neo-fascist," but it is hard to tell if this was just a handy epithet thrown in by the journalist. Regardless, the image took hold, and it did not take long for others in the scene to run with it.

Fenriz fanned the flames of the controversy in 1994 when he produced a

A PEACEVILLE
PRESS RELEASE

The **Peaceville** label has taken the unprecedented step of refusing to promote or advertise the forthcoming release of one of its own bands. The move follows outspoken comments by **Fenriz**, drummer for Norwegian terrors **Darkthrone**, in which he expresses views and opinions which **Peaceville** feel unable to support or understand.

In a fax sent to the **Peaceville** office, **Fenriz** states: 'We would like to state that 'Transilvanian Hunger' stands beyond any criticism. If any man should attempt to criticize this LP, he should be thoroughly patronized for his obvious Jewish behaviour.' The drummer insists that this statement be included on the sleeve of the forthcoming album, 'Transilvanian Hunger.'

Peaceville guru **Hammy** has responded by complying with that request, but makes it clear that neither he nor anyone involved with the label agrees with **Darkthrone's** sentiments.

'We will never censor one of our bands,' says **Hammy**, 'but we cannot condone sexist, racist or fascist views. By refusing to promote **Darkthrone's** point of view we are simply distancing ourselves from their opinions. This is not a matter of censorship, only a refusal to become associated with ideals which **Peaceville** finds abhorrent and unacceptable.'

The **Peaceville** label has faced problems with some of their acts before, notably with the sleeve artwork for the last **Banished** LP **'Deliver Me Unto Pain'**, and more famously with **Autopsy's 'Acts of the Unspeakable'** artwork, which was seized by customs officers on two continents. However, this is the first time that **Peaceville** has openly criticised the behaviour of one of its artistes.

Peaceville hopes that fans and press alike will understand that while it is not our job to censor any artist, this does not mean that we must uphold their sometimes contentious opinions

For further info contact Dan or Andy on
Tel: 0924 457821 Fax: 0924 455120

FIRST PEACEVILLE PRESS RELEASE

statement for a forthcoming Darkthrone album which he demanded be included on the record sleeve: "We would like to state that *Transylvania Hunger* stands beyond any criticism. If any man should attempt to criticize this LP, he should be thoroughly patronized for his obvious Jewish behavior."[5] His British record label was appalled, but agreed to heed the request to print the statement on the album; at the same time they publicly stated they would refuse to promote or advertise the record in any way. A controversy quickly erupted over the statement, with distributors and the press calling for a boycott of Darkthrone. With the impending loss of large sums from record sales, it didn't take long for money to decide the matter, and the band issued a public apology for Fenriz's statement. After a ludicrous explanation for the remark, they promised Darkthrone was "absolutely not a political band" and "as innocent as humanly possible."[6] Such reassurances are hard to swallow coming from someone who had previously insisted he would sacrifice his parents if necessary for the cause of the Black Metal Mafia, not to mention that the album in question still featured the words "NORWEGIAN ARYAN BLACK METAL" prominently printed across the sleeve, which no one seemed to take much notice of. Another notorious Fenriz remark a year or two earlier emphasized the apocalyptic totalitarianism of some Black Metal: "We are fascist in outlook. We

PEACEVILLE

DARKTHRONE PRESS STATEMENT/APOLOGY

This DARKTHRONE press statement is an explanation and an apology to prevent a disaster in the musical enviroment. We've been told that PEACEVILLE and Darkthrone faces a boycott/lock out because of *suspicion* that Darkthrone should be racist/fascist or Nazis. This is because of an earlier Darkthrone press statement where the word 'Jew' is used negatively.

Darkthrone can only apologize for this tragic choice of words, but PLEASE let us explain this. You see, in Norway, the word 'Jew' is used all the time to mean something that's out of order, if something breaks down, if something is stupid etc. It's always been like this. we don't know why. its just a coincidence in our slang language. When we wrote 'Jewish behaviour' in our previous press statement we could have easily have written, according to the Norwegian language. 'stupid' instead. Now we know that we should have used another word, but, as we explained, the use of the word 'Jew' is frequently used instead of 'jerk' or 'stupid' in Norway. WHY it is impossible to say, because Norwegians have always liked Jews. and racism is not a big issue in Norway. You could actually ask the entire Norwegian nation for an apology. It is a most unfortunate coincidence and we ask all parties involved to try and understand this accident. Believe us, we were as shocked as anyone else when everyone suddenly called us a Nazi band. It's so unfair, and we want to stop this A.S.A.P.

As the person responsible for the previous press statement doesn't read newspapers, music press or watch television news, he had no idea of the situation in the rest of Europe. Therefore he couldn't have had any idea that the word 'Jew' would offend anyone, it was more on impulse because it could have been *any other word*, for instance 'bad'. 'Jew' was ABSOLUTELY NOT intended to hurt or provoke anyone, and we apologize to anyone who has suffered, also to our record label PEACEVILLE who are as innocent as ourselves. This was all a result of Norwegian language customs.

DARKTHRONE APOLOGY (CONTINUED ON NEXT PAGE)

do not believe that individual thought should be allowed in the world. We want to see a return to the dark ages when Christianity and Satanism fought it out for supremacy—whatever the consequences."[7]

The similarities between Black Metal and other fascistic genres like skinhead music revolve around the role the music plays within these very specific youth cultures—in both cases prone to violence, sloganeering, and anti-social behavior. Vikernes has talked of his associations with radical skinheads via his Norwegian Heathen Front project, and Hellhammer of Mayhem also concurs that both audiences overlap to a certain small degree.

HELLHAMMER

HOW MUCH TRUTH IS THERE TO THE ACCUSATIONS OF FASCISM IN BLACK METAL?

I'll put it this way, we don't like black people here. Black Metal is for white people.

Also, it must be said that NONE of our albums have ever contained any
racism/fascism or Nazi slant at all. Everyone can check this out by simply reading
our lyrics. If you, the music press and our distributors will let Darkthrone and
Peaceville continue to release great music, we can assure you all that future releases
from Darkthrone will be totally neutral - of course. Peaceville *have never* and *will
never* spread Nazi propaganda, so PLEASE HELP US and understand to end this
horrible misunderstanding that so tragically has struck, all because of a coincidence
in our previous press statement.

Darkthrone is *absolutely not* a political band and we never were. We ask everyone
involved to look to our albums for the final proof that we are as innocent as humanly
possible. We and Peaceville apologize to all parties involved and urge you to read
this over again until you understand the coincidence that was the reason for this
tragic misunderstanding. Then we ask you not to stop a band on the grounds of
SUSPICION, because that would be truly tragic for other bands and labels - imagine
how easy it would be to stop music you dislike if a rumour or a misunderstanding
such as this is enough to be banished forever.

Please accept our apology and stop the rumours about Darkthrone if you can.
Anyone who requires further explanations of this misunderstanding can contact
Darkthrone via the Peaceville office.

THANX IN ADVANCE TO EVERYONE.

For further information contact Dan or Andy on Tel: 0924 457821 Fax: 0924 455120

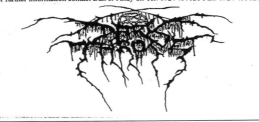

**IS THAT A GENERAL
VIEW?**

Yes.

**DO YOU CONSIDER
YOURSELF TO HAVE FAS-
CIST VIEWS, OR ARE
YOU MORE INTERESTED
JUST IN BEING WITH
YOUR OWN KIND OF
PEOPLE?**

I'm pretty con-
vinced that there are differences between races
as well as anything else. I
think that like animals,
some races are more...
you know, like a cat is
much more intelligent
than a bird or a cow, or
even a dog, and I think
that's also the case with different races.

**ARE THERE PROBLEMS IN NORWAY
WITH IMMIGRATION?**

Yes. It is a problem here, but not as
much as it is in Sweden. But they are
coming here too.

**IS THERE MUCH CONTACT BETWEEN
THE SKINHEADS AND BLACK METAL
PEOPLE?**

I know a lot of skinheads and we
get along personally very well. They are
a bit upset about the Satan stuff, and I
agree with that because I'm not a
Satanist. But we get along.

HELLHAMMER

True Norwegian Black Metal
9086-11060-2
Darkthrone
Transilvanian Hunger

Transilvanian Hunger

Transilvanian Hunger
Ouer Fjell Og Gjennom Torner
Skald Au Satans Sol
Slottet I Det Fjerne
Lyrics: Fenriz

Graven Takeheimens Saler
I En Hall Med Flesk Og Mjod
As Flittermice As Satans Spys
En As I Dype Skogen
Lyrics: Varg

Transilvanian Hunger Was Recorded In November And December 1993

Norsk Arisk Black Metal
Darkthrone
Is For All
The Euil
In Man

"Norwegian Aryan Black Metal"—Back Cover of Darkthrone CD

ARE THE SKINHEADS FANS OF THE MUSIC?

It's not so much about an interest musically, it's more about politics.

Many in the Black Metal milieu today would downplay attitudes like the above from Hellhammer, which he expressed in 1994. Even if they possibly agreed with the sentiments, they realize overt allegiance to rightist politics will not be tolerated in the world of record distributors, shops, and magazines which they rely on to sell their releases. Still, many harbor strong feelings on subjects like immigration. Bård Eithun explains:

> The connection with the extreme right wing came when people got more conscious about their own past and country; people searched for ways to hail their culture and heritage. I see a certain trend here as well. The wave of extreme political bands hailing their country has grown as fast as Black Metal grew in the beginning of the '90s.[8]

There are many divergent political views found across the spectrum of Black Metal musicians and fans (the communism of Euronymous provides a prime

AVE,

This flyer is a calling to all people who are in Black and Death Metal.

It's ... real to the true ones who are ... not braindead. So read this and spread it out – all over the whole fucking world!

"NEVER support the Black circle of Norway and other fascistic organisations! Stay away from Nazi-Scum or fuck off!!!" FASCISM REALLY SUCKS!!!!!! We don't need this brainless and idiotic pile of shit!!Start the fight!!! Now and forever they shall bleed!"

Follow this calling and spread the message! Death to COUNT GRISHFUCK AND HIS "EVIL" DISCIPLES!!!!!!!!!!!!!!!!!!!!!!!!!!!!!!!!!!!!!

ALSO A BIG FUCK OFF TO THE GERMAN BLACK METAL MAFIA!!!!!!!!!!!!!

LET THEM BLEED!!!! STOP THIS MISERY!!!! EXECUTE THEM ALL!!!!

ANTI-GRISHNACKH FLYER

example of someone taking left-ism to its utmost extreme), but no one will deny that right-wing attitudes have become a natural extension of the interests of some involved.

SAMOTH: A lot of this started because some people were fasci-nated by the extremities of the Second World War. It was noth-ing racial really, but just another fascination for the extreme. However, you'll also find "nation-al romantic" people who have serious feelings for the fatherland and its nature. But in today's soci-ety it's rather difficult to be proud of your own country and identity without being labelled a racist or neo-Nazi. It's very sad, but that's how it is.

M. W. DAOLOTH: Neo-fascism and "racism" is a logical step since the aware-ness of the ancient traditions suggests the need for a national identity. A full return to the past (in a spiritual sense) suggests a Europe for Europeans as it was in ancient times, before multi-culturalism and universalism were adopted as the official political/religious stance. And if you consider that fascism and Satanism have a lot of similarities as they both advocate power, spiritual and physical excel-lence, responsibility, survival of the fittest, elitism, etc., it's logical that some bands advocate both. This phenomenon has started to happen in Hellas [Greece] too—not on a large scale, but it's getting bigger day by day.

IHSAHN: There are of course racist and Nazi views within the Black Metal scene, all over the world. People have strong views. Personally, I don't think Black Metal should involve a lot of politics, because I see it much more as an atmos-pheric and emotional thing rather than a political one. Hardcore [Punk] bands can deal with political things; Black Metal is something else. If someone is a Nazi and plays Black Metal, that doesn't mean that everyone into Black Metal is also a Nazi. I don't see Nazism having much to do with Black Metal in general, except maybe in terms of the similarities between Satanism and Nazism about the strong individual.

With Black Metal's occasional propensity toward the far right, an intriguing question is what kind of reaction these controversial musicians have received from some of the more radical political organizations. Hellhammer stated that the only common ground between skinheads and Black Metalers was political, but that may be changing. A few of the Nazi skinhead bands—particularly Swedish and American ones—appear to be drawing subtle stylistic influences from Black Metal, though they have yet to create music which is very similar to something like Burzum or Darkthrone. They will probably never cross over too far into the genre, for to do so might defeat the point of an overtly political band. The song lyrics, a primary vehicle for propaganda, would be unintelligible if recited in "true" Black Metal fashion.

The revolutionary right, much like Black Metal, is an underground environment which maintains communication through innumerable small fanzines, journals, and leaflets. A few of these publications in different countries have begun courting the Black Metal audience, publishing articles supportive of the church burnings, murders, and even the music itself. In France the journal *Napalm Rock* is issued regularly under the auspices of the National-Bolshevist political group Nouvelle Résistance. Through the magazine they try to maintain a close connection with the cutting edge of European youth culture, steering it in a radical nationalist direction. The magazine's editor uses the pseudonym "Gungnir" [the mythological name of Odin's magical spear].

GUNGNIR OF *NAPALM ROCK*

WHAT ARE THE AIMS OF *NAPALM ROCK*?

The goals of *Napalm Rock* are:
* The creation of a pagan and nationalist European empire. We are Revolutionary Nationalists (primarily Third Way), we are pagans (Druidic and Keltic, mainly), we are Europeans. We don't support the French, Italian, or German nationalist ideas. Europe of Europeans for Europeans!

* To educate the French nationalist youth and movements, skinheads, etc., that nationalist music is not only based in Oi and "Rock Against Communism." We want to show that the musical nationalist/pagan culture is also Black and Death Metal, Industrial and Hardcore too.

* To explain to young Metalers and headbangers that they must not listen to the stupid and poor Metal scene. We want to show them that they need to sup-

port only the bands which are pagan and/or nationalist, because French listeners have to fight against the politically correct Rock mass media. We have to be proud of our culture and traditions and we must not listen to some Rap, Raï or other Arabian, Black, or Jewish types of music.

WHEN AND WHY DID YOU BEGIN THIS MAGAZINE?

We began this magazine two years ago because the true pagan/nationalist music scene did not exist. In France, nationalist movements (with the exception of Nouvelle Résistance) ignore Rock music and culture in general.

YOU HAVE ALWAYS COVERED DEATH METAL AND BLACK METAL—WHAT IS IMPORTANT ABOUT THESE KINDS OF MUSIC?

These are free and independent types of music! They are aggressive, fast, diverse, and very violent kinds of music. It is morbid, white, and unholy music. Many people—the politically correct especially—don't like these kinds of music because they are afraid of them. They say it is insane, evil, and twisted music. Black and Death Metal are uniting together everyone who thinks in a pagan way, and a nationalist and racialist way. Black and Death Metal bands are keeping alive European roots such as corpsepaint, dressing in black, and wearing occult and pagan symbols (pentagrams, Thor's hammers, Keltic crosses, etc.). A Black Metal concert is bigger and better and more magical than any other concert.

YOU HAVE EXPRESSED SUPPORT FOR VARG VIKERNES. YOU DO NOT FEEL ANY SYMPATHY FOR THOSE HE TOOK ACTION AGAINST?

No one! In fact I think highly of Varg Vikernes—he is a courageous and brave Norseman. He just wanted to free his pagan country from Judeo-Christianity. I understand his actions (church arsons and the murder of the traitor Euronymous). I am totally on the side of Varg and not that of Euronymous and Mayhem. Norway, like the rest of Europe, is under Judeo-Christian law. This murderous faith forced our ancestors to convert to a religion imported from the desert. We're not Hebrews, we are Indo-Europeans and thus we want a European spirituality!

DO YOU SUPPORT SATANISM AS AN EFFECTIVE OPPOSITION TO CHRISTIANITY?

I don't care about Satanism. For us, Satanism is the pure product of Judeo-Christianity, its opposite. Satanism is cool for blasphemous acts and to make people cry or be disgusted! It's a philosophy which is very combative against Christianity but I think there are a lot of insane people in this "religion" (for example many pedophiles and drug addicts).

In fact, we neither support Satanism in *Napalm Rock*, nor in our lifestyle. We prefer to refer to European paganism such as the Keltic, Druidic, Odinist, Greek and Latin pantheisms.

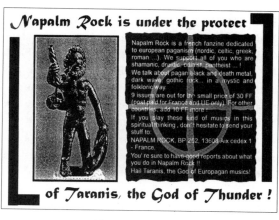

NAPALM ROCK FLYER

YOU OFTEN WRITE ABOUT TOPICS AND GROUPS CONNECTED TO PAGANISM. WHY ARE THE PRE-CHRISTIAN BELIEFS IMPORTANT?

We are from a country, a nation, or a community, and we must live within it, in harmony with the other members of the group. A French, German, or Greek man must refer to European pre-Christian religions and not to alien ones such as Judaism, Islam, Catholicism, or Protestantism. We must find our origins and firmly keep our cultural, spiritual, and ethnic roots alive. The flame must eternally burn. These pre-Christian beliefs are important to fight against the New World Order and Zionist domination. We observe the important Keltic feasts such as the solstices, equinoxes, Beltane and Samhain.

I know there are other forms of paganism such as that of the North Amerindians, and I respect them, but they are not for Europeans, they are for Indians. As we say in *Napalm Rock*: "Let us be wild! Let us be pagans!"

Kerry Bolton of New Zealand publishes a small journal called *The Nexus* that counts a significant number of Black Metal readers among its audience. He has assisted in the past with the editing of *Key of Alocer*, an occult and Black Metal related fanzine also produced in New Zealand, but receiving a substantial readership worldwide. Having been involved in underground agitation for decades, Bolton was also responsible for founding the (since defunct) Black Order, an international occult group dedicated to invoking "the shadow side of

Europe,"[9] which drew many adherents from the Black Metal scene. The Black Order is not the only such group. A more prevalent organization which seems to draw a large number of members from both Black Metal musicians and fans is the Order of the Jarls of Bælder. They publish a wide range of information on both Satanism and heathenism, and offer courses in physical fitness and "warrior arts." Kerry Bolton has also contributed to the operations of Bælder, which he sees as allied with his own goals.

Kerry Bolton

Your publications have always had an audience in what is now called the Black Metal scene. How did this come about, and was it conscious?

I began writing from a "Satanic" perspective about the time of what I consider to possibly have been a high point of interest in that subject about six years ago, which seems to have subsided gradually over the last few years. Seeing Satanism as a catalyst for change and a challenge to the status quo politically and culturally, I set up several esoteric orders and several publishing endeavors as I would a political campaign, having had some experience in the latter. Therefore my efforts were quite aboveground and easily accessible.

Having assessed that there were some serious people in the Metal scene who had a genuine desire to learn and act, a certain amount of my endeavors were with them. Anti-Christianity to some extent, especially with a Nietzschean influence, was tactically utilized, as the preoccupation of much of the Metal youth seems to be with Christianity and purging themselves of it. My efforts were meant to show that Christianity is but one product of the Western malady, and no longer today even the predominant one. Christianity is but one product of the Magian infection of Western culture, the others being plutocracy, liberalism, globalism, egalitarianism, and so forth. As Nietzsche pointed out, these are uprisings against culture.

I hoped to show a connection between them all and some doctrines which could be utilized in the rebellion many youth intuitively identify with Satanism. ... Since my agenda is to assist with the return of European culture to its "youth" or "Springtime" (in the Spenglerian cyclic sense), in repudiation of our present age of Western senility, it is most apt that any pitch should be aimed at the youth—just as Fascism itself arose as fundamentally a youth movement against the politically, culturally, and socially aged. Much of the support for my various projects continues to come from youth, including metalers.

Many Black Metal bands and publications have flirted or appeared to endorse fascistic/nationalist/racist views. Is this merely an attempt to shock, or does it reflect something deeper?

No doubt many such publications and bands are out to shock as much with fascism as with Satanism. But what if the desire to shock comes from deeper, usually at first unconscious motivations, which might themselves be quite laudable? For all the negativity and often outright childishness often involved, at least the desire to shock indicates a bit of individuality in a world which promotes uniformity even whilst promoting it in the guise of a pseudo-individuality. Often the desire to shock leads to knowledge and situations which induce maturity and something of a "conversion" when one eventually stumbles upon that which is truly rebellious.

MANY OF THE BLACK METAL PEOPLE APPEAR TO HAVE MADE A SHIFT AWAY FROM SATANISM AND TOWARDS INDIGENOUS HEATHEN RELIGIOUS FORMS, OFTEN COUPLED WITH NATIONALISM.

Yes, I have noticed a shift to native heathenism, and to nationalism. However, I would say it is heathenism in a "Satanic" context, a version of Satanism that is ethnically and culturally based, rather than of a more cosmopolitan nature of the type one often first encounters. It is a natural and heartening development, since Satanism is itself derived from heathenism. "Satan" takes many forms and is most aptly assessed via the archetypes and collective unconscious of one's own heritage, rather than wandering through a maze of multicultural esotericism, borrowing from

SATANISM
A World To Win

CALLING
YOUTH

BLACK
ORDER

World Headquarters
P.O. Box 38-262
Wellington Mail Centre
New Zealand

SATANIST LEAFLETS

ARYAN LIVING

prepares Gentlemen for the Coming noble society of Europe

Residential Courses for education & training
to restore the finest European qualities.

- ENDURANCE, MILITARY TRAINING.
- GROOMING/HEALTH-HYGIENE.
- CHANT & INCANTATION.
- STAVE MARTIAL ARTS.
- SURVIVAL IN NATURE.
- RITUAL LANDSCAPING.
- AUTONOMIS, GYMNOS.
- MANNERS, BEHAVIOUR, BEARING.
- HONOUR & NOBILITY. • AEONICS.
- EUROPEAN MUSIC. • SHAMANISM.
- SPORTS & PHYSIQUE. • ARTS & CRAFTS.
- ORGANISING GROUPS. • SPORTS MAGICK.
- WINE & BEERMAKING. • DIET & LIFE SKILLS.
- TRIBAL HISTORY. • PUBLIC SPEAKING. • NATURAL MAGICK.
- GARDENING, SELF-SUFFICIENCY. • HOMELANDS HERITAGE.

Discounts for Federation members. For complete
info.pack + Bælder Journal etc £3 or 6$ or 7 IRC's to:
Aryan Living: 60, Elmhurst Rd, Reading RG15HY. England

BÆLDER FLYER

sundry cultures and periods and throwing it all in a ragbag labelled "modern Satanism."

Since the thrust of the present civilization in its phase of senility is towards a global plutocracy, with the plutocrats and globalists utilizing consumerism and multi-culturalism to break down the different nations and cultures and the archetypes upon which they are based, it is fitting that "new" forms of Satanism are emerging with a nativist heathen basis to challenge this globalism. Anything less and Satanism would be (and in some forms actually is) a symptom of the Old Order's decadence rather than an "adversary and accuser" of it.

This move to one's heritage among Satanists is occurring for the same reasons that many other youth are trying to discover their own heritage—a search for anchorage beyond the nihilism and superficiality offered up by global plutocracy and its world consumer "culture."

Satanism and the heathenism from which it ultimately descends are themselves the products of the archetypes and differentiated psyches of nations and peoples, and they therefore spring from the same "occultic" or mystical sources as nationalism itself. Nationalism is the political manifestation of a folk's collective unconscious; heathenism/Satanism is the spiritual manifestation. Both ascend from the same source. It's therefore no coincidence that occultism and nationalism/fascism have both claimed common adherents prior to the present interest in both by youth.

WHAT ARE YOUR OWN VIEWS ON THE BLACK METAL PHENOMENON?

The major strength, it seems, is the commitment of its performers and fans, making it an enduring phenomenon. Its weakness (which also afflicted skinhead "Oi" music until recently) is not having a focus, a discipline, a long-range view of where it's going as a potential resistance to the status quo. Therefore, some of the most motivated will strike out blindly at targets which might not be the most appropriate.

There is also lack of ideological cohesion. I often read interviews, including some with older entertainers and composers, which spout "fascism" out one side of the mouth, and some type of libertarian nihilism out the other side. The rebellious impulse in Metal therefore has yet to synthesize the nihilism with the fascism, and since fascism is a synthesis itself, there's no reason this cannot eventually be achieved.

CAN IT BE COMPARED TO ANY OTHER FORMS OF AGITATIONAL MUSIC?

Yes, it can be compared to the leftist radical songs of the '60s, though fortunately from the opposite direction, and therefore not quite "kosher" to the music establishment (literally speaking). Of course the establishment will try to buy it off, but that would presumably mean a fundamental departure from its present form and content. The '60s music genres were thoroughly phony in their radicalism. Unlike Black Metal (and for that matter "Oi," and much Industrial) the '60s musicians had no fundamental difference in outlook to the establishment they were supposedly rebelling against. There was most of all an underlying ethnic affinity between the establishment and its phoney critics—whether in music, literature, or the media.

DO YOU SEE IT BEING ABSORBED INTO THE MAINSTREAM LIKE SO MANY OTHER "UNDERGROUND" ENDEAVORS, AND ENDING UP DIVESTED OF ITS MORE RADICAL ASPECTS?

Most Black Metalers appear to be worlds apart from the music establishment and a common ground is not likely to be easily reached, if they are to retain their heathen focus. The possibility of being bought off by the music business would most likely be by way of insisting on a return to the specifically anti-Christian themes at the expense of the heathen resurgence, since I'm sure many of the executives of the music industry can co-exist well enough and even utilize anti-Christianity, including Satanism, especially if it is of the nature of yet one more superficial American commodity.

Convergence of Extremes

Up until 1997, the connection between figures like Vikernes and extremist political movements appeared to be little more than the use of similar slogans and symbolism. All this has changed. Beyond his role as the driving inspiration behind the rise of church burning, Varg appears now to furnish motivational inspiration to genuine members of the revolutionary right.

On Saturday, April 12, 1997, Norwegian newspaper headlines were ablaze with a story about the so-called "Einsatzgruppe," composed of figures from the neo-Nazi scene, which had been raided by the police. Five young men were arrested at Hemnes, a small community 60–70 kilometers from Oslo. The arrests had been made the night of April 8th, and in the following three days investigators uncovered startling information about the group.

According to the police, the Einsatzgruppe was plotting direct action against prominent Norwegian politicians, bishops, and public figures. The group's plans included a scheme to break Varg Vikernes out of jail by force. The Einsatzgruppe had all the trappings of a paramilitary unit: bulletproof vests, steel helmets, cartridge belts, and ski masks. In addition, the police found a list of twelve firearms and a map for a hiding place at a mountain. However, the only weapons the police confiscated right away were some sawed-off shotguns and dynamite with blasting caps.

The police also found a war chest with 100,000 Nor-

Norwegian Headline: "Count's Mother Jailed, Planned Use of Force Against Politicians."

wegian Kroner (close to $20,000). This had been
supplied by Lene Bore, Varg Vikernes's mother. She
was also arrested and charged with financing an
illegal group. Bore confessed, but claimed she had
no idea these people were "right-wing extremists."
She expressed concerns about the treatment her
son received in jail, and claimed that he was subjected to violence by his fellow inmates. This was
dismissed as unfounded by the prison director.
However, it is true that Varg's jaw had been broken
in an altercation with another inmate in late 1996.

TOM EITERNES ON TV2

The police speculated that the 100,000
Kroner might have come from Varg Vikernes himself. According to this theory,
the money was culled out of the royalties from his substantial record sales. Bore
herself claimed the money came from the proceeds from the sale of a house.

Curiously, Bore could not be prosecuted under Norwegian law—conspiracy
to break the law is not illegal if it is done to help a close family member.

Vikernes was interviewed by the Norwegian channel TV2 and claimed that
the police involving his mother in the case was "absurd." When asked if he and his
would-be rescuers were dangerous, he replied: "[We are] nationalists and
Odinists—we represent truth. Considering that truth is a threat to the Jew
powers, then yes, we are dangerous." When asked to comment on the confiscated
military supplies, he stated that "Big boys have expensive toys."[10]

The TV2 interview caused some controversy over Vikernes's dress. He had a
shaved head, a black bomber jacket of the type favored by neo-Nazi skinheads, a
belt buckle with SS insignia, and cut quite a striking figure for the camera. As the
case unravelled, the scenario became increasingly outrageous. The group was,
according to some sources, aiming to escape with the freed Vikernes to Africa—
hardly the hideout of choice for passionate racists.

Vikernes's commitment to the group had been revealed quite some time
before the Einsatzgruppe made headlines, although very few people, if anyone,
realized this. In early 1997 a new Burzum T-shirt design was produced according
to Varg's specifications and sold by his record label, Misanthropy, in England. Due
to its imagery it attracted a bit of negative publicity and criticism, although sales
were brisk. The shirt was advertised with a photo of an unidentified skinhead
modeling the garment. The design featured a Burzum logo and SS death's-head
on the front; the slogan "Support Your Local Einsatz-Kommando" was emblazoned across the back. Most thought it was simply a nasty attempt to be offensive, entirely unaware that Vikernes wasn't kidding.

The most prominent member of the Einsatzgruppe was 22-year-old Tom
Eiternes. His earlier political career had included starting a local chapter of the Ku
Klux Klan. At the time, he claimed to have received $26,000 in financial support
from the American mother organization.

He had also served a prison sentence for robbing a gun store in Stavanger with four other members of the Einsatzgruppe. The robbery went awry and ended in the near-fatal stabbing of the store clerk. The five neo-Nazis fled towards the border of Sweden in a stolen car. When they reached the border, they found there was a customs post which hadn't appeared on the map. When customs officials tried to stop their car they just kept driving. The daring fugitives were stopped a little further into Sweden by armed police, and immediately extradited back to Norway.

While serving his sentence for the robbery and stabbing at Ila prison, Tom Eiternes met Varg Vikernes. Eiternes made public that he had converted to Odinism, presumably after talks with Vikernes. Eiternes broke contact with the Klan and forged an alliance with Vikernes. Right before his escape from prison, Eiternes was interviewed for a TV program about political extremism, where he made a series of statements that give insight into his worldview.

As one might expect from a National Socialist, he wants a one-party system. For people that have not kept up-to-date on far-right politics, some of his ideas might be surprising. Eiternes has no grudges with immigrants, seeing them as the victims of the situation just like the Norwegians. The criminals are the politicians who encourage large-scale race-mixing. Norwegian politics are controlled by "international Jewry" via the Freemasons and the United Nations. From their bases in Washington, D.C., and Tel Aviv they are plotting the world's downfall through race-mixing—"a Jewish conspiracy that wants to destroy the white race," to use his own words in the interview.[11] Far-fetched, to be sure, but it all makes sense in the head of Tom Eiternes.

This vision of the enemy might predispose him to take his actions one step further, from harassing immigrants to Baader-Meinhof-style urban guerilla warfare directed at leading power figures. To do that, he would need guns.

When arrested for the robbery, Eiternes and his accomplices claimed that they just

NORWEGIAN HEADLINE: "GAVE MONEY FOR ESCAPE PLAN: LENE BORE FEARED FOR HER SON'S LIFE"

wanted to sell the guns for money. However, this story is not very credible. On Eiternes's shopping list were items like rifles with telescopic sights and guns outfitted with silencers, which are ideal for terrorism. When he was asked directly whether the guns were to be used in a coming race war, Eiternes answered somewhat awkwardly, "That is not necessarily so very far from the truth."[12]

Eiternes stated that he thinks political violence is justified and insisted that it is necessary to defend oneself against the Norwegian regime. His National Socialism is of a radical, revolutionary brand, and he seems to look up to figures like David Lane, a prominent member of American terrorist group The Order,

VARG IN SKINHEAD STYLE

currently serving life sentence for conspiracy to commit murder and robbery.

Norwegian prisons are far more liberal than their American counterparts. Eiternes was actually able to run away while on a leave from the prison. It was during this period of freedom that the Einsatzgruppe initiated their plans.

The police were certain the group they had rounded up was a dangerous terrorist organization, a task force ready to embark on an all-out attack on Norwegian public figures. The proof cited was lists of private addresses for Bishops and government figures, including Oslo's police commissioner, Ingelin Killengreen. The police claimed these records were death lists and that the Einsatzgruppe was planning violent action against the named individuals. The defense, however, claimed that the lists were intended solely for mailing propaganda to these people. Further evidence was an article in the Einsatzgruppe's possession from the glossy weekly Se og Hør (roughly the Norwegian equivalent of People magazine) with pictures of the homes of these prominent figures. Also found were sketches of the military camp at Heistadmoen near Kongsberg, with the arms depot clearly marked.

The group was to be charged with Paragraph 104 of the Norwegian penal code, concerning participation in a conspiracy to "disturb the order of society or gain influence in public affairs by sabotage, use of force, or other illegal means." This carries a maximum sentence of two years, which can be increased to a maximum of six years in grave offenses. An armed unit would certainly constitute a grave offense, therefore it was important for the authorities to uncover the extensive weapons cache that the group was said to possess. In addition to the shotguns and dynamite

NORWEGIAN HEADLINE: "HAD WEAPONS AND WILD PLANS"

the police had found so far, in a later raid they discovered a 7.62 mm battle rifle of the kind used by the Norwegian military, a pistol, a rifle, and an old Russian AK-47 Kalashnikov. Parts of a submachine-gun were also found. There are rumors of more.

The arms capability of Norwegian rightist radicals has been a point of dispute for as long as these elements have been in the public eye. It is difficult to estimate exactly how many firearms these groups have. While gun control is quite strict in Norway, it is relatively easy to procure automatic weapons from the National Guard depots scattered around the country. Over the last ten years, 850 small arms have disappeared from the Army. Explosives, M-72 anti-tank rocket launchers, and hand grenades are also out there, somewhere in the Norwegian underworld.

How many of these are in the hands of extremists? It is the *modus operandi* of Norwegian right-wing extremists to make unrealistic claims about membership numbers and weapon stockpiles to the press. This makes them seem important and powerful, in turn making it easier for them to gain recruits and converts to their cause.

In association with the Einsatzgruppe case, members of the group *Hvit Arisk Terror* (White Aryan Terror—the initials spell "Hate" in Norwegian) claimed to have more than thirty handguns in caches spread around the Oslo area. In a country where guns are rarely ever used, this is significant. There are speculations about whether some of the weapons might have come from the rival biker groups the Bandidos and Hell's Angels, who have been engaged in a protracted war in Scandinavia. So far, twenty people have been killed in a conflict that has included drive-by shootings, bombings, and attacks with anti-tank weapons. While the early acts of hostility were confined to Denmark, in the last few years the war has spilled over into Norway.

While the Einsatzgruppe might have had the guns, the key question is whether they were really ready to take the step into the world of political terrorism. Henrik Lunde is a sociologist who works for the Norwegian *Antirasistisk Senter* (Antiracist Center), an organization that monitors racist and anti-immigration activity, and one of Norway's leading experts on these movements. Lunde doubts if the words of a group like the Einsatzgruppe would readily be translated into action:

> I think the nationalist scene has been moving in a more violent direction. But there is still one final, big step left to where they actually pick up weapons and run amok. They have been getting guns and dynamite, and they have developed an ideology that makes them ready to do rather extreme things. But they still have the final step left. It doesn't take much competence, but it does require that one sever the last ties to the real world. That is hard to do.[13]

THE NATIONALIST FRINGE

A brief look at the history of Norwegian right-wing extremism might be helpful. It is a movement comprised of myriad small organizations ranging from relatively moderate anti-immigration groups to militant skinhead gangs with overtly neo-Nazi overtones. These organizations are very fluid, with new groups starting up as old ones disband. This makes an overview difficult, as it can be very hard to tell which name is a functioning organization and which is merely a post office box.

Another potential minefield is classifying what the political agendas of these groups are. Most prefer the label "nationalist." Some see themselves as "opponents of Norwegian immigration policy." A very few are overtly National Socialist. The stigma associated with Nazism is much stronger in Norway than it is in neighboring Sweden or the U.S., where most of the Norwegian Nazis draw their inspiration from. This is largely due to the fact that Norway was occupied by Nazi Germany from 1940 to 1945. Vidkun Quisling, the leader of the National Union party at the time, chose to set up a collaborationist regime. As a result, outright Nazi imagery and ideology has never been very popular in Norwegian right-wing circles. Some elements have used Nazi imagery but this is more often a result of a desire for shock value and powerful symbolism than outright subscription to National Socialist dogma.

This is starting to change. Many younger groups have a marked National Socialist tinge to their symbolism and ideology. A good indication of this is the pronounced anti-Semitism which has appeared over the last few years. Part of this development was that Norwegian neo-Nazis imported the American (though rather classic Nazi) idea that the country is run by "ZOG," the Zionist Occupation Government. This is somewhat curious noting that the Jewish population is very low in Norway. Out of nearly 4.5 million Norwegians, approximately 1500 are Jews. Jews were refused entry into the Kingdom of Norway until 1851. Of those

that made their home in the country, large numbers were deported during the
Occupation from 1940 to 1945 to Germany, whence few returned.

If the far-right alliance might seem shaky, conflicts are usually avoided due
to a sense of common beliefs: the resentment of non-White immigrants. While
the older anti-immigrationists are mostly concerned with writing letters to the
local newspaper editor and spreading flyers, some of the younger activists are
arming themselves and preparing for violent conflict.

So far, relatively few people have been hurt. There have been serious
episodes, like throwing bombs at May 1st socialist parades, and the dynamiting of
a mosque in Oslo and some leftist bookshops, but these incidents are few and far
between. While the violence is serious enough for the ones at the receiving end,
the scenario has yet to resemble actual, armed political violence in any "urban
guerilla" sense. The one notable exception was the so-called "Hadeland killings"
at the start of the 1980s when a dispute erupted between members of a group calling itself the Norwegian Germanic Army and two young men who were enlisted
to steal weapons for them. Panic over whether these assistants might talk to the
police led to them being liquidated.

This is the historical backdrop the Einsatzgruppe emerged out of. They were
originally composed of the remnants of the Birkebeiner Group, a neo-Nazi aggre-
gation which took its name from the *Birkibeinar* (literally "Birch Legs," stemming
from the fact they wrapped birch bark around their legs to keep warm), a group
of rebel warriors in the late 1100s which eventually fought under King Sverre. The
Birkebeiner Group disbanded when Jan Holthe, its leader and a seminal figure on
the young neo-Nazi scene, left the movement to devote himself to family life. The
remains of his group reorganized under the name Einsatzgruppe.

The name was chosen both to establish a historical continuity and for shock
value. *Einsatzgruppen* (Action Groups) was the name given to units of the SS
responsible for the killings of civilian partisans, a large number of whom were
Jews. The *Einsatzgruppen* carved a bloody reputation for themselves at Babi Yar in
Russia, where 40,000 people were massacred. To emphasize its connection with
this legacy, the Norwegian Einsatzgruppe even named its sub-units *Sonder-
kommando*, Special Commandos. It is dubious how much this classical military
structure had to do with reality; Norwegian extremists have always been good at
producing lots of organizational titles, something that makes them look much
more numerous.

All in all, there has often been a considerable gap between talk and action in
Norwegian neo-Nazi circles. Henrik Lunde explains:

> The Einsatzgruppe came out of the scene in Brumunddal, where Arne Myrdal (a famous anti-
> immigration activist with a conviction for intending to dynamite a refugee center) had politicized
> gangs that were hanging around the gas station there. Other people joined them, including Jan
> Holthe. Holthe started several groups. One of them was the *Hvit Arisk Motstand*, (White Aryan
> Resistance), modeled after *Vitt Ariskt Motstånd* in Sweden. He also started the Birkebeiner Group,

which formed the basis of the Einsatzgruppe later. He published a magazine called *Vikingen* ("The Viking"). Holthe was good at producing paper, but very little was put into action.

The Mayor of Brumunddal was subjected to what one would called low-level harassment. No physical attacks, no real serious vandalism, but an endless stream of mailorder merchandise, pizzas and ambulances ordered in his name. Pornographic photo montages were also posted along the route his children walked to school. Two of the activists from Brumunddal defecated on the steps of the town hall to express their discontent with municipal policy. They thought this was really smart, so they did it once more, and then were caught.

It never really went any further than this. After Holthe pulled out, things died down a little. Down in Stavanger, the Einsatzgruppe continued. And the few members there were extremely active. They all have endless convictions, especially Tom Eiternes.

They've been posting flyers and stickers and working to get contacts. Then they turned violent. On one occasion a group of them simply ran down the street and beat up every immigrant they saw. They ran and hit, ran and hit, until they were apprehended.

The case became strange when it reached court. One of their victims, a Vietnamese man, insisted that he only had fallen from his bike; he had not been beaten up, he said. But there were witnesses to what had happened so the judge overruled his statement on the grounds that the man was afraid of reprisal.[14]

It sounds odd that so few men would try something almost approaching a *coup d'etat*. Lunde estimates the hardcore of the Einsatzgruppe at four or five individuals, the ones arrested by the police. There were also others:

In all scenes, there is a certain contingent of "coattail hangers." The Einsatzgruppe had perhaps fifteen to twenty of them. The numbers would typically fluctuate, because many of them will end up in the scene somewhat unwittingly. In one relatively recent case, this circle had plans to disrupt a meeting of the Israel Mission up in Stavanger. In that case, they had some younger boys with them. This is a typical example of what these more peripheral members will participate in; something "tough" and exciting. But when you start stabbing arms dealers and stealing assault rifles to shoot "traitors," that's another ball game.[15]

With regards to the Einsatzgruppe, however, the court was unable to prove any behavior of this type having been initiated. When the case came to trial in 1998, the charges against the Einsatzgruppe were eventually dropped, as the court failed to produce any concrete evidence of actual plans for terrorist strikes. Some of the accused nationalists implicated in the case even subsequently decided to bring counter-lawsuits against the state for wrongful imprisonment.

Whether the Einsatzgruppe really were ready to move from rhetoric into action and whether they were materially and psychologically prepared for such a high level of violent conflict is impossible to know for sure. There is no doubt, however, that in certain nationalist circles the fervor of the rhetoric is quite strong.

Henrik Lunde

How has the contact between the Black Metal scene and the nationalists been established?

In Black Metal fanzines there have been ads for things like NorEffekter (an outlet for books like *The Turner Diaries* and neo-Nazi skinhead music) and some of the political groups. There have also been articles that have strengthened the ideological connections. So there is contact and people switching from one scene to another. There are examples where people have changed their politics, and definitely their hairstyle, from one day to another.

Many political movements in our time have used music as a glue to keep activists together. The extreme rightist scene is very aware of its potential, and many of the contacts have been through music, with Black Metal bands using slogans like "Norwegian Aryan Black Metal" on their records. The most important though is probably Varg Vikernes's development. Vikernes was supposed to contribute a track to a compilation CD released by Boot Boy Records. This never worked out, however. Perhaps just as well for him. The CD was the first I've seen to be really slammed in *Nordland* [the most prestigious European neo-Nazi magazine].

Shouldn't one assume that these scenes are incompatible, ideologically speaking?

Well, yes, at least I think so. But these scenes write very little about what they want. They mostly complain about immigration and immigrants.

This strange marriage seem reasonable to me. In a Hitler T-shirt, hand in hand with Varg Vikernes, Norway's most famous church burner—it's not possible to place yourself further out.

On one hand, they can kiss all chance of mainstream respectability goodbye, but on the other hand, they get a very good potential for recruiting people from the Black Metal scene.

One thing people often forget with the extreme rightist scene is that they think in a completely different way from other political movements. If you look at the sometimes extremely offensive and crude propaganda they produce, it's clear that they're not after the man in the street or the schools. They're after the ones who can fight.

UNIDENTIFIED ARMED BLACK METALER

Katrine Fangen is a sociologist whose primary field of expertise is the Norwegian right-wing extremist scene. Her work has been published in a report entitled *Skinheads i rødt, hvitt og blått* ("Skinheads in Red, White and Blue"—a reference to the colors of the Norwegian flag), an investigation of young people's involvement in this scene. The report also deals with contacts between the skinheads and Black Metalers.

KATRINE FANGEN

WHAT KIND OF YOUTHS WOULD FIND THEIR WAY INTO THE BLACK METAL SCENE?

My impression is that they come from the middle class or the bourgeoisie, more intellectually endowed youths than the ones recruited to far-right scenes. So they're motivated by other things than having played themselves out in school. Rather, they seem to be youths who find it exciting to explore the dark sides of life. I've seen interviews where they talk about walking in the forest at night. They're exploring the mystical aspects of life. In a way, it's more of an intellectual quest than simply getting out frustration and aggression.

RACIST FLYER CIRCULATING IN BLACK METAL UNDERGROUND

WHAT ABOUT THE STATE OF MIND OF THESE YOUTHS?

I will presume that these are "seekers." When they get into an environment like the Black Metal scene, one thing can lead to another. After a while, things can get pretty tough. They can get caught up in rituals and trying to outdo each other in daring to be extreme. For some, that can become a one-way path, with no way of backing out.

SO IT CAN BECOME A SITUATION WHERE THEY COMPETE IN STEPPING OVER PROGRESSIVELY HIGHER THRESHOLDS?

Yes. They will have to prove themselves by participating in rituals and group activities without moral inhibitions.

DO YOU FEEL SOME KIDS BECOME ATTRACTED TO THE IDEOLOGICAL ASPECTS OF BLACK METAL, AND THROUGH SENSATIONALIST PRESS ARTICLES?

Then they start hanging out in places that the musicians frequent. There are pubs in Oslo that have served as meeting places for the Black Metal scene. These have also been meeting points for other subcultures, like right-wing extremists. As a result, there is a certain mobility between these groups.

IS THERE SOME KIND OF HIERARCHY?

Yes, with some musicians and senior figures in the scene on the top. This hierarchy might get very serious. If one sees the scene as having worth, one might go quite far to rise in status and recognition within it. Being the leading figure may get very important. This can lead to extreme cases, like the "Count's" murder of Aarseth. To me, this looked like a struggle for status.

> ## WARNING TO ALL TRUE BLACK AND DEATH FREAKS:
>
> Are you sick of rip-off bastards ? Then you have to be warned about the most disgusting scenes in the underground: the Asian, the South- and East-European and the South-American scenes. Do not buy stuff from these big rip-off countries !!!!!! Don't support bands that trade the true Aryan North-European and North-American bands !!!!!! They poison our music !!!!!! Fuck them up the ass and let them know that our true scene has no need of such DICK SUCKING PIGS !!!
> DEATH TO FALSE METAL !!!!!!!!!!!!!!!!!!!
> DEATH TO ALL NOT-ARYAN PEOPLE !!!!!!!!!!!!!!!!!!!!!!
> (signed: WIKING HORDES, mai '95)

RACIST FLYER

WHAT MECHANISMS CAUSE OTHERWISE ORDINARY YOUTHS TO BURN CHURCHES AND KILL EACH OTHER? IS IT PEER PRESSURE?

Yes, but the peer pressure is fictitious, as we say, because it isn't actually so that they have to do these things to get respect from the others. Still, they *believe* that the others expect them to act in such a way. So to assert themselves, they try to outdo each other. And because the scene is so closed to the outside world, they develop their own norms and rules of conduct.

WHAT SPECIFIC ACTS MAKE ONE RECOGNIZED WITHIN THE SCENE?

This will vary. In subcultures like Black Metal, there will usually be disagreements about what is important. To some, it will be important to dare to take part in the rituals and carry these out, while others will think it is more important to know a lot about the music or be a good musician. This might be a central thing in the Vikernes and Aarseth case. My impression is that in this case, the music was the most important thing for Aarseth, not the other things. Whereas for the "Count," the ritual sides were important too. Both had the charisma necessary to be setting the fashion about what should be important.

SO IT DOESN'T HAVE TO DO WITH BEING "IDEOLOGICALLY PURE"?

No, my impressions of the Black Metal scene is that it has more to do with daring to be "evil," and to let oneself be directed by mystical forces and similar things. Daring to be destructive.

How do you think the use of symbolism and rituals will affect the mental state of the people within the scene?

It will definitely do something to a person to participate in ritual acts involving blood, etc. There is powerful symbolism in such acts, and they challenge forces in the unconscious. Some might lose their foothold here.

What kind of contacts exist between the Black Metal scene and the right-wingers?

There is no formal contact. That should really go without saying, because the nationalists claim they are bravely fighting for a good cause. They also claim most people deep down support this cause, but don't dare say it out loud. To be associated with Satanists fighting for the cause of "evil" would be very compromising for the nationalists. So there is no formal contact. Still, there is a kind of fluctuation of people from the Black Metal scene into nationalism. They get fed up with Satanism and see it as a kind of juvenile thing. Instead, they want to get into something "serious" and "real," something political. There have been quite a few people who've gone this way over the last couple of years.

This transition seems to be relatively painless. Why is this?

I think it is because the Black Metal scene doesn't primarily function from ideological premises, but is usually motivated by a desire for excitement. Fascination with Norse mythology is common in Black Metal circles. The next step for many will be to get into something that is more ideologically defined. Though it should be said that the ones that take this route are usually not the ones seen by their peers as "serious activists." They tend to be out for excitement— they're ones that like to use provocative symbols, drink a lot and go, *"Sieg heil!"*

What is the common ground between Black Metal and the nationalists?

Both scenes let people cultivate their dark sides. The right-wing people admit that they have prejudices and are proud of them. Other people would suppress them, circumvent them, or forget them. Instead, these extreme right-wingers scream out their prejudices. And with romanticizing violence, the extreme right wing is more open to irrationalism and forces that aren't governed by common morality. It's permissible to hate.

This makes sense, as one of the last taboos in society is hating people for their origin. The Black Metal scene has always been very concerned with breaking taboos. Now that they seem to be dropping devil worship in favor of Norse mythology, and the right-wingers at

It is a continuation of the fascination with Norse culture to say that the
Norse things are somehow elevated. For many, it is merely another step along the
same axis.

Certain circles of the revolutionary right and some elements of Black Metal
have achieved an ambiguous but undeniable level of interaction. Much of this
centers on Vikernes, who is outspoken in his nationalist views. It is difficult to say
how much influence he still has on the Black Metal scene, but if the sales of his
records are an accurate barometer, it is considerable. In the nationalist realm, the
Einsatzgruppe clearly supported Vikernes, and a few radical skinhead magazines
have begun to publish interviews and articles about him. Beyond this, it is unclear
if his views or controversial public persona are widely accepted by more established groups of the extreme right. Regardless, Vikernes continues to spread his
opinions via the media and through private channels. He has easy access to the
press due to his infamy, and he clearly
sees the new potential in presenting a
strong image of himself through television interviews. Still, he is restricted
by which of his comments the media
allows to reach the public, and often
complains of being inaccurately portrayed. Not long after the alleged
breakout scheme by the Einsatzgruppe
failed in the spring of 1997, he
achieved one substantial propaganda
victory—his *Vargsmål* book was finally published.

VARG'S BOOK

It is unclear who was behind the
production of the 156-page paperback
book, which appears to have been
printed in Italy. The cover features a
motif of the Norwegian flag,
redesigned into a nationalist sunwheel
cross. Vikernes has added a recent
foreword to the text, which urges
readers to write to the Nazi organization Zorn 88 for further "good Nor-

wegian literature."[16] Varg has also included a dedication to his adopted namesake: "*Vargsmål* is in its entirety dedicated to Vidkun Abraham Lauritz Jonssøn Quisling, for his effort and struggle for his people and fatherland in the hardest of times. May he receive a seat near Odin's, in Valhalla!"[17]

GÖTTERDÄMMERUNG

If Black Metalers and extreme rightists could agree upon an allegory for the coming apocalypse they await, it would surely be the Norse mythological tale of *Ragnarök*. This legend dramatically divulges all of the blood, fire, and warfare which can be expected as the present world reaches its demise. The skaldic poems of the *Elder Edda* relate how the events are to unfold, and a cynical observer might conclude *Ragnarök* is already upon us:

Brothers will battle to bloody end,
and sisters' sons their sib betray;
woe's in the world, much wantonness;
axe-age, sword-age—sundered are shields;
wind-age, wolf-age—ere the world crumbles;
will the spear of no man spare the other?[18]

In the prophecy, these portents signal even stormier trouble on the horizon—the cataclysmic battle leading to the Twilight of the Gods. Odin and the rest of the Æsir pantheon must war against the forces of darkness, despite the fact their own doom is foretold. Diabolical Loki, the impetuous and mischievous trickster, is unleashed from his chains and joins the fray. His son, the terrifying wolf Fenris, defeats Odin and swallows the sun, casting the earth into shadow. Surtr, the demonic fire giant, carries aloft his blazing sword and lays waste to the world with flames of purification.

In the myth, the destruction of the earth is followed by its ultimate rejuvenation and rebirth. Fields grow green and bloom again; the sun god Balder returns. A hall for the "righteous rulers" now stands on the mountain of Gimli. A perfect parallel to *Ragnarök* can be seen in the legends of the mythical Egyptian bird, the phoenix, which consumes itself in fire only to rise again, renewed in beautiful plumage, from the ashes.

At one point in time, the prime movers in Black Metal dreamt of *Ragnarök*, and hoped to accelerate its arrival. They attempted to light the fuse on the powderkeg of alienated resentment which lies behind the façade of twentieth-century civilization—as their occasional allies, the right-wing revolutionaries, have also tried to do. Neither of them succeeded. This does not mean the powderkeg is not there, just that no one has found the end of the fuse yet.

A verse by Tarjei Vesaas, one of Norway's most treasured writers and poets of this century, prefaced our lengthy investigation into extreme junctions of music, crime, and infernal spirituality. In it he writes of the "bird in the flames," the compelling phoenix of legend. Such inspired words may reveal more about the operant forces, compulsions, and convulsions of the world than any amount of theorizing and research can hope to provide, for they convey the ineffable. They also allude to the cyclical nature of human existence: the endless organic undulation of life, death, birth. It is here in the realm of symbols—and man's terrifying need to assert himself symbolically—where the keys to an otherwise inexplicable phenomenon like Black Metal may be found.

It is fitting that the uprisings in Scandinavia were marked by the insistence upon fire as their weapon. Fire embodies the intrinsic forces which are apparent under the surface of all such outbursts. According to the noble Greek philosopher Heraclitus, "Everything becomes fire, and from fire everything is born."[19] In his book *The Psychoanalysis of Fire,* Gaston Bachelard elaborates on its function:

> If all that changes slowly is explained by life, all that changes quickly is explained by fire. Fire is the ultra-living element. It is intimate and it is universal. It lives in our heart. It lives in the sky. It rises from the depths of the substance and offers itself with the warmth of love. Or it can go back down into the substance and hide there, latent and pent-up, like hate and vengeance.[20]

The European fire myths express well the energies we have seen at work in our investigations. The Titan Prometheus stole fire from the gods and gave it to man; he is the example of the defiant, questing rebel who abhors stasis and stagnancy. He serves as an ideal for the visionary and artist, the seeker. Prometheus moreover represents an important archetype for the Satanist: he is the adversary, the willful iconoclast who spurs change with his actions. Another mythical giant comes in the form of Surtr, guardian of the thermal realm of *Muspellheim,* who controls the destructive capabilities of fire. He wipes away the old and weakened, that something pristine might appear in their stead. Surtr is another patron of the rebellious, but his efforts must lead to renewal. Without this, the rebellion is little more than nihilism made tangible.

Fire stirs the spirit of human artistry; it is the spark of the will-to-create. It expresses the polarity of emotions, as Bachelard notes, and represents both the passionate higher ideals, as well as the hot and consuming tempers of irrationality. The political revolutionary is possessed of flaming disposition, and for him a corrupt world destroyed by fire has great appeal. The religious fanatic—be he Christian or Satanist—also dreams in visions of a grotesque, burning hell.

Fire is not appreciated in our civilized society, either in its literal or spiritual manifestation. Most people have lost interaction with real fire; the once universal, mystical experience of blazing night fires is gone from their lives. Stoking the flames of resentment or dissension is frowned upon in a world which depends on the smooth exchange of services. Those possessed of unrestrained spirit are silenced, or ordered to fit in. Their tendencies must be stifled. Extreme emotions are shunned; those who act on them become outcasts. Mainstream culture produces a bulging sea of quaint diversions, the ostensible rewards for good behavior. The music and art made available to the masses has the consistency of soft, damp pulp—hardly a conducive medium for fire.

Despite all this, the fire is still there. It has been locked away, its coals covered over—yet it cannot be extinguished. The forces of finance and materialism attempt to root it out and then stamp it out. But the more the lid is put on fire, the more intense the pressure builds for its release. Rather than dying away and flickering out, rebellious embers glow brighter. They begin to move, searing a path toward any source of oxygen. The burning sparks of mind, spirit, and emotion seek one another. Their ultimate hope is that they the may catch hold again, to unleash their full powers. With the necessary fuel they could illumine the darkness and incinerate that which is stagnant.

In his poetry Tarjei Vesaas speaks often of fire, that untamed energy in our midst. He tells of an allegorical "land of many fires." It is a place one can visit, but not in the external world. It lies within man. To end with another quote from Vesaas's pen seems appropriate:

> Heaps of cinder all around—
> eruptions half-forgotten.
> Dead refuse.
> And the dim remembrance
> of another time, another place
> —the land of many fires.
> Hidden under heavy crust
> waiting for eruption,
> and the heat of the netherworld
> —fires that feed upon themselves.[21]

APPENDICES

APPENDIX I

"WE LIT THE FIRES" by Finn Bjørn Tønder

[Front page story, *Bergens Tidende* newspaper January 20, 1993]

Devil Worshippers Take Responsibility for Eight Church Fires.

"We are behind all church fires in Norway. It started with Fantoft Stave Church. And we're not stopping now."
—Anonymous youth from Bergen, about 20 years old.

"Our intention is to spread fear and devilry. Fear of the powers of darkness—that is why we are telling this to *Bergens Tidende*. It started with Fantoft Stave Church. And we're not stopping with the eight church fires so far."

The person behind these words is an anonymous man from Bergen, about 20 years of age. By way of two youths that knew him, *Bergens Tidende* was able to meet him at nighttime in his apartment in the southern part of the city.

"Call us what you want. We worship the Devil, but prefer to not use the word Satan. That name has been made ridiculous by foolish groups of poseurs. Morons who think they are tough."

The youth's story is cruel and perhaps not immediately believable. However, he can give details about several of the fires. Among the details is information which has not been made public—information that *Bergens Tidende* had confirmed by police and the Gades Institute (the Forensic Science Institute at Haukeland hospital) yesterday. Therefore, much indicates that *BT*'s interviewee is telling the truth. In that case, there are groups in Norway that the public needs to take very seriously.

He Hates the Light
It is completely dark in the halls while we ascend to his loft apartment at the hour of midnight. We have also been given the message that the youth is armed—"In case you have contacted the police."

The apartment is clearly not the residence of an ordinary person. It is either just an overgrown kid who finds Nazi paraphernalia, weapons, and Satanic symbols exciting, or *BT*'s reporters have come into a "world" few people understand.

The windows are completely covered by carpets. "I hate the daylight," explains the thin, long-haired creature that introduces himself with an unintelligible name. [Translator's note: This was obviously "Count Grishnackh," Kristian Vikernes's preferred alias at the time.] We quickly get the feeling that the youth simply likes excitement. It is difficult for us to grasp that he can be speaking the truth.

Later, we check the details he gives us about the church fires. One of the investigators of the fires tells us that he finds the youth's description of the torching of Åsane Church to be credible. At the same time, Associate Professor Inge Morild at the Gades Institute, confirms information about the burned rabbit that was found by Fantoft Stave Church.

Fantoft
"We caught a rabbit by the Fana mountain. It was much more laborious than burning down Fantoft Stave Church. By the church we decapitated the now dead rabbit. We lay the body on the church steps. The head was laid on the ground next to it. The point was to spread more sorrow. Our hope was that the innocent rabbit would be found," says the youth, "a symbol of goodness to be burned on the fire," as the youth describes it.

Associate Professor Morild confirmed to *BT* yesterday that the rabbit carcass which was found was headless.

He says this is information that has not been made public before. "I don't even think the police knew it," says Morild. He cannot determine whether the head was cut or burned off the body. "Our examinations cannot determine this."

One Man
The Devil worshipper tells us that there was only one man that set fire to Fantoft Stave Church. "He wanted to do it himself, he didn't want to share the sacrifice with anyone. A church that had been revered for 800 years was something really big for us, and had more power. The day itself was carefully planned. The Eve of Pentecost, 1992 revealed the Satanic symbol 666. [Note: The arson took place on the sixth day of the sixth month, at six o'clock] The intention was that our contacts all over Norway should do the same with other churches at exactly the same time. But the others chickened out. They let it remain just talk. Luckily, their cowardice led to us gaining more power over them. Therefore they became easier to manipulate later."

A Dead Student
He gives a detailed description of how the church was ignited. The information corresponds with the police investigation of the fire.

"We had been there for a long while before the arsonist stepped into the open hall on the East side of the church. We had planned to assault the first person that came through the forest. We knew that students [Translator's note: Bergen is a university town] often walk that way. Unfortunately, no one came. It would have had greater effect to sacrifice a dead student than a rabbit," he says.

He neither laughs nor looks sad. The brutal sentences just keep coming.

Åsane Church

The Devil worshipper talks in "we" form. He says there are six persons that have participated in the eight church fires in Norway. Even if he does not want to confirm it, *BT* gets the impression that he was himself present when Åsane Church was burned to the ground the night before Christmas Eve.

"That Åsane Church was ignited the night before Christmas Eve was just a coincidence. The fire was not planned. Åsane Church went up in flames because the word "peaceful" was said on TV. We got so irately mad at all the righteousness in society. A less intelligent person was utilized. He came with one of "us." Tried to get into the church through the windows. That didn't work. Even with an axe. The door, however, quickly gave in to the axe blows," he says.

Gasoline

BT's source tells that the two doused gasoline on the altar and on a Jesus figure. "If the church didn't go up in flames, at least Jesus would burn." He claims that psalm books were torn up and piled up against the walls. Under the church tower they poured extra amounts of gasoline. It didn't take many matches before the whole church was in flames.

"After a few seconds, the church bells started tolling. The fire engines were there after two or three minutes. We were nearby. The descriptions of us in the press were almost accurate. The poor sucker that was called in for questioning had nothing to do with us," grins the youth. The smile quickly stiffens: "It's not good for us to laugh. We have nothing to laugh at in this laughable society."

[Reprinted by courtesy of Finn Bjørn Tønder. Translated by Didrik Søderlind.]

APPENDIX II

[The following essay is an intriguing investigation into the correlation between elements of modern Black Metal culture and older folk practices of the Germanic peoples. It is written by the Austrian researcher and musician Kadmon, and originally appeared in his journal concerned with varied esoteric subjects, *Aorta*.]

"OSKOREI" by Kadmon

I

In my childhood in the lake district of Upper Austria I was fascinated by the *Perchten* who haunted the villages and towns in the dark nights of winter. There were the beautiful *Perchten* with colorful clothes and glittering ornaments, and the *Schiachperchten*—bold forms, ghostly apparitions with masks of wood or bark, enveloped in furs, moss, lichen... demons represented by the inhabitants. These *Schiachperchten* were particularly amazing to me. They emanated an aura of panic. Centuries ago, and in some distant valleys only decades ago, these masked customs—done today mainly for show, kitsch, or to entertain strangers—were a sincere cultic practice which survived from pre-Christian cultures. It was uncanny. Not only children felt a dark fear when they saw these demonic creatures with their animal masks and disguises. In the *Perchten* the werewolf culture of pagan antiquity, the pagan Dark Ages, could survive even into the modern world. The adults recognized who was behind the masks, and yet there was a sinister suspicion that the neighborhood boy, whom they thought they knew well in everyday life, was another person when wearing the specter's disguise.

"Whoever dares to perform in the dangerous disguise exposes himself to the spell of sinister, incalculable forces. Dark demonic powers awaken inside him; he himself becomes a demon. ... The disguised performers of this nightmare are 'possessed,' they become bearers of demonism." (Otto Höfler, *Kultische Geheimbünde der Germanen* [Cultic Secret Societies of the Germans], 14)

In shamanic cultures there were dances of animal powers. The shaman cloaked himself in a fur, adorning himself with teeth, claws, feathers, or painting himself to awaken qualities of a specific animal. This ritual often had a dynamism of its own. The mere imitation of an animal became a metamorphosis.

In this psychodrama, mythology united with depth-psychology. In his consciousness, and that of the outer world, the psyche of the performer became one with the psyche of the creature he represented. An active imagination changed into a mystical identification. The mask not only changed the outer appearance, it also influenced the behavior and affected perception. It short-circuited everyday consciousness and reality for hours, days or even weeks: the wilderness came into appearance... A "psymbolic" magic took effect, negating the boundary between the performer and creature being evoked.

This metamorphosis also played an essential part in the world of the Berserkers and werewolves—it occurred partly intentionally, partly involuntarily, when members of these communities draped themselves in the fur of a wolf, wore a belt made from wolf hair, or drank a certain beverage. Possibly a drug was used.

In a case that took place in 1691, in what is now Latvia, an old farmer named Thies talked extensively about the customs of the werewolf community of which he was a member, the metamorphosis into the wolf, and the powers he and the other werewolves possessed when they fought with real or imagined enemies, ripped apart animals, or escaped from dogs.

This 80-year-old man was still a werewolf but intended to give this power to a younger man, through special initiation, before he died. He himself had been initiated by an old farmer who had given him his wolf pelt. Since then he had to become a wolf at certain times of the year—especially summer and winter solstice—whether he chose to or not. He had no choice and it did not matter whether he wanted this power or decided to struggle against it.

"In ancient times there were many young men who had to put on a magic fur at special times to become a werewolf. Usually they were like all the others, maybe even better; they were good and friendly and harmed no one. But if they were werewolves one had to beware of them. Many of these poor men wished to get rid of the disastrous fur, but..." (G. Goyert/R. Wolter, *Vlämische Sagen* [Flemish Tales], 129)

II

The wild hunt appeared in many legends—a ghostly flock of dark, martial shapes riding through the night on their horses through the woods, lead by Odin, the one-eyed ruler of the dead, or sometimes by a female rider... a perception that in Christian times was transposed onto the Archangel Michael and his hosts. The black riders on the storm were dead souls, dead warriors returning to their homeland at special times—especially winter solstice, the twelve nights when spirits walk—and during the *Fasching* carnival.

The Austrian folklorist Otto Höfler was able to prove in his books *Kultische Geheimbünde der Germanen* and *Verwandlungskulte* (Transformation Cults) that the wild hunt was not at all a mythological interpretation of storms, thunder, or flocks of birds—as many researchers thought—but a union of mythology and folklore, of myth and reality which was of great importance in the Nordic mystery cults.

In these legends he saw reminiscences of the raw, at times even violent customs of cult societies in which young men, usually unmarried, participated. They were initiated into these alliances. What they were taught had to remain secret—a striking similarity to the mystery cults of the Mediterranean.

Otto Höfler also referred to some resemblances between these cults of metamorphosis with the animal or demonic disguises and the Mithras cult in which certain initiatory degrees wore the masks of ravens and lions. In this way the young men embodied the souls of their ancestors. Höfler stressed that in the Germanic *Weltanschauung*, like that of most pre-Christian cultures, there was no sharp distinction between this world and the one beyond—the borders were fluid. The folklore of the cult groups was often very brutal. With or without drugs the members felt a *furor teutonicus* which Höfler called a "decidedly terroristic ecstasy" with various excesses:

"This type of cultic amplification of existence did not signify debauched gratification but ... a duty for the dead. .... In this ecstasy the boundaries of the individual are broken down—but not to detach it from from the boundaries of order; rather it should take part in the meta-individual community of confederation with the dead." (Höfler, IX)

"In the life of the archaic Germanic societies the Berserkers fulfilled the function of imagination, commotion, and violence which is as important for the social balance as the conservative function ensured by the more mature—probably the old men." (Georges Dumézil in *Tumult* 18, 98)

I discovered fascinating details about the wild hunt as harsh and violent folklore in a dissertation by Christine Johannessen on Norse youth customs. In Norway the wild hunt was called *Oskorei, Oskoreien, Oskoreidi*. This word, no longer extant in contemporary Norwegian, was interpreted as a horrific ride, a thunderous ride, but also as a ride of *Asgard* [the realm of the gods]—there were connotations with all of these concepts.

In Norway too there were cult communities, circles of young men wearing masks and furs ... until the beginning of this century.

"The wild rage which also included destruction seems to be a right of these men. A specific justification was not always necessary. ... Yet there is a certain order, a certain rule and certainly a tradition; it is not possible to psychologically explain the wildness of the young men as just the temper of youth." (Johanessen, 335)

They usually appeared during the nights surrounding winter solstice. They wore disguises, assumed false names to remain unknown, and went by foot or on horseback. Their task was to punish those who violated rural traditions. Their acts of vengeance were malicious—they hid or destroyed tools, plugged up chimneys, nailed up doors, or locked the he-goat up in the kitchen. Beer was was their special goal—kegs were stolen or secretly emptied, sometimes to be refilled with water or horse urine, or they themselves urinated back into the barrels. Often horses were also stolen; they became the property of the *Oskorei*. In the morning the farmers found their horses completely exhausted, or they had to search for them because the apocalyptic riders had set them free somewhere. In *Nordisk Jul* ("Nordic Yule"), the Swedish researcher Hilding Celander presents a description of St. Stephen's Day [December 26] from the Swedish village of Blekinge. This saint appears to have taken over some characteristics of Odin and the *Oskorei:*

"... Like madmen we were riding on the meadows and fields without concern for the paths. Some were kneeling on the horses' backs and roared as they galloped, some could even stand up on the backs without falling down ... In this way we raced, and it was dangerous for men and animals. ... We also sang songs but none of them were about Staffan [St. Stephen], although the whole thing was called "Staffan's Race." ... The farmer used to come out with the brandy bottle, to entertain and praise us. The whole time we remained sitting on the horses. ... If it was possible one of us rode into the room and drank brandy, never dismounting. ... We drank the liquor on the horses. Then we rode to the next farm and the same scenario again occurred. ... Finally we were of course very drunk. When we returned the horses often were covered by foam and sweat. Many accidents happened, and it was not good for the horses either." (Celander, 280 ff.)

Apart from punishment, the wild rites of the *Oskorei* had further significance. If the demons were given food and drinks, they brought prosperity. Sometimes the farmers left their horses with headgear in the stable—the nighttime theft of the animals should secure the fertility of the fields. Hoping for a rich harvest, one accepted the demands and offenses of the *Oskorei* as part of the bargain. Similar perceptions existed in the Alps when the *Perchten* were given nourishment as they went from house to house, or they were allowed to plunder the pantry. The Latvian werewolf Thies talked about the cultic background of their thefts—the stolen food, the drinks, and the ripped-apart animals were a sacrifice which had to be given, voluntarily or involuntarily; the sacred theft provided fertility.

Gradually, however, many farmers were no longer willing to accept the outrages of the *Oskorei*. The cultic background of the thefts and pranks fell into oblivion, becoming superstition. The sympathy of the populace disappeared—now the disguised young men were no longer considered embodiments of the dead or fertility demons, but rather troublemakers and evil-doers.

"This flock [the *Oskorei*] is usually riding through the air and most often has a female rider as leader, sometimes with the attributes of a mare. ... It breaks into the cellars and steals the beer; steals horses and rides them almost to pieces; it robs men who are found again many kilometers away, or who return to their homes half dead. ... The appearance of the *Oskorei* is much wilder, more vehement and terrifying than that of the Yule he-goats and other demonic creatures. If they arrive it is no visit but rather a burglary, a raid, an act of harmful destruction to men and animals." (Johannessen, 331)

In their works, Otto Höfler and Christine Johannessen give examples of arson used as punishment. Höfler wrote about the Swedish secret community of the *Öja-bursar* in Södermanland, which demanded strict secrecy from its members:

"It is an especially strange characteristic of the demonic mask cult that those so disguised even set buildings on fire, among other acts of terror during their wild, ecstatic processions. ... The arsons of this group had a sacred origin." (Höfler, 107 ff.)

In Norway as well Christine Johannessen was able to find hints of destruction by fire caused by members of the *Oskorei* in a combination of custom, wantonness, and drunkenness:

"It means bad luck if everything is not prepared as it should be. They destroy everything, or as in Voss (Hordaland), harm the animals or even burn the farm." (Johannessen, 243)

III

Noise played an essential role in the wild hunt, as it did in many pagan celebrations... magical noise as an archaic technique of ecstasy was a characteristic of many non-Christian cultic activities. Bonifatius, later canonized after cutting down the "Thor oak tree" for which he was killed by pagans for this outrage, cursed the noisy processions of the Germans in winter. The German language uses the term *Heidenlärm*, heathen noise. Deadly silence and murmuring apparently seemed to be the trademark of the Christian liturgy... The louder the drums, bells, cries, rattles, and whips, the more effective the noise magic became. The farther north, the longer the winter nights and the the wilder and more grim the demonic rites had to be in order to ward away the evil spirits or awaken nature, which slept in the frozen earth:

"One of the most effective means to stimulate the organism into an ecstatic state is the use of noise instruments. ... The use of roaring iron cymbals and other loud percussion instruments is known in antique processions and ecstatic mysteries. Bells are also an indispensable means of stimulation in the fury and frenzy of the masks in the wild noise processions of our homeland, the ecstatic *Perchten* and *Shembart* processions and their relatives. ... Often legends tell of the wild hunt approaching with wonderful music that frequently becomes noisy, wild shouting. ... One of the most prominent characteristics of the host is the hellish din." (Höfler, 12, 108, 110)

IV

"These groups have various means to approach the other world, to reach a religious ecstasy: disguises, masks; noise (bells, drums, etc.); intoxicating drinks (especially beer and liquor); movement (such as dance) and music (singing, but also invocatory formulas, similar to magical chants, spoken in a falsetto voice), etc. ... With their disguises as well as their behavior the masked ones want to demonstrate they represent supernatural entities and not human beings. They dress as ghostly as possible, speaking with a falsetto voice, reaching ecstasy by dancing, music and noise. ... Their clothes should be as nightmarish as possible. They attempted to dress as ugly as they were able. They had terrible eyes, with big white rings or painted up with coal." (Johannessen, 13, 95)

All these characteristics are also elements in the Black Metal music which came into existence in Scandinavia, and above all Norway, at the beginning of the '90s. Many Black Metal musicians paint their faces in demonic black-and-white grimaces, dress in ancient Nordic clothes or adorn themselves with emblems of death... which often results in kitsch. The falsetto voices of the *Oskorei* are recalled in the ghostly voices of many singers, usually a sinister blend of whispered words and hoarse cries. The disguised members of the *Oskorei* altered their voices and gave themselves false names—they represented demons and had to remain unknown. In Black Metal as well only a few musicians use their real names; many take pseudonyms from Nordic history and mythology and in the meantime it is possible to find in Black Metal culture almost all deities of the *Eddas*. Even the age is similar—the members of the *Oskorei* were usually between 15 and 25 years old.

But Black Metal is above all heathen noise, electronically enhanced. The music is powerful, violent, dark and grim; a demonic sonic art with several elements in common with the Norwegian expressionist painter Edvard Munch, whose famous work "The Scream" would fit well on a record cover. The eternal recurrence of certain leitmotifs, the dark blazing atmosphere, the obscure, viscous sonic landscape of many songs—often lasting more than ten minutes—have at times an almost psychedelic effect. In the heaviness and darkness of certain compositions it is possible to realize some subliminal melodies only after listening to these works several times. Black Metal is a werewolf culture, a werewolf romanticism. In this it comes close to the *Oskorei*. Is Black Metal in this tradition, is it a recurrence of ancient and medieval Nordic folklore? Is Black Metal with its hard, austere sound the *Oskorei* of the Iron Age? There are several similarities but also big differences: the musicians of this century are no longer members of a rural cultural landscape, of a village community. Black Metal is primarily an underground culture of Scandinavian cities. But consciously or unconsciously, the Nordic cosmology is still effective in the music of the last decade of the twentieth century... a fascinating phenomenon, even if many Germanicists and folklorists would deny this continuity.

There is a strange connection between the folklore of the *Oskorei* and the many arsons of churches in Norway in 1992. In Storetveit, Fantoft, Holmenkollen, Stavanger, Ormøya, Skjold, Hauketo, and Sarpsborg churches were set on fire. While extinguishing the fire in Sarpsborg a member of the fire department died in the flames. Amongst the churches was also one of the few remaining stave churches—the Fantoft Kirke. Some Black Metal musicians viewed these destructions as acts of vengeance against the malicious magic of Kristianity which, centuries ago, used similarly violent methods to destroy or Christianize sacred woods, clearings, sources, stones—it crucified the ancient sanctuaries of the Nordic population.

"If I had done it I would not regret it. The stave churches were built in the time of passage from proud heathendom to ludicrous Christianity. By destroying them we start a new beginning. I myself never burned a church. But I hail all who do or did. Whoever builds a Christian temple on our heathen ground desecrates the land of Odin." —Varg Vikernes

Black Metal is *Oskorei* romanticism. Many songs deal with Nordic mythology, heathenism, the fight against Christianity and also partially the fight against the Americanism afflicting all areas of European life today. Of course there are many Black

Metal musicians embellishing their songs with Nordic expressions, and their record covers with runes and images of the *Irminsul* [the Germanic world-tree] and *Mjöllnir* [Thor's Hammer], without any serious study of the spiritual background of the symbols. For them, Nordic cosmology is cosmetic make-up, decoration. But there are others who take Nordic cosmology seriously, linking ariosophic mythology together in their work with a mental attitude of self-respect and resistance, uniting them in a Nordic Nietzscheanism... Here Black Metal becomes a pagan avant-garde, a Nordic "occulture" reconciling both myth and modern world.

"A hard heart was placed in my breast by Wotan." (Nietzsche, *Beyond Good and Evil*, aphorism 260)

V

One of those musicians taking the Nordic belief and worldview very seriously is 22-year-old Varg Vikernes. Using the name Count Grishnackh he founded the musical project Burzum in 1991. He discovered this name, which means "darkness," as well as his pseudonym, in J.R.R. Tolkien's *Lord of the Rings*, a work that impressed him greatly in his youth.

I became interested in Varg Vikernes when I saw photos showing him in a shirt of chain mail, holding ancient Nordic weapons; and by reading grim, warlike statements he made in various interviews. To date, several records by Burzum have been released. The first two, the LP *Burzum* and the *Aske* 12", came out in 1992 on the Norwegian Deathlike Silence label run by Øystein Aarseth, who also owned the Helvete record shop in Oslo. In 1993 the LP *Det som engang var* (That Which Once Was) was released on Cymophane, and one year later the CD *Hvis lyset tar oss* (If the Light Takes Us) on the British label Misanthropy, who have since re-released all the previous records on CD. On the first records he still sang in English, then he decided to solely use his mother tongue.

The first song I heard by Burzum was "Det Som Engang Var" on the CD *Hvis lyset tar oss*. Even now this song remains for me the most beautiful and powerful work of Burzum; its symphonic sonic violence is impressive over and over again. It is a fourteen-minute-long composition full of grim, blazing beauty—dark and fateful. The uniquely hair-raising, screaming-at-the-heavens vocal of Varg Vikernes turns the piece into an expressionistic shriek-opera, the words of which are probably incomprehensible even for Norwegians. The song was composed in the spring of 1992. Another work which fascinates me very much is "Tomhet" (Emptiness), on the same CD. This song too has an extraordinary length; from my point of view it is an exceptional soundtrack to the Norwegian landscape—that is, Norway as I imagine it, a country ruled by silence and storm, solitude and natural violence.

The songs of Varg Vikernes are about dreams, visions, the past, about light and darkness, winter and war... Conceptions and expressions from Nordic mythology do not appear directly in the texts, but they are very clear and distinct in many interviews and in texts he has written in the last two years. In one of these texts about the Nordic belief system he also discusses the *Oskorei*. Provocative statements in some interviews gave him the image of a National Socialist and/or a Satanist:

"I am no racist because I do not hate other races. I am no Nazi either, but I am a fascist. I love my race, my culture, and myself. I am a follower of Odin, god of war and death. He is also the god of wisdom, magic, and poetry. Those are the things I am searching for. Burzum exists only for Odin, the cyclopian enemy of the Kristian god. I do not consider my ideas to be extreme at all. That which stupid people call evil is for me the actual reason to survive. Conflict is evolution, peace degeneration. Only blind people can deny that."

When all the churches were set on fire in 1992, the officials soon suspected the Black Metal musicians. Some were arrested and sentenced. Varg Vikernes was also accused of having burnt two churches. From January to March of 1993 he was in prison, but had to be set free as they could not prove he had any connection to the arsons. However, his sympathy for the torchings was evident—the destruction corresponded to his Nordic Nietzscheanism.

On August 10, 1993, Varg Vikernes had a conflict with Øystein Aarseth, who had released his first records. The reason seems to have been the rights of the Burzum works and a large sum of money. The dispute escalated; they started to fight one another with knives and Varg Vikernes stabbed Øystein Aarseth to death. Some days later he was arrested. In spring, 1994, he was sentenced to twenty-one years in prison, the highest penalty in Norway. The trial created quite a stir; headlines about the deed, and Black Metal "occulture," were in many newspapers and magazines. Several record shops and distributors refused to stock Burzum and some other Norwegian bands; at the same time Burzum bootlegs appeared on the market. I distrusted the many rumors which I read in newspapers and magazines and decided to contact Varg Vikernes directly.

VI

"Let us look ourselves in the face. We are Hyperboreans—we know well enough how far apart we live. 'Neither on land nor at sea shall you find the road to the Hyperboreans': Pindar already knew that of us. Beyond the North, beyond the ice, beyond death—*our* life, *our* happiness. ... We have discovered happiness, we know the path, we have found the exit out of entire millennia of labyrinth." (Friedrich Nietzsche, *The Antichrist)*

[The essay was originally followed by an interview with Varg Vikernes]

Sources:

Aske. Metz, 1994 (leaflet).
Daniel Bernard, *Wolf und Mensch.* Saarbrücken, 1983.
Hilding Celander, *Nordisk Jul.* Stockholm, 1928.
Hans Peter Duerr, *Traumzeit.* Frankfurt, 1978.
Mircea Eliade, *Shamanismus und archaische Ekstasetechnik.* Frankfurt, 1991.
Filosofem. Metz, 1994 (journal).
G. Goyert / R. Wolther, *Vlämische Sagen, Legenden und Volksmärchen.* Jena, 1917.
Otto Höfler, *Kultische Geheimbünde der Germanen.* Frankfurt, 1934.
Otto Höfler, *Verwandlungskulte: Volkssagen und Mythen.* Wien, 1974.
Michael Jacoby, *Wargus, Vargr—Verbrecher, Wolf: Eine Sprach- und Rechtsgeschichtliche Untersuchung.* Uppsala, 1974.
Christine Johannessen, *Norwegisches Burschenbrauchtum. Kult und Saga.* Wien, 1967 (dissertation).
Paul Kaufmann, *Brauchtum in Österreich.* Wien, 1982.
Friedrich Nietzsche, *Götzendämmerung/Der Antichrist/Ecce Homo/Gedichte.* Stuttgart, 1978.

Friedrich Nietzsche, *Jenseits von Gut und Böse.* Stuttgart, 1988.

Martha Paul, *Wolf, Hund und Fuchs bei den Germanen.* Wien, 1976 (dissertation).

Will-Erich Peuckert, *Geheimkulte.* Hildesheim, 1984.

Rudolf Simek, *Lexikon der Germanischen Mythologie.* Stuttgart, 1984.

Tumult 18: Georges Dumézil, Historiker, Seher. Wien, 1993 (journal).

Lily Weiser, *Alt Germanische Jünglingsweihen und Männerbünde.* Bühl, 1927.

[Originally published in the journal *Aorta*, PO Box 778, A-1011 Wien, Austria. This version is a revised translation by Kadmon and Michael Moynihan.]

APPENDIX III

"SATANISM IN NORWAY"
written and translated by Simen Midgaard

If, by the turn of the century, someone chooses to publish a work entitled "The Wooden Churches of Norway," several of the descriptions will stick to some standardized phrase like "burnt by Satanists in 199-." The word "Satanist" will at that time be commonly understood, if not in its full breadth.

Before this decade, knowledge about Satanists was the province of few, and it was not the Norwegian, black-clad and long-haired church-burners that would appear before one's inner eye. There was a Church of Satan in the U.S.A., publicly recognized and entitled to tax exemption, as well as some smaller groups spread around the Christian world, usually with a hedonistic, life-approving philosophy. The darker element would indicate that they had read Jung's theory about the "Shadow," the repressed archetype in man.

The type of Satanist that has become commonly known in this country is a quite unique Norwegian variety. They make music, and they probably believe in Satan, being Satanists. During the night they might get the idea of going out to play with candles in churchyards, knock over tombstones, or simply burn the entire church down, especially if there are holidays coming up. Fortunately for them, most Norwegian churches are made of wood, so they can soak the wooden walls with gasoline, light it, and run off. What probably fills their head when, at a safe distance, they enjoy the church spire's silhouette turning black in a fiery column, is the delight of genuine power, that they have demonstrated it, and that they have wreaked revenge. They despise people in general, whom they view as sheep. "God" is just the god of a hypocritical society and state that attempts to cleanse people's brains with spiritual chlorine.

Satan opposes this head-on. He is the individual that does not acquiesce, that is not tempted and fooled by sweet lies, falsely associated with the term "spirit" and disgracefully given the name "religion." He is the metaphysical opposite of everything feeble and dorky, to put it in popular youthful terms, and awakens the memory of the Italian poet from the turn of the century, Carducci, who initiated his "Hymn to Satan" by lauding the latter as the origin of the clear, rational thought.

The kick these modern Devil worshippers get when contemplating a successful arson attack on a church, is a juvenile boost of subverting the pathetically frail security of the domesticated and truth-fearing herd. Let us say that this is the case, and dwell a little on such a perspective. What does it mean for this subculture's ability to survive? If they keep going like this ten more years, that could mean that they will amuse themselves with ten more churches each year. That would amount to a hundred, and I see no reason that it should not happen. The history of the Church will then look more like a history of war. But at that time the movement will have made itself thoroughly noticed, and succeeded in making the term "Satanist" a part of the index of Church history. They will simultaneously have made themselves exemplary for new heroes of the same ilk.

It is the ultimate rebellion, executed with a spiteful sneer and harsh grin, against a metaphysic that shows a so-called almighty, but oh-so-deedless god indeed, so inconsequential that you must have maggots in the brain to really believe in, or do so because you are a hysterical coward—afraid of death, of loneliness and darkness, the core of what these well-fed youngsters have established as true and real, and which they worship with skulls, ritual murders of hamsters, Saturnian music, and all kinds of petty sadistic acts that hardly escape attention in a small town, where it seems that most Satanists are inhabitants.

Let it be known: these *Fauves* definitely have a point. If the Christian god should be given metaphysical status as something fundamental, then the opposite must also exist, if only as an overcharged symbol. It is a point which makes me think that these "youthful pranks" will continue for a long time to come, as the message is simple, easy to fathom, and already understood.

A cult has arisen. Without proper arguments or any established philosophy, but with an aesthetic as tough as weeds, which is significant of kitsch. Elvis-worshippers have no ideology, either. If the teachings of the Satanists are rejected as idealistic kitsch, then the Church from which their sectarian condition has originated should be vulnerable to similar criticism.

Technically speaking the Satanists, if they can be said to be organized at all, form a Christian sect. The only alternative godhead within the dominating religion in Norway is Satan. He is as Christian as Jesus, if viewed as a phenomenon of religious history. And the church-burners are probably members or ex-members of, if not the State Church, at least a comparable Lutheran variation, baptised and confirmed. From a bird's-eye view there will then be no doubt: the youthful Satanism is an extreme breed of Christianity where serenity, truth, and honesty exchange gods for their opposite. Dogmas disappear in the sect's teachings, but that is what signifies sects. This is a banality, but it should be better understood.

Society has no idea of what it is dealing with. By the Church's thousand-year anniversary it has not grasped that the demand for logical consequence and rationality also can find a religious variety, which—contrary to the lie of eternal life—worships the ecstatic contemplation of truth, which is death, for nothing is more true. With that within sight, reality will suddenly feel close and near. To make it even more intense, one worships it in all shapes and colors, with texts, pictures, and music, like any other religion. The Truthful as the Good, and therefore the Beautiful, is a basic Aristotelian principle that has definitely not passed the black-clad by. When this seems to be the reality in the heads of these self-styled fog-bursters, it would be naive to think that they are moved by a weaker force than one that has always made enthusiasts force the truth, contrary to society's beliefs.

My conclusion is that this society is facing a movement that it will take a long time to establish a clear view upon, and that any lightly considered action against it may be like putting out a fire with gasoline.

[Originally published in *Morgenbladet*, 1995.]

BIBLIOGRAPHY

Alvsvåg, Martin. *Rock og satanisme—destruktive elementer i tungrocken.* Oslo: Credo, 1995.

Anderson, Rasmus. *Norse Mythology.* Chicago: S. C. Griggs, 1876.

Anker, Peter. *The Art of Scandinavia.* London: Peter Hamlyn, 1970.

Arnett, Jeffrey Jensen. *Metalheads: Heavy Metal Music and Adolescent Alienation.* Boulder, CO: Westview, 1996.

Aschehoug og Gyldendals store norske leksikon. Olaf Kortner, Preben Munthe, and Egil Tveterås, editors. Oslo: Kunnskapsforlaget, 1989.

Bachelard, Gaston. *The Psychoanalysis of Fire.* London: Quartet, 1987.

Baring-Gould, Sabine. *The Book of Werewolves.* New York: Causeway, 1973.

Barth, Else Margarete. *Gud, det er meg: Vidkun Quisling som politisk filosof.* Oslo: Pax, 1996.

Barton, Blanche. *The Church of Satan.* New York: Hell's Kitchen, 1990.

Barton, Blanche. *The Secret Life of a Satanist.* Los Angeles: Feral House, 1990.

Bashe, Philip. *Heavy Metal Thunder.* New York: Dolphin, 1985.

Baskin, Wade. *Dictionary of Satanism.* New York: Philosophical Library, 1972.

Bataille, Georges. *Death and Sensuality: A Study of Eroticism and the Taboo.* New York: Walker and Co., 1962.

Billerbeck, Liane v. and Frank Nordhausen. *Satanskinder: Der Mordfall Sandro B.* Berlin: Ch. Links Verlag, 1994.

Bjørgo, Tore. *Politisk terrorisme.* Oslo: Tano, 1993.

Booth, Stanley. *Dance With the Devil: The Rolling Stones and Their Times.* New York: Random House, 1984.

Bourre, Jean-Paul. *Les Profanateurs.* France, n.p.: Le Comptour Editions, 1997.

Calt, Stephen & Gayle Wardlow. *King of the Delta Blues: The Life and Music of Charlie Patton.* Newton, NJ: Rock Chapel Press, 1988.

Carus, Paul. *The History of the Devil and the Idea of Evil.* Chicago: Open Court, 1990. Reprint, Avenel, NJ: Gramercy, 1996.

Chadwick, H. M. *The Cult of Othin: An Essay in the Ancient Religion of the North.* Stockholm: Looking Glass Press, 1994.

Dahl, Hans Fredrik. *Vidkun Quisling: En fører blir til/Vidkun Quisling: En fører for fall.* Oslo: Aschehoug, 1991/92.

Davenport, Guy, transl. *Herakleitos and Diogenes.* San Francisco: Grey Fox, 1990.

Davidson, H. R. Ellis. *Gods and Myths of the Viking Age.* New York: Bell Publishing, 1981.

Davis, Stephen. *Hammer of the Gods: The Led Zeppelin Saga.* New York: William Morrow, 1985.

Dumézil, Georges. *Gods of the Ancient Northmen.* Berkeley: University of California Press, 1973.

Dyrendal, Asbjørn. "Media Constructions of 'Satanism' in Norway (1988-1997)" *Friend of a Friend (FOAF) Tale News: Newsletter of the Contemporary Legend Society.* Summer/Fall 1997 Issue.

Eisler, Robert. *Man Into Wolf: An Anthropological Interpretation of Sadism, Masochism and Lycanthropy.* London: Spring Books, n.d.

Fangen, Katrine. *Skinheads i rødt, hvitt og blått : en sosiologisk studie fra "innsiden."* Oslo: Program for Ungdomsforskning, Norges Forskningsråd, 1995.

Flatin, Kjetil A. *Tussar og trolldom.* Oslo: Norsk folkeminnelag, 1930.

Gerstein, Mary R. "Germanic Warg: The Outlaw as Werewolf." In *Myth in Indo-European Antiquity,* ed. Gerald Larson, pgs. 157-168. Berkeley, CA: University of California Press, 1974.

Grimm, Jacob. *Teutonic Mythology* (4 Vols). Magnolia, MA: Peter Smith, 1976.

Gummere, Francis B. *Germanic Origins: A Study in Primitive Culture.* London: David Nutt, 1892.

Gundarsson, Kveldulfr Hagen. "The Folklore of the Wild Hunt." In *Mountain Thunder,* issue 7, pgs. 11-18. Boulder, CO: Mountain Thunder, 1992.

Hoidal, Oddvar K. *Quisling: A Study in Treason.* Oslo: Norwegian University Press, 1989.

Jacoby, Michael. *Wargus, Vargr—'Verbrecher' 'Wolf': eine sprach- und rechtsgeschichtliche Untersuchung.* Uppsala, Sweden: Almqvist and Wiksell, 1974.

Jones, Gwyn. *A History of the Vikings.* Revised Ed. Oxford: Oxford University Press, 1984.

Jung, C. G. *Two Essays on Analytical Psychology.* New York: Meridian, 1956.

Kadmon. "Oskorei." *Aorta,* No. 20. Vienna: Aorta Publications, 1995.

Kaplan, Jeffrey. *Radical Religion in America: Millenarian Movements from the Far Right to the Children of Noah.* Syracuse, NY: Syracuse University Press, 1997.

Kennedy, John. *Fire and Arson Investigation.* Chicago: Investigations Institute, 1962.

King, Francis. *The Magical World of Aleister Crowley.* New York: Coward McCann & Geoghegan, 1977.

Landis, Bill. *Anger: The Unauthorized Biography of Kenneth Anger.* New York: HarperCollins, 1995.

LaVey, Anton Szandor. *The Satanic Bible.* New York: Avon, 1969.

LaVey, Anton Szandor. *The Satanic Rituals.* New York: Avon, 1972.

Lewis, Nolan D. C. and Helen Yarnell. *Pathological Firesetting (Pyromania).* New York: Nervous and Mental Disease Monographs, 1951.

Lunde, Henrik. *Aller ytterst : De rasistiske grupperinger i dagens Norge.* Oslo: Antirasistisk senter, 1993

Lyons, Arthur. *The Second Coming: Satanism in America.* New York: Dodd, Mead, 1970.

Marsden, John. *Fury of the Northmen.* New York: St. Martin's, 1993.

Martin, John Stanley. *Ragnarok: An Investigation into Old Norse Concepts of the Fate of the Gods.* Assen, Netherlands: Van Gorcum, 1972.

Michelet, Jules. *Satanism and Witchcraft: A Study in Medieval Superstition.* Translated by A. R. Allinson. New York: Citadel, 1946.

Norman, Philip. *Symphony for the Devil: The Rolling Stones Story.* New York: Linden Press, 1984.

Olrik, Axel. *Viking Civilization.* New York: American-Scandinavian Foundation, 1930.

Otten, Charlotte F., ed. *A Lycanthropy Reader: Werewolves in Western Culture.* New York: Dorset, 1989.

Owen, Francis. *The Germanic People: Their Origin, Expansion and Culture.* New York: Barnes and Noble, 1993.

Parker, John. *At the Heart of Darkness: Witchcraft, Black Magic and Satanism Today.* Secaucus, NJ: Carol, 1993.

The Poetic Edda. Translated by Henry Adams Bellows. New York: American-Scandinavian Foundation, 1968.

The Poetic Edda. Translated by Lee M. Hollander. Second edition, revised. Austin: University of Texas Press, 1988.

Rhodes, H. T. F. The Satanic Mass. London: Jarrolds, 1968.

Rooth, Anna Birgitta. Loki in Scandinavian Mythology. Lund, Sweden. C.W.K. Gleerups Förlag, 1961.

Rudwin, Maximilian. The Devil in Legend and Literature. La Salle, IL: Open Court, 1989.

Rydberg, Viktor. Teutonic Mythology: Gods and Goddesses of the Northland. 3 Vols. Translated by Rasmus Anderson. New York: Norrœna Society, 1907.

Simek, Rudolf. Dictionary of Northern Mythology. Cambridge, UK: D. S. Brewer, 1996.

Stekel, Wilhelm, M. D. Peculiarities of Behavior. Vol. 2. Translated by James S. Van Teslaar. New York: Grove Press, 1964.

Sturluson, Snorre. Heimskringla. Translated by Lee M. Hollander. Austin: University of Texas Press, 1964.

Sturluson, Snorre. The Heimskringla. 2 Vols. Translated by Samuel Laing. New York: Norroena Society, 1911.

Summers, Montague. The Werewolf. New Hyde Park, NY: University Books, 1966.

Terry, Patricia, trans. Poems of the Elder Edda. Revised ed. Philadelphia: University of Pennsylvania Press, 1990.

Vesaas, Tarjei. Land of Hidden Fires (Løynde eldars land). Translated by Fritz König and Jerry Crisp. Detroit, MI: Wayne State Univ. Press, 1973.

Vikernes, Varg. Vargsmål. n.p., 1997.

Walser, Robert. Running with the Devil: Power, Gender, and Madness in Heavy Metal Music. Middletown, CT: Wesleyan Univ. Press, 1993.

Walsten, David. Stave Churches of the World: An Introduction. Denmark, WI: Madsen Press, 1994.

Ward, Robert. "The Wild Hunt." In Vor Tru, issue 55, pgs. 28-35. Payson, AZ: World Tree, 1996.

Weinstein, Deena. Heavy Metal: A Cultural Sociology. New York: Lexington Books, 1991.

Wolfe, Burton H. The Devil's Avenger: A Biography of Anton Szandor LaVey. New York: Pyramid, 1974.

MUSIC RESOURCES

For those wishing to investigate the netherworlds of Black Metal in all its guises, the following addresses (mostly online) are provided:

MAIL-ORDER SERVICE

www.blackmetal.com

www.redstream.org

www.theendrecords.com

www.relapse.com

LABELS

Nuclear Blast
www.nuclearblastusa.com

Cacophonous Records
www.visiblenoise.com/cacoph

Moonfog Productions
www.moonfog.no

Nocturnal Art Productions
www.nocturnalart.com

Prophecy Productions
www.prophecy.cd

Merciless Records
www.merciless-records.de

Iron Pegasus
www.iron-pegasus.com

No Colours Records
www.no-colours-records.de

Napalm Records
www.napalmrecords.com

Avantgarde Music
www.avantgardemusic.com

Osmose Productions
www.osmoseproductions.com

Black Mark Productions
www.blackmark.net

MISCELLANEOUS

Norwegian Heathen Front
www.heathenfront.org

www.burzum.com

ENDNOTES

INTRODUCTION

1 Tarjei Vesaas, *Land of Hidden Fires*, pg. 121.

2 Quoted in John Marsden, *Fury of the Northmen*, pg. xiii.

3 John Marsden, *Fury of the Northmen*, pg. 61.

4 Ibid., pg. 42.

5 Francis Owen, *The Germanic People: Their Origin, Expansion and Culture*, pg. 204.

CHAPTER ONE

1 Arthur Lyons, *The Second Coming: Satanism in America*, pg. 124.

2 Quoted in Stanley Booth, *Dance With the Devil: The Rolling Stones and Their Times*, pg. 26.

3 Stephen Davis, *Hammer of the Gods: The Led Zeppelin Saga*, pg. 229.

4 Ibid.

5 Ibid., pg. 175.

6 *Seconds* Magazine, Issue 29, 1994, pg. 61.

7 *Seconds* Magazine, Issue 39, 1996, pg. 64.

8 Coven, *Witchcraft*, Mercury Records, SR 61239.

9 Descent Magazine, Issue III, 1996.

10 Interviewed by M. Moynihan, 1993.

11 Interviewed by M. Moynihan, 1994.

12 Ibid.

13 Interviewed by Elden M., 1997. Tape supplied to the authors.

14 Ibid.

15 Ibid.

16 Venom, *Black Metal*, Combat Records, MX 8030.

17 Interviewed by Elden M., 1997.

18 *Kerrang!* , Issue 94, 1985.

19 Interviewed by M. Moynihan, 1993.

20 Mercyful Fate, *Don't Break the Oath*, Roadrunner Records, RCD 9835

21 Interviewed by M. Moynihan, 1993.

22 Interviewed by M. Moynihan, 1993.

23 Ibid.

24 Ibid.

25 Bathory, *Blood Fire Death*, Kraze Records, ML 1063.

26 Interviewed by M. Moynihan, 1993.

27 Ibid.

CHAPTER TWO

1 Slayer, *Hell Awaits*. Lyrical transcriptions at: http://www.slaytanic.com.

2 Interviewed by Elden M., 1997.

3 Interviewed by M. Moynihan, 1994.

4 Interviewed by Elden M., 1997.

CHAPTER THREE

1 Translation by the authors.

2 Letter to M. Moynihan, 1997.

3 Interviewed by the authors, 1995.

4 Ibid.

5 Ibid.

6 Ibid.

7 Ibid.

8 Ibid.

9 Ibid.

10 *Rock Furore*, February 1993.

CHAPTER FOUR

1 Georges Bataille, *Death and Sensuality: A Study of Eroticism and the Taboo*, pg. 46.

2 *Slayer* Magazine, Vol. 3/4, 1986, pg. 41.

3 C. O. T. I. M. Magazine, #5, 1985.

4 Found at: http://www.intercom.no/~kulde/dead.html

5 Interviewed by the authors, 1995.

6 Interviewed by Kurt Hubert in *Pit* Magazine, 1994.

7 Ibid.

8 *Orcustus*. Issue 2, 1992, pg. 36.

9 Reproduced on *Dawn of the Black Hearts: Live in Sarpsborg* bootleg CD. Quote is credited "Euronymous, April 1991, two weeks after Dead's suicide."

10 Interviewed by M. Moynihan, 1995.

11 C. O. T. I. M. Magazine, #5, 1985.

12 *Spin,* February 1996, pg. 65.

CHAPTER FIVE

1 George Bernard Shaw, *Man and Superman*. New York: Brentano's, 1975, pg. 99.

2 *Orcustus,* Issue 2, 1992, pg. 36.

3 Ibid.

4 Interviewed by the authors, 1995.

5 Interviewed by the authors, 1995.

6 Ibid.

7 Interviewed by M. Moynihan, 1995.

8 Interviewed by the authors, 1995.

9 C. O. T. I. M. Magazine, #3.

10 Interviewed by the authors, 1995.

11 Ibid.

12 Excerpt from original *Vargsmål* manuscript given to the authors by Vikernes, translated by D. Søderlind. This passage appears to have been excised from the published version.

13 C. O. T. I. M. Magazine, #3.

14 *Orcustus*. Issue 2, 1992, pg. 39.

CHAPTER SIX

1 *Filosofem,* Vol. 1, Issue 1, 1994. The lyric was here misleadingly credited to Vikernes.

2 David M. Walsten, *Stave Churches of the World,* pg. 28.

3 John Kennedy, *Fire and Arson Investigation,* pg. 61.

4 Nolan D. C. Lewis, and Helen Yarnell. *Pathological Firesetting (Pyromania),* pg. 4.

5 Ibid., pg. 63.

6 Ibid., pg. 342.

7 Ibid., pg. 89.

8 Ibid., pg. 273.

9 Ibid., pg. 274.

10 Wilhelm Stekel, *Peculiarities of Behavior,* Vol. 2, pg. 125.

11 Ibid., pg. 135 ff.

12 Quoted on official Burzum biography sheet issued by Misanthropy Records, UK.

13 Wilhelm Stekel, *Peculiarities of Behavior,* Vol. 2, pg. 131.

14 Ibid., pg. 139.

15 Ibid., pg. 229.

16 David M. Walsten, *Stave Churches of the World,* pg. 30.

17 Quoted in *Sounds of Death* Magazine, Issue 4, 1994.

18 Ibid.

19 Ibid.

20 *Bergens Tidende,* 1/20/93. See Appendix I.

21 Ibid.

22 *Kerrang!,* No. 436. March 27, 1993.

23 Ibid., pg. 42.

24 Ibid.

25 Ibid.

26 Ibid.

27 Ibid., pg. 42 ff.

28 Ibid., pg. 43.

29 Ibid.

30 Ibid.

31 Ibid., pg. 44.

32 Ibid., pg. 43.

33 Interviewed by the authors, 1995.

34 *An Phoblacht,* Sraith Nua Iml 16, Uimhir 28 (April, 1997).

CHAPTER SEVEN

1 Snorre Sturlason, *Heimskringla,* translated by Lee M. Hollander, pg. 124.

2 Interviewed by M. Moynihan, 1995.

3 Unpublished *Bolt* Magazine interview by Geir Larsen.

4 *Spin,* February 1996, pg. 70.

5 Quoted in liner notes to *Nordic Metal,* Necropolis Records, NR-009.

6 Interviewed by M. Moynihan, 1997.

7 Quoted in *Sounds of Death* Magazine,

Issue 4, 1994.

8 Ibid.

9 Ibid.

10 Interviewed by M. Moynihan, 1995.

11 Interviewed by the authors, 1995.

12 Interviewed by the authors, 1995.

13 Varg Vikernes, *Vargsmål*, pg. 52. Translated by D. Søderlind.

14 *Slayer* Magazine, Vol. X, pg. 25.

15 *Filosofem*, Vol. 1, Issue 1, 1994.

16 *Ultrakill!* Magazine, No. 1, 1994.

17 *Slayer* Magazine, Vol. X, pg. 25.

18 Interviewed by M. Moynihan, 1997.

19 Excerpt from original *Vargsmål* manuscript, translated by D. Søderlind. This passage appears to have been excised from the published version.

CHAPTER EIGHT

1 *The Poetic Edda*, translated by Ursula Dronke. Oxford: The Clarendon Press, 1969. Stanza 8.

2 Interviewed by Roberto C. Sanchez in *Terrorizer* magazine, Issue 28, 1996.

3 Interviewed by the authors, 1995.

4 Ibid.

5 *Ultrakill!* Magazine, No. 1, 1994.

6 Interviewed by Roberto C. Sanchez in *Terrorizer* magazine, Issue 28, 1996.

7 Interviewed by the authors, 1995.

8 Ibid.
9 Ibid.

10 Excerpt from original *Vargsmål* manuscript, translated by D. Søderlind. This passage appears to have been excised from the published version.

11 Oddvar K. Hoidal, *Quisling: A Study in Treason*, pg. 58.

12 *American Heritage Dictionary,* Second College Edition. Boston: Houghton Mifflin, 1982. Pg. 898.

13 Oddvar K. Hoidal, *Quisling: A Study in Treason*, pg. 213.

14 Interviewed by the authors, 1995.

15 Excerpt from original *Vargsmål* manuscript, translated by D. Søderlind. This passage appears to have been excised from the published version.

16 Interviewed by the authors, 1995.

CHAPTER NINE

1 *Random House Dictionary of the English Language,* Unabridged Edition. New York: Random House, 1967. Pgs. 1223, 93.

2 C.G. Jung, *Collected Works of C.G. Jung,* Vol. 10, pg. 189.

3 "Morituri Te Salutant" by "Hofding Warge" [Varg Vikernes], *Filosofem,* Vol. 1, Issue 2, 1994.

4 *Aschehoug og Gyldendals store norske leksikon,* Second Edition, Volume 10, pg. 562. English translation found at: http//oskoreia.studby.uio.no/english/oskoreia.html.

5 Interviewed by M. Moynihan, 1997.

6 Interviewed by the authors, 1995.

7 *Descent* Magazine, Vol. One, May 1994.

8 C. G. Jung, *Two Essays on Analytical Psychology*, pg. 75 ff.

9 Interviewed by M. Moynihan, 1991.

10 Interviewed by Roberto C. Sanchez in *Terrorizer* magazine, Issue 28, 1996.

11 C. G. Jung, *Collected Works of C.G. Jung*, Vol. 10, pg. 180.

12 Ibid., pg. 192.

13 Interviewed by the authors, 1995.

14 Ibid.

15 Kjetil A. Flatin, *Tussar og trolldom*, pg. 76. English translation found at: http://faeryland.etsu.edu/~earendil/faerie/story/oskorei.html

16 Mary R. Gerstein, "Germanic Warg: The Outlaw as Werewolf." *Myth in Indo-European Antiquity*, pg. 137.

17 Ibid., pg. 139.

18 Quoted in Sabine Baring-Gould, *The Book of Werewolves*, pg. 49.

19 Ibid., pg. 48 ff.

20 Interviewed by M. Moynihan, 1997.

21 Sabine Baring-Gould, *The Book of Werewolves*, pg. 40.

22 *The Poetic Edda*, translated by Henry Adams Bellows, pg. 11.

23 Georges Dumézil, *Gods of the Ancient Northmen*, pg. 30.

24 Mary R. Gerstein, "Germanic Warg: The Outlaw as Werewolf." *Myth in Indo-European Antiquity*, pg. 143.

25 Snorri Sturlason, *Heimskringla*, translated by Lee M. Hollander, pg. 11.

26 Mary R. Gerstein, "Germanic Warg: The Outlaw as Werewolf." *Myth in Indo-European Antiquity*, pg. 143.

27 Ibid.

28 F. B. Gummere, *Germanic Origins*, pg. 425.

CHAPTER TEN

1 Paul Carus, *The History of the Devil and the Idea of Evil*, pg. 482.

2 Interviewed by D. Søderlind, 1997.

3 Interviewed by M. Moynihan, 1997.

4 Interviewed by M. Moynihan, 1997.

5 Interviewed by M. Moynihan, 1997.

6 Asbjørn Dyrendal, "Media Constructions of 'Satanism' in Norway (1988-1997)" *Friend of a Friend (FOAF) Tale News*, Summer/Fall 1997 Issue.

7 Ibid.

8 Ibid.

CHAPTER ELEVEN

1 *C. O. T. I. M.* Magazine, Issue 4.

2 *Der Spiegel*, Issue 41, 1994, pg. 91 ff.

3 Ibid.

4 Ibid.

5 Liane von Billerbeck and Frank Nordhausen, *Satanskinder*, pg. 63.

6 Ibid., pg. 66.

7 Ibid., pg. 106.

8 Ibid.

9 Ibid., pg. 36.

10 Ibid., pg. 280.

11 Ibid., pg. 293.

12 Ibid., pg. 232.

13 Ibid., pg. 234.

14 Interviewed by the authors, 1995.

15 Absurd, *Facta Loquuntur,* No Colours Records/Silencelike Death, NC 007/SDP 3001.

16 Letter to M. Moynihan, 1997.

17 Ibid.

18 Ibid.

19 Ibid.

20 Absurd, *Facta Loquuntur,* No Colours Records/Silencelike Death, NC 007/SDP 3001.

21 A sarcastic acronym for "Zionist Occupational Government," often employed in radical political circles to describe any of the present-day Western democratic states.

CHAPTER TWELVE

1 Quoted in Gwyn Jones, *A History of the Vikings,* pg. 195.

2 From a facsimile of the Animal Militia letter provided by Roadrunner Records.

3 *Slayer* Magazine, Issue X, pg. 52.

4 *L'Express,* 18/7/96, pg. 43.

5 Ibid.

6 Ibid.

7 *L'Express,* 7/11/96.

8 *France-Soir,* 7/2/97, pg. 5.

9 Ibid.

10 Ibid.
11 Ibid.

12 Ibid.

13 Ibid.

14 *Kerrang!,* No. 514, October 1, 1994, pg. 16.

15 "This Music Must be Banned" *Kent Messenger,* UK daily paper, circa October, 1994.

16 Ibid.

17 *Kerrang!,* No. 514, October 1, 1994, pg. 16.

18 "This Music Must be Banned" *Kent Messenger,* UK daily paper, circa October, 1994.

19 *Kerrang!,* No. 514, October 1, 1994, pg. 17.

20 *Kerrang!,* No. 514, October 1, 1994, pg. 16.

21 Ibid.

22 "This Music Must be Banned" *Kent Messenger,* UK daily paper, circa October, 1994.

23 Ibid.

24 Interviewed by M. Moynihan, 1997.

25 *Terrorizer*, Issue 29, April, 1996. pg. 28.

26 Ibid.

27 *Wall Street Journal*, 2/18/93, pg. A1.

28 *Penthouse*, September, 1993, pgs. 121, 186.

29 Ibid., pg. 121.

30 Ibid., pg. 120.

31 Ibid., pg. 186.

32 *Penthouse*, September, 1993, pg. 116.

33 *Wall Street Journal*, 2/18/93, pg. A1.

34 *Penthouse*, September, 1993, pg. 190.

35 Ibid.

36 Ibid., pg. 116.

37 *Resistance* Magazine, Issue 7, pg. 53.

38 Ibid., pg. 54.

39 Ibid., pg. 55.

40 *Petrified Zine*, 1994.

41 Ibid.

42 From press release material supplied by Roadrunner Records.

43 *The Rocket* biweekly newspaper, November 5-19, 1997, Issue #265, pg. 21ff.

44 *New Times* weekly newspaper, May 23-30, 1996 issue, pg. 22.

45 The Electric Hellfire Club, *Burn, Baby, Burn*, Cleopatra Records, 1993, CLEO 7269-2.

46 Quoted from transcript of interview which appeared in *Seconds* Magazine, Issue 43, 1997.

47 Ibid.

48 *San Francisco Chronicle*, 5/10/96, pg. A14.

49 Ibid.

50 *Fort Myers News-Press*, 6/22/96.

51 Ibid.

52 Ibid.

53 Ibid.

54 Ibid.

55 *San Francisco Chronicle*, 5/10/96, pg. A14.

56 From an essay on Tom Ascoll's Internet Site circa July, 1997, titled "Lords of Chaos: Where Do They Come From? Reflections on Sin and Evil."

57 *20/20* TV news program, second week of October, 1997.

58 Ibid.

59 Ibid.

60 *People* Magazine, October 1, 1997, downloaded from *People* website.

CHAPTER THIRTEEN

1 John Stanley Martin, *Ragnarok*, pg. 3.

2 Fenriz quote from *Thy Kingdom Come* Magazine, Issue 4, 1995.

3 Jeffrey Jensen Arnett, *Metalheads*, pg. 7.

4 Quoted in *Fortean Times*, Issue 80, pg. 34.